COASTLINE

LANDFALL – FIRST PASSAGE

*Based on the True Story of a Vietnamese
Woman and Her Fight to Survive*

TIM WILCOX

ISBN: 978-1-944566-11-1
Published in the United States by Bush Publishing

Library of Congress Cataloging-in-publication data
Wilcox, Tim
Coastline: Landfall – First Passage

Printed in the United States of America

DEDICATION

This is dedicated first to Loan. Additionally this is dedicated to the remarkable Vietnamese, Laotians and Cambodians who fled Southeast Asia and the countries, charitable organizations and citizens that took them in. This is further dedicated to the 600,000+ Vietnamese that left Viet Nam but never it made it to another country or crossed another coastline.

TABLE OF CONTENTS

DECLARATION

I consider myself to be one of the luckiest recipients of America's version of the Viet Nam War. Through horrendous circumstance, it propelled people of Viet Nam to America in order to escape the chaos. My luck: I met one of them and she has enriched my life beyond measure and expectation.

I owe this in part to the hubris of CBS News Anchor Walter Chronkite. During the 1968 Tet Invasion by the Viet Cong, he stated on the nightly news to the horror of President LBJ that the war appeared unwinnable.

I owe additional gratitude for the toxic management of Congresswoman Bella Abzug and other reckless democrats as she and others abruptly cut the funding from the war without a managed withdrawal of support and enhanced refugee program. The sudden disruption of funding enabled the chaos that fell upon South Viet Nam in 1975.

If not for them and their reckless arrogance, I would never have met Nguyên Xuân Loan and experienced the Viet Nam I ran from over four decades ago.

Tim Wilcox, January 2015

Author's Vietnamese and American Nomenclature

Names and locations in Viet Nam, the Philippines and The United States have been changed to avoid undue attention to real people living or dead involved in this history.

Since some Vietnamese names such as Nguyên are used by over 35% of the Asian and North American Vietnamese populations. Identification with other Vietnamese by the same name is likely and merely coincidental.

Vietnamese Names of Locations:

True to the people, culture and language, terms such as Viet Nam and Sai Gon are represented in the form used by the Vietnamese. Just as New York and St. Louis are not Newyork or Stlouis,

Viet Nam is truly Viet Nam (meaning South Region). Sai Gon is truly Sai Gon. While Sai Gon was changed to Ho Chi Minh City after May 1, 1975, many Vietnamese continue to call the city Sai Gon.

Vietnamese Writing:

Where possible, I have endeavored to use the five and six diacritics (example: á,â,ã,ä,å) above vowels and some change in consonants true to the Vietnamese written language wherever possible. The diacritics were added to the Roman letters to adopt western writing to the language in the 1800s. It is complicated to western ears but necessary to understanding Vietnamese conversations and some of their difficulties with the use of English. Much as I have attempted to be precise, I will get some spelling of Vietnamese names and locations with the diacritics wrong. I apologize in advance.

Tim Wilcox, January 2015

AUTHOR'S NOTE

According to Philip Cavuto's seminal personal narrative, *A Rumor of War*, he landed in Da Nang, Viet Nam on March 8, 1965 as an infantry officer of the United States Marine's 9th Expeditionary Brigade. A decade later, civilian Philip Cavuto returned to Viet Nam as a reporter for the Chicago Tribune in April 1975 as Sai Gon was about to fall to the Communist offensive. He flew out of Viet Nam on one of the last evacuation helicopters on April 29, 1975 landing on the U.S.S Denver in The South China Sea. The last paragraph of his book reads:

"The next day, April 30, (1975) the ship's captain announced that the Sai Gon government had surrendered to the North Vietnamese. We took the news quietly. It was over."

For the Vietnamese stranded in their country by awful circumstance, April 30, 1975 was not the end of anything. "It" was not "over." At minimum, for those Vietnamese alive that last day and living now, it is not over until their hearts cease pumping.

April 30, 1975 marked the beginning of everything really bad for millions of Vietnamese who wanted to live out their lives better than before. Many migrated from North Viet Nam and Southern China over the previous half century. Unfortunately, many bet on the losing side of the fight.

In fact, each side of the conflict backed the wrong side that failed to achieve their hopes for an acceptable peace. Viet Nam took decades to emerge from its new and self-imposed Dark Age.

Tensions between neighbors and communities remain palpable, especially on April 30 of each year. The conflict between Southeast Asia's "North" and "South" simmers to this day.

Many Vietnamese expected Americans to be heroic strangers enabling opportunities to sustain if not improve their lives. Others drank the Hanoi "Kool-Aid," so to speak, believing Americans and the Western world stood against them as slavers if not devils. They fought to consolidate Viet Nam in order to save South Viet Nam from itself.

The American version of the Viet Nam War spent good people on both sides for nothing. There would be a Chinese and Cambodian version of the war in subsequent years and twenty years of persecution despite early amnesties declared for former combatants and political opposition.

When Sai Gon fell on April 30, 1975, the entire country went medieval in a week for the losers. Yet, the affliction respected no side of the conflict. All Vietnamese who remained in Viet Nam discovered a new version of hell after May 1975. Anyone of means made plans to escape. They constructed strategies to cross many coastlines in search of a better life.

Everyone transitions when as if rolling on waves of a body of water; adjust to life as it is, floating on the variable surface of what they expect. Then they make landfall.

There are emotional levels crossing from sea to land depending on the interface between two environments. Why else separately call it "land" and "fall"? It is a term by itself that summarizes important change.

Deep down, we know if not remember our first transition which was by all accounts a horrific experience. **_We were born_**.

Our mothers pushed us out after eight or nine months of ease literally floating in a warm bath with every want and care met well. Abruptly, we were squeezed if not seemingly crushed into a cold, bright and noisy world where crying is the first word in our nascent vocabulary.

Birth is our first landfall, so to speak. All of us crossed a clear boundary delineated by land and water, by comfort and immense displeasure. Making it to the living is our first coastline.

As you read this, remember or realize you are among those who made it ashore and scrambled to life among the living. Like me, like you, there were thousands of things to know and skills to develop, hopefully among loving family in a stable world where food and shelter were provided well enough such that we prospered and advanced to this moment in relative ease.

We continue to cross many coastlines hopefully less extreme than birth itself. And if we are blessed with energy, luck and providence, we make the final transition in peace after a long and prosperous life surrounded by a comforting family as we pass into oblivion.

For many, life has been a series of rough landfalls from one alien shoreline to another. Meals and shelter were uncertain at every hour. Their circumstances tested endurance and their survival challenges beliefs. Of the exceptional survivals, spectators such as me wonder whether unseen forces were at work.

For a period, one of these people lived naked and alone in a rugged jungle coast of the Philippines until the age of 12. She slept in trees and lived on fruits and crickets until she found her way out to civilization and eventually to America.

I know this person. Her informal and public name is Loan.

Arriving in the United States as an inadvertent orphan, she eventually reconnected to her family two decades later. Thereafter, she contemplated returning to Viet Nam to recapture something of her lost childhood.

After her mother passed away in 2007 in Sai Gon, she settled the conflict of residence. She became an American.

I witnessed her American naturalization ceremony in middle-America in 2008. Of the thirty six people in the ceremony, many were Vietnamese. Thirty nine years after Sai Gon and South Viet Nam fell to a communist regime on April 30, 975, life begins anew.

Vietnamese continue to immigrate to America. Instead of escaping by foot and flimsy sea craft, they petition Hanoi and the United States consulates. They make landfall in America by commercial aircraft after spending every resource they have to leave a land they once loved.

Why? Why do these people make so much effort to be here?

I never intended to be a writer of anything beyond engineering documents on how to operate mechanical and electrical systems in buildings. Loan's remarkable life has transformed mine.

My brothers and I endeavored to avoid an all-expense paid trip to Viet Nam in the early 1970s. 40-plus years later, I have become immersed in all things Viet Nam and look forward to the next visit to put at rest how she came to be here along with a million other Vietnamese.

I have become her scribe and attempt to communicate a measure of human fortitude like I have never known. Her anti-fragile circumstances compelled me to record a larger history that greatly affected America as much as it affected the Vietnamese.

This is partly written from a Vietnamese viewpoint that I have attempted to convey. America gave South Viet Nam hope in the 1960s and then wistfully abandoned loyalists as they were called to their doom in the 1970s. I do not speak of this idly.

Vietnamese men who fought beside Americans, Brits and Aussies spend their remaining years in Sai Gon *(Ho Chi Minh City)* contemplating the mysteries of that difficult past. In July 2012, one of these aging Vietnamese veterans asked, "Why did we (Americans) leave? "

In our first meeting in 2009, he asked for my help to locate his American comrades-in-arms and reconnect to them. He had bonded with foreign brothers in arms fighting for South Viet Nam's independence. As it was, I failed miserably. I could not locate his American comrades.

Among the living US veterans, he did not understand that these men, if still living, might not want to hear again of Viet Nam. There is much to understand and convey on both sides of the world.

It has taken the better part of a decade to record Loans memories, dissect her lexicon that is part 8-year old totally-unschooled girl-on-the-run and lessons learned unmanaged and parentless in 1980s America to the present. Best as possible, I fill in the personal history of southern Asia, Viet Nam and America to build the context of a remarkable history.

I projected the silhouette of her descriptions against the perceptions of other Vietnamese of every age and profession. I mix thin understanding of Asian culture and attitudes to expand the context. At best, I've painted a Rorschach print subject to interpretation by most anyone qualified with a valid driver's license. Start with my template of mixed cultures and build your own view as you wish.

There is nothing unremarkable about her. She endured many situations that would have killed my large white self. She entered the larger world at 8 and emerged with a riveting approach to everything by the age of 14 as she learned her fourth language, English, in New York.

This is not about me other than as interrupter-in-training of Asian issues in an effort to convey an initial understanding of a world we lived in but seldom understood. Americans generated some of the future she later had to embrace. I cannot answer whether this is better than if she had remained in Viet Nam. Yet for me, she has enriched my life and her family in Viet Nam beyond measure.

Formerly big issues in my life now seem petty. This has compelled me to share her story.

COASTLINE is about her, 1930s China, 1950s Viet Nam and the many tragedies of conflict in that region in the last century. America played a part and by happenstance, there are nearly two million Vietnamese in the United States as of the census of 2010.

Many of the Asians that are present in North America are here because life was not good there. America was among other countries that offered a bastion of hope for a better life.

Achieving sanctuary required perilous travel. The Asians crossed many coastlines to make life in America and a dozen other countries. Most of them headed for America.

This narrative summarizes many of the issues and stories in the incredible real-life account of Nguyên Xuân Loan and her Chinese-Vietnamese family as they crossed endless coastlines from Asia to America starting in 1937 China. The history flows through Viet Nam in the 1950s to 1977 and then to the near-present when Loan reconnects to her family in Viet Nam.

I am grateful for the privilege of this experience with her life and the lives of others brought into contact. It is often exhausting for an American-born person to engage the complexity of other-born cultures.

I seldom view an approaching coastline the same. I will never view people who risked much to be here as anything but worthy of acceptance.

This is not an advocacy of open borders. It is recognition that true immigrants for quality of life add to America's phenomenal story.

Loan's life redefines perceptions of comfort and importance. Recording her story has required many thousands of hours across eight years borrowed from other tasks and routines. I used to keep a good lawn and competed with neighbors on the best Christmas light display. The house remains darker than normal and appears as if Viet Nam vets landscaped my yard with defoliant.

Waves of life's expectations crash into the shoreline of an immensely variable universe. Fluid hopes fall back to the sea, wets the beach or refills tidal pools. Creatures of the waves crashed on the shore may be stranded to die or meant to thrive anew on the surface of mother earth.

Loan held on. She thrived ... turning disaster into existence and then some.

There may be a comforting deity looking over us. I don't really know enough to say with 100% assurance. I can only believe she is here in life by providence and a bit of pluck. The main question is whether I satisfy her purpose and goals in life by telling this well.

Loan's existence suggests forces of nature beyond my grasp. This may not be as much a narrative as a plea for help. Perhaps you can help me understand this remarkable story of tragedy and triumph. How did this small ignorant girl of no material capability survive?

Explain this better so that I may understand. I will be forever in your debt.

Tim Wilcox
January 2015

PREFACE

Memories of big events depend on when and where they were made. Vietnamese that fled Sai Gon before April 30, 1975 may reject the record of events recalled by others that survived the city's last days and endured the days to follow. Fixed-wing aircraft, helicopters, barges, and commercial sea craft removed roughly 80,000 South Vietnamese out to waiting ships in South Viet Nam's final hours of independence from Hanoi.

Several hundred thousand "at-risk" Vietnamese remained behind in Sai Gon. Not all of them remained by an easy choice. Some of them, Vietnamese civic leaders to girlfriends of Americans who believed life verged on the unbearable under the rule of Hanoi committed suicide at the end of April 1975.

Tuesday, the 30th of April 1975 marked the beginning of abysmal times for South Vietnamese. Vietnamese know a different story of Sai Gon in the last 72 hours of April 1975. Many lived in outer regions of the city that survived the invasion to undergo life in a conquered realm. Thousands fled by walking west to Thailand. Hundreds of thousands sailed south and east to Hong Kong, the Philippines, and Malaysia for years.

Few Vietnamese knew how to swim in Southeast Asia of 1975. Hundreds of thousands of Vietnamese drowned in the South China Sea. Others died of starvation, dehydration or at the hands of Thai and Vietnamese pirates.

Captured in the escape attempt by Vietnamese patrols, would-be refugees spent years in prisons relabeled "re-education camps." Some disappeared forever without their final moments recorded.

Coastline is about the people who made it out and the history that drove them to desperate measures. In particular, this initially relies on the memory of an ethnic Chinese Vietnamese eight-year old girl Nguyên Xuân Loan (Loan).

Against all odds, Loan survived more than a day clinging to boat lumber in the South China Sea, years in the trees of a tropical jungle and life as an inadvertent orphan alone in an alien wilderness known as the United States of America.

I have assembled the following dramatized narrative from Loan's memories. Lacking formal education until she made her way to the United States at the age of fourteen in 1984, the record of her early days is in her head. I am her "grunt," her interpreter, inadequate to the task as I might be. I write her memories down and tie it to the history around her.

Loan knew only what her mother, Nguyên Maï (Maï), and the lessons of a falling country could impart to her. Stranded in the jungle, she expanded her skills of survival not realizing the extent her mother had prepared her to endure.

Struggling to the next moment and the next day, she was too young to understand the role of her mother in the fight to preserve South Viet Nam from Communism. Two decades passed before Loan learned the history of the circumstances of her family that propelled her to America.

Lessons on the streets of Sai Gon and the jungle villages of surrounding communities filled the void in Loan's vacant education and enabled her to survive extreme hardship. After all of Viet Nam plunged into barbaric re-organization on April 30, 1975, she entered a new chapter of calamity to become an inadvertent orphan in 1977 cast into a wide foreign world alone.

While Loan's family remained in Sai Gon, they had essentially traded Loan's servitude to another family in exchange for two hundred kilos of rice. The rice fed her siblings as Viet Nam's civilization went dark. The unfamiliar family she served fled Viet Nam taking her with them in an over-loaded fishing boat that broke up in heavy seas and sank off a rugged section of the Philippine coast.

The South China Sea and the jungles of the Bataan Peninsula completed her informal training. It also prepared her for challenges in the foreign land of North America.

I constructed this narrative around the personal story of Loan and the greatest exodus across oceans and through tropical forests that the world has ever known. The term mass exodus is somewhat inappropriate. It occurred in numbers of two to over a hundred at a time. Some were caught and returned to Viet Nam only to try again months later. This is a story about the flight of the incredible Vietnamese as roughly detailed in part by a young girl's indelible memories.

This is also about America and the positive roles many might not realize Americans played in the change of lives in Southeast Asia. There have been numerous first-person narratives of difficult passages out of Viet Nam. This story ties together the tragic events and remarkable experiences that ties Viet Nam to North America and to each hour of every day in the present.

I sorted through Loan's words as if constructing a ten-thousand-piece puzzle composed of more than three dimensions. She spent decades traveling tens of thousands of miles largely alone starting at the age of seven. Unschooled, she believed she was in still in Viet Nam for nearly four years as she dwelled in the Philippine jungles. Besides her search for better food, one goal dominated her … embrace her mother again.

Another piece of the puzzle is summarized in a basic question: "By what providence or state of mind of a young unschooled girl enabled her to survive?

The next-to-final piece is the story of the unending pain of her family. Six months after her disappearance, they resigned themselves to accept her mysterious disappearance which only meant death. There had been so many calamities and death. How could her family think they were immune to one more tragedy? They could not bear the rift in their hearts for much longer. Civilization in Viet Nam deteriorated rapidly adding new burdens to the living.

They wanted closure. Her family's mystery ran for eighteen years.

Besides starvation, extreme isolation, packs of wild dogs, a near miss with land mines and NVA artillery, by the age of 14, Loan had lived out the calamities and stresses of a lifetime. By then, she entered the United States as an orphaned refugee from Viet Nam with zero knowledge of language or western culture. Simply, her childhood, if anyone can call it that, was inconceivable. No one should have survived it.

This story pieced together by listening to Nguyên Xuân Loan in every minute she shared a memory or thought. Without notice, she emotes or recalls something. I interrupt my day job to listen and record.

Recording her words is hard as the mangled English and mixed up lexicon do not result in clear text. We needed a Rosetta stone to sort her historical references from hysterical conclusions.

Time often passes between related memories. I dutifully collected and cataloged them. Since 2006, I covered a wall with shifting time-lines, sticky notes on research and wore out my welcome with the local library system keeping books far longer than allowed. Eventually, one event tied to another and a corner of the puzzle formed. Another corner developed. Islands of assembled memories and historical notes formed in the middle.

Like the assembly of complex puzzle, a sizable framework developed at the edges. The left boundary of the timeline expanded back to essential earlier history in China and World War II.

The challenge became sorting out annoying inner pieces and overcoming my limited understanding of Asian culture and language. Her use of terms baffled me as if the puzzle was all of one color with every piece unique.

As a student of Nguyên Xuên Loan and Viet Nam, you have to sort between the lexicon of her fourth language, English, modified with a thick Asian accent and pronunciations that require a better "Rosetta stone." Mix that in by fathoming unfamiliar ways of eastern culture viewed through the lens of my western upbringing and racial misperceptions.

The term "inscrutable Asian" applies wholesale. The language and writing of all Asia is 90 degrees askew and every expression sounds intense to western ears. Asian tongues sound as if the speaker is angry or about to vomit. They often three words in Vietnamese where one will do in English.

Interviews with American veterans and Vietnamese refugees eventually added enough information to form a "Loan's Guidebook" of sorts. It was hazardous to interview some Vietnamese in Viet Nam. A white American's attention to a Vietnamese war veteran might draw unfavorable notice from the regime. We made do in America with limited conversations in Viet Nam.

Many American Viet Nam vets that were in the thick of "it" are hesitant to plow up their memories. Yet, as some get older, they feel compelled to talk before they can no longer do so.

Breakthroughs came rapidly after spending nine weeks in three different trips living with her family in Sai Gon. Working from a hotel room would have been far less productive. Living in the Cholon, the Chinatown of Sai Gon, I saw again and again the places where a bomb landed here or there. Or a trench was excavated for mass burial in May 1975. I have met some of the survivors that lost nearly all they held dear in 1975.

Finally, declassified documents and books on the war enabled corroboration of events. I have read and re-read some of them, corresponding with some of the authors who are generous to respond.

For lack of a better term, the last pieces focus on providence. By what miracle or strength did she survive? If she had a guardian angel, there had to be a least three of which two retired to permanent emotional therapy treatments.

There was luck and pluck to be sure. The mystery binds together by her personal determination to press on to the next moment. I kid you not. Few American-born children today could survive her journey.

The challenge is properly conveying Loan's puzzle into print. Her first husband paid a writer $15,000 eighteen years ago to develop the narrative. He and the writer travelled to the Bataan Peninsula looking for evidence she had made by marking rocks in an effort to find her way out. Having found some of her scratches in the rocks, the writer struggled to build the story from her memories. Viet Nam was still emerging from its isolation since 1975 and wary of foreign journalists.

As it were, there were many Vietnamese that were stranded for a time before the United States processed them to America through Thailand, Malaysian and Philippine refugee programs. It took Loan more than five years in the Philippines to cross the American coastline.

Out of fear of being stranded again in the jungle, Loan refused to return to the Philippines with the writer and her husband. They found some of the evidence. Unfortunately, her husband died shortly after that trip in a construction accident in Nebraska.

Loan's English was still a work in progress with two small children to manage. Her husband had not "Americanized" her well enough and lacked the mindset to put down her memories on paper. The writer disappeared. His notes, if they were cogent, were lost after she made several moves to other states.

After piecing together hundreds of events and comments, I did not know how to present this other than a back and forth narrative between events just as Loan told me. Telling this sequentially loses the flavor of the surprise as I learned each part the same way.

From that process, I concluded that the first writer did not have enough time. He did not live with Loan, which is a necessity due to the variability of when she feels like talking about her story.

As it turns out from when I first started this project in 2006, time in the jungle is significant component but not the whole story. The Asian migrations, Viet Nam, the Vietnamese, and America's role after April 30, 1975 are the story. Additionally, the story starts in 1937 China when Japan invaded Shanghai and put lives in motion that ended up in Southern Viet Nam and then in North America and half a dozen countries.

Ten years ago, if someone told me I would research and document a life and a history such as follows, I'd ask a simple "How?" Writing is not in an engineer's DNA. Loan's story is a retrovirus, a life-long infection that transformed my intellect and view of a much larger world.

Her story owns me. If you don't understand this, let me rephrase the statement. Her story owns me.

I have attempted to flesh this in with the facts of Viet Nam between 1945 and 1995, 1970s Philippines and numerous accounts of other survivors in their transition to other countries. Tragically, I lack the record of 600,000-plus Vietnamese that failed to make the transit. Their legacies are their bones lying at the bottom of the South China Sea or underneath over-grown jungle paths leading to Thailand.

Many sources are difficult to confirm. Interviews with vital living witnesses in Viet Nam are hazardous. To this day, attention of an American interviewing a former combatant, even in what passes for a nursing home in Viet Nam can jeopardize the welfare of the Vietnamese citizen and put the American on an early flight home.

Nearly four decades after Sai Gon fell, many refugees have passed away. Among the survivors, memories remain painful to explore. Only by living with a witness do I know most any of the incredible events of this story.

When in Viet Nam, engage any internet search-engine about the grim afterlife of Viet Nam's war. Google finds a fraction of the existing articles sanitized of anything unfavorable to Hanoi.

Censorship is alive and well in the 21st century. Where American media may under-report or distort events unfavorable to an agenda, official "press" in other countries re-writes history if not shout down contrary evidence.

Evidence of western affiliations of any sort held by South Vietnamese was dangerous to possess. Papers, photographs, memorabilia, or any sort became a liability after 30 April 1975. What may still remain is hidden to this day.

Vital interviews with living witnesses are gone. The experiences of significant people in this story are dead and their remarkable part in this story, if not told to someone else, is lost to history.

This book serves another purpose. Loan's story will elicit the memories if not the living testimony of over-looked participants in this event. This may serve as a hub to call in orphaned memories that deserve a home.

I have done my best to narrate this phenomenal story. I also have much to learn.

What can be more complicated than deciding to leave a beloved country? What can be more difficult than to leave a warm fertile land for an alien environment half a world away, 99% populated by other races, language, and culture?

COASTLINE Landfall – First Passage represents in a simplified version of immensely complicated lives of the native-born Vietnamese that now populate other parts of the worlds. It also reveals their remarkable adaptive nature.

Learning of Loan's passage altered my sense of comfort. The cruelty of her circumstances shattered my construct of the world. I am at the same time, less secure but more encouraged. Her life's story improves my view of human resilience and charity.

I have shed untold tears in my attempt to wrap my mind around Loan's and Viet Nam's difficult circumstances over five tortuous decades. I have spent time and thought concerning Vietnamese/Asian culture and the history of Viet Nam between 1945 and 1995. After three trips to Viet Nam and dwelling in the heart of Sai Gon where this narrative begins, this is only a beginning.

My American frame of reference worked poorly to explain Vietnamese or for that matter, Asians. As an aging Caucasian male from a prosperous family in Middle America, I have attempted to discard earlier assumptions about what makes people "tick."

The biggest stress in my formative years in the 1960s was about avoiding the meat-grinder that was the American period of the Viet Nam War. I have had an easy life with minimal drama and no tragedies. Taking on this project is still a bit of personal mystery.

I cannot really tell you why I started recording her story other than I could. I have access to her and am somewhat literate. What other qualifications should I need?

Through interpretation of her story, Loan's life is the thread that weaves a map of recent history of Viet Nam. The unfolded guide shows two main paths, noted with question marks and stained with tears.

One path, if the reader is non-Vietnamese, reveals their starkly different world. It is nothing like I expected. Previous books, documentaries and movies area rough representations. Perhaps, this improves the portrayal short of traveling there.

The other path reveals some of the categories of Vietnamese that vary based on when they left, how they fled the country, their generation and their politics. There are many types of Vietnamese that reside in North America and other parts of the world. From expatriates that arrived in 1975 that never looked back to ones that desire to go home if they could make a better living, they are here. There even those who have "walked" the Viet Nam War here with both sides of the conflict nursing resentment if not hostility in many Vietnamese communities across North America.

On my first trip to Viet Nam in 2009, one of my sons predicted that I was about to take a sip from a "cultural fire hose." He was half-right. I have taken a plunge into a torrent of history between Viet Nam, America, and the world as revealed by the Vietnamese "boat people."

The Author's Risk

We are taking a risk in writing this if it is perceived as critical of Viet Nam's current state of government. This is a history of conditions no longer in existence. There is a shameful component of history that should not be forgotten and this narrative will be dishonest if facts and evidence are edited from this text.

I may not be able to return, or if there, I may suffer some discomfort by those advocating a sanitized history that differs substantially from what I know. Therefore, I have changed the names of significant people and shifted the locations of some of the significant events.

Know this. The people I describe existed and at this writing are still alive. Lastly, I could not invent this story. I am merely its scribe.

Tim Wilcox
January 2015

SECTION ONE: SAI GON

28 April 1975 Sai Gon, Viet Nam The Cholon Districts *(Chinatown)*
Traffic – Sai Gon Style
__Ho Chi Minh City__ (Formerly Sai Gon and to many, still Sai Gon)
__Latitude:__ 10.8º North. Longitude: 106.7º East. Elevation: 3 meters (10 feet.) above sea level.
__Weather:__ Tropical: Daily temperature range 365 days of the year: 70º F. to 90º F.
__Humidity:__ 8,760 hours out of 8,760 hours of the year (8,784 hours in leap years).
__Time difference from Rocky Mountain Time:__ Summer: 13 Hours ahead, Winter ahead: 14 Hours.

An eclectic stream of motorized vehicles blended with pedestrians and peddlers displaying their wares arrayed on the sides of the road. The often-clogged narrow and wide arteries moved the life-blood of Sai Gon.

Morning Sai Gon traffic flowed as if a river of people and things. Motor scooters darted in and out among bicycles and three-wheel carts that served as any man's truck transported every form of commerce. Wiry sweating Asian men pushed and pedaled their three-wheel handcarts laden, often to over-flowing, with market produce, construction materials, and refuse. Occasionally, a cart overloaded with rice straw or lemon grass crept among the throng of vehicles. An unseen driver steered the mobile ball of hay via limited vision through narrow slots cut into the front and sides.

The cumbersome over-loaded carts and bicycles set the pace of urban flow resembling bobbing flotsam in a turbulent stream of humanity. To western eyes, this was chaos in slow motion.

Women of all ages wore the ubiquitous non-la, a practical conical rice-straw hat, and a common outfit that westerners thought more as pajamas mixed with other women in their Aoi Dai, elegant apron-like dresses unique to Viet Nam. They gently wove their bicycles around the slow tricycle-carts and turned just in time to avoid pedestrians making a practiced crossing of the street.

Sai Gon Street Crossing

Seasoned pedestrians waded into the traffic as if fording a swollen river. Rather than waiting hopelessly for a gap in the flow to dash for the other side, they step off in front of the oncoming traffic. Seasoned pedestrians expected bicycles, motorcycles, and small trucks to navigate around them. Pedestrians need only pace their transit. Predictable movements gave drivers options to weave right or left. Impulsive darting pedestrians seldom lasted very long.

Babies swinging in back-slings clung to their mother's ribs as they dozed off or suckled an exposed nipple. Their mothers wove their bicycles haltingly in the traffic being the first to concede other vehicles a path ahead of them. Mothers on motor scooters with children of every age sitting in front or clinging to their back moved tentatively in the traffic mingled with other bicycles and food carts pushed by men and women of every age and infirmity.

Nuc maum, a distinct Vietnamese form of the Asian sauce flavored dried and steamed fish and scented the morning air. The food-carts vendors threaded the congestion only long enough to steer to the next side street to peddle their wares. The hint of rough kerosene wafted from their carts as they heated varieties of Vietnamese foods out of blackened tin cans stamped in America. The aromas of spices and steam rice mixed with engine exhaust and over-ripe sweat.

Motor scooters and small motorcycles with one, two, or more people zipped through the street. 3-wheel Xe Lams, iconic Italian-made mini utility-vehicles with a one-man cab in front bobbed in the oozing flow of people and cargo. The Xe Lam worked well in the narrow streets of Italy cities constructed centuries before based on horse-drawn carts. The vehicles found a working home in narrow passages of Asian side-streets and dotted broad thoroughfares.

The Xe Lam possessed a universal load-bearing platform that provided utility from truck bed to bench seats. The ubiquitous Xe Lams provided everything from bus service of up to a dozen or more passengers to overloaded transport, the suspension springs fully compressed.

Sai Gon Traffic Control: *(None)*

Bells, horns, and voices mixed in Vietnamese and Cantonese constantly expressed, "I'm here! I'm here!" and marked the intersection of streets and near collisions. Few angry words characterized the events. Citizens beeped and called out caution at every turn, intersection, or adjoining street. The flow managed congestion liberally with a mildly-enforced stay-on-the-right-side-of-traffic rule.

In a jam, the left side of the road and any sidewalk, left or right provided acceptable passage. Again, seasoned pedestrians crossed streets steadily made their slow progress predictable. All manner of wheeled traffic flowed around them.

The mixture of pedestrians and motorized traffic worked in slow motion. Rush hour traffic rarely averaged more than 33 kilometers per hour *(~20 miles per hour)*. Higher traffic speeds assured injuries and death.

Few wore helmets on the small displacement French, Italian, French and Japanese motorcycles. Traffic lights sorting most intersections remained decades away from replacing Sai Gon police officers directing the flow. Infamous European traffic circles worked well enough to sort out the cross-roads of up to seven intersecting streets.

Vietnamese writing, the only Asian language using Roman letters modified with five or six diacritics and several dozen combinations to apply sounds unfamiliar in western languages. Business signs, usually written in red letters on a yellow background, declared an enterprise that could be as small as two-meter square space on the side of the road. Enterprise occurred wherever there was traffic and an acceptable working space to the side.

Some of the signage bore Chinese characters, written in Cantonese. Some sections of Sai Gon barely spoke Southern Vietnamese. They immigrated to Viet Nam from southern China earlier in the century.

Commerce in languages varied. Vietnamese prevailed in most of the city. In the Cholon, Cantonese dominated daily conversation.

To a westerner, many roads and businesses seemed to have similar names. One word with one of the six inflections had six different meanings. The word "ma" with one inflection meant mother, with another inflection, it meant horse.

Half of everybody in Viet Nam seemed to have the family name "Nguyên" pronounced "win" with a barely audible "n" sound in front. It was the name of one of the last emperors of Viet Nam before the French colonized the country more than a century before.

South Viet Nam had divorced itself from France in one form or another for three decades. Of the eight basic "ethnic" groups classified by language, Viet is spoken by the largest population. The Vietnamese identified themselves among 54 people types that spread among the eight language groupings. North Vietnamese differed from South Vietnamese such that odd words made idioms incompatible. One phrase in Hanoi that asked the question, "Where are you going?" translated to "Go wash your hands" in South Viet Nam. North Viet Nam had an additional meaningful tonal quality that affected many the meaning of many phrases.

The chaotic rhythm of traffic set the hum of Sai Gon from 4 AM to midnight every day of the year. A venerable Chinese saying: "When the traffic ceases, so does Sai Gon."

Traffic Stop

Few events short of typhoons and war throttled traffic or commerce in Sai Gon. Density and pace swelled and ebbed according to the day. There was more of it when the Americans were engaged in the war and less after they withdrew the bulk of their forces by the end of 1973.

Traffic swelled again as the population of Sai Gon and surrounding communities exploded with refugees fleeing the North. The North Vietnamese Army (NVA) or People's Army of Viet Nam (PAVN) overwhelmed cities and villages between the 17th parallel and Sai Gon. By Tuesday, April 2nd, Da Nang fell with minimal resistance. The cities of Huë and Nah Trang fell with fleeting resistance.

The Army of the Republic of Viet Nam (ARVN) played a limited delaying action. Even the courageous battles east and northeast of the city bought only weeks.

Many Vietnamese hoped if not expected America to return to salvage South Viet Nam. By mid-April, if they weren't in coming in time to for the cities to the north, at least America will protect Sai Gon.

In a few days, the flow of traditional street traffic ground to a halt. Sai Gon, the "Paris" of Southeast Asia as the world somewhat knew it, was about to die.

The cresting first wave of Hanoi's invasion verged on the edges of Sai Gon by mid-April. The first waves to follow swept into the remnants of South Viet Nam and gutted its political, social and economic structure over-night by May 1, 1975.

Hanoi won out in consolidating the country and saving South Vietnamese citizens from themselves as they described their conquest. The arrogance of the victors eventually initiated a series of tragedies in Cambodia and Laos.

The sad consequence of the fall of Sai Gon was a string of assassinations in the tens of thousands, suicides, mass destruction, and the hazardous flight of millions of people to other countries. The population of entire villages and much of the cities emptied out to seek anonymity in the new wilderness of South Viet Nam until they could leave the country.

South Viet Nam lived through decades of depravity. It took decades to resume previous levels of industry and commerce as measured by the flow of Sai Gon traffic before April 30, 1975.

Sai Gon became Ho Chi Minh City, a euphemism for "city of the lost" to many Vietnamese. No one dare desecrate the name of "Father Ho" in public, under their breath, the continued to call it "Sai Gon." They do so even to this day.

Sai Gon was about to fall to its enemy, Hanoi, and persistent instructions of the late Ho Chi Minh, plunging Southeast Asia into darkness, and scatter objecting Vietnamese populations to far reaches of the planet. Even members of the victorious Viet Cong and NVA found conditions disappointing. Many left the country in the coming decades. The bitterness of the war walked, floated, and flew to other countries. Animosities between Vietnamese on both sides of the conflict smolder to this day.

Sai Gon's traffic diminished. A new traffic emerged, the one of flight from the country. In the next hours, days and years, a 7-year old ethnic-Chinese Vietnamese girl became part of the exodus from Viet Nam. She spoke Cantonese and Vietnamese. In a few years she learned Philippine Spanish and eventually English. Two decades later, she returned from the "dead" to lift her family out of poverty.

Loan's "Big Day" *(April 26, 1975)*

Before sunrise on Saturday, April 26, 1975, six-year old Loan stood below her father holding up a small cardboard box of rusted metal nails and screws above her head. She stood in the flickering light of white-gas lanterns swaying on the top of thin bamboo rods hastily erected to illuminate the courtyard of their home.

Roosters throughout their neighborhood began to crow an hour before. Lacking a working clock in the household, Loan believed it was around 4:00 am. She had been up for an hour.

Her difficult father, Toan, balanced his five-foot thin frame on an upturned metal bucket as he tied stiff wire around two thick hardwood posts. Toan blindly reached down to pick something from the box expecting Loan to hold the box precisely where his hand landed. If he had to grope for the box, he cursed Loan for her lack of attention to him. She focused on his left hand and after an hour, Loan had his hand signals down to an art. His fingers seldom missed the box. She "insured" her service by having a wad of nails and screws in her right hand if Toan missed his mark on the box.

They normally secured the tie-down wire with nails and screws to reduce theft. Toan was in a terrible hurry to finish this task neglecting to screw all the wire wrapping on the inside of the enclosure.

She had never seen her father in a frantic state. She sensed something in the air. He was a difficult man at all times but his urgency was palpable.

A thin handsome man, some might call him sophisticated to the point of being "cool." His charm with women stemmed from a disconnected confidence. Toan was a bit of a playboy. Maï was the principal bread-winner.

Toan's behavior vexed his marriage and relationship with his children throughout his life. He acted as the standard bearer for moral behavior as he transgressed low standards on fidelity and industry on a weekly basis. He was above criticism even as he critiqued everyone in the family at every opportunity.

He seldom raised his voice. He expressed crushing dissatisfaction in a terse manner to steer vulnerable offspring to his will. When that failed, he struck them when they were young and incapable of defense. Traditional Asian respect for elder males gave him a pass on senseless punishments of his family for virtually no offense. Toan corrected young children with various forms of stinging punishment. As they grew older, he added hurtful words and stern looks to keep them in line. All of this usually occurred without loss of composure. Until now.

Many things in this dark morning were terribly different. Toan was frantic. He had been up since 2 AM working furiously in the dark save for the lanterns. He sweated profusely which was odd for a thin man accustomed to the tropics.

He moved about the work on the wall as if in a race for his life. This was the first time Loan saw her father lose composure. His alien behavior made him a stranger.

Before sunset on Friday, her father appeared calm as the family settled in for the evening. Everyone performed their chores tending to any of Toan's immediate requests.

Loan's mother appeared at twilight and talked to Toan in whispers. Maï's intense expression implied urgency but she said nothing to anyone else besides her husband.

After half an hour of conversation with Toan, Maï went to each of her children milling in the house and kissed them on the head in what seemed a solemn ritual to the Loan's older brothers. She told them to listen to their father and take care of each other. Her comments seemed disconnected by the quiet sunset and routine of the household.

By 9 PM, Maï left the house. It was dark save for distant thunder and flashes of light on the eastern horizon. Maï stayed somewhere in Sai Gon unknown to most of the children. They were accustomed to their mother's unexplained comings and goings. It was one more evening without Maï sleeping in the family household. This was unpleasant but normal.

Toan's demeanor had mysteriously shifted that night. He instructed everyone to sleep now. He owned an American alarm clock with the embossed label WestClock. Toan assumed WestClock meant "alarm" in English. He wound it up each night and set it guessing at the actual hour most of the time. *(It had an annoying clacking ring and he was glad it didn't work after Sai Gon fell.)*

He expected them to wake up with a few hours after midnight. They had to start new chores.

True to his word, he woke up everyone before the roosters began to crow. Toan instructed Loan's brothers to reinforce the wall and gate of the courtyard. He told his 17-year old daughter to prepare rice, sweet potatoes and bean curd for everyone to eat at sunrise.

Toan directed Loan to assist him with work on the gate. Normally, she helped her older sister. She followed her father's instruction without question lest he strike her with something.

Loan's arms tired as she held the tin can full of nails above her head. She said nothing to avoid a stern word or a slap on the head. Even as the youngest girl of many siblings, Toan treated her as if she was an older brother. Tonight, he treated her older brothers as slaves.

Toan was a difficult and unforgiving man. He was "Aba"... a.k.a. "father." He commanded blind obedience and expected respect despite minimal show of affection to his children.

Rigid male hierarchy characterized Chinese culture going back thousands of years. Senior males dominated all aspects of family as they chose. This principal also applied to the next tier or generation as western culture labeled it.

Sons had numbers in addition to their names making rank clear among siblings. The number one son possessed substantially more authority than subsequent brothers. The rule of dominance by birth order applied less stringently among sisters.

Toan was the absolute ruler of his house. He acted as he pleased or thought. Older sons seldom challenged him unless an extreme situation required a contest of his will.

While Toan's sons were young, the rest of his children lacked an agency of relief when their mother was absent. Maï managed Toan through her guile, her purse strings and resolve to prevent his autocratic tendencies from doing great harm.

Toan was well-schooled in China although his training meant little to their adopted life in Viet Nam. He was educated in Shanghai, China before civilization disintegrated when Japan invaded in 1937.

For the next five decades, Chairman Mao and his barbarous communist state advanced an inhuman male autocracy to a whole new level. By Mao's direction, China murdered and imprisoned hundreds of millions of independent-thinking productive citizens. It shuttered the advancement of a billion people for 40 years as the rest of the world lived out the future.

Self-serving dogmatic and autocratic men unraveled the morality of China for decades to come. Half of their civilization lived shuttered away in China in the shadows. The hidden humans were all Chinese women and girls.

The measure of morality is subjective among cultures. Asian men might appear more selfish and self-serving to western mores. The distinctions break down when examined more closely. Men with charm and money tend to appear the same the world over when confronted with temptation. Toan was selfish and self-serving.

Toan possesses a charm with women that pervaded his life and continues to this day as he approaches the tenth decade of his life. He was married only once to Nguyên Maï. In their immediate marriage, she bore eleven children. He sired twice that many by most accounts.

By 1975, Loan had five half-brothers she knew about because her mother had adopted them into the family. In Asia, distinction is seldom made between all-blood and half-blood when a parent such as Loan's mother accepted the offspring of her husband's dalliances.

By current estimates, Toan has sired at least twenty-three children in his 91 years. If there are sons or daughters that reject him outright for his dalliances, it is not evident in his house. After all it is his house whether or not he built it by himself.

Asia practiced polygamy openly for millennia. Where it became technically illegal, it has been tolerated in less overt forms. In a land that had 1st wives, 2nd wives and 3rd wives for millennia, having a girlfriend is a term of historical (*if not hysterical*) distinction.

Welfare of offspring born in any circumstance of relationship measures a culture's level of civilization. The reverse proves the point. During warfare, the guardians of a child's future are always compromised thus diminishing a civil world.

Viet Nam hardly knew peace since the 1930s. When not abandoned outright by stressed families, many children orphaned by war migrated to communities. Orphanages managed by Buddhist and Christian organizations took on orphans as best they could. Toward the end of Sai Gon and limited by resources, many facilities turned away older children capable of living on the streets of Sai Gon and other communities.

The fate of bastard children varied. Toan produced more than a dozen of them. Incredibly, Maï eventually accepted six of them into her care and remained married to her husband thoughout her life.

Loan had come into the world in 1968 and knew little of a civilized world. She expected nothing gentle from her father. Mai labored tirelessly to provide shelter and food to more than a dozen children by the time Loan was born. Outside of the Chinese New Year (TET) celebration, Loan seldom enjoyed a full stomach. Three square meals a day was a fantasy

Toan achieved the status of a jerk by most world measures. He is not all to blame in this. Ancient culture removed him from immediate condemnation. Single women that shared their favors with him played a part and the war accommodated excuses for poor character endlessly. Above all, Maê's loyalty to her marriage defied cold logic.

Loan knew nothing of this history. She knew only to avoid being slapped and cursed. Her father let few objections go unpunished. She obeyed Toan as best as possible. Harsh words and slaps on the head handed out for invisible transgressions kept her guessing on how to act. She attempted to figure out the proper way to hold up the tin of nails to avoid Toan's reprisals.

Six of her older brothers ranging from ages 8 to 27 stood on short bamboo ladders as they worked on the posts next to her binding old and new bamboo side by side to form a vertical wall that formed the front entrance of their house. They bound the posts with rusty fragile wire, twisting it with one pair of pliers shared among them. The Chinese-made baling wire stained their hands orange and snapped easily when stressed too often.

The brothers asked among themselves if there was wire that did not break so easily. They knew their father made a bargain against their mother's advice to pay more for American and Japanese products.

Toan excused his decisions by saying the "black market" dried up of better goods. Fact: he spent the difference on girlfriends. As Sai Gon's future worsened, Toan discovered that his pocket money went further. He sustained a girlfriend or two as easily as ever.

As the piaster inflated, the desperation of people on the fringes grew. At some point, gold and American money mattered. Eventually, American money became too dangerous to hold.

Normally, if Toan had overheard his sons' challenging questions, he stopped and berated if not beat them for insolence. In this case, over the last week, lectures shortened and the beatings almost stopped with a command: "Make it work. We have no choices."

Up to then, Toan droned on with his endless repetition about his children's inadequacies. This followed and preceded a slap or whack of his infamous broom handle on the top of their heads or backs.

Today, the children heard none of Toan's lectures. Toan gave them encouragement to get the task done. The tension in Toan's face and voice was evident to everyone.

The end of American military participation in Viet Nam started in early 1972. America re-assigned most of the military on the ground to advisory duties. Soldiers finished out their "tour" and returned to civilian life in North America by the end of 1973. With the Americans went the cadres of non-military support staff, contractors, and equipment. With the Americans went the abundance of high-quality construction materials.

Vietnamese black markets in recycled or stolen American goods dried up. Few trusted the street vendors who claimed "special access." Outside of low-fired clay bricks, jungle-cut bamboo and coconut leaves, durable manufactured building materials disappeared.

Toan exhausted his supply of decent construction materials. He resorted to using mud bricks and bamboo tied with knife-resisting wire in lieu of bamboo strips. He bound the bamboo to strengthen the front wall and reduce theft from neighbors. When he neglected to tie everything down, some of the materials in the front of the house disappeared at night.

The clay/mud bricks added shrapnel-stopping mass to the wall. Toan had served with the French army in Hanoi in the early 1950s. Before France surrendered the colony in 1954, he recalled the last days of French operations and the horrific damage of mortars shredding flimsy rural dwellings. Many non-combatants died as they huddled helplessly in their homes of bamboo, rice straw, and coconut fronds.

Toan cursed himself for missing the opportunity to store American plywood. It made the job of building up the front wall much easier. To avoid knowledge of his connections, Toan disguised American products with a clay/mud covering and mended it after heavy rains. Few were the wiser, so Toan thought.

Toan was distracted this morning. As he coerced everyone to finish their chores, he let small infractions pass by unnoticed. Loan and her brothers appreciated their father's distraction. They were yet to realize their family had run out of time.

The flashes last night to the northeast were not lightning. The distant rumbles were not thunder. The outlying communities adjacent to Sai Gon were under attack.

Bombardment

The barrage began as a low vibration in their chest they felt first in a low rumble in their feet a split second before they heard the explosions. The NVA began shelling the Cholon neighborhoods.

Loan was more curious than afraid. The first sounds reminded her of a large sack of rice hitting the floor. "Wuummppp." Then thunder. In succession, the series of sounds came from the southeast. Mortars shells exploded on the fringes of Sai Gon and "walked" toward them.

Another sound similar to a New Year's rocket flew overhead with a spitting swishing sound. Rockets! Whooshing 122mm Katyusha rockets flew overhead landing a block away.

North Viet Nam made its final assault on Sai Gon. The NVA shelled the neighborhoods they believed might offer resistance. They bombarded the Chinese neighborhoods of the Cholon.

Loan's father looked up turning his head to locate the direction of new sounds. Toan heard an ominous "foom!" from blocks away, followed by another. Toan knew these sounds too well. He distinguished the "foom" of mortars and the "crack" of mobile artillery. There was more to follow as the explosions grew close.

Tracking mortar rounds wasted precious seconds seeking safety. Explosions erupted a few hundred meters to the north. Time had run out.

Lot Hui! Lot Hui! (*Hide! Hide!*)

Toan shouted before the mortars exploded in a neighboring street, "Lot Hui! Lot Hui!" Cantonese: "Hide! Hide!" As he focused on the direction of the explosions, Loan and her younger brothers had stepped through the gate to look up or down the narrow road to see what was coming their way.

Toan losing composure screamed at everyone to get inside the gate immediately. None of them had ever heard him sound as he did now. From his earliest days, he had summoned his "command voice." That alone made them obedient.

He resumed his command voice ordering them to come into the house to take cover. He herded the younger children into the front of the house telling them to stand at his bed mat.

The bewildered children stared at their father. In the flimsy long and narrow single story one-room house constructed with flammable bamboo, thatch, and coconut leaves, where do they hide?

The thin small man strained to contain himself. There would be time enough to punish them if they survived what was heading their way. In one form or another, everyone in the family knew the horrors of high explosives.

TET Land Mine

Number three son, 18-year old Cüõng, was bright and eager to please. Three months before, Cüõng helped a farmer plow a peanut field Maï had inherited from her father outside of Tay Ninh, two hours north-west of Sai Gon. The remote plot of open land was suitable for sweet potatoes and peanuts. If not farmed, the jungle quickly reclaimed it.

Three teenagers of other families and Cüõng gathered the peanuts out of the upturned soil. They worked close to the small tractor as its rake unearthed legumes from the soft earth.

They worked quickly to harvest their share of the peanuts in order to prepare meals for Tet, the Chinese New Year celebrated on the second new moon after the winter solstice. Tet is the biggest holiday of the year and among the few times Viet Nam sets aside work *(and warfare)* in order to enjoy the holiday.

Buddhist Viet Nam shut down to celebrate the holiday. Christian Vietnamese took it in stride and celebrated with the rest of the country. Tet was a Day of Atonement, New Year's and Christmas rolled into one big holiday. Everyone made an effort to put on the best celebration possible.

Loan and three of her older brothers crouched low to the ground 30 yards behind the tractor taking time to pick out peanuts the others had missed. Loan's mother had been inside the one-room house preparing other meals with Loan's older sister, also called Maï. Late morning, they took a break to step out and watch the primitive tractor creep along as it turned the soil. Late morning, the machine struck a mine as Cüõng's mother and sister looked on from the porch of the farmhouse.

The mine was large. By its size, it was designed to destroy a disable a vehicle. By 1975, Viet Nam was peppered with thousands of anti-personnel mines that varied from the M14-type "toe-poppers" *(đạp lôi "step mine")* that disabled a soldier to sophisticated mines that killed a dozen.

This mine was much larger. It was a tank mine.

As Loan's brothers bent over looking for missed peanuts, the shock wave shoved them and Loan to the dirt. Other than blood seeping from her right ear, Loan was unharmed. She lay face down in the dirt as her senses recovered from the shock. Except for burst eardrums, her three younger brothers were unharmed.

Adrenaline raced her heart. Loan could feel a pulse in her temples as she spit dirt and wiped soil from her face. She tried to stand up before her sense of balance recovered. She stumbled aimlessly for a minute. As her vision cleared, she saw that her other brothers in the field attempted to stand up. Cüõng and the others around the tractor had disappeared in a red fog.

Indiscernible remains of the four children, the old man, the tractor, and clouds of dirt rained down into a cloud of dust and smoke. Maï and her daughter had been shoved against the thatch wall but remained standing, staring, mouths open in a long exhale. Leaning against the wall, they stared where the tractor had been moving. It took five seconds for their expressions to thaw into horror. Incoherent noises rose from their gut.

Loan and her brothers stood on unsteady legs unable to hear. Each instinctively wanted to run toward the spot where the five had been plowing. Nothing was visible but smoke, a wet red-brown mist and a yawning crater littered with grisly debris. They turned and stumbled off the field toward the house. Their screams stuck in their throats as they gasped for air. Cüõng along with the others was gone.

There was hardly enough of the five to construct an entire adult body. A day after the explosion, a neighbor returned an object their dog had found and carried around. It was most of Cüõng head.

The five families and neighboring friends scoured the jungle and located a few more remains. They added it to a singular off-white cotton burial shroud. Decay set in on the flesh. They had to bury everything soon.

The families buried the four children and the farmer next to Maï's house in a common grave. Maï donated her property and a wad of cash to start the process of making a site. In exchange for perpetual rights to visit the site, the four other grieving families chipped in what they could for a mass grave marker. South Viet Nam in January 1975 was in turmoil verging on absolute chaos. Only rough grave markers were available.

Crushed in grief, Maï instructed Toan to handle the grim duty of transporting the red pumice grave markers from a stone cutter in Sai Gon. The families worked together to complete the grave whose site sits overgrown by jungle to this day. The grave sits 30 meters from where the mine turned them into casualties of war.

Loan's family grieved for weeks. To the end of her days, Maï never enjoyed the Tet holiday again. Everyone suspected but no one said, it was payback by Hanoi. Maï, the warrior-mother, had stayed in one place too long. Thirty-two years later, Maï returned to Tay Ninh permanently to watch over Cüóng. In the fall of 2007, Loan's family interned her remains next to the humble grave markers of the five.

Besides expressed anger and perpetual dissatisfaction, Toan seldom showed softer emotions. Loan remembered her father's anger over Cüóng death, little more. Much like her oldest brother, Huang, Cüóng made everyone laugh as he competed for attention among his many brothers. He made the day easier with his unchallenged humor and perpetual enthusiasm.

At her age, Loan knew little of the world. She knew that she enjoyed Cüóng and his sense of humor. She knew also that Cüóng was gone. This loss crushed her universe. Her favorite older brother was dead. He was one among five of senseless casualties of political objectives.

Cüóng's death loomed disproportionately large. The family's world dimmed a bit with his loss. Yet, his father barely acknowledged that sadness. He was angry with Cüóng for making the ultimate mistake of recklessness.

The small farm plots were an unlikely place for such large ordnance. The sheer size and depth of the crater indicated that it was a tank mine. It was expensive ordnance for the Viet Cong to deploy in such a wayward location. Maï's father had purchased the land in 1958, there had been no history of battles or on the way to anywhere a heavy vehicle might travel. American armament never traveled there. Someone placed the mine for other purposes.

They knew of no reason why the field was mined or if there were more buried in the fields. It could have been buried in December after the ground had been sown for peanuts.

No one wanted to find the culprit. Curiosity elicited unwanted attention from the NVA as the area was rife with VC and NVA. Maï's plot of land ceased being farmed for over two decades. It would not return to agriculture until the mid-1990s as Viet Nam cleared farmland of mines and booby-traps.

Toan believed Cüöng was reckless, working too quickly, too close to the tractor. His complaints were irrational. Unmarked minefields plagued Viet Nam. Yet, Toan thought Cüöng should have known better. Toan was all wise about his son's tragic mistake. *(Author's Note: Personally, as a father of three and parent of five, the loss of a child would crush me. If I had sired 23 children, still, the loss of a single child would crush me. Toan only exhibited anger over Cüöng recklessness. Perhaps he had deeper sentiments but it was not the way of Chinese culture for a man to be so exposed.)*

Explosions in the Neighborhood

As the neighborhood received mortars and rockets, Toan cursed his wife for her absence. Despite the chaos emerging around him, he privately demanded her presence. Between commands, he muttered curses under his breath as he winced as from the new concussions in the neighborhood. To anyone unfamiliar with Toan, they thought he was losing his mind.

Maï had abandoned her duty to the children, so Toan believed. She had dumped one hundred percent of the responsibility on him in what amounted to the greatest danger the large family had ever faced.

He could not imagine what kept her away. He was unable to know that Maï watched in horror from a few kilometers to the east as deadly rockets flew overhead toward the Cholon neighborhoods. Perched in a church steeple at an abandoned Christian orphanage, she was spotting NVA movement on the fringes of Sai Gon when the barrage began. She watched the flares of the rocket engines as the Russian-made ordnance flew into her neighborhood.

Toan's lapse into delirious mutterings stopped as he made the one decision he hoped to avoid. There was simply no choice but to expose his best kept secret.

He ignored the sound of the rocket warheads and mortar rounds detonating and turned to his children clustered together. Toan ordered his children to stand by the bed mat.

He directed his older sons to secure the front gate. He was about to reveal a secret he had managed to keep from most of the children for the last three years. Now his secret might be their only chance of survival.

Nearly a dozen children ranging from young Loan to 17-year-old big sister, Maï assembled in the front of the long structure. Older brothers joined them.

The interior was dark with a triangular opening in the back facing south. The glare of the morning sky rendered everything interior in black until eyes adjusted to the space. In this oversized jungle hut populated mostly with children, Toan prepared to reveal a hidden structural feature of the house.

Rural Housing – Viet Nam, 1975

1975-vintage "rural" housing on the boundaries of what defined Sai Gon, were constructed similar to long pole-barn structures on might see on a western farm. The simple construction stood on hardwood or thick bamboo columns. The "A"-frame roof structure utilized bamboo and softwood for cross-ties and pole rafters. The roofing, composed of thatched vines or thin bamboo lashed with strips of rattan and covered with coconut fronds, needed only to shed the rain.

If the families had means, the roofing was made of galvanized or raw corrugated iron. Red-brick and mortar replaced thatch walls. Families of means covered the brick with cement plaster, usually sans a matrix of steel or bamboo mesh to hold the coating together.

The narrow ends of the houses were often open below the roof to ventilate the interior. On larger homes and businesses, an additional story was added to accommodate cooking smoke and enable sunlight to penetrate the interior of the house.

Coarse cotton sheets covered two-meter tall bamboo partitions along the sides and the rear of the house to provide a measure of privacy. The latrine and bathing area possessed the only mortared brick in the floor and rear wall for sanitary needs.

Toan's house contained some unusual features. Half a dozen American-made 55-gallon oil drums lined the east wall of the house. This provided water for bathing and extinguishing fires on the frequent occasion when the walls or roof began to burn. Several of the drums were lined with plastic to reduce the taste of petroleum residue and rust when the water was used for cooking. Any stored water tasted of polyethylene plastic that spices rarely neutralized.

The house lacked blast-resistant structure. A close strike could shove the entire structure to the ground. A direct hit would likely injure if not kill all the inhabitants. There was nothing in typical construction to stop a bullet or deflect shrapnel. Except for the bricks and water-storage in oil drums, everything in the construction was flammable.

Where to Hide

No one hid. No one took cover. Their best option above ground: hug the water-filled drums inside. It gave some of them a 50/50 chance of surviving the barrage. The other option: jump into the latrine. Third option, dig a hole. There was not enough time to make a hole in the ground.

As they puzzled over what Toan was preparing to do next, a rocket arced out of the sky into a similarly constructed house twenty meters *(sixty feet)* to the west of them. Ball bearings and pieces of hot metal zinged through the air. The concussion shook everyone.

Loan later remembered that it felt as if someone shoved her down to the ground. It instantly reminded her of when Cüöng, brother number three, and four others were blown up by the landmine near Tay Ninh.

Deadly shrapnel pierced the neighbor's house blowing the structure apart. Unprotected flesh separated from bone, body parts fell disconnected to blend in with the debris. Twisted pieces of hot metal split apart people and livestock. Fragments of coconut fronds and bamboo rained down in the shadows of the clouds of dust and smoke rising into the air.

As the shock of the explosion faded in their ears, they heard the screams of neighbors as the remainder of the house collapsed. Rattan bindings split by the shrapnel disconnect post and beam. Crumpled roof tiled in dry coconut leaves began to smoke and burn.

Impulsive Curiosity

Ever curious, Loan impulsively darted through the heavy bamboo gate as oldest brothers lifted it to swing it the opposite post. As the smallest member of the family, they didn't see her pass through the gate. They first noticed successive brothers chasing after their baby sister. She led a rush out the front gate to see the aftermath. Her brothers followed.

Toan realized too slowly that he once again lost control of his brood. In the dark interior, he had been frantically fussing with something around his bed-matt as his younger children bolted into the narrow road. The gaggle of children rounded the left corner of their front gate to see the aftermath of the large mortar. The unfamiliarity of their neighbor's collapsed house silenced them.

Amidst the series of long one-story rural houses mixed with open land with gardens and orchards, the largest house in the neighborhood with several dozen members of six families laid blown apart and starting to burn. The mangled and shredded bodies of their neighbors lay twisted in the wreckage. Shattered bamboo posts and rafter structure lay in pieces. Odd pieces of material stained nearby walls as if painted red. Injured chickens and a dog mixed in with debris blown into the road.

Twenty-four people were either dead or dying. Some of the still-living rolled and moaned in agony. Rocket shrapnel and bamboo shards bloodied the still-living. All but one died. As remains of the fractured construction burned, stunned victims and spectators began to scream.

The firework-novelty of the explosions transformed to horror. Loan's brothers and sisters ran back to the house screaming only to face another problem ... their father with his wire-wrapped broom and limitless anger. They had disobeyed him. Despite the chaos and tragedies emerging around them, their biggest fear was of their father and his unbridled punishments.

Toan, who by now had sired at least fifteen children within and outside of his marriage, had one other talent. He had mastered the art of intimidating his children. He added one more credential. He provided what amounted to be a bomb-resistant shelter.

Unexpected Blessing

Her father's self-centered universe probably saved her life. Loan recalled this blessing three-plus decades later. *(Author's Note: After years of recording her memories, she told me this. It finally put in perspective why she has treated him with respect as she does to this day.)*

In Toan's ceaseless effort to create a sanctuary for his creature comforts, he inadvertently constructed a durable shelter for his children. He had made a place in which they could hide.

Toan's Pit

Loan's father began excavating a shallow pit starting in 1972. Initially, he excavated the hole to hide his creature comforts, not for the protection of his family. He created the cavity under his bed-mat after he stumbled into dangerous activities conducted by his wife.

Toan, Maï and their two oldest sons alone knew about the pit. She had been aiding the South Vietnamese government who in turn cooperated with the American CIA in neutralizing Viet Cong Infrastructure (VCI). Nguyên Maï began her secret career for the CIA around 1966. This was six years passed before Toan realized the scale and hazards of her actions.

Toan started the pit in secret. He did most of the work drawing on his oldest sons Huang and Seip to pitch in while Maï and the rest of the children lived in a sequence of villages to the north. For fear of unwanted disclosure, they kept knowledge of it from the rest of the family. Since the early 1960s, an unguarded word could invite theft if not destruction of an entire family in the Cholon.

Maï stole enemy weapons among other activities. She "recovered" V.C. guns and explosives and sold the weapons to South Vietnamese and American military for bounty.

Until Maï could deliver the weapons to the Americans or South Vietnamese forces, Toan had to conceal them. In basically a single room barn-like house, there was no other option than burial.

He braced the top with bamboo poles, covered the bracing with American plywood and applied half an inch of smoothed clay to blend in with the rest of the floor. He eventually dug one meter square holes on the north and south sides to access the void without disturbing his sleeping matt each time.

Toan expanded the pit as Maï's clandestine military activities continued. The function of the pit grew as Maï was often paid in American canned goods as well as piasters. She preferred gold but settled for boxes of C-rations and foods stored in aluminum cans.

Flashing sudden wealth in any form invited questions as Viet Nam's economy declined with the exit of the Americans. Sai Gon was infiltrated with North Viet Nam sympathizers and spies for decades. The districts that made up the Cholon largely backed South Viet Nam, Many family's loyalties split between the Hanoi and Sai Gon. The loyalties often shifted based on which side had more power or won large battles. Bottom-line: Anything of western origin or American-made attracted attention.

Boxes of American food products required more head room. Every so often, Toan scraped down another three to six inches in order to stack more on the sides. With a little reinforcement, the thick clay walls held up well.

By the end of 1974, he had excavated over four feet of depth from under the 90" by 90" sleeping mat. He lined the east and west walls with rough-hewn slats to stabilize the side walls and reinforced the bamboo "roof structure".

Standing 4'-10", Toan added a thin bamboo ladder on each end to improve entry and exit. An additional woven mat covered a simple plywood hatch. Covered in a thin layer of clay, a little water and rubbed to smoothness rendered the edges of the hatch invisible.

As America's role in South Viet Nam declined, the nature of contraband changed. Boxes of canned meats (Spam, Vienna sausage), self-contained meals (U.S. C-Rations) and American peanut butter replaced guns, ammunition and grenades.

Toan cut recesses into the firm clay sides to hold money, gold and jewelry. He transferred anything absolutely incriminating such as stolen VC weapons to a similar buried cache in Tay Ninh.

Candles and Zippo butane lighters sat on the boxes, ready to provide illumination when he needed light to sort storage or make inventory. In the tropics, mildew and rot was a constant problem. Toan cut some slots on the east side that penetrated the raised earth of the clay "foundation" to enable air exchange if and when the pit got wet during the monsoon season.

Without planning for it, Toan had built a bomb-shelter of sorts. It was barely large enough to protect the seven residing sons and two daughters as NVA leveled the neighborhood. But it might just work.

Returning Children

The children returned through the gate a minute after they rushed out. Toan stood to one side to confront his wayward offspring. His red-broom handle at the ready, he whacked each child as they entered the front enclosure. Mind-numbed to the point of shame, none dodged the beating. No one questioned his spitting anger. Per Asian culture, an angry father's acts to reinforce discipline went unchallenged.

The beatings occurred as another round of explosions "walked" across the neighborhood. The orderly progression of the concussions indicated something else more ominous. NVA artillery shelled the neighborhood.

Smoke rose from burning debris all around them. People screamed, called out or shouted instructions from all directions. New explosions erupted on all sides fragmenting the flimsy construction of the Vietnamese rural community through-out the fringe of Sai Gon.

Punishments had to wait on something else. For the first time in living memory, something took priority over Toan's process of enforcing discipline on errant Children.

They had to take cover lest his offspring die. Action had a compelling argument.

In the brief lull from the mortar attack in their area, Toan instructed them to obey lest they come to harm. It was not the usual threat that they could be replaced, that he could make new children. It was a common threat that had a different meaning. They were in a bad way.

Children ranging from Loan's six years to Huang's 27 years listened, chastened by the obliteration of six families to the west in one well-placed weapon. Everyone knew the families at all generations. Most everyone was gone in those homes. If still among the living, they were crippled and maimed beyond a productive life. This tragedy occurred throughout Cholon on that day. They weren't combatants, they were victims of Hanoi.

Toan recovered some humanity as the children stood in the house hurting from strikes of the broom and slaps on their heads. He stopped his muttering curses. He motioned the children to make room for him as he approached his sleeping mat.

Pointing at his bed mat lying flat on the clay floor, he calmly said "We have to hide in this hole. We have get in this hole now," waving his hands around to signify the mat.

He studied the quizzical looks in some of their faces. The younger children didn't understand his motion toward the mat and the instruction to get into the hole.

Up to then, there was no "hole–in-the-ground." Until now.

Into the Pit

Toan motioned them to stand aside as he pulled aside a smaller rice-straw floor covering. He pulled on the side of the bed and drew out heavy twine that disappeared into the floor's clay covering.

As Toan lifted the twine, the clay floor split. His actions cleaved the clay/mud in a rough line that formed a one-meter square. An end of the twine tied in a knot to a thick vine that came up in a loop with both ends disappearing into the floor. Toan grabbed the loop with both hands and pulled hard on it. With effort, the closest side of the clay square lifted as if on a hinge.

The split clay line revealed the outline of a hatch-door.

The wooden hatch had been concealed by a thin layer of clay. The bottom of the hatch revealed a portion of an American logo stenciled in black ink: "U.S. Plywood".

Toan raised the hatch to rest standing straight up above a square dark hole. In one motion, Toan now on his hands and knees on the edge of the hole reached down into the hole with his left arm. In a moment, he drew up a bamboo ladder setting it against the edge at a slant.

Loan as well as the rest of her siblings stared blankly at the hole. Not in silence. In the background as Toan miraculously created a hole in the ground, concussions of NVA artillery walked toward them. The sound of the muffled explosions competed with shouts and screams of neighbors. The succession of explosions sounded as if the rounds headed toward their house. Destruction came their way.

Oldest brothers, Huang and Siep, were not amazed. They were busy. Siep ignited a white-gas lantern and held it to one side to provide some light over the hole. It was morning in daylight but the interior of the house darkened as smoke and haze dimmed the sky and obscured the sun.

Toan motioned Loan's oldest brothers to guide the children into the opening starting with her. He pointed to the dark hole and told her to "Go." He saw her uncertainty and explained, "This is a ladder with six rungs. Go. Get to the bottom and move to the back."

In the dim light of the interior of the house, the hole appeared bottomless. Loan paused and swiftly considered her next options. She had to drop down the hole or feel her father's broom handle slap on her back.

Fearing the broom handle more than falling down the hole, Loan moved to the ladder and fumbled climbing down backwards. The bamboo was cool to the touch. The dank air in the hole carried the odors of mildew and wet wood. She stepped onto a cool clay floor and turned to move into the blackness. Hands moving about, she felt cardboard boxes on both sides, moving slowly feeling for the next object.

Toan brandished the broom handle motioning Loan's youngest brother, Que, to follow. Then another brother, Doc, followed Que. Then brother Anam came down, and so on running up the ages of siblings.

Siep, holding the lantern over the hole, instructed his younger brothers and two sisters, "Move to the back." He repeated the instruction, "Move to the back." Loan paused a second as her brother, Que, was moving feeling his way backward down the bamboo ladder. Loan's vision improved enough with the limited light from the torch to see a narrow channel lined with stacks of boxes. She moved back into the hole with her hands outstretched probing the darkness.

She touched a flat wood surface. It was the back end of the hole. In a moment, Que, breathing heavily out of anxiety, not exhaustion, bumped into her. Then next brother, Doc, stood next to Que. No one spoke. They listened for the next instruction from their father and glad to be away from the broom handle.

The forty-nine year old Chinese man carried a heavy broom handle fashioned from bundles of rice straw wrapped in twine and rusted baling wire. The thin rusty wire left parallel welts on the back of an errant child. The working end of the handle was barren of rice-straw. This was no longer a broom, it was a motivational tool.

Toan's chiseled features on a wiry frame rendered him handsome by Asian standards. His good looks concealed a mean streak known well by his children. They tracked the broom handle more than their father's facial expressions just as a dog focuses on a master's cruel hand.

He seldom used it. As each child grew older, their regard for that broom handle grew as well. Toan held the handle menacingly as they clambered into the pit. He stood over the entrance of the dark canopy as the older children shoved the younger ones into the darkness.

Loan felt around the darkness to learn its dimension. The boxes stacked on the sides of the pit to the top of the dimensionless space. The ceiling of the cavity was perhaps more than a meter high, (44" or so). The top was lined with thick bamboo poles laid side by side to form a roof that supported Toan's bed matt above.

Her father called out instructions as the children piled into the hole. He told them to make space for the others. Cardboard boxes stacked and packed with dense heavy things lined the cavity. The sides of the boxes yielded no room. The narrow space between the boxes was less than a meter wide.

The cardboard containers were western and likely from North America. The cardboard was made of cellulose different from rice-straw or Vietnamese pulp woods. It had a distinctive woody smell unlike rice-stalk-cardboard.

The boxes were packed with western products called Spam and Vienna sausage acquired through Maï in her work with the Americans. If the children could read English and if there had been enough light, they could see labels that read "C-Rations." Toan stored smaller items in voids above the boxes including individual cans, duct tape, boxes of screws and nails.

"Dragonflys" and A-1H Skyraiders

Over the noise of chaos, another ominous sound came from the sky. It was the drone of large radial engines powering 1940s-vintage propeller aircraft making low passes over the neighborhood. Several A-1H Skyraiders flew over the neighborhoods roiling columns of smoke rising the first rockets and artillery.

The American-made aircraft were formerly the property of South Viet Nam's Air Force (VNAF). North Vietnamese and defectors of the VNAF piloted the war craft.

The aircraft skirted the center of Sai Gon unsure if the airport or the airbase had anti-aircraft batteries. They reasoned that non-military targets lacked anti-aircraft batteries. The VPAF A-1 pilots of the slower propeller-driven aircraft sorted among targets as smoke rose from the shelled neighborhoods. The Cholon districts held no military assets. It was Chinatown. It was occupied by Sino-Vietnamese civilians who backed the government of South Viet Nam and its allies.

Over-run northern VNAF bases at Da Nang, Bien Mai, and Nah Trang had transported most of the jets and larger arsenal prior to falling to the communists. The airbases lacked sufficient warning and capable pilots to move the remainder of the aircraft to remote air bases to the South and Thailand. The A-1s and A-37 "Dragonfly" aircraft bore VNAF markings. The NVA had not bothered to change to Viet Nam People's Air Force (VPAF).

On Sunday, April 28, 1975, three A-37s commandeered by VPAF pilots bombed the VNAF flight-line at Tan Son Nhut Air Base damaging aircraft and some of the runways. The destruction of the runways forced the evacuation of Americans and vulnerable South Vietnamese by helicopter known as "Operation Frequent Wind."

VNAF personnel attempted to destroy weapons as they abandoned the bases in the north. As in many cases, army and air force officers had moved their families with them. As the NVA moved south, key command personnel abandoned their posts to manage their family's safety.

In haste, some of the smaller armament remained intact. Among the half-dozen air bases, enough arsenal and bomb-fuses were available to put up A-37 "Dragonfly" and the slower A-1s with armament to add to the assault on Sai Gon. Hanoi was able to intimidate Sai Gon resistance with South Viet Nam's own weapons.

An unknown number of 250-pound MK81 iron bombs fell on the fringes of the Sai Gon in advance of the NVA ground troops. Other than creating confusion to quell layers of defense that South Viet Nam might have mustered, the bombing was limited and random. Despite current arguments to the contrary, Loan remembers the aircraft and the bombs. To her, it happened.

While some may argue the amount of harm inflicted on the Cholon was insignificant, Loan's memories and that of her surviving family are indelible. Hanoi and the NVA set out to punish Cholon with explosives. Ignorant ambitious men conquered Sai Gon by any means possible. The final horrific blow to Loan's neighborhood developed from the confusion of bomb fuses.

Bomb Fuses

Unguided "dumb" iron bombs utilize one or two small propellers to arm the weapon after it is released from the wing of aircraft. The arming propeller, located on the front and rear of the bomb between fixed guidance fins used to orient the weapon nose down, prevented the bomb from becoming "live" until it was dropped from the wing mount from a sufficient height.

Released from the wing, safety pins on stiff wires attached to the wings yanked off the bomb as it fell from the wing mount. This permitted the arming propeller to spin. The propeller turned a threaded rod to enable the bomb to become "live" to detonate on impact, at a specific altitude or timed out its detonation to occur hours to days later. The weapon must fall a specific distance which varied according the type and purpose.

Dropped from too low of altitude, the weapon remained un-armed and became a **UXB**, an **Un-eXploded Bomb**. Time-delay fuses on bombs dropped from sufficient height buried in debris tick away until the fuse ignites the explosive charge.

Former American equipment assigned to VNAF had English and Vietnamese instructions that fell into NVA hands. North Vietnamese and South Vietnamese as a common language possess differing idioms, colloquialisms and tonal differences distinguishing regional use. Confusion reigned on how to use the abandoned bombs and arming equipment.

The VPAF mustered pilots with minimal experience in aerial armament. Few North Vietnamese read English well enough to sort the complicated arming instructions of American ordnance. Confusion on arming the weapons for VPAF use against Sai Gon reigned as the last days of April approached.

South Viet Nam and America dominated the skies throughout the war. North Viet Nam fought a ground war with a limited source of VPAF fighters engaging South Vietnamese ground forces and naval ships. There were few instances where North Vietnamese aircraft bombed ground forces or southern communities.

Infiltrators from Hanoi had become VNAF pilots in previous years. As South Viet Nam's collapse appeared imminent, some of them "defected." It might explain why ARVN forward air controllers were often leery of calling in airstrikes from their brothers in the VNAF.

The NVA assembled their ad hoc Air Force assembled with a mixture of unfamiliar aircraft, weapons technology, conflicts in languages and a head-long rush to crush the resistance of South Viet Nam. Consequently, they deployed the use of weapons on undefended civilian regions of Sai Gon recklessly. They deployed the weapons on the Loan's neighborhood.

VNAF pilots were well trained in the A-1 Skyraiders. Except for the defectors, little is known about the quality of VPAF pilots that literally had to master the flight characteristics of straight wing aircraft in days.

Three decades old, the Skyraider was designed as a bomb platform that carried more than its weight in armament. It was designed to go in close and accurately place munitions, usually in support of ground troops. Fusing of the bombs depended on the method of attack. Simpler ordnance (MK81) was dropped from greater height or utilized drag inducing "wings" *(American Ordnance MK81 "Snakeye")* to slow the weapon's descent. Otherwise, an inappropriate close-in detonation could destroy the aircraft along with the target.

As the skills of North Viet Nam's anti-aircraft systems improved, the low-flying and vulnerable A-1s role in tactical warfare changed. VNAF relegated its role to a number of bases between Sai Gon and Da Nang. As the NVA approached the VNAF air bases, South Vietnamese piloted higher value aircraft to bases in Thailand. Lacking enough "ferry pilots," a number of viable aircraft remained behind including A-1s. As command and control fell apart, flight officers failed to scuttle *(detonate or neutralize)* the aircraft and MK81s iron-bombs in the ordnance bunkers.

In the last days of April 1975, The A-1s final role was that of terrorizing a passive population unable to fight back. By some accounts, it was probably also payback for the horrific bombing of the NVA forces in the battles of Xuân Lộc between April 9 and April 21.

If Sai Gon had anti-aircraft batteries in Cholon, no one in Loan's family knew of it. Amidst the chaos, no one recalled hearing ground fire from Sai Gon toward the low-flying aircraft. No one had ever seen such a plane on a bomb run on Sai Gon. It never happened before.

Some of the ordnance did not explode as VPAF pilots expected. They could see white smoke rising from NVA rockets and artillery igniting houses and businesses. Burning vehicles produced black oily smoke. Larger explosions from aerial bombs failed to materialize. Detonation of a larger explosion created a spreading white blossom of air compressed at the edge of the shock-wave. It was hard to miss. However, many dropped bombs failed to perform.

Unfamiliar with the radio settings, the few planes the VPAF put up could not advise other pilots to drop their ordnance from greater height. In some cases, the arming "envelope" did not matter. Fusing of each bomb affected its viability.

At least one of the bombs that landed in Loan's neighborhood dropped the sufficient distance and armed. It had a time-delay fuse. South Viet Nam and its allies frequently deployed ordnance designed to detonate minutes, hours or days later. The uncertainty of a UXB's detonation tied up NVA resources until the weapon's lethality could be managed. This was designed for the Ho Chi Minh Trail that delivered NVA and munitions to South Viet Nam. It was never intended to land in a Sai Gon suburb.

The time-delay bomb in Loan's neighborhood buried itself in debris along the road one hundred meters from their house. Another impact-fuse bomb landed less than fifteen meters from where they hid.

From the slotted air vents in the pit, they could see a lozenge-shape form sticking up on the far edge of their garden plot to the east. The gray iron bomb lay half-imbedded in the sandy clay field with the motionless propeller-arming device between the fins.

One of the rockets and a MK-81 250-pounder that fell close to the house failed or failed to arm before striking the ground. The buried weapon farther away was fused to detonate in less than two days. It had armed and unless discovered and defused in time, it would detonate.

The bomb went undiscovered and as the citizens of Sai Gon were marshaled out to line the streets arm-in-arm to "cheer at gunpoint" the new regime's parade a few days later, the bomb exploded. Loan's memory: the bomb killed and maimed dozens on May 1, 1975. Her brothers closer to the explosion carry tiny shrapnel in their legs to this day.

Loan's Information Resources

Loan was unaware of dangers she and her family faced. As a six-year old girl and the youngest child in a male-centered Asian culture, she was the last to know anything.

The oldest brothers learned something first. They determined information that should be passed to sisters.

Loan's older sister at seventeen dwelled in the gossip of other girls and women in the neighborhood. She was an unreliable source.

Loan had few friends among the girls in the neighborhood. She had moved back to Sai Gon two months before and had lived elsewhere for so long, she was a stranger. Having friends mattered little in knowing more about the world. The young girls were ignorant and compliant.

Loan's mother was her best resource on what happened in their world. Nguyên Maï's energies and time were limited. She appeared after sunset and disappeared before sunrise. As she was absent most of the time, Loan relied on her temperamental father for information.

Toan could not be bothered with a young daughter's questions. Females were servile, for household maintenance, a man's pleasure, and children. Steeped in male-centered Chinese culture and bias, females stood on a lower plane of existence.

When he did not slap Loan for disrupting his indulgences, he told her to ask her mother or one of her brothers closest in age. Unschooled and trapped in a cycle of denied information, she was unafraid of the impending calamity falling on Sai Gon. No one told her what to fear.

Loan did not have to know what to fear to have a sense of change in the city. Similar to her mother, she was curious and enterprising. Curiosity made Loan precocious and at times annoying among her peers including her brothers. She asked too many questions.

Urgency was everywhere and building up ever since they returned to Sai Gon two months ago. People of means steadily left the Chinese neighborhoods to places unknown. Others were selling belongings in exchange for gold. Even as the refugees from over-run villages and cities to the North flowed in to crowd the city, people who had lived in the city for decades fled Sai Gon.

An air of nameless tension was palpable even to Loan. The nature of traffic changed. Motorized vehicles ran faster. People on bicycles strained to stay up with rushing traffic. Pedestrians no longer walked leisurely. Everyone on the street moved with increasing urgency.

The purpose of everyone changed. The humor and patience of everyone dimmed to intolerance of any delay or disappointment. To a little girl kept in the dark and little else to do but serve the family, she saw the city mood change. She didn't know why.

Nguyên Maï

Nguyën Mai (Mai), visited her youngest child and daughter, Loan, less and then only at night. She was more exhausted as ever and had little time to talk. Mai responded to Loan's questions with shorter answers. Sometimes, she nodded off in mid-sentence as she talked to Loan.

Maï had gone into hiding south of Sai Gon. 27-year old Nguyên Huang *("Hung")*, Loan's oldest brother, tended to his mother during her infrequent appearances. Maï entrusted Huang with information she denied her husband. For safety of the family, she shared nothing of importance with Loan or other young children.

Trustworthy as he was, brother Huang was a weak liar. He told his siblings fictions to calm them. "Mother is okay and will return soon. Mother brings fresh fat chickens to the house and money to spend in the market. Mother is in the city locating better resources."

Loan's aunts, her mother's sisters, arrived on occasion with food and stories that reinforced Huang's fictions. Loan plied her aunts with questions to which she received conflicting answers. Her aunts were not particularly good liars either. Or it may be simple that Maï's sisters knew nothing about their warrior-sister other than she operated a bit on the edge of civilized Sai Gon.

Fresh chickens began to appear in the family menu at the beginning of April as Vietnamese unloaded their possessions across the city for gold and American cash. Gold and to a lesser extent silver, dominated Vietnamese interest. Precious metals held value in other countries. The interest in precious metals betrayed the biggest secret older brothers kept. People trading goods for precious metals planned to leave Viet Nam.

Many Vietnamese accumulated precious metals. To be sure, it hedged inflation. The French-originated piaster fluctuated constantly and fell weekly if not daily in the last months of Sai Gon.

North Viet Nam replaced the French-based currency with its currency, the dong. Worldly Vietnamese expected the piaster to be replaced in a consolidated Viet Nam. South Vietnamese paper money lost value and was doomed to become worthless.

North Viet Nam initiated a series of devaluations of the dong that rattled the economy for decades. Vietnamese paper currency became worthless, especially outside of Viet Nam. Gold and silver were the only currency of value for those planning to leave the country.

Conversations dwelled more on the question of the amount of gold needed to start life over in Hong Kong, Manila, Malaysia, Australia or North America. By late 1974, many considered the unthinkable and sorting options of leaving Southeast Asia. Options varied depending on one of the four main languages spoken in Viet Nam.

Cantonese speaking Vietnamese knew of the Asian communities, the Chinatowns, of larger cities in North America. They could ease their way into American life via the buffer of their first language. They moved into an insulated environment that made life in America easier.

Vietnamese-only-speakers expected to struggle. A small number of Vietnamese living abroad had married French, American, British and Australian personnel. There was little "easy" 1970s foreign sanctuary for Vietnamese immigrants at first. The same was even truer for Hmong and the Montenyards. *(As Sai Gon fell, Montenyard parents begged Americans to evacuate their children. They gave up their small babies as they knew they would be slaughtered by the NVA when Sai Gon fell. The outcome of this was never fully known other than some inadvertent "orphans" made it to other countries.)*

South Viet Nam's struggle ran between 1954 and 1975. They were about to lose the 21-year war since convention established South Viet Nam below the 17th parallel.

Vietnamese loyalists of South Viet Nam dreaded the future as America withdrew. The American component of the war ran between 1959 and 1973. British, Australian and Korean allies that played a part in the 1960s also withdrew as well.

Few held illusions that the quality of life in South Viet Nam could improve once Hanoi took over. A socialist command economy was incapable of duplicating the bounty of the free-market system operating in the South. Everyone expected cronyism of a one-party political system to replace semi-democratic processes. One form of corruption replaced another with a new level of institutional cruelty not seen in South Viet Nam. (** *Tens of thousands died in the months following the collapse of Viet Nam. Cause: Unknown. By some measures of empty hamlets, villages and communities, the slaughter numbered more than 300,000.*)

Everyone expected Hanoi to distribute the spoils of war to the leaders of North Vietnamese forces. Property, industry and business of South Viet Nam's loyalists were forfeit, particularly of those who prominently opposed consolidation with North Viet Nam.

Atrocities littered both sides of the conflict for decades leaving deep emotional wounds and seething resentment for generations. Worst of all, payback loomed as the central issue with a conquering force. Everyone expected the NVA and Hanoi to exact wholesale revenge.

On every level on both sides it was a brutal war. The 1968 wholesale massacre of 4,000-6,500 civilians in the City of Huë and the Viet Cong death squads that terrorized Sai Gon over the years reminded everyone of the unforgiving capability of North Viet Nam to exact revenge.

South Viet Nam with its allies had lay waste the country side with the heaviest bombing campaign in world history. Captured Viet Cong and NVA seldom survived interrogation by South Vietnamese and South Korean army personnel.

Reluctant western allies were obligated to turn over captured VC and NVA to South Vietnamese and South Korean forces. They knew prisoners of war seldom survived to return to North Viet Nam. On occasion, interrogated high-ranking enemy were disposed of during flights over the South China Sea as a matter of South Vietnamese military policy.

In South Viet Nam, every administrator, merchant and soldier expected that their lives and the lives of their families to be persecuted, if not punished or extinguished by Hanoi. America's military and CIA shared the same concerns. As capricious liberal American politics unraveled promises of support as US military withdrew from the fight, remaining western personnel in Viet Nam watched the world betray South Vietnamese hopes and aspirations.

Americans, no matter their view of the Viet Nam War, had engaged Viet Nam in duty and heart. Duty ended after their service was over. The obligation of the heart persists to this day. Time and incompetence betrayed everyone. Sai Gon prepared to go it alone and managed poorly. Hanoi succeeded quickly. The rest was a study in cruelty and punishment of the victor over the vanquished.

A few Vietnamese with foresight and means began leaving by the end of 1974 and headed for Asian communities in Australia, Hong Kong, Malaysia, France and North America. They left carrying gold and bundles of green American cash.

American money held minimal value to civilians when Hanoi ran all of Viet Nam in a few months. Possession of any form of foreign papers and American money earned trouble. Word traveled down from Da Nang after it fell in early April: "At risk" Vietnamese should bury or destroy incriminating documents and swap dollars for gold before Sai Gon fell. American money traded at a fraction of its value as it was collected by the "state" to buy foreign resources such as oil and medicine. Viet Nam consolidated into one country of sorry economics, immorality and cruelty.

Worse yet, after Da Nang fell, whispers began in early April that Hanoi had a "hit list." Destroying documents for "at risk" Vietnamese might not be enough. And if they could leave the country, leave now. If they could not escape or buy their way out, change identity, become a rice-farmer or fisherman.

In simple: hide.

American currency spent freely well into April. It held its value better than the local piaster. Nguyên Maï had access to American dollars and as conditions deteriorated, she broke with traditional frugal habits. She spent money on "trade-worthy" goods as quickly as she received it. The stocks of American canned goods, soap and shampoo could be traded for rice if not buy off government officials of either side of the war.

By late October 1974, Maï steadily bought gold in flat stamped plates hiding the purchases and the gold from her husband. She increased gold purchases in January 1975 and stocked durable goods including additional clothing for the children. Just ahead of the run up on the cost of Asian's staple in their foods, she told Toan to store more rice in the house in Sai Gon.

For the first time in memory, they had canned foods stored in the cooking area including tomatoes and corn. Foods with foreign names, Jif, Del Monte and Green Giant stacked up along the walls.

Toan lacked a can opener. A screw driver and hammer sufficed. Cans of SPAM opened with a key that wound up a strip of metal on the top.

Disposable Income

Maï seldom used the curious western term "disposable income" (*Cantonese: chùm râu lieu or Vietnamese: còn thêm tiền*) as every piaster was spent on daily basics. The currency lost value and had to be spent as soon as possible. Maï distributed American and Vietnamese currency to her sisters and oldest sons with specific instructions to spend it on needed items.

Maï gave the remainder of the "disposable income" to her husband. She asked that some of it go to the children to spend in the markets. Most of the money went to her father. Some of it dribbled down to Loan's brothers who shared it with her in a smaller trickle of nearly-useless local cash.

As "baby sister," older siblings shared with her readily. It was rare to have money to spend and be encouraged to spend the funds quickly.

It was the first time the younger children handled American cash. Strange images of white American leaders were printed on thick durable paper. Vendors in the open-air markets took the money without question.

Every few days, they were informed of the equivalent value in piasters. A one dollar bill in America money had increasing value trading for multiples in Vietnamese currency. The purchasing power of a single bill made Loan feel rich. The weathered bill had an image of "George Washington," a white American with peculiar hair and clothing. It spent easily.

The thick green bills that spent easily in early April purchased less as the next month approached. The American money that had the highest value a month before became hazardous to possess in any quantity. Hanoi's hatred of anything American permeated Viet Nam for decades. The money had to be spent before it could spend no longer.

In increasingly rare evenings, Nguyên Maï returned to the house after sunset. She met first with the older children sorting household business. She took a small bowl of rice and sweet potatoes and talked to everyone inspecting the stores of food and condition of the house.

Every now and then, she would gather the children and teach them a song in Cantonese or Vietnamese. They would rehearse a few times and it was time to sleep. There were many rituals of the evening they used to do including reciting mathematics and language skills. In the spring of 1975, there was no longer enough family time before they slept. There was no longer enough time.

Then she lay down next to Loan on her rice-straw sleeping mat shared with her big sister. This started after the family extinguished the house's meager lighting: white-gas lanterns with a conical lamp shade made of rice paste.

Electricity

Few in the neighborhood afforded the erratic electricity utility. Sai Gon's electrical reliability on the fringes of the city waned steadily after the Americans began a systematic exit from Viet Nam in 1972. The Americans enlarged the electrical system where needed for political and military purposes during their participation of the war. Maintenance fell upon Sai Gon's government after the United States withdrew its support.

South Viet Nam's larger weakness emanated from the corruption and semi-ethnic divides. Often considered an Asian cultural strength, the hierarchal male-centered attitudes hamstrung adaptive thinking. Older men are automatically smarter than younger men. Women in general had no say. The cultural paralysis inevitability unraveled their ability to oppose Hanoi.

In Loan's neighborhood, one family used the intermittent electricity. They used the power mostly for manufacturing and commerce. Sai Gon's fragile electrical grid on city fringes barely sustained large electrical loads. Air conditioning was considered obscene use of the utility even if someone could afford the electricity. Ceiling fans returned as the western technology proved too expensive on generating companies reliant on oil post the Arab-Embargo of 1973.

Sai Gon maintained street lights at major intersections intermittently. A light rain knocked out the power for hours. During the monsoon season from May to October, electric service was out for days.

Civilian electricity was unreliable, more off than on and expensive. Common electrification for urban homes remained decades away.

Most everyone slept at night waving hand-fans fashioned from banana leaves on themselves as the air motion relieved the cloying humidity. Even the small cost of running overhead ceiling fan became a luxury out of reach. Nights were spent in darkness when the white-gas lamps were extinguished. Loan listened to the small sounds of sleeping family, the hand-fans occasionally heard as one of the family fanned themselves back to sleep.

Open flame presented constant fire hazard. A spark could ignite dried leaves of the roof and walls—fires occurred almost weekly. Wood fires used for cooking caused most of the fires.

Typical to this type of construction, the roofs of the houses and business caught fire. A family water-brigade limited the extent of the fire when possible letting the affected portion burn out. Family and neighbors replaced it within hours with fresh bamboo rafters and a new layer of coconut leaves. Housing was organic in those days with bamboo, coconut and palm fronds remaking a structure in hours.

When they extinguished the white-gas lanterns, everyone went to sleep nursing their energy for another day of toil. Some bathed with water drawn from an open well. The unheated water chilled enough to cool the skin and made sleeping side-by-side with family easier. Up until 1975, a bath using a white bar of soap with the English word "Ivory" scented their skin. They saw less of this soap after the Americans ceased fighting alongside the Vietnamese in 1973.

Married brothers

Loan's two oldest brothers were married and slept on woven rice-straw floor mats with everyone else. Huang and Siep slept with their wives among a throng of siblings.

Darkness and stealth provided limited conjugal privacy. Loan occasionally woke up in the middle of the night to hear odd sounds from her married brothers. She assumed brother number 1 or 2 played a game with his wife in the darkness. She heard muffled laughs and whispers. It must be a good game. They did it often after everyone went to sleep.

Decades later, she realized Huang and Siep had been intimate with their wives lying side-by-side in the middle of the rest of the family. Loan had clever brothers and sisters-in-law to be sure.

At times, Loan's oldest brothers relented from tradition and answered her questions about her mother's absences. They ended many discussions with the same phrase Maï used so often, "You must be strong for the future." The wisdom seldom improved Loan's understanding of anything.

Sanitation

In the back end of the narrow long household, family relieved themselves in a slit latrine. They covered it on occasion with lemon grass and a layer of soil when flies became a problem.

Each family hand-pumped potable water from water well that was boiled daily. At times, they penetrated the well with a primitive "piledriver," a car wheel on a shaft filled with concrete. Distributed city water and sanitary sewers were decades away even though this house was within the domain of Sai Gon.

Soft red bricks lined the edges of the slit trench and floor which was recessed about three inches. A wide wooden plank with a 14" diameter hole covered the trench with a circular lid that covered the opening.

A galvanized bucket full of rain or well water with an aluminum ladle the size of a small fry pan sat next to the hole provided bodily maintenance. There was no such thing as toilet paper in rural Viet Nam. Toilet paper is remains uncommon except for westerners including the Russians that live in the city to this day.

In the perpetual humidity of Sai Gon, frequent dousing of the body brought a measure of comfort. Since clothing was light and limited, a brief wash of water took little time.

The male population lived in shorts and sandals. Women wore cotton blouses. Fashionable women wore the Ao Di, the elegant apron-like dress famously Vietnamese. Western undergarments beyond underwear were luxuries and a source of discomfort in the permanent humidity.

Calendar

While Asia kept the western Gregorian calendar with its seven-day week, they toiled all seven neglecting half days on Saturdays and all of Sunday as a day of rest. Despite the influence of western religions throughout Asia, there was virtually no "day of rest" for most of the population. Saturday and Sunday were other work days of the week. There was no such thing as a "week end".

The industrious Vietnamese rested in the dark. The darkness gave everyone a chance, if not an excuse, to rest. When the sun set on houses and industry that lacked electricity or reliable forms of it, production ground to a halt. White gas lanterns and candles extended hours into the night despite constant risk of fire. For manual tasks, labors might go for a few more hours. Yet, darkness gave blessed excuse to rest.

A Mother's Council

Loan expected her older sister to fall asleep early. Maï, as the oldest daughter in a large Asian family dominated by a 5:1 ratio of sons to daughters, spent her waking hours on endless tasks. Her mother's daytime absence placed a constant burden on Maï. Maï's father made it no easier as daughters were expected to serve their fathers. Most of this fell upon older-sister Maï.

Loan's mother spoke briefly with Maï who preferred sleep to conversation. Maï then spoke quietly to Loan after the lanterns were extinguished. She invariably whispered her personal secrets with Loan. Her perpetual message had become routine in the last six months.

"You are the curious strong one, the smart one, Loan." She'd whisper into her ear. "Difficult days are coming. Mother and I are close to watch over you. You may not see her in the day. Yet, I watch over you."

When Loan's mother, Maï, talked to the youngest daughter, she often paused as she gathered herself to limit the emotion in her voice. "In the coming days, you will not be able to find me but I will always find you. I do this for your protection. I watch over you."

Her mother could barely contain her grief as she spoke to Loan. In the dark, Maï's tears silently ran down her dusty face. Loan sensed her mother was crying. Her voice cracked and often a tear tapped on Loan's forehead. She remained quiet recording every nuance of her mother's words.

Maï was uncertain whether she and her family could survive the next few days. Her foreboding of an end-time loomed large by the end of October of 1974. Fragmented intelligence from Hmong and Montenyard refugees streaming toward South Viet Nam implied massive

NVA build-up despite the "peace agreement." After she learned the estimated size of NVA forces moving along the western border of Viet Nam and the stores of weapons stockpiled in Laos and Cambodia, she formed a single conclusion. Hanoi prepared to violate all Paris peace agreements and the worthless good words of politicians. North Viet Nam would attack and win.

South Viet Nam boots on the ground.

South Viet Nam possessed considerable forces on paper. Yet, in the field or even in the open markets of Tay Ninh, there were young men sporting ARVN uniforms that appeared to be free to come and go as they pleased. They were in fact deserters no longer reporting to their units.

South Viet Nam had a plan to systematically reduce their forces by 100,000 per year from a war-time number above one million at the same time drafting young men into service. In fact, South Viet Nam was hemorrhaging troops while North Viet Nam was building up forces in sanctuaries to the west in Laos and Cambodia.

Maï read the body language of her interpreter if not that of the American advisers earlier in 1974. Among those she could ask, no one seemed to know who was in charge. Worse, they seemed unconcerned with the growing imbalance of forces that in all actuality surrounded Sai Gon. Sai Gon was doomed.

For several years, Maï knew that South Viet Nam might not hold out. By January 1975, collapse appeared certain even though South Vietnamese media proclaimed the strength of government forces. It was all fiction.

The Paris Peace Accords were a sham. Hanoi had no intention of continuing the stalemate created by peace agreements. With the Americans out of the fight, Hanoi had a clear field of fire, so to speak. South Viet Nam's government was thoroughly infiltrated with spies. Hanoi knew every move and decision before South Viet Nam did.

The collapse of South Viet Nam forces occurred much faster than expected. North Viet Nam took Huë and Da Nang without a fight by late March 1975. They had some slugging further south as they approached Sai Gon but the outcome was obvious, South Viet Nam would fall by late spring.

Telling a Child of Danger

What, Maï asked herself, do you tell a child about the impending calamity that was South Viet Nam? Sai Gon had become an island alone in a nation infiltrated with spies and defectors-in-waiting. The city was rife with treachery among the Viet-Viet. No one non-Chinese could be trusted. Each community and ethnicity closed ranks. Inter-ethnic cooperation in Sai Gon ceased out of fear and caution.

They faced a vengeful and intractable enemy whose numbers and arms grew after being nearly crushed a few years before. The great successes of South Viet Nam's fight to remain independent of consolidation with Hanoi resulted in fragile accomplishment. Without the aid of American wealth and military capabilities, Hanoi systematically dismantled South Viet Nam's frontier as they chewed through South Viet Nam on their way to Sai Gon.

For many reasons analyzed in writings and declassified documents in over three decades since 1975, South Viet Nam squandered the accomplishments of successful warriors and campaigns. In short, many sacrifices in time, treasure and life amounted to nothing. The effort of western civilization with all the Americans, British and Australian forces would be wasted along with the sacrifices of the South Koreans.

In truth, both sides felt the incredible waste of war. The losses of North Vietnamese were estimated to exceed two million. For several decades following their victory and even to this day, the price of victory paid meager dividends. All-in estimates are that Viet Nam wasted millions in blood and billions in dollars due to wander politics on both sides. The drain of blood and treasure would continue.

All of South Viet Nam's allies were essentially absent. The Americans, British, Australians and Koreans had left the fight two years before. The amazing brave Americans Maï served deep into the jungles north of Sai Gon had returned to America in 1973. She would never see them again but some of them would return to honor her on her death in 2006.

The U.S. Navy SEALS had finished their "tours" as they called their participation. They returned home. Mai's service to Viet Nam was not a "tour," it was a fight for her country. Her obligation was life-long and permanent. As a birth-mother of ten by 1975 and eventually eleven, the biggest role she bore was not of children but of the fight for her adopted country. She fought for South Viet Nam.

By the incompetence of men and politics of nations, South Viet Nam ceased to exist as an independent nation. There was a North Korea and a South Korea thanks to the Americans. South Viet Nam existed for another decade thanks to American involvement. It could not last much longer because the critical factor of America was gone. Russia and China propelled Hanoi to success.

What does a mother tell a young child of the impending disaster? Maï knew she could not personally be near Loan to shelter her.

Maï's presence near any family could rain down disaster for everyone. She could only advise Loan to be strong and smart. She could not be with her in person without jeopardizing the family. Her presence assured destruction.

She shadowed her children more than before. After years "on the run" as an operative, she believed she and her family could prevail the coming destruction. There were basic rules she had worked out to remain a parent no longer in residence. Yet, a parent she would be.

Maï often repeated Buddha's simple directives **"Follow the eight-fold path in your own moment. Look to no one else for your final consolidation of wisdom. If you are wise and certain, execute your plan with all confidence. If you are uncertain and have the luxury of time, seek more knowledge. If there is no time, act quickly and well rather than cower and suffer."**

This was Maï's strange repeated conversations with six-year old Loan as all hell was about to break loose. She was about learning her ways in an Asian culture too young to be interested in adult life such as boys and children and a peaceful abundant life.

Loan was a thin ethnic-Chinese child. Now she was a child who had to be wise and strong per her mother's instruction. This made her less than a child. Her childhood, such as western civilization might call it, was now ending.

Peace might be defined as a period when neighborhood children grow up to adulthood without having to learn too early how to fire a weapon against another person or stave off starvation. At six, Loan already knew hunger. Eventually she became expert on firing a weapon on another person.

As Sai Gon falls, so does South Viet Nam. Those fully vested in Sai Gon's future took extreme measures to flee beforehand or as often occurred, ended their lives with poison or a bullet.

Witless Warriors

North Viet Nam, backed by Russia and China, fought South Viet Nam with singular purpose to conquer and re-establish colonial boundaries. Maï knew from interrogations of captured Viet Cong and NVA, Hanoi propaganda promoted that North Viet Nam was saving South Vietnamese from South Viet Nam. Many Vietnamese were unaware of the noble mission of Hanoi despite the propaganda meetings in outlying villages and rural communities.

Boys, "pre-teen young men," drafted into the North Vietnamese Army from hamlets and villages in North Viet Nam experienced little formal education other than political indoctrination. They weren't brain-washed as their minds were not yet fully formed. Their view was a blank canvas. Hanoi molded their minds in the formative years with absolute communist doctrine that denied curiosity.

Asian cultural strength resided in family. The future of North Viet Nam relied on de-constructing a recruit's family and replacing it with the state. When dragooned into the NVA by force at an early age, young men and women of promise in a civilized time became dedicated soldiers in a politic they only knew as doctrine. Few ever returned to North Viet Nam. Hanoi's draft into service and sent south was a death sentence.

Even after the United States pulled out, Hanoi's distortions continued to portray America's support as one of returning Viet Nam to a colony. The "Imperialist Interests" of America was brilliant dogma. Hanoi distorted artifacts of history that conveyed America and the west as imperialists working to colonize all of Viet Nam. The fact that America backed France in the disposition of Viet Nam in the 1950s reinforced Hanoi's dogma. The fact that a conquered Japan remained an independent nation eluded NVA cadre.

The only foreign soil held by Americans was that of the graveyard in all the countries the United States defended in WWI and WWII. In absence of better information, young men stripped of their families believed the doctrine of Hanoi. Americans were colonialists and therefore evil.

Maï fought long and hard in ways perhaps offensive to western mores to stem the tide of Hanoi and the legacy of Ho Chi Minh. Both Toan and her had taken AK-47 bullets and left for dead three years earlier. She and family witnessed the murder of 16-year old Cüöng, son number three, along with three other children and an old farmer to a land mine three months before in Tay Ninh.

North Viet Nam would win. They were virtually at the city "gates." Her fight for South Viet Nam ended in a few days. The ugliness of living under an egregious conqueror was about to begin.

Compromised Operatives

America's CIA failed to destroy sensitive files before NVA invaded Huë and Da Nang. Those files listed Maï as a highly-successful operative of the counter-insurgency. The extent of compromising information was unknown.

Maï's "handler," a Vietnamese interpreter that worked with her from 1966 to 1972 sent a message to her to take extreme precautions. He advised her that other Vietnamese operatives had been assassinated along with their families in the Cholon in the preceding weeks. The killings were specific to Vietnamese in the employ of a CIA program called "Phoenix."

Precautions

Maï avoided capture among her family at all costs. Hanoi punished all they did not kill. Confusion of names adopted by Chinese Vietnamese decades before confounded Hanoi's spies in Sai Gon. Husband and wife often had different family names. Property titles had different names for the owner. As for record research, Toan and Maï married in China lacked a proper record of them in Sai Gon as husband and wife.

Mai listed her address in error by design. It was a park called Dem Sen situated in the south of Sai Gon. In the grid-less street layout of an ancient village that became a city, Hanoi's operatives located Nguyên Maï's address. Maï lived at a traffic sign.

Toan occasionally encountered "committed officials." These were humorless men looking for his wife. He fretted about those moments for decades. He had taken two rounds from an AK-47 years before when caught with stolen VC weapons he transported for Maï.

The wounds proved non-life-threatening but had lasting effects on Toan's attitude. He believed Maï's activities endangered them if not kill them. To silence opposition, he pointed to his wounds as if to win the argument. Maï carried similar wounds but said nothing. Arguing with him was always fruitless.

Toan wanted nothing to do with the war. Often, it seemed as if he wanted nothing to do with the children. Contradiction was truer. The war overwhelmed Toan's life. He was task-saturated just getting to the next day. His escape from duty appeared to be in his girlfriends.

Maï's over-sexed husband often acted and did as he wished. She had to be the last best answer for her children. Practical burdens of keeping them safe fell upon her. Her essential directive, such as an Asian woman could provide to a husband, was to stay close to the children and pray to Buddha that his parental instincts kicked in.

Maï wept in the dark as she sorted among the words to tell her daughter to be brave and have faith in her resources. She debated whether to tell Loan that Viet Nam had less than a week to exist as they knew it.

Resourceful people fled to Honk Kong, The Philippines and Malaysia. Word trickled in that some had already made it to Australia and North America.

Mai wondered that if the well-connected and rich had stayed in Viet Nam to fight, would Sai Gon's situation be so desperate? She did not understand the larger workings of Sai Gon and America, South Viet Nam's mercurial partner in the fight for South Viet Nam. To this day, many Vietnamese never learned the history of America's abandonment of Viet Nam.

Emerging Exodus

The early exodus was small. The ripple of migration before April 30, 1975 was invisible as Vietnamese purchased flights and passage on ships. The waves of boat people began after May 1, 1975.

No one projected the inconceivable numbers that left in over-crowded boats, flimsy sea-craft or hike to Thailand in coming months

63

and years. One solution while Sai Gon remained free: leave with the aid of the Americans.

American processing of Vietnamese for exit Visas was slow. Vietnamese needed sponsorships and background checks to qualify for immigration as a refugee. As South Viet Nam came apart by the day, the U.S. Embassy applied plodding passport procedures with overworked staff.

In the last two weeks of April, the U.S. Embassy finally stripped away red-tape and accelerated processing. The U.S. government debated on how much the Vietnamese knew as America planned its own departure. They were afraid some of the ARVN soldiers might fire on them for evacuating.

Many of the Vietnamese flew out of Sai Gon on fixed-wing aircraft until NVA rockets rendered the runways inoperable. Operation Frequent Wind began in the final days as the largest helicopter airlift in history evacuated 7,000 of the 130,000 Vietnamese able to get out before May 1, 1975. At least several million Vietnamese truly "at risk" were left behind even though the Americans put the number at several hundred thousand.

As South Viet Nam ran out of time, VNAF pilots commandeered military aircraft to transport families and friends. Fixed wing aircraft flew to airbases in Thailand and helicopters flew to U.S. Navy ships stationed east of Vung Tau in the South China Sea.

Standard rules of flight safety of every kind were broken. The daily thread of helicopters shuttling between the airport and the U.S. Embassy ran all day as weather allowed.

If Not by Air, Then by Boat

The CIA had sent out instructions to accessible Vietnamese operatives. Some had gone into hiding abandoning the Americans as reliable allies. Maï depended on her South Vietnamese army connection for communication. She could ill afford having an American making contact with her in the neighborhood with all the communist sympathizer's infiltrated into Sai Gon.

U.S. Navy provided Mai with approval papers to take to the U.S. Embassy to fly out. Barring that option, she could escape by boat in the Sai Gon harbor. In this case, barges had been set up in the Sai Gon River to take refugees to the U.S. Navy ships stationed off of Vung Tau.

Three key elements stood in Maï's way of getting out of Viet Nam.

(1) Crowds at the U.S. Embassy,
(2) Toan and Maï's two-dozen-plus family members,
(3) Inadequate ground transportation
(4) Obstinate Toan
(5) Obstinate Toan,
(6) Obstinate Toan.

The crowds of Vietnamese outside of the U.S. Embassy swelled making getting to the gates problematic. Maï's immediate family numbered over twenty. Her sisters and their husbands along with their children brought the number to thirty four.

How do you move thirty-four people together to the U.S. Embassy, the airport or the harbor when ground transportation was breaking down? The airport and the embassy were eight kilometers to the north. The Americans positioned barges in the Sai Gon harbor ten kilometers to the southeast. And there was no time left.

Of all travel logistics, Toan remained Maï's biggest obstacle. She knew what to do if it wasn't for her damnable husband. For some reason, he believed it better to hunker down and "get through this." Toan believed they could "weather" this situation just like they did in every other circumstance.

This wasn't like every other circumstance they had endured. Viet Nam descended into unimaginable darkness.

Toan suffered a principal flaw in his thinking. He believed he was the head of the family.

Maï was the one that pulled them through every situation. She petitioned and cajoled him through every event. He often failed to realize how much she manipulated him. She even let him appear to be in charge.

Toan was never in charge of the family. He was the principal disappointment in family management.

She figured that at least two of their children resulted from negotiations with him. Save those events for another discussion, Maï used every mechanism at her disposal to bribe Toan to do the right thing. They had to leave the country in order to assure survival of all of them.

Overcoming Toan

Leaving Viet Nam presented too high a hurdle to clear in such a short time. This time Toan balked. He could not be reasoned into moving the family to the barges, let alone to the U.S. Embassy or the airport. South Viet Nam and the Americans had made the evacuation arrangements too late. Maï believed she could have persuaded Toan if there were a few more days.

Maï had sustained hope of getting the family to the barges. She competed with other Vietnamese to establish a place for their large family. There were hundreds of thousands of Vietnamese at immediate risk. A percentage of them had accommodating spouses and made it to the docks to wait for others to join them.

The next day would tell Maï whether the flight from Sai Gon might still work. Effective city transportation ground to a halt. Escape depended on the family working together as a unit. She knew in her heart, it was too little too late.

She tried. As always, and always, Maï would try.

Each day in April 1975 brought disappointment either from NVA success or failure of South Vietnamese leadership. Key people in the know with connections simply disappeared the next day. Leadership ranks decimated by unexpected or unannounced abandonment as they talked a good story of defending Sai Gon to the last man…and then removed themselves by the next morning on a helicopter.

Those with aircraft training commandeered VNAF helicopters and flew their families to aircraft carriers stationed east of Vung Tau. South Viet Nam's command and control fell apart as key leadership fled Sai Gon's fraying civilization. The male-hierarchical structure of Asia made things more fragile when key men in government and even among family disappeared.

South Vietnamese civilization broke down quickly as the male-dominated dominos of Asian culture disintegrated into societal dysfunction. The last days of Sai Gon were chaos on every level.

Americans safe at home watched the nightly news as "acquired" Huey helicopters ditched in the South China Sea or were pitched over the side of flight decks to make room for more aircraft. VNAF pilots hijacked fix-winged aircraft and flew all the family they could carry to airbases in Thailand.

Maï and family had no such option of flying out of Sai Gon. It came down to the barges in the river or nothing. After sunset on the 26th, there was little else in the defense of Sai Gon but return to her house and prepare for the next days.

Toan was nearly paralyzed with fear and loathing. He would be nothing in America. At least in Sai Gon, he was someone with property and an elder position. To shift the Asian-culture dynamic of not challenging the senior male of the family, she seriously considered shooting him to release her family to act well. Maï killed seven enemy of South Viet Nam. Her husband might become one more casualty of a difficult and protracted war.

Mai's Words Before the "Fall"

"Just know that you are smart and strong." That said, Maï rubbed her daughter's scalp and back as Loan nuzzled in her mother's blouse. Loan knew the sweet-sour smell of her mother's diabetic sweat and the sandpaper roughness of her toil-worn hands.

Then there was the familiar smell of fireworks on her skin. Her mother had been playing with fireworks, according to a six-year-old girl's assessment. She smelled the remnants of gunpowder.

Sometimes, Loan's mother smelled of fireworks. Maï's skin occasionally carried the fragrance of spent gunpowder and wondered where she went during the day. Someone had to make the fireworks that sparked the Chinese New Year and other celebrations. Perhaps it was her mother.

Maï never answered any question along the line of her "work" with the Americans. Loan had given up the question months before.

Two decades later, Loan learned that her mother could field-strip an American M-16 or a Russian AK-47 and re-assemble it under fire. She had carried four American M61 grenades with a "jungle-clip" in a banana-belt strapped under her breasts and under her blouse. Two slim curving knifes were often wrapped in leather sheaths along her ribs. She had used the knives and grenades to good effect. Her ARVN handlers made sure she had ample supply.

At 4'-11", the compact woman strapped two .32 caliber revolvers on her thighs. Maï struggled with carrying a .45 caliber pistol known as a "1911" that was heavy for her small hands. The Americans eventually supplied her with the compact .32 caliber revolvers. By April 1975, she had carried these weapons for eight years and deployed the grenades in two instances saving the lives of Americans as well as her.

Most important, Nguyên Maï never brandished her weapons or openly talked about it. Her children never saw her carry so much as a knife other than to prepare a meal. She was a pacifist by all appearances, a mother of ten and sponsor to other children not of her womb. There were no bandoliers full of bullets wrapped on her body or grenades hanging off clips on the front of her black pajama-blouse. She was the "anti-Rambo," so to speak in American culture-de-jour, the warrior-woman in hiding.

Maï diverted the questions by asking another question. She asked her young daughter if her brothers treated her well or if she had made any friends since returning to Sai Gon. Loan had specific answers for the good and bad behavior of each of her brothers and a tired "no" in regard to friends. Little else besides those issues were discussed as curled up in the darkness against her mother's neck and breasts. The smell of her mother's perspiring skin put Loan to sleep.

Warrior-Mother to Daughter

Maï ached to tell Loan more. What does a mother tell a young daughter about the impending fall of South Viet Nam? Loan was too young to manage the burden of fear of an uncertain future. The girl barely knew of her legacy including why her Cantonese-speaking family lived in Viet Nam.

Contrary to myth, Americans sought a woman's advice. It surprised and delighted her that they desired her council. American men even took instruction when it was smarter than their own.

These over-sized human beings appeared Witless about Viet Nam and Asia in general. Yet, Americans of white and black skin possessed the ability to unleash the deadliest technologies. For all that, they relied on her skills of information and strategy.

They realized Maï's potential and rewarded her with cash and materials. Since 1967, she steadily purchased property in Sai Gon with her "earnings" from the Americans.

If only the Americans had been able to speak Cantonese, she could have made a larger difference. Interpreters often translated poorly both in message and intensity.

Maï's ideas of counter-insurgency were often mangled. Essential emphasis of a statement was missed. It took much effort to communicate with the western people. Her best wisdom went untold.

Fortunately, the Americans were open to solution and patient with the limits of their communication with her. They had the same goal: preserve South Viet Nam as an independent capitalistic democracy. Corrupt as it was, South Viet Nam was worth saving.

Maï's perpetual concern with the Americans was their "tour." They fought for so much time and returned home. How can somebody execute a war if essential warriors go home never to return? The Vietnamese were defending their home with a capricious ally.

She knew there was a time when her American brothers-in-arms returned home. Hanoi's propaganda that the United States intended to colonize Viet Nam was a lie. If the Americans wanted to colonize Viet Nam, they should have held the ground they won. They only won the fight and retreated to their bases. How can you colonize a country and not hold ground? Western involvement in Viet Nam never made sense if South Vietnamese forces conquered territory only to relinquish it months later.

The ugly over-sized men she admired were temporary combatants. South Viet Nam was doomed from the start of western escalation in 1964. For all that it did, America only postponed the inevitable capitulation to Ho Chi Minh and Hanoi.

Some of their missions were wasted simply because of language and gender. They gave ground to protect her when she was ready to finish the mission. A few Americans and Maï ended up with shrapnel wounds and retreated for her sake. She believed they lost an opportunity because their culture believed she was fragile.

The American and Vietnamese soldiers she guided accomplished much without loss of a single man. In effect, her alliance with the strange people of the west "kicked butt" as the lower ranked Americans might say. She knew they could have accomplished more.

The combination of American Special Forces and Vietnamese operatives enjoyed great success in the six years they worked together. When each mission was completed, a Vietnamese driver in a worn-out Xe Lam drove her to the outskirts of her neighborhood.

She unloaded her bicycle and loaded it with C-Rations, Spam and a mixture of other goods wrapped in banana leaves. She walked the bicycle home as if coming from the market. If in Sai Gon, Toan removed the goods.

Maï stashed cash in one of the thatched walls. If in Tay Ninh or another hamlet, she buried the money in a tin cracker box buried under her sleeping mat.

Nguyên Maï seldom spoke about the missions she conducted with the Americans. Knowledge was dangerous in Sai Gon with so many spies infiltrating every community of South Viet Nam. The most trusted of neighbors had split-family. Some served Hanoi. Few were above suspicion. Neighbors traded gossip about Maï's frequent absence from the family. The most common rumors speculated that she had affairs with American soldiers. Given Toan's reputation, few women blamed her for indulgence with the generous and over-sized Americans.

Maï let the rumors persist about the exotic attraction to the Americans that seemed to be twice her height and weight. Their attention to the Asian women made up for what they lacked in attractive skin color. These strange men of a wealthy country with the power to destroy gave unexpected attention to Asian women who walked three meters behind their husbands and had small voice in large family affairs.

Maï could not see the political strings that manipulated the endeavors of some of the smartest non-Asian men she would ever know. The U.S. Navy SEALS were "in country" longer than others. Inevitably, all of the Americans "rotated" out of Viet Nam. Some returned for another "tour" but in the end, every American returned home alive or dead.

She did not understand the concept of rotation. It was a word the Americans used. How can you be in a fight and then leave when your "rotation" was "up"? South Viet Nam was in a fight for its life. Vietnamese had no option to "rotate out." Vietnamese could only flee, endure or die.

The American military along with the British and Australian force evacuated at the height of incredible success. Hanoi's forces were demoralized and "on their heels" as the Americans said. Hanoi used the peace discussions to recover, re-arm and reset the conflict

The timing of the American exit seemed incredibly odd to the Vietnamese. Eight years before, the timing of the American "intrusion" was unexpected after U.S. President Lyndon Banes Johnson

(LBJ) escalated America's presence after the "Gulf of Tonkin" incident. Nearly all at once in late 1964, there were Americans everywhere.

South Viet Nam had won large at several periods of the conflict. Their American allies and Vietnamese forces failed to close on a win and purse the enemy as it dissolved into the jungle after a fight. They seldom held the ground they won.

The Rules Of Engagement (ROE) plagued them to avoid a nuclear war was one excuse. Lack of a clear "end game" was another. It was said that the Americans conducted the Viet Nam War based on the last war they won which was in 1945.

She had a flickering hope: the Americans and the rest of the allies would return and fight. Her over-sized naïve white and black men would return and change the inevitable course of South Viet Nam running on its own resources. It was a foolish wish as the last days of April burned off. Americans had romanced Viet Nam into believing "We were there for the long term." It didn't happen.

With days left and watching the helicopters fly in and out to the waiting ships off the coast of Vung Tau, she sorted among the few facts of the day. The Americans weren't coming back to save Sai Gon. The immensely capable America as she knew and imagined them to be were not coming back to save South Viet Nam.

Brief Embrace

With her face pressed into her mother's bosom, Loan invariably fell asleep in mid-sentence. Those minutes were all Maï could spare her daughter. Loan was the youngest and as "baby-sister," her older siblings did not begrudge their mother's attention to her. Maï gently unwound her embrace with Loan.

In the darkness, one of Maï's older sons approached them and whispered to her. They were still awake and heard her rise from the Loan's bed matt. "Ama (*Vietnamese: Mother*), what about tomorrow, what do we do?"

Maï repeated the instructions as before, "Watch over your sisters and brothers. Be strong for them. Know everything that you can and make good decisions."

Maï often paused before she asked them to help their father. As often at night as she left the house, with hell breaking loose on all sides of Sai

Gon, he was not there. She had given him some money for the household, part of which, of course, sustained his penchant for girlfriends.

Toan's self-centered life was about to change drastically. Old Sai Gon, the "Paris of Asia," with its blend of Asian architecture, French influences and artifacts of the American military had a few days left. Hanoi would take the city vigorously and lock it down for fear of an uprising. Few predicted how far North Viet Nam would go to keep the population under control. All knew it could be bad. It turned out to be worse.

Toan spent his resources assuming something better around the corner would bail him out. On Friday, April 26, 1975, Maï told him to reinforce the front gate and buy as much rice as he could. She said that the NVA might shell the neighborhoods just as they did in Da Nang. It was the last thing she told him before sunrise on Saturday.

Loan usually slept until well after midnight. Wrapped in coarse cotton and her day clothing, she stirred from her fetal position. She felt the cooling humid night air intrude her thin blanket. The coolness afforded some comfort a few hours before sunrise.

Traces of her mother's scent lingered on her face and in her nose. In the blackness, she groped for her mother's warmth. "Ama" had left.

The moon was full on Friday, April 25, 1975, just before collapse the next week. The sky was clear.

The moonlight penetrated openings in the woven structure of the roof salting the black room with spots of light. After the lanterns were extinguished, Loan's eyes took minutes to adapt to the low light level. It revealed shadowy lumps of her family in the dark room as they lay on their sleeping mats.

Typically from 10:00 PM to 4:00 AM, their community rested. Several hours before sunrise, the roosters in every household crowed. Every household had chickens, often for commerce if not for themselves.

The roosters had yet to crow. It was well before 4:00 am. That was the only measure of time she had, sunset, her mother's temporary visits, the noisy roosters and then sunrise. Another day of toil was about to start.

The empty space on the woven sleeping mat between her and her sister was cool to the touch. Her mother left hours before.

Maï had returned to the ranks of the soldiers on what was the crumbling eastern front holding off NVA forces. The last battle at

Xuân Lôc had ended on April 21. The NVA were massing for a final assault on Sai Gon on the eastern fringes. They set up artillery and rocket batteries to suppress loyalists in the Cholon from striking back.

During the Tet Offensive of 1968, Viet Cong insurgents expected the citizens of South Viet Nam to arise and help them. The uprising never occurred and the Viet Cong were nearly wiped out. The NVA absorbed the remnants of the VC and seven years later, as they approached Sai Gon, they expected the citizens to attack them. They prepared to shell their neighborhoods to keep them the civilians at bay.

Mai's absences from the household were mistaken for liaisons with other men. Perhaps, given her husband's transgressions, who could blame her? Yet, there was no evidence of dishonorable conduct. Among the amorphous combatants, Mai, the least likely due to her large family, fought for South Viet Nam and when all appeared lost, fought to delay the inevitable: The Fall of Sai Gon.

Mai did what she could to delay the North Vietnamese Army (NVA) so the family could board one of the barges the Americans conscripted for evacuation. They positioned the shallow draft barges where Vietnamese allies could reach them on the Sai Gon River.

The barges were not advertised to anyone other than the people who worked for South Vietnamese or American agencies. The barges were meant to save those at high risk. Still, word leaked out that large transport awaited anyone who could get to them.

Loan's mother ceased fighting to preserve an independent South Viet Nam months ago. That fight was hopeless without the return of American support.

It has been estimated that even as far back as January of 1975 after she lost son number three, Cüông, to a landmine in Tay Ninh, she had come to realize she and her family had paid too high a price for South Viet Nam. She had immigrated as a young woman to Viet Nam. Mai had invested much including all the land she held in the neighborhood. With her back to the sea, she ran out of options but to hold on.

Attitude - Mai's Life-long Fight

Nguyên Mai fought for South Viet Nam largely in secret, even secret to her husband, since 1964. Like so many ethnic Chinese or

Chinese-Vietnamese that settled in South Viet Nam from North Viet Nam in the 1950s, Maï hated communism. Many knew or directly experienced the scale of cruelty and destruction in Southern China that drove them to Southeast Asia after WWII.

Toan misread Maï's militia activities as something else. Until 1972, he was caught up in his own world to the point he over-looked the odd behavior of his wife.

Ethnic Chinese wives tolerated errant husbands to a point. They may be a result of a long-held acceptance of polygamy otherwise discouraged due to influence of Christianity over the last few centuries in Asia. Viet Nam fluctuated between 7 and 10 percent Christian with a significant Catholic population. Polygamy was outlawed but culturally tolerated.

Maï tolerated Toan's girlfriends not so much by choice but by necessity. It worked well for her "cover." Her hatred of the communist ambitions exceeded her despise of Toan's penchant for Vietnamese women that aimed their loins at him. As it was, she lived a dual existence as dutiful mother of a large family and warrior-combatant.

Shanghai 1937

Maï's origins as a South Vietnamese loyalist and insurgent fighter, for lack of a better term, began in China at eleven years of age when Japan assaulted Shanghai in that last half of 1937. With superior weaponry, the Japanese invaded China's eastern coastline with impunity. Ill-equipped Chinese forces defended the city with small arms against well-equipped Japanese air force, navy and ground forces. The Japanese brought along with them an added feature of remarkable cruelty toward non-combatants *(civilians)*.

The Chinese forces attempted to delay the Japanese intrusion to move industries and skilled work force further inland and in hopes of receiving international aid. Shanghai's Chinese forces lost over a quarter million soldiers along with tens of thousands of civilians as Japan brutalized the entire Chinese coastline. China's WWII civilian and military death toll ran in the millions.

WWII ended September 1945 a few months after Mai turned 19. She faced new conflicts as communism fought for the future of China. Mao Zedong emerged victorious driving many capitalist Chinese to Taiwan, Indo-China, Malaysia and beyond.

Maï aided her father as he tended Chinese casualties throughout the war which, for China, ran over eight years. While not accustomed to the horror, she seldom flinched at the site of dismembered men, women, and children. Chinese atrocities exchanged for Japanese atrocities as the end of WWII continued with civil war.

After World War II, China won over Japan to find itself in civil war as nationalists and communists fought over the future of the mainland. Her father, a physician-in-training, was well educated including exposure to European and North American medical practices. His western education, interrupted by war and social turmoil, contaminated his future in the emerging China of the late 1940s.

As communism emerged, his professional ambitions formed under old regime antagonized the new order. The working classes condemned anything "western" including religions, culture, engineering, and medicine. His record of service during World War II mattered little. He found another career. He became a police officer.

China's political reformation drove the country into medieval hell. Decades of strife and the new politics of communism under Mao Zedong's dictatorship forced many to flee to the rest of the world. Speaking Cantonese, Huang was reluctant to move his family to Taiwan where Mandarin dominated the language. He remained near Shanghai hoping the political and civil chaos could subside.

As a member of the police, he concealed his "western training." It worked to a point. Huang ended up with a front-row seat on a rising display of "state barbarism."

From 1945 to the early 1950s, China crushed civil disobedience of any form with appalling brutality. In what Chairman Mao characterized as "land reform" distributing land to the masses and creating communes, the regime suppressed even mild civil objection by state murder.

Stripped of their properties, former property owners that refused to commit suicide were beheaded in public for their "crimes." Others starved to death in labor camps.

As a police officer, Huang and his cadre received quotas for punishment of decadent Chinese. The state forced him to humiliate civilians selected from a list of formerly wealthy landowners and professional classes. Humiliation was euphemism for something far worse. It meant anything from labor camps to summary execution in public.

Among the many races of man, Asians tend to be the most suicide-prone. "Saving face" was steeped in millennia of Chinese culture and legendary in Japan during World War II.

The prospects of public humiliation drove many to suicide. The aspects of starvation in labor camps compelled others to end their lives by whatever means available. Everything from jumping off a tall building in Shanghai to self-inflicted injury became epidemic.

For the more resilient citizens-become-criminals hanging on to life by whatever means, public beheadings sent a chilling message to the populace. If senior males of a prominent family stood their ground or publically expressed their objections, the local authority of the new regime beheaded them. Mainland Chinese had zero agency of relief once their names were on a list and the quota for executions remained unfulfilled. If they could flee, they did.

Huang's age and exhaustive works as a front-line "doctor" during the Battle of Shanghai in 1937 earned him unpleasant responsibility. As a ranking police officer with shadowy western training, he became executioner. He knew best how to slit a throat in public. He was merciful and quick on the "criminal."

If he failed his job, someone stepped up and relieved him of his duty in a similar manner. Unwilling Chinese executioners were bound in a chain of terror to carry out their duty.

China's descent into hell pressed him into becoming the devil's servants. From the first moment he realized the outcome of his choice of an alternate career, he did what he could to preserve his family. Refusal of his appointed obligations meant personal destruction.

Before his first public execution, Le Huang made plans to escape to somewhere else in China. There was no refuge.

By the end of the 1940s, he planned to flee his beloved China. Sorting among his options as circumstances changed, move south to the border, toward the former French colony known as Viet Nam. There were Cantonese-speaking Chinese in Hanoi. He might be able to make a life there.

They delayed moving south until a blessed event occurred. In late 1949, one his daughter's, Maï, bore her number one son. They named him Le Huang after his grandfather.

His daughter had married a well-educated young man from an upper-class family in Shanghai. He seemed a bit self-centered. That was something for Chinese men to say of other Chinese men.

The son-in-law took another name once in Viet Nam as was the practice over centuries. He became Nguyên Toan. For simplicity of public identification, Le Huang's daughter became Nguyên Maï.

Hanoi – Temporary Residence

Starting with Maï's father, Nguyên Huang, when they lived in North Viet Nam until 1956, the egregious expectations of Hanoi's party officials exploited the labors of others. Huang changed the family name to Nguyên in an adaptation of a similar name when they emigrated from Shanghai, China a decade before. He changed the family name to Nguyên and became Nguyên Huang as was the practice of many migrating Chinese.

The name-change made them less obvious they were ethnic Chinese. Nobody in Viet Nam actually bought the distortion. Subtle differences in face alone distinguished Viet from Sino-Vietnamese.

His move to North Viet Nam and lack of socialist membership further reduced his qualifications. Viet Nam became inundated with western-educated Chinese escaping the civil purges under Chairman Mao. Studied in medicine in Shanghai before World War II, the changes in China stripped him of his medical credentials. North Viet Nam lacked the educational infrastructure to assimilate and re-qualify him.

Huang's lofty hopes for a medical career re-started at the bottom in a new country. The language barrier alone made recertification in medicine impossible. Cantonese and Vietnamese were distinct languages. Huang's French proved of little value as anything French was considered unseemly in North Viet Nam in the 1950s.

As a former police officer under Chairman Mao that beheaded "criminals" per state quota, Huang knew how to butcher livestock. Much as he loved science and medicine, he applied his training to another useful trade. He became a butcher.

A capable butcher of chickens, swine, and cattle made a difference in the health of its customers. Private electricity and refrigeration in post WWII North Viet Nam remained erratic if not rare. Huang purchased ice to chill his vulnerable meats reducing the rate of loss. Wealthier patrons sought out Huang's small tidy shop. His thin precooked and chilled slices of pork spiced with ginger and horseradish became a popular delicacy. Huang prospered.

After the pivotal battle of Điện Biên Phủ (*Vietnamese: Chiến dịch Điện Biên Phủ*) in May 1954, Viet Nam split at the 17th parallel by 1957. Ho Chi Minh's socialist regime assumed full control of North Viet Nam. Hanoi made plans to consolidate South Viet Nam.

Huang expected open elections as French nationals returned to France. Expectations clashed with reality. The hand of Chairman Mao held sway on North Viet Nam delivering arms, guidance, and money to Ho Chi Minh.

Promises of open elections withered as Hanoi became a one-party socialist system. Huang knew the drill. Conform or die. Or flee.

Huang had to flee for the third time in two decades. Surely, there must be a place to find where one can dwell without threat or retreat. Perhaps, the future is in South Viet Nam. Perhaps it is in Sai Gon with its better weather.

Until the fall of 1954, the French and their ever-passionate love of fine food paid for Huang's services. He learned to speak French while in school in the 1920s and knew something of western culture.

Huang tolerated their endless self-praise of everything French. Unlike Asian clientele, the Europeans paid his price with little negotiation. When possible, he negotiated for precious metals and gems. The French became preferred clientele.

Huang's wife prepared a popular offering called phó bo (*"fuhh! – bo" aka phenomenal beef soup*) or phó ga (*"fuhh! Ga" aka phenomenal chicken soup*). Privately, the French told him that Vietnamese cuisine almost rivaled French cooking. Huang nodded, smiled, and took their piaster.

After 1954, North Viet Nam's political consolidation chilled the social atmosphere. Harsh land reforms distributed estates to regime and ranking peasants. New elite surfaced among the throng that had defeated arrogant French management and French-descendant citizens of North Viet Nam.

As the French nationals left the country, Nguyên Huang's clientele split between two types: the traditional Asian customer and the party official. Asian customers negotiated. Party officials and political minions exploited recent émigré's such as Huang.

After the French surrendered Viet Nam to the Vietnamese in 1954, party officials expected entrepreneurs such as Nguyên Huang's butchery to provide services at zero profit.

In order to sustain a living, Huang returned to butchering live-stock on a daily basis. Hanoi stood decades away of reliable electricity and private refrigeration. His shop returned to the open-air market mechanism of slaughtering animals for daily consumption. Process efficiencies and simmering delicacies disappeared as North Viet Nam once again went medieval.

The infection of mainland China's "land reforms" flowed south by 1955. The barbarity that drove Huang to immigrate repeated itself in North Viet Nam. Nguyën Maï's father opposed what he considered state theft. Imprisoning and executing land owners as happened before in Shanghai was nothing less than state-sanctioned murder.

By mid-April 1956, most of the remaining French Nationals left Viet Nam. Nearly a million Catholic Vietnamese migrated to South Viet Nam. Similar numbers of disillusioned Buddhist Chinese-Viet-namese moved south.

From the first moment in 1950, Huang suspected North Viet Nam to repeat the cruel legacy of communist China. By 1956, it became obvious. Move to the fertile regions of South Viet Nam and put 1,700 kilometers *(1,000 miles)* between Huang's family and Hanoi.

Per Asian standards, Nguyên Huang regretted having no sons. He enjoyed his daughters. Little is known about Huang's wife other than she was a good and loyal mate.

As if a son to him, his youngest daughter, the ever-curious Nguyên Maï followed his council. Her older sisters were lost on the issues of politics and planning. From her first day, Huang knew his youngest daughter was different from her sisters. Huang, in principle, had real-ized a man-like thinking in the young woman. He could not sire a son for all his effort. Maï became every bit the equivalent of his only son.

In time, Maï's older sisters followed her lead. Their father advised Maï's sibling to follow Maï's council. She was strong and gifted of mind. They should listen to her.

Steeped in the Buddhist traditions of the eight-fold path to wis-dom and inner peace, Nguyên Huang advised on the principals of Buddha. Nguyên was the name of one of the last dynasties of Viet Nam and many Viet-Vietnamese as well as Chinese-Vietnamese assumed that family name prior to the end of the colonial period under the rule of France.

Nguyên Huang had said that they must support a dependable leader. More important, they must support their chosen leadership by whatever means possible. Huang put his "stock" in the youngest daughter, Maï. He instructed his older daughters to support her endeavors.

Chinese fathers of his generation and religion picked their words carefully. Right thinking and right action was important. His children adhered to rational instruction.

Nguyên Huang knew of Ho Chi Minh before he set foot in Viet Nam in 1950. Ho Chi Minh had made a name for himself since the 1920s petitioning for an independent Viet Nam. Huang believed he was too willing to trade politics for independence. Huang knew from experience that when the state was made more important that the people, humanity will suffer.

Father Ho turned to China for support when the Americans backed France up to the final days of colonial Viet Nam in 1954. Despite the fact that Americans saved Ho Chi Minh's life at the end of World War II, predisposed alliances and Chinese influence prevailed.

Ho Chi Minh sought the help of the United States in establishing a free Viet Nam appealing to its legacy as the first breakaway colony in world history in the late 1700s. Unfortunately, America stood by France assuming it had the ability to manage the Viet Minh insurgents in the North.

France underestimated the strength of the guerillas, the deployment of weapons acquired from China and the cunning of a "primitive" enemy. America backed an incapable ally.

The United States first notions of "containment" of the communist threat began with Korea and transmogrified into the conditions of Viet Nam. The failure of the French during the siege at Điện Biên Phủ became a template of future warfare through to the fall of Sai Gon in 1975.

The situation was understandable given the times and circumstances of a world emerging from World War II. By 1954, Korea split into North and South. Korea set an expectation that disappointed future conflicts.

America, a British colony that broke away from England two centuries before, supported an egregious France in lieu of the independent Viet Nam. Father Ho never forgave that error. China and

Russia exploited that conflict and backed Hanoi centering its propaganda on the first break-away colony in the history of the world. The country was America.

Nguyên Huang could not support Father Ho's side when the struggle to free Viet Nam from France emerged. He did not immigrate to North Viet Nam to reside in another communist state. In 1956, he moved his family to Sai Gon, the "Paris of Southeast Asia" to build again a new life for his children. He hoped this was finally the last move.

By that time, his youngest daughter, Nguyên Maï, was married to Toan, also of Shanghai, China. His first grandson was born near Shanghai. The second was born in Hanoi. After that, all the rest were born in South Viet Nam.

In reality, Maï did not take Toan's family name with some of her children. Part of this was due to the confusion of language. She used another family name most of the time and for anonymity of her family in Sai Gon as of 2014. That name is not mentioned.

South Viet Nam was their last place of refuge on the Asia continent. They migrated to the last independent region of Southeast Asia. To the west, Cambodia and Lao were kingdoms. To the east, they faced The South China Sea. To the south and east of the southern tip of South Viet Nam, they faced The Gulf of Thailand and Malaysia.

They put their stock in South Viet Nam. They had their backs to the sea.

Russia/China vs. South Viet Nam

Without allied support, massive communist-bloc influence and material support overwhelmed South Viet Nam. South Viet Nam was doomed.

Backed by Russia and China, North Viet Nam issued directives to young men and women starting before adolescence. They knew all that was required about South Viet Nam: it was evil and corrupt. The mantra: South Vietnamese needed salvation from its government.

When the United States substantially escalated support in August 1994, Hanoi indoctrinated its cadres of youth dragooned into service telling them the struggle for the entire country was at hand. They repeated a simple propaganda: The United States had imperial designs on Viet Nam and Southeast Asia. Viet Nam was infected by western culture and dogma. They must save the South Vietnamese from themselves.

History with the white race re-enforced the propaganda with the fact that France colonized much of indo-China a century ago. Europe and North America sent missionaries throughout Asia for centuries converting segments of the population into Christians. In the mid-1800s, a French Jesuit priest, Alexandre de Rhodes, developed a dictionary of Vietnamese (*quôc ngif*) using a substantially enhanced Roman alphabet. White imperialists left their mark on Viet Nam as Vietnamese is the only Asian language written with western characters. According to Hanoi, it was primary evidence of western desire to permanently dominate Viet Nam.

Authoritarian states thrive by limiting information. A tightly controlled broadcast and printed press repeated the dogma. The internet was decades away. In absence of other information, the evidence made compelling arguments that South Viet Nam, in cahoots with western countries, was up to no good.

Anecdotal: "John L," a Chinese-cum-American friend of mine, emigrated from Beijing to live in a small community in Kentucky in1978 at the age of 14. While still living in China, the regime jailed his father for teaching western music. A decade earlier, his father might have been executed for a crime such as teaching a western art form.

John is an engineer that works for a manufacturing firm in Maryland in his "day job" and plays the violin for a prominent university orchestra in Baltimore. He learned to play the "western instrument" in secret, taught by his father as he grew up in Beijing.

He spoke of spending time as a young boy in idle moments on street corners watching the thin city traffic pass with cars and occupants of any kind. On occasion, he saw white women wearing red lipstick. That was sensational. In the evening, he reported to his family what he saw.

Peers reminded him that the capitalist woman's red lips were evidence that she sucked the blood of the working class in Europe and North America. China imprisoned his father for teaching and playing western music. John had little information to the contrary.

John believed the reasoning. He had no other sources of information to offset the theory of women's lips being painted red. Chairman Mao had reduced all form of extravagance including the form of clothing and visual enhancement as inappropriate decadent western influences. The first explanation of the scandalous red lips of western women was the only explanation John heard until he immigrated to the United States.

Extrapolate that propaganda to North Viet Nam between 1945 and 1975 and the cadre of youth indoctrinated without alternative information. America, similar to France come to Viet Nam to subjugate Southeast Asia.

John's highest ambition at the age of 13 (c. 1977) living in Beijing was ride one time in a car sometime in his life. He told this story as drove me from BWI Airport in Maryland to a meeting in 2011. He said as he drove his beautiful western-built car on the 495 beltway around Washington D.C. that he had achieved his lifetime goal of being in a car. Owning a car exceeded his lifetime expectations.

On a high school trip in 1981, John visited Georgia where he visited a marvelous hotel in downtown Atlanta. As a young boy, he dreamed of riding in a car and visiting such a hotel. Today, he owns several cars and has stayed at that hotel achieving his childhood dreams.

For many reasons, South Viet Nam was doomed.

A mindless army populated by cadres that knew of little else but sacrifice for "Father Ho" and remove the western blue-eyed devils at all cost infiltrated South Viet Nam's open society. North Viet Nam forged an army hardened by deprivation and rote instruction prepared to save South Viet Nam from itself.

For many reasons, South Viet Nam was doomed.

By 1974, North Viet Nam possessed the will and means to win. South Viet Nam might have possessed the will to prevail but the United States withdrew its considerable financial and material aid. The imbalance was obvious. South Viet Nam was doomed.

It takes money to wage a war. Short of that, it takes a will to win at all costs. North Viet Nam had more of both assets than South Viet Nam.

Without resources to buy and sustain military, South Viet Nam was doomed.

As the Watergate scandal evolved in early 1974, President Richard M. Nixon lost political capital necessary to deliver his promised support of Viet Nam's President Thieu. Nixon resigned on August 9, 1974. The domino that was South Viet Nam teetered large and unbalanced as Nixon left office unable to finish his promises to Viet Nam.

While Nixon escalated America's involvement in the war at the beginning of his term in 1969, he is credited with reducing U.S. forces. To the contrary, Nixon did not end America's involvement as often cited.

It takes money to wage a war. An unwilling U.S. Congress defunded the unpopular war in 1974.

Saudi Arabia's King Fiasal made an offer of $25 million in aid to South Viet Nam. Unfortunately, one of his nephews assassinated him on March 25, 1975 before Saudi Arabia transferred the funds to Sai Gon. It is unlikely that money for armament alone could have done little more than buy a few more weeks for Sai Gon. (*After South Viet Nam fell, large caches of weapons and ammunition turned up as ARVN hoarded ammunition declaring "shortages" in the months running up to April 30, 1975.*)

An essential question in the inevitable fall of South Viet Nam was time. How long could South Viet Nam hold out? The speed of the South Viet Nam's collapse surprised America's CIA and Hanoi. Despite heroic sacrifice at Xuân Lôc up to April 21, 1975 and other battles, the NVA surged on Sai Gon's perimeter virtually unchallenged.

Maï's Exit Papers

The American navy offered Nguyên Maï and family an expense-paid relocation to America. The date of this offer is uncertain. Possession of U.S. Navy "exit" papers by Vietnamese citizens is dangerous up to the present (2015). The author estimates that Mai received the papers in the first week after Da Nang fell to NVA forces. She probably received refugee documents before April 7, 1975.

The papers might as well promised passage to the planet Mars. All she had to do was move her family to the airport or failing that, to a barge or ship in the Sai Gon harbor.

Evacuating large Chinese-Vietnamese families in Sai Gon circa 1975 requires a doctoral study in logistics. To put it simply, fleeing Viet Nam was complicated.

On short notice, Nguyên Maï was reluctant to flee Viet Nam. There were many family members to persuade if not confront. Imagine trying to mobilize your family and extended relations to leave a community such as Albuquerque and leave for Australia. It required a big reason to evacuate. Imminent personal destruction is a good reason. Still, it wasn't believed enough.

For Mai's family, there was zero knowledge of the western world except through the lens of Hollywood movies and western-made products promoted throughout Asia. The first non-Chinese people she ever saw were British and American personnel on gunboats plying the Yangtze River in the early 1930s. She eventually saw white Frenchmen that did business with her father in Hanoi confusing them with Americans for a time. *(All white people look alike.)*

The image of America 1975 appeared to her world as B-52 bombers, spaceships to the moon, Coca Cola and Mickey Mouse. While she traveled "in-country" with American service members for days on end between 1966 and 1972, she spoke to them through an interpreter. Maï extrapolated America as a version of Viet Nam unable to integrate images of "tract housing," "tornadoes" and "rodeos."

The American military bases she visited improved nothing of her images of American life. The officers had better manners than enlisted men. Overall, they were good men but naïve and a bit lazy if left to themselves. No different from her husband as she saw them, men were men as dogs are dogs. If she could not love a dog, she could not appreciate a man.

American sloth and wealth offended her even as she embraced their spirit of independence and commerce. The best of them were tough. "In country," there was no better fighter than the Americans she knew. Rich and lazy as they were, they knew how to fight.

It was hard to conceive of a life with few Asians among the population. White and black people populated the United States. Few Asians appeared in movies as other than bad guys along with indigenous Americans inappropriately labeled "Indians" which really didn't appear as if they came from India.

Large people populated a large continent 18,000 kilometers (11,000 miles) away. They had come here to fight the egregious people of North Viet Nam to prevent, as she understood, the invasion of people expecting undeserved-sharing of her efforts. America sent their forces to Viet Nam to contain communism. Maï hardly knew how they could accomplish that if they didn't hold the ground they won.

These over-sized people with unhealthy light skin, red and blond hair, and ghostly eyes colored brown, blue and green came to fight beside and die with strangers, her golden-skinned people, to defend the right to reap benefits from personal effort. Maï expected South Viet Nam to win.

She never contemplated going to America to make another life. Her back was literally to the sea. She took her stand with South Viet Nam. She knew from the start that she could not accept the generous offer from the American navy unless she was about to die.

Maï's hard life seldom gave her time to learn the size of the planet and the arrangement of continents. She had a vague idea of the size of earth as compared to the size of Viet Nam. Having fled the immense world of China, she knew that Viet Nam was physically a small country.

She often questioned why so much of the world had concentrated interests in her adoptive South Viet Nam. Viet Nam became a crucible focusing much human energy and treasure from across the globe. The reasons for such large interest varied between ideals and ambitions for world domination. She only wanted an ally on whom she could depend.

America was a perpetual contradiction. The United States was the first of the colonies to revolt two centuries before. It was portrayed as imperialist even though she never witnessed the expectations of the SEALS to do anything but do their "tour" and return home. They were tourists in every sense of the world looking to be back in the U. S. of A. at the first opportunity.

The Americans along with their allies were temporary combatants highly spoiled and among many of them, undisciplined. Their personal hygiene and quality of food was at times abysmal. Yet, among the richest people she ever knew, the best of their soldiers were the most skilled and dedicated she ever met.

She knew more of what the Americans did than where and how they lived their lives. The "westerns" invented everything. From phones to television and flights into space, the "westerns" made it all happen. Top of the list of innovators were the Americans.

America was the inventor of everything big in the human universe, the atomic bomb, and victory in WWII over the Japanese. The Americans landed on the moon and ended polio. Their marvelous DDT saved millions from malaria. The free world rocked to their infectious music.

Western civilization generated most discoveries and innovations of the 20th century. Yet, Mai confused the Australians and British with American largesse.

She had one simple term: "The Americans." They invented everything even as she knew that the 220 Volt 50 Hertz electric system that powered Viet Nam was developed in Europe. Yet, she extrapolated that their form of electricity was invented by the Americans.

Mai didn't know much about Europe and WWII. To her, all things essential were Asian. As South Viet Nam verged on collapse, the Americans figured as her only option. The Americans who had sacrificed over 50,000 of their kin for her country could preserve her family.

In fact, America could not spare her family from misery save one, her youngest daughter, Nguyên Xuân Loan, who returned from the "dead" two decades later from America. Nguyên Maï should have and could have relied on America to preserve her family from chaos. Unfortunately, she faced immense ethnic, cultural and logistical hurdles ahead to flee a falling government.

Nguyên Maï faced vexing details of Chinese tradition and one immense obstacle to leaving Viet Nam: her intractable husband. The traditional responsibility for the remains of ancestors was nearly as large a problem as Toan.

In Chinese tradition, descendants were obligated to steward the remains of their ancestors. Her parents were buried in Sai Gon. She had to exhume their remains and have them cremated. She attempted to bribe officials to expedite the process. By late March, she realized how large the potential exodus had become. A number of people were ahead of her paid officials to do the same thing. She was in a bidding-war for processing her parent's remains.

Again, there was her intractable husband. She needed Toan to agree and apply his full support to leave the country.

Mai knew there was no persuading Toan. After living in Viet Nam for over two decades, he spoke mainly Cantonese. He was all things Chinese living in Viet Nam.

One of Toan's brothers prepared to take to his wife and children to the barges. He had been selling off everything of value. As it was a buyer's market, he could barely give his property away.

Toan's brother sealed up the house just in case they failed to board a barge and had to return home. His preparations for the house sealed their doom instead. *(Author's Note: The family didn't make to the barges on time and had to return to their house. After Sai Gon fell, the new regime discovered he attempted to flee. The entire family was summarily executed. For years, Toan cited that event as the justification for his reluctance to leave the country.)*

Starting in late March, Mai's Vietnamese US connections pleaded with her to leave the country. Their earnest advice seemed out of character. They withheld the reasons for their emotional pleas. They knew more than they were telling her.

They neglected to tell her that the Americans duplicated their files on Vietnamese collaborators and maintained them in other locations besides Sai Gon. Maï had operated between Tay Ninh and Nah Trang 400 km to the North since 1966. She had an impressive record of accomplishments. The CIA documented her participation well. Too well.

The Americans she knew were all about paperwork. They seemed to have more than enough of it. Most damning were the photographs. She was uncomfortable about her "Polaroid" portraits that they clipped to her files. The Americans made three copies of everything.

The Americans made triplicate files as necessary and kept them in other locations besides Sai Gon. In late March, Da Nang was about to fall. They kept a dossier on Maï in Da Nang among files on thousands of Vietnamese. Da Nang fell fast, too fast for America's CIA to evacuate or destroy the files.

Mai's Vietnamese liaison with the Americans finally convinced her that the entire family was in danger. On April 7, 1975, a Vietnamese operative known as Vo gave her a manila envelope with papers written in Vietnamese and English stating the United States Navy authorized her and her family to immigrate to Guam where they could be processed to the United States.

Mai spoke and wrote Cantonese and struggled with written Vietnamese. Of the American documents she possessed, she only knew it was from the American Navy and passage for all family out of Viet Nam.

This paperwork was immensely valuable. It was also a death sentence if discovered by communist forces.

Maï was certain that once Sai Gon fell, discovery of the papers by the communists condemned the entire family. Few Americans knew what she did. They would return to America unable to provide witness to Hanoi had they been captured. The papers were condemnation enough.

A piece of inappropriate paperwork in the wrong hands meant destruction. There were many pieces of dangerous paperwork distributed throughout South Viet Nam.

Maï believed they could have reached the cargo ships or the barges had Toan listened to her pleas. It was do-able, save for him.

Loan puzzled over the secrets her mother kept from Toan. Asian tradition of respect for the father clashed with the effort everyone spent steering around Toan. Few sought his council. He was all expert on hygiene and how to eat a meal. Fastidious about cleanliness, he berated his children about poor personal maintenance. Drinking too much water or tea during a meal elicited another series of lectures on how to eat. Beyond those admirable traits, Toan appeared to be short on marketable skills.

Toan received a good education in China such as it was before Japan invaded Shanghai in 1937. Yet, he dabbled in jobs that mostly provided cover for his penchant with girlfriends. Maï was the producer of the family.

Toan possessed charm in abundance. Women respond to his charisma even to this day. Without cash, charisma alone stumbles Asia. Even a toad with money does better than a poor charming prince.

Girlfriends require maintenance. Attention and adoration alone are not enough to keep most females of any species. The male has to provide. In simple parlance, it takes cash to keep a girlfriend.

In order for Toan to have his girlfriends, he needed cash and a cover story for where it came from. His industrious wife could not be the source of his gifts. He lost face if everyone understood Maï generated his income.

In the mid-1960s, Maï purchased a 3-wheel Lambretta or Xe Lam, as it was called, for Toan. He used it as a taxi and truck-for-hire. It is not known if he ever made much income. He went to Maï for money knowing she had it but not fully understanding how she made it.

She operated for the CIA for five years before he realized the scale of her role with the ARVN forces and the Americans. He only learned that after discovering VC weapons hidden under the bottom of his Xe Lam.

A Girl's Questions

When Loan awoke in the middle of the night, she meant to interrogate her mother about family secrets. Asians conduct directness unfamiliar to "western" people who often characterize the interaction as rude. To some Asian cultures, it is just efficient communication.

On a phone call where western culture ends it with "Goodbye" or "bye-bye," a short form of conversational exit that has evolved from the old English phrase "God be with Ye," many born-there Asians just hang up when the conversation appears at an end. It is hard for western culture not to take offense when someone just hangs up without so much as a "Goodbye." *(Author's Note: It took me years of talking to Loan to get comfortable with the affront.)*

Loan interrogated her mother at every opportunity by the age of four. Her mother was her lifeline to the universe as her brothers and older sister were often unreliable sources of information. No subject was out of range of questions from Loan's perspective. She had to know everything.

By late night, her mother was gone. In a city of millions of people in distress, there was no one for Loan to ask anything. Even among her older sister and many brothers, she was alone in her curiosity. No one gave her answers to which she could expand her limited knowledge at six years of age.

To this moment in her life today in her mid-40s, she drills through weak answers and calls out deceits and liars without regard to polite conduct. Loan seldom suffers inappropriate politeness where a business or family matter is concerned. No answer is not an answer.

Only time limited Loan with her mother. Maï answered most anything as long as she could be there. The one answer she could not give is why she had so little time to spend in the house. Loan's mother did not dwell in her house for long lest her enemies catch her.

The Mystery of Maï

Loan suspected Maï might return to their 4 hectares (10 acres) of land near Tay Ninh, 80 kilometers north-and-northwest of Sai Gon. They had left their farm in such a hurry weeks before abandoning half-harvested crops.

Each night Maï returned, she brought sacks of peanuts, sweet potatoes and rice. Loan figured her mother made trips to the small farm and gathered the crops in secret. In fact, by late April, outlying areas of Tay Ninh were over-run with NVA forces. South Vietnamese crops fed the enemy.

With frequency, Maï arrived with sacks of rice and heavy boxes marked in American words. Toan stacked them near his bed matt instructing the children to leave the boxes alone. In the morning, some of the sacks remained stacked on the water drums. The boxes along with her mother were gone.

Nguyên Huang, Loan's oldest brother was special. He was the number one son and the only sibling born in Shanghai. He knew that the NVA had overrun many of the Northern provinces. Maï told him to stay close to the family and help his father.

Huang as the only child born in southern China before Toan and Mai moved south to Viet Nam took pride in being the only sibling "from China." He has a marvelous sense of humor and among the family; he is tall. He has a broad-faced smile and laugh that reminds of the 1930s American actor Joe E. Brown.

His humor is a ruse. His smile and jokes mask an extensive knowledge of the family's tragic history of upheaval and unfortunate death.

As the oldest male, he knows most of Maï's travels and many of her actions. He knew the situation better than his father. If the NVA identified her for who she was, they would execute her on the spot. The VC retribution might extend beyond her execution to her family.

Huang's larger fears had merit. Maï's capture threatened the entire family with destruction.

Most of the younger children sensed an anxiety Huang could barely contain. If Maï didn't appear as promised, he became an emotional wreck. His younger siblings measured his stress by his show of relief when Maï returned after sunset.

In his mid-twenties, married and struggling with his own concerns, bearing the knowledge of his mother's risks overwhelmed him. Chinese culture heaped great responsibility on the eldest son.

Huang privately cursed his position in life as a first born male's life script is written far in advance. Other brothers had pre-assigned duties in life. The number one son had the most to bear in administering the family's future.

Huang covered for his mother and served his difficult father with a dozen-plus siblings in tow. He attempted to fill the role of two parents and keep Maï's secrets in a country about to fall. Maï trusted heavily in number one son. Her trust was well-placed.

Huang fretted over discussion of any of his mother's activities. For a mother of so many children, the long periods of her absence drew curiosity. Huang exercised the standard story during daylight hours that she was always there. Most of the time, she was elsewhere.

At night, Maï checked in with Huang and the children. Then, she went out to the street to exchange gossip and small talk sustaining the façade of normalcy. The rest of the children were instructed to never talk about Mai's location whether she was at the house or elsewhere.

Huang covered probing questions about apparent long absences that Mai was at the market or ill and unable to talk. As a diabetic for decades, Maï's frequent "illnesses" appeared likely to acquaintances. Diabetes killed many unable to access medication and dietary council.

After Sai Gon fell, former combatants declared they had always been just rice farmers, shop keepers and taxi drivers. A litany of standard lies emerged: They never carried a gun or launched a mortar. None knew Americans or worked for the government of South Viet Nam. Industrial or farming accidents explained away scars or missing limbs. Lying became an art form in Viet Nam.

Poor luck excused obvious combat wounds. Just say they were at the wrong place and wrong time. A well placed curse on the Americans or ARVN soldiers reduced suspicion. That strategy worked for a while until the CIA and ARVN records caught up with the victim.

Best of all covers was gender and motherhood. It worked to Maï's benefit in a country rife with spies and informants. Maï was a mother of ten children and a growing number of half-blood offspring from their errant father. How could a mother of so many be a combatant?

The Viet Cong and NVA cadre might have been brain-washed and poorly educated. They were anything but stupid. They didn't suffer the miasma of western culture in regard to women. Women combatants populated NVA forces throughout the war and were as fierce as any man.

Women played a large role in North Viet Nam's conquest of South Viet Nam. Black-and-white propaganda films showed women as combatants fighting beside the men. More than a few duped gullible Americans misunderstood the culture and the lethality of women.

In turn, Hanoi was skeptical of any façade or pretense. If Maï was proved as an enemy of the newly consolidated Viet Nam, a mother of many was easy to execute.

Da Nang and CIA Records

In the northern districts of South Viet Nam, something went bad-wrong in March. The Americans heavily fortified Da Nang with facilities and armament during the 1960s. Da Nang was a central operating point for the CIA's northern field stations including maintenance of records on Vietnamese operatives in the Phoenix programs and its Vietnamese parallel operations.

The CIA maintained records on operations with Nguyên Maï along with her liaisons among Chinese-Vietnamese who translated her Cantonese into Vietnamese and English. Maï spoke Vietnamese as a second language learned as a young adult. Translators sorted among the idioms between Vietnamese spoken in the north and south. CIA files listed those translators, most often ARVN soldiers from the Cholon who became Maï's "handlers".

Maï provided information on the Viet Cong cells operating north of Sai Gon from Tay Ninh to the northwest and up to Nah Trang on the coast. As an industrious mother of many children with an errant husband in Sai Gon, she appeared to be the least likely of spies. By 1967, her track record as a reliable source of information blended with an unexpected attribute among South Vietnamese women. Maï emerged as a "combatant" in the CIA files.

Records described operations with counter-insurgent teams in which a small Vietnamese woman traveled as "guide and back-up combatant." The records noted her pregnancies working "in country" with U.S. Navy SEALS between 1966 and 1971. She worked to the beginning of her third trimester when her energy flagged and returned to Sai Gon to have a baby.

She was back "in country" two months after the birth. Her older sisters and children took care of the newborn in stride as she disappeared for as long a week.

Some of the operations described her actions serving as scout, cook and steward of men trained to need nothing of the sort. Diabetic since the late 1950s, she brought her own food disdaining American processed foods untrusting of the sugar and salt content. Depending on the mission, she carried more than she needed sharing it with her ARVN interpreter and the SEALS being careful to withhold some of the spices. The Americans were largely unaccustomed to the spices in traditional Asian foods. They were tough men but not that tough.

Maï carried four grenades that she could deploy to good effect. The CIA provided her with small revolvers. Grenades remained her weapon of choice. Grenades required less aiming.

Nguyên Maï was a nearly invisible combatant. On paper, she worked for the CIA. In reality, she worked for her adopted South Viet Nam. The Americans did not exploit her. She exploited the Americans.

It took her ARVN and American "handlers" a few years to realize she was handling them. She played every card in the deck. She was the ultimate river-boat gambler in Viet Nam.

Mai nursed an immense hatred of communism and she sought to stop the communists by all mechanisms short of prostitution. Even that function might be deployed if it delivered useful results. She was in total war with the rape of human endeavor disguised as communism and egregious socialism. All of her humanity was sacrifice if their goal of independence for her offspring could be maintained.

The intensity was hard to fathom without knowing her history going back to the 1937 when Japan invaded Shanghai and started the devolution of Chinese civilization. At the age of crystallizations of most humans which is around ten to twelve years of age, she decided to never suffer an egregious society that condoned the drain of human endeavor. Theft of any kind deserved no quarter. Make no mistake about it; communism was state-sanctioned theft.

South Viet Nam wandered into chaos until the Americans showed up with all their resources. Since 1965, South Viet Nam appeared to have more than an even chance of remaining independent of Hanoi. The witless Americans showed up to rescue South Viet Nam.

By the end of 1967, South Viet Nam seemed to hold its own. A sympathetic press supported this endeavor despite the American body-count reported every week. Young Americans at risk began to petition as each City and State reported the growing tally of casualties.

South Viet Nam and the Americans seldom kept won territory and by handicapped politics, permitted the perpetual NVA invasion along the Ho Chi Minh trail along the western border.

Viet Nam was a war of wandering ambivalence. Hanoi decided to exploit this in singular event known as the Tet Offensive to unsettle the stalemate if not turn the tide of the war.

The Tet offensive of 1968 went badly for the Viet Cong. The VC nearly ceased to function as a force. North Viet Nam lost the Tet Offensive but it had the desired effect on unsettling America.

Hanoi was clever and untrustworthy. They never kept a promise or upheld an agreement. Never. A diplomatic solution could never be expected to hold without destroying Hanoi's capability to fight in the South.

Her best hope lay in aiding ARVN and Americans disrupt the remnants of Viet Cong and emerging cells of NVA forces. Maï had what the Americans and ARVN forces needed. She possessed excellent information on the enemy.

The Americans and ARVN forces had what she needed, firepower and capability. They both possessed the same goal: neutralize North Viet Nam's intrusion to preserve an independent South Viet Nam.

Nobody was above suspicion throughout the history of Viet Nam between 1945 and 1975. By design, Maï appeared as a meek Chinese-Vietnamese woman in service to South Viet Nam and its western allies. ARVN and Americans scrutinized Mai's unflagging hatred of Hanoi.

The CIA analyzed motives of its Vietnamese operatives. They questioned why oppose other Vietnamese aligned with Hanoi? Track records mattered as a test of fealty.

Did Mai walk the talk? Answer: She did. In American parlance, she was the real deal, the whole "enchilada".

In time, Maï's information generated phenomenal results establishing her motives above reproach. The unfortunate event is that the CIA recorded details and analysis of the Vietnamese operatives in detail in volumes of documents. Little as they might know about Nguyên Maï, they wrote down everything they could know or guess. The mere existence of the records scripted a death-sentence on Mai and her family once South Viet Nam fell.

Nguyën Maï "neutralized" Viet Cong either by information or in fact by deed. Her remarkable history was analyzed, recorded and duplicated. America's record-prone CIA kept duplicate files in Da Nang. Even with time to destroy records in Sai Gon, the CIA was unable to destroy everything before April 30, 1975.

NVA routed the South Vietnamese Army (ARVN) at almost every position. NVA had the "high-ground" in the marble mountain(s) northwest of Da Nang where NVA spotters directed artillery and rockets when the weather was clear. NVA had been routing or over-running ARVN defenses almost unopposed by March 1975.

Family Policy Toxic to Warfare

Above all factors, family influences rational actions in Asian culture. Poorly managed, "family" often contributes to irrational policy among Asians.

Vietnamese military leadership dragged their families to the "front-lines" of a poorly managed war with Hanoi. In a decades-long war with few permanent battle fronts or physical limitations, moving family to the war zones for the convenience of male officers appeared idiotic.

It was reckless to the level of stupid. South Vietnamese military allowed officers to move their families with them. Of all the wars in the 20th century, what other conflict permitted military leadership to bring wives and children to reside near where they served? Research shows little of this in any other conflict.

ARVN leadership was functionally compromised when Hanoi launched its campaign in January 1975. They had lodged their family scant miles behind front lines. If the front line(s) suddenly collapsed, military leadership fell apart.

Desertion of leadership began in Da Nang in March 1975. Leaderless ARVN forces in the northern sectors evaporated as North Viet Nam initiated the final phase of their conquest of South Viet Nam.

Sai Gon fortified Da Nang as a South Vietnamese strong point. They stocked it with weapons, personnel and records of operations. The Americans left behind a huge arsenal. It had the wherewithal to hold then line save one key element of durability. The Americans needed to be there to back up the as-yet prepared South Vietnamese army.

Despite the inability to eliminate North Vietnamese artillery spotters in the high ground, the city was considered "safe." How somebody holds the "high ground" above a city with artillery and calls it "safe" eludes explanation. In a famous region in 1954 in North Viet Nam, the Viet Minh fired on a French air base from concealed tunnels in a mountain overlooking the valley. It proved to be the undoing of the French.

In short, Da Nang was doomed. By March, the NVA executed a complete rout in northern regions. Disorganized ARVN units managed a poor retreat. They were slaughtered.

As the threat fell upon Da Nang, defense of the city fell apart. Many officers abandoned their positions to move family to the south. This left ARVN forces uncoordinated if not leaderless.

We'll never know the full extent of the failure. Leaderless platoons of loyalists of South Viet Nam were killed often to a man. Often in the rout, the man and his family were killed. NVA gave no quarter.

Human Deluge

Civilians fleeing south flooded limited roads in central Viet Nam. This compromised what remained of organized military movement of South Vietnamese forces.

NVA forces moved south seemingly uncontested despite the number of ARVN forces in the region. Consequently, Americans with "listening posts" and operational offices of the Central Information Agency (CIA) in Da Nang had days if that to destroy tens of tens of thousands of documents. In the best circumstances, the CIA needed weeks if not a month to remove or destroy documents and destroy arsenal.

Paper Inertia

Fragile paper in bulk is very durable. It is hard to destroy well and quickly.

The CIA left behind tens of thousands of files listing Vietnamese agents that aided the Americans and South Vietnamese forces. The files included photographs of the operative, descriptions, assessments, debriefings all made of 20-pound paper stock in paper folders.

Accounting ledgers listing expenses and payments document everything in American life. Da Nang documentation was no exception. The documents were a prosecutor's dream. It becomes the work-list of Hanoi's appointed executioners of enemies of the state.

America's litigious culture left behind records that readily condemned any Vietnamese that halfway fit the description. Commonality of names and unrestrained license to kill formulated a prescription for slaughter throughout South Viet Nam after April 30, 1975.

Record Destruction Made Simple

A sheet of fragile 8.5" x 11" paper is easy to render destroyed with a single match. Different issues arise with a few million sheets of paper stacked and packed in filing cabinets.

That difference factored in Loan's life. She contemplated this history three decades later in America. Among the many factors that sent Loan on an incredible journey was the management, if you can call it that, of the records of war. The CIA's management of her mother's history on paper propelled her into an alien world known simply as "America."

Burning the Paperwork

In quantity, reams of paper are difficult objects to destroy. This claim is easy to test.

> (1) Take stacks of paper and fill a 55-gallon oil drum with holes punch in the bottom to introduce combustion air below.
> (2) Set the paper on fire. *(It won't burn well for long without "stirring" the pile. It never does.)*

The fire on the stacked paper will penetrate 5% of the papers and either smolder for a time or go out. The thin layer of each page needs open exposure to oxygen to page. To get this right, crumple the paper a few sheets at a time or shred it.

The rules of document destruction are simple: No air and space to burn = no incineration. Stacks of paper require mechanical work to mangle sufficient separation to expose the cellulose to heat and air. Somebody or something has to crumple or shred the paper into combustible form.

Apply lighter fluid to accelerate incineration. Stir the burning documents occasionally to ensure exposure of paper to flame. It is messy, time-consuming and unpleasant on all levels.

In Viet Nam, it took time and "grunts" to make this happen well. CIA weren't very good at stirring oil-drums with papers to burn to oblivion. They were short of personnel, grunts-in-training, proper incineration drums and time.

In Sai Gon as in the northern military provinces near Da Nang, there was a huge shortage of trusted paper "crumplers." Low-cost labor fled south as the NVA closed in on the city.

NVA artillery shelled "safe" Da Nang from the Marble Mountains with impunity. Hanoi owned the high ground in late March 1975. A shattered South Vietnamese army fled south in the jammed highways of the narrow country. At least 120,000 were killed, wounded or captured by April 1, 1975. ARVN soldiers threw off their uniforms and assumed status as wayward peasants as the immense resources of that region of South Viet Nam withered in the onslaught.

Americans were out of the fight able only to watch. Da Nang was cut-off by the end of March. Everyone marched south. A few ships over-loaded with Vietnamese escaped only to live another horror at sea as many starved to death on the way to Sai Gon. The last commercial jet aircraft left Da Nang over-loaded and flew to Hong Kong with the rear door open holding refugees that hadn't fall off the platform or out of the landing-gear wells as the flight took off.

The CIA's evacuation helicopters made attractive targets unable to linger longer than to remove personnel and electronics. Sensitive documents remained intact along with tons of military hardware and ammunition.

Document destruction re-appeared a month later in Sai Gon as the CIA generated a snowfall of cinders that fell in the courtyard of the U.S. Embassy in the final days of April 1975. They were better prepared this time able to destroy more of the documents including thousands of dollars of American cash. Foreign currency posed a liability in the hands of NVA. It was also part of the April payroll that went undistributed to Vietnamese employed by the United States.

The paper-work-prolific CIA created thousands of records with the names of over 20,000 Vietnamese "employed" in their aid. From Da Nang to Sai Gon down to Rac Ghia at the southern tip, poorly destroyed files listing South Vietnamese operatives fell into NVA hands.

Nobody planned for Viet Nam's collapse at such a speed. In the 1970s, the document management of the CIA was the biggest blunder of the decade. Document mismanagement contributed untold harm to South Vietnamese loyalists. Political necessity met practical hurdles no one prepared to manage.

Frank Snepp, formerly of the CIA, documents his witness of the last days of Sai Gon in his seminal book, "Decent Interval." The CIA's central office in Sai Gon forewarned that South Viet Nam would fall

18 months after America's exit. That turned out to be insufficient. The document-burning oil-drums ran 24/7 including green American cash. The infamous "snow" of ashes littered the U.S. Embassy compound in the last weeks of April 1975.

The destruction of condemning documents began too late with insufficient resources. The CIA by proxy gave Hanoi its "kill list" on stranded South Vietnamese. Nguyên Maï was on that list. Why else did the new regime visit the house and punish Toan for not knowing the location of Maï.

Price on Her Head

The CIA material listed Mai's participation against the Viet Cong and NVA. She knew Da Nang had fallen on April 2, 1975 but wasn't told how her ARVN liaison learned she was a likely target for assassination. Her last recorded location was in Tay Ninh.

She had abandoned her small farm more than a month before. Hanoi pursued this woman and her family for years based on confusing information thanks much to Americans knew hardly how to say her name.

Sai Gon itself was falling. Maï's daytime contacts jeopardized the entire family. She could not be captured with them. All would be imprisoned or executed on the spot. Entire families were being slaughtered in Cholon in sporadic locations. Sai Gon police, such as they were, became over-whelmed with murders they would never solve.

Maï mistrusted her neighbors, well-meaning as they might be. Her nighttime visitations were the only time she could see her brood with a degree of safety. She was a mother of ten children and stepmother to at least four more at the time. She bore most of them, suckled many and provided for all.

Maï embodied motherhood. Yet, she seldom risked being among her brood for more than a few hours each night. Her physical presence threatened all she held dear in the world.

A mother's protection of offspring's is a remarkable thing. Maï juggled between surviving and functioning as a mother to her children. It was a difficult and exhausting choreography of a life she believed might end all at once.

Maï had led the "good fight." She was effective by all accounts. Due to the incompetence of men, South Viet Nam was lost. All that left was buying as much time as possible to stall the fall of Sai Gon to secure something for her family.

Xuân Lôc Sai Gon's "Last Stand"

On April 9, 1975, ARVN forces set up a defensive line against NVA forces northeast of Sai Gon at Xuân Lôc. *(Soon Lock)* Outnumbered, the ARVN forces held off the NVA for over a week until finally abandoning the center of Xuân Lôc on April 21. The next city was Sai Gon. It was a matter of days before North Viet Nam prevailed over all of a divided Viet Nam.

Americans dithered on making arrangements to evacuate loyalist-Vietnamese until early April. The effort gradually stepped up. Unfortunately, it did take into account Asian culture of tending to the graves of ancestors and the size of "immediate" family.

Evacuation also meant taking other assets including favored pigs and chickens. Families leaving for the airport and the harbor carried small livestock making for a bizarre parade of humans and animals. All of the abandoned animals ended up wandering the streets of Sai Gon on May 1, 1975.

The term family meant different things between western and Asian cultures. A Vietnamese couple with four children was often a family of a dozen or more including parents and grandparents. They expanded the meaning to include aunts, uncles, adult siblings, and cousins. Unrelated close friends were also "family."

Unspecific evacuation plans and cultural mores clashed. Ignorance blended with uncertainty and hesitation. The mixture assured disappointment and failure.

Loan's oldest brothers, Huang or perhaps the younger Siep knew Mai had word from the Americans on where to go. The airport and U.S. Embassy were over run. The barges became their next best bet. The oldest sons were married and lived close by, bringing food in cardboard boxes to the family during the days when their mother was elsewhere.

Maï had been in constant contact with the oldest sons until a few weeks ago. As South Viet Nam's army fell apart, days passed between contacts.

By April 7, 1975, she mentioned one item. Xuân Lôc must hold out as long as possible.

The rapid fall of Da Nang and Hue emboldened the NVA that originally planned to take Sai Gon by late October 1975. The NVA had more than bravado, they moved south with American-made stocks of weapons captured at Da Nang including tanks and aircraft. The American-made weapons were operated and flown by defecting South Vietnamese military.

After two weeks, on April 21, she returned in the night to tell them the family must prepare to leave. Nguyên Maï and her difficult husband, Toan, argued bitterly over the options. Until 1974, he beat her for arguing with him.

Authoritarian Chinese male-culture had its limits. Toan discovered how far his cultural support sustained him. Toan could not overcome the anger of oldest sons who no longer stood by as he exercised his oldest-male rights on his errant wife.

His older sons changed that dynamic by beating him and threatened him with greater harm if he hit their mother one more time. As if a blinding light illuminated the family, as Sai Gon was falling apart, Maï's sons ended the abuse with a threat. Toan ceased his physical abuse of Mai as his oldest sons assumed true Asian manhood. From that day forward, they gave their father tacit respect but no more unbounded tirades were allowed.

Toan naively believed that the Americans would step in as they had in the past. Maï knew better of America. She had worked for them, fought with them, almost died with them. If the soldiers she knew could be there, they should have intervened by now. Circumstances beyond their knowledge restrained the remarkable Americans from acting.

The Americans were out of the fight for South Viet Nam never to return. Explaining her limited knowledge of American politics to Toan was useless. His isolated arrogance presented too high a hurdle. She couldn't seduce him with cash or lie on her back for him one more time in an endeavor to convince him the rightness of her plan. His fears energized resistance immune to all manners of persuasion.

He only knew of the westerners by their abundance of material goods. At least at a subconscious level, he knew his "income" over a decade came from Maï's money. Much of Maï's "extra" resources that helped him maintain girlfriends were made working with CIA and ARVN operations.

Americans provided transport out of Sai Gon for anybody who showed up as best they could. They lacked skills in Asian-family logistics. They offered to transport Maï, Toan, their fourteen children and other family out of Viet Nam. Mai had to figure out how to get their family to the Sai Gon River or out to the Sai Gon harbor. Her biggest dilemma was whether she should kill Toan.

The Americans arranged barges on the Sai Gon River and in the Sai Gon harbor for any operatives and allies and their families. Flying out of Sai Gon became a poor option. NVA had shut down Ton Son Hut Airport runways with rockets and egregious "turn-coats," the ARVN saboteurs that destroyed the runways.

Sai Gon's airport became a staging area for helicopters that continually flew back and forth to the American ships waiting in The South China Sea on the last days of April. The U.S. Embassy swarmed with Vietnamese who had been advised to go there to be air-lifted from helicopters of the embassy roof. Stories of chaos at the American's embassy gates discouraged Mai.

Maï believed her best chance of getting two dozen of their "family" out of Viet Nam was by water. Her contacts told her to get to the docks on the Sai Gon Harbor. The problem was logistics, transportation, food and worst of all, Toan.

Toan

Toan dug in as Maï prepared to flee. As she argued with him, she gained full measure of his insecurity. His arrogance and frequent cruelty concealed his isolation. His indulgences comforted him and reinforced his rejection of changing reality. To aggravate Toan's situation, the Chinese tradition of honoring the father reduced outward criticism and the view that outward criticism was valid. Family silence enabled him to expand his errors of judgment, virtually unchallenged.

For the first time, the younger children heard the hard words. Their mother loomed large as she broke the shackles of tradition and screamed at him much as he did to her all of their lives. In the long one-room shelter, there was little privacy. She berated him openly.

They seldom heard Maï raise her voice to her husband. Asian ancient limited a woman's public expression of outrage. She could not physically move the family by herself. She needed a compliant Toan.

Even if she didn't need Toan, she could not leave him behind. It was in her culture to preserve all family much as she hated his behavior.

Maï was desperate to convince Toan that it was time to leave. She played the only option she had left. She told him the larger story in front of silent awe-struck children.

Maï's Pronouncement

Everyone heard her scream at him that South Viet Nam was lost. Worse, she predicted that the harsh regime under Hanoi will punish ethnic-Chinese-become-Vietnamese that backed South Viet Nam and American involvement. She told him clearly for all to hear that Hanoi was coming to kill her and all connected to her. Given her secretive comings and goings for months, no one could argue with her declaration of doom.

The stories of persecution from the over-run villages and cities trickled into Sai Gon. Hanoi had lists of enemies. South Viet Nam and its American allies failed to destroy all the records in Da Nang. Families were being slaughter across three and four generations.

Mai shouted, "Was the brutal travesty at Huë in 1968 not demonstration enough of Hanoi's capability to destroy us? We are facing a virulent political and selfish disease that will reduce us to nothing! They will end our line!"

Going outside of her comfort zone, in the Cantonese equivalent, she shouted at Toan that "The Americans screwed up in Da Nang. My name is on a list. My actions are described."

Stunned by her outburst, Toan was silent as she continued in an intensity he never witnessed, "They will go to Tay Ninh to find me. Then they'll come to Sai Gon. They will come to the Cholon looking for me and all connected with me. They will end our line!"

Maï rattled off the name of a few families in the Cholon which lost relatives, usually a nephew or cousin that collaborated for the CIA. The NVA infiltrators and 'sleeper cells' killed the husband, wife and children and all other relatives in the household. The attacks picked up in January as Hanoi launched its final offensive on South Viet Nam. Maï ended the list of names by saying with a frozen scowl in a terse voice "That will be us."

Maï paused to let that sink in. In a calmer tone, "I don't know if the records list this house. I never met with the Americans in Sai Gon after 1967. They may only have a vague idea of where we live. Despite all that, if they find me here, they will kill us all."

Toan stood numb and did not respond. Maï was right, but he wasn't going out to the barge on river to leave Sai Gon to go to Honk Kong or even to America. The "dumah" (*Vietnamese epithet*) dug in.

The Viet Cong and NVA death squads that had acted in Sai Gon over the last decade had grown in number and activity. Whole families of government officials and CIA operatives were being slaughtered in the north. Since 1968, residents of the Cholon remembered the roving death squads of the TET offensive. The horror never ended after that with sporadic assassinations occurring monthly.

Nguyên Maï's name was on one of those lists. The family must flee or die. She could put the situation in no better terms.

Normally, Toan would have struck his insolent wife. His sons were ready to strike him if raised a hand. He knew the truth of her words.

Frightened as he was, he could not leave the crumbling sanctuary of South Viet Nam. He put too much "personal stock" as it were into Sai Gon. He was frozen in terror.

Preparation for Invasion

Accurate information grew scare. Its absence told more. Loan's oldest brothers: No. 1 brother, Huang and No. 2 brother, Siep, could not conceal their growing fears. The expression in their faces spoke volumes even if their words failed. The country fell to Hanoi. Sai Gon was the last hold-out. It could not last.

Loan's brothers told her their singular secret. Bad men were coming. She asked if it was the Viet Cong, the people her mother hated. Her oldest brother filled in a few facts.

The North Vietnamese Army came on. It was no longer the Viet Cong as the remnants of them had been absorbed into the NVA. Despite the actual identity of the enemy, the forces of Hanoi hated the ethnic-Chinese Vietnamese that backed South Viet Nam and the Americans.

(Similar to other habits of speech, one term encapsulated many creating some confusion to western ears. Loan referred to Viet Cong without distinction of history. The NVA absorbed the remnants of the Viet Cong after the Tet Offensive in 1968. To this day, Loan always refers to any version of the North Vietnamese forces as "Viet

Cong." In public settings to this day, the term is not used openly referring only to them as "VC" as the regime retains spies to watch the population for unrest.)

Maï's children avoided talking to strangers. If someone asked about her mother, Loan was told to say nothing. If forced to talk, she told people her mother died in 1970. Everyone knew to say Nguyên Maï died in 1970. They rehearsed the phrase frequently as the end of April approached. It was an obvious lie but in some cases, it bought time to make up another answer.

From a western perspective, the lie about a mother's death seems at least a bid odd. In wartime Viet Nam, distortions and lies became necessary to foster confusion as a matter of survival. Confusion and obfuscation were necessary skills to Vietnamese that defended the losing side of the war.

Advantages of Multiple Names

Nguyên is a common family name. There might be hundreds of women in Sai Gon by the name of Nguyên Maï. For reasons unknown (author's limitation), Toan's family name was different. Although she owned all the property, the Sai Gon records listed Toan as the owner. This gave some measure of confusion to the NVA that might have pulled her records pulled from the CIA office that failed to understand Vietnamese cultural logistics.

This mother of ten children sans son number 3 and parent of fourteen-plus children further increased the confusion. She also listed herself as divorced or single and childless in some of the records. Having bore ten offspring herself, her figure showed minimal impact of childbearing.

The lie of marital status put the Americans as well as AVRN operatives at ease when she travelled with them on missions. It was inconceivable to Americans that a mother of a large family took such risks.

Maï bore three children between 1965 and 1969 while in-country with the ARVN and American forces. She told them the father of her children was already married failing to tell them he was married to her. The naïve Americans had no way to sort her fictions. Her children share one of three family names. Their names diagramed on a family tree make little sense to western culture.

Birthdates were also another matter of confusion for Sai Gon census takers. Some Asian culture refers to the date of conception in the determination of a person's age. Even the calendar and time-zone changed slightly in the 1960s aligning geographically with mainland China.

Idiomatic and inflection differences between North and South Vietnamese speech further complicated answers. In the Cholon, the Sino-Vietnamese adopted the Vietnamese language in changing circumstances. For many reasons, recorded information in city ledgers and CIA documents could be misleading which provided another measure of protection to Maï's family.

South: Good. North: Bad

At six, Loan understood minimum of the politics of South and North Viet Nam. Her understanding was limited as a matter of survival. South Vietnamese: Good. North Vietnamese: Bad. Viet Cong: Very Bad. Above all, trust no one. That was her political universe.

She was told to withhold information. If strange people asked her something, it was simple enough for her to protect the family. She didn't know anything.

Americans? Westerners? The white and black people? She didn't know who these people were. She seldom actually saw a white or black person in daylight. The Americans that visited their homes in the villages north of Sai Gon came only in the dark of night.

She saw that the men were large, seemingly twice the size of Vietnamese men. She never actually saw the color of their skin in daylight. She over-heard her older brother whisper about the western men of different color. Were there also blue, green or purple men?

The last contingents of Americans and fortunate Vietnamese left the country by helicopter. The evacuation of Sai Gon became the largest helicopter-based evacuation in world history.

Helicopters shuttled in from the east, picked up Americans and Vietnamese at the airport and embassy roof and returned west to aircraft carriers stationed in the South China Sea. In the last days of Sai Gon, the city witnessed helicopters spaced across an invisible east-west running oval racetrack in the sky. The distinctive the whop-whop-whop sound of the blades and whine of turbines started an hour before dawn and ended just after sunset.

As the end of April approached, the noise of the helicopters faded in the darkness to be replaced by thunder as the flashes of exploding artillery delineated the horizon to the east. Unlike the blue-white flashes of lightning, the illumination was a warm incandescence illuminating the bottom of clouds and columns of smoke from burning buildings.

South East Asian Geography

Loan assumed the American's were going home, somewhere on the other side of Sai Gon. The helicopters ran back and forth, from Sai Gon somewhere to the east over the South China Sea. She knew nothing of the size of the planet, the layout of continents and oceans. Everyone she knew of was a neighbor either in Sai Gon or nearby.

Loan was six years old. Unschooled, she knew nothing of world geography or of distance. Travel between villages and cities in Viet Nam was measured in hours and days, not kilometers. That has not changed much even to this day. Distance "as the crow flies" has thin meaning in Viet Nam when it came to describing the length of travel.

Loan's geographical perception: There was Viet Nam and there was "somewhere else." The western people, the Americans, near as she could figure, were neighbors that lived east of Sai Gon.

The big secret Maï hinted to Loan is they might travel on a boat in a few days. Maï arranged travel to America but only if Loan could keep a secret.

The South Vietnamese Navy and Americans positioned industrial barges in the Sai Gon River to evacuate Vietnamese to ships in the South China Sea. Loan knew she might get to travel on the water and envisioned it was like the fishing boats with the sails.

She had never been in water deeper than a tub of bath water and only watched her brothers wade in a stream or river. The prospect of an adventure on a boat lightened her heart even though she knew she could not swim.

To protect her and the family, Maï minimized the family's knowledge of her personal role in fighting Viet Cong. A child's unmanaged knowledge could unwittingly put the entire family at risk.

Moving from village to village as they had, Loan knew only of the village's name in the unlikely event she became lost. She remembered the time it took to travel from one village to another but little else. Yet, she knew it was not far.

Any errant comment by a family member or a neighbor was dangerous. Geographical identity spoke volumes and was therefore concealed. Other than Buddhism, religious identity presented additional risks, particularly Christianity. In a political move to change the support structure of South Viet Nam, Catholic Vietnamese relocated in the 1950s in large numbers from North Viet Nam which carried a political identity distinct from Protestant Christians.

North Viet Nam considered anyone working with the South Viet Nam government or Americans as a mark of the enemy. Nobody in affiliation with South Viet Nam was immune to reprisal from Hanoi.

Murders occurred sporadically over a fifteen-year period. It happened from time to time and most often among ethnic-Chinese that had immigrated to South Viet Nam two decades before.

The ethnic-Chinese closed ranks treating unfamiliar people as potential threats. Loan's father had always lived in Sai Gon along with his oldest sons. Neighbors accepted the return of Maï and the children without question. Yet, everyone guarded their comments as the frequency of the assassinations increased.

Hanoi endorsed the assassinations as a means to communicate to the population in the Cholon. Support South Viet Nam at your peril. Every victim of Hanoi's grievance worked for the Americans or high up in the South Vietnamese government.

Tragically, sensitive lists of Vietnamese and the ethnic-Chinese collaborators fell into NVA hands in the last two months. After the first spate of killings, word spread through the Cholon that Hanoi targeted any Vietnamese supporter of South Viet Nam.

Nguyên Maï was on those lists. Through an interpreter, she described herself as someone else in an entirely different life. She gave no detail about Toan and reluctantly posed for a Polaroid picture that went into a file somewhere in 1967. The Polaroid picture bothered her the most.

Maï and Toan did not share the same last name. His family name was different. Due to confusion with the Vietnamese language, their children had different last names based on Maï's answer each time she had another child.

Toan was never present when each child was born and Maï, often delirious from the pain of childbirth, answered Vietnamese mid-wives inconsistently. When the midwife recorded the child's family name mangled by Maï's broken Vietnamese, the name became permanent.

The confusion in names confused Maï's enemies and probably saved their lives. As the war escalated, Maï's activities attracted attention. Frustrated by the disappearance of Viet Cong cells north of Sai Gon, Hanoi directed VC operatives to stem the leaks of information. They began to suspect anyone that did "business" with the VC. They eventually targeted an unlikely candidate. They targeted the unmarried bottle-woman with a dozen children under her care.

Khêń Đùć Ambush

Viet Cong confronted six-month pregnant Maï in August 1967 outside of Khêń Đùć. She walked her bicycle laden with re-cycled intravenous bottles acquired from a trash dump outside of an American installation. As she headed to the house two kilometers up a winding jungle path, two young men wearing black shorts and sandals with AK-47s slung on their backs stepped out of a bamboo thicket. They had been waiting for Maï *(aka "the bottle woman".)*

They spoke to her in Vietnamese. After a decade of living in South Viet Nam, she struggled with much of the language. Cantonese had nothing in common with spoken or written Vietnamese. North Viet Nam differed from South Vietnamese by an extra inflection and varying idioms.

For example, one phrase in the North was a question "Where are you going" and in the South was a directive, "Go wash your hands." Many common phrases meant different things.

Maï had lived in the North and understood this. Communication was not the issue. These men were threatening her. She was in grave danger. They were there to kill her.

Feigning poor understanding, she asked them to repeat their questions as they stood face to face. Frustrated by her responses, one of the men began to make his point by shoving her backward. The bicycle toppled with its load of glass IV bottles. The bottles clattered noisily. Maï contained her anger. If the fall cracked the bottles, they could not be sold. She was more concerned about her fetus that was kicking up a storm. *(Author's Note: She succeeded in bearing another son, Quy, which is a bit of a contrary person. Perhaps his contrary nature came from that moment in the womb.)*

One of the young men broke her distraction by shoving her roughly on her shoulders. Then the other young man pushed on her. With no place to set her feet, Maï lost her balance.

Maï fell backward on the bicycle feeling the frame and seat against her back. The second man pressed in with the first yelling at her, leaning over her as she held out her arms to keep them back.

Angry and afraid, she yelled back, "Xin lois, toi knong biết!" (*Excuse me, I don't know."*). As they yelled more, Maï pleaded, "Xin lois, toi khong hiêụ!" (*Excuse me, I don't understand!*)

She understood all too well. These men were executioners. They were there to sort the mystery of so many losses of VC cadre.

If they killed her and the mysterious losses continued, they had wasted a life. It was a small risk. She was a poor Chinese woman of no importance.

These were young men in their early twenties barely taller than Maï, standing over her in the afternoon heat. VC leadership directed them to find and kill one peasant woman. The leader of their VC cell failed to tell them their target was a pregnant woman.

Her pregnancy made the young men uncertain, hesitant. Family mattered significantly to Asians. (*Author's note: Through numerous introductions between western and Asian men, one of the first questions that come through the translator is how many children I have. The Asian men are invariably pleased that I have more than two.*)

Viet Cong recruits were torn from their families as early as 12. Viet Cong reconstructed their family in the jungles in order to indoctrinate them in Ho Chi Minh's revolution. They referred to the patriarch of their new family as "Father Ho" or "Uncle Ho." Children were given candy at holidays including Christmas that was celebrated by Christian Vietnamese and told to say "Thank you Uncle Ho" in order to receive the treat.

Killing a pregnant woman was unsettling. To most Asians, life starts at conception. They were asked to kill not one, but two human beings that day. If she was carrying twins, they would be killing three people.

They knew little about her other than she and her family arrived a few months at settled on a small plot of farmland outside the village. She rented a farm and house outside of Khêń Đừć. With no apparent husband, her means of support apparently came from selling black-market medical supplies. Christian and Buddhist missions and village medical facilities in Khếń Đùć bought her re-cycled intravenous (IV) bottles and other medical supplies. The increase in warfare made it a booming business.

The Viet Cong made contact with her a month after she had arrived. Competing with the missions, the VC negotiated for her supplies for their underground hospitals and bunkers that peppered the region north of Sai Gon.

Hanoi supplied the VC via the Ho Chi Minh trail that snaked down the west side of Viet Nam or by ships unloading in Cambodia. American and Vietnamese airstrikes frequently interrupted the flow of supplies. As the war escalated, demand for medical supplies grew forcing the VC to fill in their shortages by other means. The "bottle-woman" showed up at the right time.

One month after buying Nguyên Maï's "products," South Vietnamese and American forces discovered and destroyed well-hidden Viet Cong bunkers. Cells of VC were typically insulated from knowing about each other to prevent a compromised unit from betraying the location of other Viet Cong cells. Captured VC were interrogated briefly by the Americans and reluctantly turned over to South Viet Nam and worse, to the South Koreans. It was usually a death-sentence. Few captured North Vietnamese ever returned to Hanoi.

AVRN forces along with American Special Forces became dangerously effective. South Viet Nam's counter-insurgent strikes were precise. The losses were total and unprecedented. Somebody guided Hanoi's enemies straight to the VC bunkers. A new form of soldier began operating around Sai Gon named after an aquatic mammal called a U.S. Navy SEAL.

Viet Cong had a different name for the U.S. Navy SEALS. They called them "The devil with the green face." They were not like standard American GIs. Yet that could not explain their success in uncovering and destroying VC assets. They suspected the woman of aiding the Americans.

AK-47s hung across their backs as they bent over the small woman. They had pinned her down lying backwards on the side of the bicycle and the black plastic sacks loaded with empty glass bottles.

In the afternoon sunlight, they were shifting threatening dark silhouettes against a bright tropical sky. One of the men questioned her repeatedly in a string of Vietnamese she barely understood, the other had his right hand out as if about to slap her. His left hand menacingly held the end of knife in a scabbard loosely belted on his waist. He turned his head left and right from time to time to see if anyone was on coming up the jungle path.

Maï carried two curving filet knives under her black blouse. Razor sharp, she tucked the knives into leather wrappings on each side of her breasts. As they continued to yell at her pushing on the front of her shoulders to keep her from getting off her back, she folded her arms across her breasts as if to protect them.

She felt the handles of the knives under her blouse. As they yelled in her face, she winced keeping her eyes down as if submissive. She was not submissive. She focused on the position of their necks in relation to the reach of her hand filled with knife.

They were now shouting in unison, something about whether she talked to ARVN or American soldiers. One of them was blowing spittle from his lips as he screamed at her. She maintained a simple response as they shouted at her, their faces barely a foot away from hers.

In one motion, Maï unfolded her arms with the knives flashing in each hand. Left-handed, Maï whipped the blade across the neck of the man on her left. A thin red line appeared running from behind his right ear and down to his wind pipe. The line cleaved open spurting blood. She severed his right common carotid artery. The loss of blood pressure in his brain rendered him unconscious. No longer yelling, he slumped forward falling on Maï's left side driving her back into the handlebars.

The man on her right jerked back grabbing the front of his neck. She had missed the softer tissues on the side of neck. The thin blade in Maï's right hand penetrated his windpipe and stopped on his neck bones. Eyes wide with shock, he stood up with the blade and handle sticking out the front of his Adam's apple (throat). The blade lodged in his wind-pipe. He could not talk. He raised his right hand to grab the knife but switched to his left hand fumbling for the knife handle.

His AK-47 was slung on his right shoulder requiring his right hand to bring it forward. The knife handle in his left hand, he grabbed the stock of the AK-47 to swing the gun forward. He staggered backward doing two things at once, trying to remove the knife and kill the woman.

Shoving the dying man off her left side, Maï rolled off the bicycle holding the knife in her left hand. The second man needed both hands on the rifle. He yanked the knife out of his throat and dropped it. His neck wound spurted red droplets and air as he gasped for breath. Blood ran into his lungs.

The gun was still behind him as he reached back with both hands to swing the muzzle forward. He turned his head to the right to see where the rifle was. As he attempted to grab the rifle with his left hand, she used her free right hand to move up from the bicycle. She lunged spewing an epithet in Cantonese. It was in reference to an inappropriate act the young man might have with his mother.

His hands were full as he staggered back raising the gun toward her. Maï closed the space between them and drove the blade in her left hand into his stomach below the sternum. She shoved it and drove it in until it stopped with her fist in his belly.

As the barrel of the AK-47 came up, Maï threw her left knee into the barrel. He had not placed his finger on the trigger. As he groped for the trigger, she jerked the knife out and drove it lower into his stomach. He collapsed with Mai falling on top of him.

She had severed his aorta. His blood pressure collapsed. He fell unconscious. He was dead.

The struggle was over. Two minutes had elapsed from the first challenge from the VC.

She rolled over him on to her back on the dirt path gasping for air. She lay there for a few seconds staring up at the cloudless blue-white sky. Her mind screamed, "Get up! Get up! Sort this out!"

Shaking from the rush of adrenalin, Maï turned over to her side and worked up to her hands and knees. Then she stood feeling the baby kick up a storm. The fetus was responding to the hormonal rush in her blood stream.

Her blouse was covered in dust and blood from the second man's chest wounds. She felt the coolness of the congealing blood on her forearms, breasts and belly.

Her pulse pounded in her temples. She stood for a moment between the two men, their wounds bleeding into an expanding dark stain in the dust. Blood pooled on the second man's stomach and drained off one side. The wounds bled rapidly from their still-pumping hearts.

Maï looked up and down the path. No one appeared. Except for their shouting, the incident made no other noise. Few used this back-path into Khên Đùć in the afternoon heat.

Holding one of his feet, she dragged the first body into the bamboo thicket they used to conceal their ambush. Tucked into hollow area of the thicket, Maï found a rice sack converted into a crude backpack. It held balls of sticky rice and bean curd wrapped in banana leaves. Another backpack contained VC "canteens," glass Coca-Cola bottles filled with hazy water corked with a bamboo shoot. A third satchel held four curved 30-round "banana clips."

Wrapped in another leaf was bánh bao, a ball of rice-flour filled with meat, the Vietnamese equivalent of a sausage role. It was still warm from someone's oven.

This VC cadre had come from Khên Đùć within the last few hours. They must have contacts there and by the looks of their hiding place, they planned to wait for her for days, maybe a week.

Maï became all business. She cleared the evidence quickly.

She returned to the second body and dragged it to the other side of the path to where it was concealed by brush. She turned the body face down so that the blood would drain into the soil.

Mai estimated the men had to "check in" on an interval. She figured that other VC might check on their cadre in a few days. As she was about to toss their sandals deeper into the brush, she thought better of it. There was nothing distinctly VC about them. Her older sons could wear them.

Her mouth was parched from the adrenaline. She wanted to take a drink but thought better of it as the water was a bit cloudy. She couldn't afford to get sick from bad water. Her thirst could wait.

She removed the seals from one of the Coca-Cola bottles and emptied it over her hands and forearms. Then she washed her neck dousing it on her breasts and belly to cool down. Blood spots on her blouse darkened in the heat and began to blend in. If the stains remained, she planned to burn the blouse.

She moved their guns and hid them in another bamboo thicket removing the banana-clips. She gathered the ammunition and tucked the clips into another grass clump across the path.

The Americans paid a decent bounty for AK-47s. Mai might make more selling them to a hamlet or village if she found a leader she could trust.

Possessing one or selling it to non-combatant Vietnamese might lead the VC to her. She was not sure who to trust in the village. She planned to retrieve them later and take them to the Americans.

She stirred the dirt in the road to hide the blood with clumps of grass. Flies already buzzed over the ground immediately drawn by the scent. In the tropical heat, flies swarmed the bodies within minutes. On second thought, she moved the guns farther up the road and broke off some thin bamboo to mark the thicket.

She gathered lemon grass and threw it on the bodies to cover the scent at least for a while. It didn't fool the flies that collected on the seeping wounds.

She looked up and down the path. It was still empty. Time for more tasks.

She waded into the brush and stripped the bodies of their shorts and non la, the conical "Chinaman's Hat." Unlike the ARVN and American soldiers, they did not have dog tags.

She straightened up her bicycle after inspecting the IV bottles. Nothing broke. She packed the black shorts around the bottles to keep them from clinking.

She moved her bicycle up the road about ten meters away from the blood stains. She surveyed the scene. Apart from some grass on the dirt trail, it looked like any other walking path in the non-descript jungle fringes around the village.

The baby inside her settled down. Still, she was unsteady and though better of riding the bicycle. She walked it down the road going through her mind what had to be done. She had to send a message to Toan to bring the Xe Lam to Khêń Đùć. She planned to sell the AK-47s and use the bounty to pay the landlord for an extra month to buy some silence. They would leave the farmhouse at night as soon as she found another farm to rent in the next village.

By the time Maï had walked the laden bicycle into Khêń Đùć, her black blouse had dried. In the heat of the afternoon, everyone stayed in the shade. Wearing her non la, she was just another peasant woman moving her trade-goods to the next village.

An old woman crouched on the side of the road selling Vietnamese lemonade made from crushed sugar cane and lime. Maï traded one of the non la she recovered from her assassins for a paper cup of the warm sticky drink.

The old woman had no sandals. She traded one of the pair of VC sandals with her for another cup and moved on before sunset.

One of the ARVN contacts was supposed to see her after sunset. She debated whether to tell him of the incident. Maï told him that VC in the area were nosing around as to who was who. That would be enough to say. He would find a small farm to rent up the road.

Vo let everyone know Nguyên Maï was relocating again. There was no profit in telling him about the assassins. He learned about it soon enough when the bodies were discovered. He suspected it was her since each naked decomposing body still had its head. Had they been hapless South Vietnamese soldiers, the heads might have been missing. It was curious there were no clothes to be found. Since there no weapons, it was hard to confirm which side they served.

Before Vo was knew of the discovery of the bodies, Maï told him that they needed to move to another location and be settled before the baby came due. That seemed logical as well since the VC cells they know of had been neutralized. It was a good time to relocate Maï and her brood.

Loan's closest-in-age brother was born in the next hamlet in late 1967.

Move from Tay Ninh District

Happier days in the Tay Ninh district north of Sai Gon ended in late January 1975. Loan, her older sister and many brothers had stayed in one place for almost two years. Her earliest memories were of moving to another village north of Sai Gon every few months. Just when she made a friend or two, the family moved to another village. Until Tay Ninh, they stayed in each preceding village or hamlet less than six months.

The constant moves went unexplained. They just happened. When it happened, Maï was all business instructing everyone to "break camp." In Cantonese or Vietnamese, the phrase had no meaning. It was a "western" term.

All was well until suddenly, Maï instructed her sons to "break camp." Their temperamental father showed up in the three-wheel Xe Lam along with a brother, several of Maï's sisters with borrowed transportation in various forms. The family possessed mostly cooking pots, utensils, woven bed mats and three sets of cloths. The bulkiest objects were livestock that varied in number but limited to chickens and diminutive pigs. More often than not, she sold off the pigs buying new stock in the next village.

The move was usually to a single room farmhouse that functioned as single-room home for a dozen people, a chicken coop and a pig sty on arable land. A farm was any place with open land. The red soils were easy to spot against the verdant jungle indicating a working plot of land.

South Viet Nam enjoyed year round growing weather with one variable, the monsoon season that ran between May and October. Planting and harvesting occurred with the luck of dry days. Crop growth depended on the luck of abundant sunshine and beneficial rains. Protracted dry weather was rare. Monsoon rains often flooded out seeds and plants or made harvest impossible.

Maï made strategic choices of what they planted. Short-ripening plants served best. They might not be able to harvest a planting that took long to ripen. Sweet potatoes, tomatoes, carrots, peanuts, peppers and herbs sufficed if they lived there more than a few months.

On several occasions, Loan remembered having to move as some of the plants were close to harvest. Everyone looked forward to harvesting fresh ripe foods. The burgeoning fruit of their labor delighted everyone. In abundant times, they mixed in the spices and sweet potatoes with rice and every now and then, some meat. They had meat in the diet if a chicken was too sickly for market.

The move was often less than 10 km (7 miles). Loan's younger brothers whispered to themselves that is was a waste of time. "Why pick up and leave so often?" they asked. Huang, the oldest brother seemed to know more not objecting to their mother's instruction. He said little more than "It is time to move." When the eldest son said it, it had to be so.

The moves from village to village occurred since 1965, three years before Loan was born. Neighbors in Sai Gon believed Maï moved to the countryside to distance herself from her errant husband who remained in Sai Gon. He visited the family on occasion, mostly to move a load to justify his three-wheel "truck," beg for money from Maï and occasionally sire another child when he was not berating her for leaving Sai Gon.

Maï always had money to share with Toan. Mostly in the Vietnamese Piasters, in a pinch, she gave him American cash. Money silenced his complaints and emerging suspicions for a time. He returned to Sai Gon in the Xe Lam only to return when more pressing needs forced him to become momentarily civil, mount her, sire another child and then return to Sai Gon and his girlfriends.

When Loan was four, her father showed up with a toddler, one of his "productions" with a woman unable to manage motherhood. Tran became brother number nine. This life continued until early February 1975 when they "broke camp" for the last time and moved to Sai Gon.

As the youngest child in a line of a dozen siblings, Loan began to determine her father was a jerk of the first order. She developed the notion that adult men were little different that noisy roosters strutting their "stuff" around a hen house. She puzzled over the growing stress of her mother as measured by Maï's waning energy and time for her children.

Tay Ninh, Viet Nam and Schooling

Prolonged family residence near the city of Tay Ninh enabled Loan's brothers to do something historic. They attended school. Brothers 6, 7 and 8 were able to finish more than one uninterrupted year.

Loan remained home with her older sister to work on the plot of land. Loan always had chores from dawn to dark, tending chickens and small pigs, planting or harvesting sweet potatoes and peanuts. Sunset relieved her of one set of tasks only to have other chores, preparing rice and sweet potatoes for her brothers or sweeping the straw sleeping mats and clay floor of the house. There was little time for play. Developing hobbies or outside interests was alien.

Toil in the field had its rewards. Maï was home with family for the longest stretch of time Loan could recall. She remembered the constant hugs and touches as she worked beside her mother in preparing a meal or tending chickens and pigs. Her biggest days were at the open markets in Tay Ninh when they sold peanuts and the best of their chickens. Unless her mother assigned a chore, she was free to play with the other children.

Maï was up with the roosters and worked tirelessly to keep the family in motion. The sun was the clock and the moon set the calendar. The shadows of a particular tree or the house were the hour-hands telling them what part of the day was left. When living near Tay Ninh,

Maï instructed her sons to install a tall bamboo pole in the middle of open ground she could view from the front door. The pole's only purpose was to tell time. It was a form of sun dial and calendar with stones placed at key positions according to the location of the shadow. It made sense in the north in Shanghai than in Southern Viet Nam where the sun seemed always overhead.

The phases of the moon told them when a holiday was coming up. The Chinese New Year, Tet, came on the second new moon after the winter solstice. Other holidays centered on cycles of the moon. Maï commented often about the cycle of the moon. Per Chinese tradition, the moon's appearance foretold their future.

As a parent, Maï was firm but fair. She dealt harshly with irrational behavior but rarely slapped a child for mild transgressions. When she showed her "claws" as her sons joked, arguments withered.

Maï disappeared less often as she had over the preceding years. The strange-talking white men no longer appeared in the dark to talk to her mother. VO, a Vietnamese man that spoke English well enough, always attended the meetings. The "western" men never entered the house. Loan never actually saw them in the light of day.

Loan's older brothers call VO "Uncle." On occasion, he sat with them for a meal. He brought them sacks of rice and boxes of canned foods with "western" writing on the sides of the boxes. Decades later in America, Loan recalled the western writing on the shelves in grocery stores. The boxes were printed with the words "Hormel" and "Spam."

On special events, Mai mixed in the tangy processed meet with rice and sweet potatoes. Other than a sickly chicken that ended up in the day's meal, she and her brothers rarely had meat in their diet. Now and then, chunks of chopped-up "mystery-meat" ended up in a dish. It was American "spam." Spam provided a rare salty treat in their otherwise vegetarian diet.

By January 1974, the occasional mid-night meetings between Maï and the American soldier-men in green uniforms ended. Up until 1973, the strange men came to the farmhouse after sunset, often after everyone had gone to sleep. In a day or two, one of Maï's sisters came to stay and Maï disappeared for a few days to a week. These memories were on the loftiest edge of what Loan could recall about her early life.

Her two oldest brothers came up from Sai Gon with their wives and children to help with the farming and bring news of Sai Gon.

Neighbors from the Cholon neighborhood came to visit, sometimes staying over-night. Toan seldom came to Tay Ninh unless he was short of cash. They had no electricity. Phone service was at the postal station in the village. They managed their own water and sewer. Living on the fringes had no on-going utility bills.

Mai's husband imposed the largest drain on income. When Toan needed money for girlfriends, he became the doting father and attentive husband. Cash in hand, he returned to Sai Gon.

Toan came up from Sai Gon to visit them. His stays turned mostly into arguments with Mai and requests for money. At times, Toan raised his voice. Mai spoke only in hushed tones. There was perpetual friction between them. Maï was more-often happy to see him leave with his money, some of the harvest of peanuts, sweet potatoes and a few chickens.

Deception in oppressive societies is essential to the maintenance of family unable to defend themselves. Maï had separated her broods of chickens and pens containing her pigs. Toan harvested a portion from he believed she had not realizing another group of hens or pigs sustained the family. Maï sold the meat in the local market. It seldom made it into their daily meals.

As in Chinese culture, Loan was compelled to respect her father. It did not prevent her from resenting his visits. She learned from her brothers a Vietnamese name for him: "dumahh." It was not a kind reference.

Toan returned to Sai Gon to the house in the truck she bought for him. She knew he had several girlfriends. Some of the money went to them. By 1975, four of her sons were born by other women. The Asian tradition of polygamy never quite disappeared.

Divorce in Viet Nam was less common than in other parts of the world. Many women endured their husband's dalliances.

Maï showed no apparent romantic interest in other men. With many mouths to feed, there was no time or resources for indulging a different life. By all measures in life, Maï was the ultimate producer, nurturing parent and faithful wife.

To Loan and her family, half-blood was all blood and half-brothers were brothers just the same. Another brother showed up even though her mother showed no pregnancy, Loan called him brother. Loan was the youngest of the children between Maï and Toan. Brothers showed up she never knew her mother bore.

Hanoi's Push, February 1975

Tet celebrations shut down most of South Viet Nam making travel difficult until early February 1975. As soon as the celebrations ended, everything else changed. Armies on both sides were on the march, the South in retreat, the North in advance. Hanoi's force steadily advanced on the Northern provinces of South Viet Nam.

South Viet Nam's President Thieu attempted to micro-manage forces better left to competent generals. South Viet Nam yielded through poorly coordinated strategies and break down in discipline. Three major cities, over a hundred thousand irreplaceable troops, and tons of armament were lost in a month.

Loan's father showed up in Tay Ninh with his three-wheel truck/taxi and loaded up their belongings to head back to Sai Gon. Being the youngest, she rode in the front with her father and the youngest brother hanging out the right door. The back of the truck loaded to over-flowing with brothers and the few goods they could carry crept along the road barely in 2nd gear. They left behind a house and a blended grave of number three brother and four others.

Twenty years passed before Loan would pay her respects to Cûông's grave. *(Author's Note: I have visited the grave four times. The red pumice markers are over-grown by the jungle. It is a sad place to see knowing that fragments of an old man and four boys are interred there.)*

Her mother was largely absent for the move to Sai Gon. She showed up now and then checking on arrangements Toan made to exit Tay Ninh.

Toan complained to Maï about the plans. She stuffed money in his hands and told him there were no options. Move everyone to Sai Gon.

For the first time, she whispered to him that they might have to flee Sai Gon.

"Leave Sai Gon?" he asked. "Move To Where in Viet Nam?"

Rolling up eyes was a facial expression that showed disbelief in western cultures. When a spouse expresses something wholesale stupid, the other spouse might roll their eyes to show disbelief at the other's stupidity.

Among some Asian cultures, a similar expression is too look down and be silent for a moment. Mai looked down and paused. She told Toan simply, "We go to America."

Toan looked down at his feet for an interminable moment and uttered in a sigh, "America." It was too much of a subject to argue with her.

He knew the topic was coming. Many in the Sai Gon neighborhood talked about America or Australia. Malaysia and the Philippines would not welcome them.

Mai advised him that the situation in the north had deteriorated. There was no good news.

He challenged her and for the first of many to come, she shouted down his ignorance. Her boldness shocked anyone within hearing. "We go to America or let the VC kill us."

Traditional Asian men limited instruction or direction from women without cause. Toan had little choice but to comply. Maï had the money and more grit than her 95 pounds implied.

For men in a man's world, saving face dominated daily conduct. Toan avoided any demonstration of weakness. Maï went along with the ruse as she had over decades but the stakes were high and they were out of time to make easy choices.

Maï seldom displayed her anger in public. She was the docile Asian wife by most appearances but anyone close to them knew where the strength in the family lay.

Usually submissive to Toan in public, Maï was openly in charge of the exodus from Tay Ninh. Her older sons had never seen their mother act as large as now.

Loan's brothers thought her change in demeanor was due to the loss of number three son, Cûông, in the landmine incident in January. She was an angry Chinese mother in grief ready to challenge Buddha if necessary. This bought Maï some social license among the community.

It had been hardly a month since Cûông died. She had sworn her life to avoid losing another child to political machinations. Maï had more than a dozen in her care to preserve and would nurse her grief when she the luxury of time and comfort permitted.

Hanoi's ambitions to consolidate a separate South Viet Nam cost millions of lives including that of Mai's third son. She had killed witless young men drafted from their villages at gunpoint to fill the ranks of Viet Cong and NVA. On the Cambodian border, she walked the moonscape left by B-52 bomb runs after witnessing the destruction of hundreds of NVA the night before. From her view at the top of a tree two miles away, 2,000 bombs ripped a hole in the night along the border.

They were indoctrinated young men carrying little more than an AK-47, a few balls of sticky rice and the dogma of father Ho. Hundreds of thousands of adolescent boys were drafted from their villages and sent down the Ho Chi Minh trail never to be seen or heard from again.

She never saw the B-52s up close. They were specs of pepper leading white ropes of condensing exhaust 35,000 feet overhead as they headed back to Guam after an early morning raid on the Ho Chi Minh trail. She knew in part that her information fed into a network that eventually influenced the target selection of the large bombers that raked the stratosphere with their contrails.

As a mother of many boys and caring for their half-brothers, she felt the grief of the mothers in North Viet Nam who lost their sons. She often wondered if parents of the north knew what happened to their sons and daughters.

By their conduct, there was no way in which the VC could have advised families in North Viet Nam of how or where many of their sons died. The Ho Chi Minh trail was a one-way ticket to South Viet Nam. There was minimal evidence of wounded traffic returning to Hanoi other than to pick up more weapons. Unlike Sai Gon, there were few wounded warriors milling about in Hanoi.

The VC turned them into lethal cadre beyond hope of redemption. They must be stopped. Her sorrow was the waste of the verdant jungle more than the lives of young men turned to evil.

By the time the young Viet Cong had migrated to take up a position in a cell of three to eight men, there was no reasoning with them and the error of their training. There was no easy option other than destroy them before they destroyed her and hoped-for way of life.

Maï had given up any sense of luxury and thus a part of her life to sustain an independent South Viet Nam. Mai's hatred of theft of honest effort consumed her. She saw too much of it in her forty-eight years.

Western colonialism and Christianity ravaged Southeast Asia for centuries. France and Spain opened up influence by deploying Christianity and its priests to convert Asians uncertain in their own faith and culture. The serial process that conquered South America in the 1500s continued in Asia starting in the 1700s. When the Christian missions became threatened by real or contrived events, Spain and France marshaled in their armies to protect its citizens. It was only a matter of time before colonial conversion began.

The Philippines became a vassal state of Spain. Indo-China as Viet Nam, Laos, and Cambodia came under the influence of France. The French made Viet Nam its only colony but the French influence persisted throughout Southeast Asia.

Asians referred to the Dutch, English and French as "blued-eyed devils." The "westerns" made an indelible imprint on Asia. Catholic and Protestant conversions of the heathen Asians took effect. Spain won over the Philippines. France had Viet Nam and pockets of influence in southern China. England gains were mainly in India and around Hong Kong but they plied influence throughout Asia. Strangely enough, the Dutch traders did business with the region colonizing little territory. The remnants of religious conversion continue to this day in Asia as well as their Asian churches in North America, France and Australia.

For centuries, western-driven cultural and economic disruption laid bare Asian societies as fertile ground for communism and fascism. Japan alone in its quest for ethnic purity adopted an imperial version of fascism that fostered and produced the Asian half of World War II. Japan's millennial conflict with China initiated a conversion to communism as Japan surrendered in 1945.

With its backside bordering Russia, China embraced communism and social dogma that murdered dissident populations by the tens of millions between the 1930s and the 1980s. The seductive dogma of socialism flowed into Indo-China and persists to this day in Viet Nam, Laos and Cambodia.

Once the shackles of colonialism were removed, Southeast Asia became contested ground for political ideals. The untested appeal of Communism took hold of China and, in turn, North Viet Nam. Viet Nam became the crucible that tested civilization nearly to the extreme of ending any sense of civil life.

Mai did what she could to preserve a piece of Southeast Asia that was open and free. As one woman in a male-dominated society, she accomplished more than many men in stemming the communist tide.

From the age of eleven when Japan invaded Shanghai in 1937, she resented any system of governance that enabled political elite to harvest other people's production at will. Hanoi's minions attempted to compel Vietnamese under lofty notions of brotherhood and shared sacrifice.

Mai knew that political brotherhood was an illusion as one man will try to dominate another. The concept of shared sacrifice nauseated her. She personally witnessed her share of state theft both from China and Hanoi. At times, Sai Gon's loose democracy seemed no better when men tweaked military strategy for financial gain. Yet, they seldom confiscated land and industry to the scale of Beijing and Hanoi.

South Viet Nam was their last refuge in Asia. Yet, her expectations of a future Viet Nam slipped away. She knew at minimum, the fragile quality of life would wither after Hanoi assumed control of Sai Gon.

Life was hard enough. Having come from Shanghai and then from North Viet Nam, she knew of the horrible circumstance that awaited the whole of Viet Nam, North and South.

Russia and China backed an unaccountable monster of a one-party system with a mutated concept of fairness in "civilized society." With the "Godhead of Ho Chi Minh," Hanoi's directive became a predictable formula for cruelty and destruction of South Viet Nam. She knew better than anyone the shocking future that lay in store for complacent and misled Vietnamese.

There were rumors that Mai's life might be at great risk. Worse, her entire family might be at risk. America kept records of people in service to South Viet Nam. Uncle "Lau" had raised concerns about what the Americans might leave behind should they vacate Viet Nam.

She knew this above all and it compelled her surprising displays of intensity in front of her children and in public. She had to convince Toan to flee Viet Nam. They had the "tickets" from the American Navy to leave Asia. She could gamble wholesale on living in an alien world such as America given the circumstances she faced. Fearless Nguyên Maï planned to flee by barge, helicopter or walk out of the country save for her obligation to dead ancestors and an intractable husband.

Ancestors and Anchors

Asian tradition imposed a number of obligations on potential refugees. Maï as well as Toan was obligated to watch over the remains of ancestors. The obligation went past remembrance. Gifts were sent to the deceased.

Buddhist priests provided packages of "copied" money, rice-board houses and cardboard cars to burn in ceremony to send to money and convenience to the after-life ... for a small fee of course. Today in Viet Nam, Buddhists burn Xeroxed copies of American $100 bills as the money probably holds better value in the afterlife than the Vietnamese Dong.

Leaving Asia altogether created a new burden on the living. There were various levels of expectation to take ancestral remains to the new country.

Maï's parents were buried in Sai Gon while Toan's ancestral remains were interred near inaccessible Shanghai. Leaving behind buried family perhaps never to return factored in many thoughts as she contemplated fleeing Viet Nam.

She determined that she could exhume the remains of her mother and father, cremate them and leave the country with their ashes. Unfortunately, the corrupt Sai Gon government was in disarray but functioning as expected.

Maï bribed officials to get that done. It took too much time and costs for such a service rose to unacceptable levels.

Wealthier Vietnamese bid up the process pricing exhumation out of reach. Maï balanced her efforts between deceased family and the living seeking a new life in another country. There was also the problem of returning to Tay Ninh to exhume Cûông's remains, such as they were, mixed in with four other people. Sorting the remains between individuals was impossible. She expected the other families to object.

Like so many other situations in South Viet Nam in the spring of 1975, few anticipated the speed at which North Viet Nam invaded the south. In a protracted war over decades that seldom yield large gains for either side, South Viet Nam fell apart quickly.

The rate of decline was accelerating. The best military experts in the world were stunned by the speed at which South Viet Nam collapsed.

Loan and her older brothers interrogated number one brother, Huang, about their mother's distractions with the remains of family. At twenty seven, Huang had yet to achieve the lofty attitude of oldest males in ethnic-Chinese families. In fact, he never assumed the traditional leadership of the oldest son deferring his rightful position to younger brothers.

He shook his head and told his siblings that their mother's behavior is about something else. It was the first time Loan heard the term "The VC comes."

Loan's family didn't make distinctions between the North Viet Nam Army and Viet Cong. All were Viet Cong (VC). (*The VC fundamentally ceased to exist as a cohesive fighting force after the Tet Offensive in 1968. NVA absorbed the remainder of VC. Despite all that, the "VC" title persists to this day.*)

Huang said the VC moved rapidly on Sai Gon. With a sad certainty, he declared "VC could win and life will change."

Loan knew little of the world. There was South Viet Nam and North Viet Nam. Evidence of the war permeated life at every level. Mangled people, mostly young men missing a leg or an arm populated every community they knew. Everyone had a family member or close friend that disappeared into the grisly maw that was the war with Hanoi.

She was a few dozen meters in the peanut field when her brother Cûồng was killed along with three other children and the old man on the small tractor. Landmines were a part of Vietnamese existence. One of them killed her most-favorite brother.

The threat of destruction was always near. There were bad people, Viet Cong as she knew them…were always nearby and threatening. The threat had risen in January 1975 killing one brother and forcing them to move back to the big city she barely knew. She was born there but beyond intermittent visits in her six years, it was barely home. Yet, Sai Gon was the only place she could call home.

They moved back to Sai Gon. At six, Loan had her first notion that they had no place else to go. The VC had chased them back to Sai Gon.

Oldest brother Huang said the family fled Shanghai to Hanoi. Then they fled Hanoi to Tay Ninh. And then they fled Tay Ninh to Sai Gon. He joked their next move was to the South China Sea. Loan had an image of life on the edge of the sea. It was hard for her to imagine how people lived on a coastline with all that scary deep water so near.

The Crowded Road to Sai Gon

The unpaved two-lane road that connected with the main highway led to Sai Gon was usually rutted during the monsoons and scraped flat during the dry seasons. Late February marked the tail-end of the dry season. Rains occurred throughout the year but the monsoon season turned anything of soil into mud. North Viet Nam most likely initiated its offensive in January 1975 part because it was the dry season for most of the country.

Loan's family "caravan" merged on to Highway 22 south of Tay Ninh. It was one of the best roads paved with crushed laterite. Three months before the beginning of the monsoon rains, this road widened as southerly traffic swelled. Jammed with pedestrians, bicycles and vehicles, peasants widened the road by peasants spreading the laterite to the sides. Ad hoc road crews popped up as citizens widened the road to dislodge their vehicles from a ditch or mired in a rut.

The volume of traffic in the country-side surprised everyone. Northwestern provinces of South Viet Nam moved southeast. The countryside fled to Sai Gon.

All manner of pedestrians, bicycles laden with possessions wrapped in rice sacks, coconut leaves and lashed with twine moved steadily south. Hand carts and tricycle carts with a motorcycle in front or back sputtered in the slow traffic. A few private vehicles and the three-wheel Xe Lams honked to move the slower traffic aside.

Lighter traffic headed north, mostly ARVN military, the Army of South Viet Nam, loaded with grim men. Since early January, South Viet Nam's military either failed to hold a line or retreated to the south. Of a million Vietnamese military personnel in South Viet Nam with sufficient stockpiles of American armament, there was no counter attack. The Americans no longer flew in air support. The planes were flown by Vietnamese.

The normal four-hour trip covering 60 kilometers (35 miles) between Tay Ninh and southern Sai Gon consumed a long day. At one point, Loan's mother, Nguyên Maï, showed up in an American-made jeep painted in dark camouflage driven by an ARVN soldier. Another ARVN soldier sat in back with an American-made M16 resting in his arms. Everyone was dusted and dirty from the travel on dry roads. Loan's mother seemed almost a stranger covered in dust turned to a thin layer of mud mixed with her sweat.

Maï wore the iconic non la rice-straw hat, black "pajamas" and sandals. Her bicycle was strapped on the back of the vehicle. To the casual observer, she appeared as a peasant woman in tow with the provincial ARVN soldiers. American soldiers called her a "mamasan," an inappropriate Japanese idiom adopted in Viet Nam.

The opposite was true. The ARVN soldiers were under her command. Few Asian men accepted the instruction of women. Maï's credentials as a combatant changed convention. Completely out of character among Asian society in South Viet Nam, Maï directed military movement to the north even as she had no position or rank among South Vietnamese military. Her knowledge of Tay Ninh and surrounding areas gave her rank above most everyone else.

Maï's Belly Weapons

Wrapped under her dark blouse, Maï carried four American MK-2 grenades wrapped in a sleeve made from banana leaf strapped to her belly. At times, she carried 9mm versions of the "1911" pistol but complained of the weight of the gun wrapped in cotton and strapped to her thighs. Four 8-round clips and some bundles of bean-curd wrapped in banana leaf weighed down a satchel she carried on her side. Her over-sized blouse provided reasonable concealment of the grenades. She was seldom comfortable with the pistols.

Maï was the "anti-Rambo" so to speak never sporting her weapons openly. She was about guile and stealth. Her gender and motherhood gained concealment. She played her role to her culture's blinds spots. Appearing tough and threatening betrayed her strengths in stealth as a woman. Her best asset lay in apparent impotence.

Loan learned decades later that her mother "packed heat" most of the time until May 1975. The left-handed Mai could remove the pin on a grenade and hurl it with her right hand as she emptied an eight-round clip in the general direction of the "enemy." Causalities of Maï's aim with a heavy American pistol were unknown.

Her grenades proved much more effective and documented well enough when she died in October 2006 by her American "brothers-in-arms." The retired US Navy SEALS said of her, "She walked a talk she never spoke."

Nguyên Maï spoke to the driver as if she was in charge because … she was in charge. The driver of the jeep was her driver. The soldier holding the M16 was her body guard. She appeared as a peasant woman in service to the soldiers by design.

Maï spoke a few minutes to Loan's father handing him a shiny packet wrapped in banana leaves. The leaf color was appropriate. It wrapped green American cash. Before offending him with a woman's instruction, she gave him money. Outside of Sai Gon, Toan moderated his tendency to play all dominant male. His drinking buddies and girlfriends might not recognize him in this situation.

Maï owned the marital high ground when living "in country" in the hamlets and villages north of the city. Toan knew his place much as he hated the situation.

By outward appearances, a western person would hardly assume that Toan and Mai were husband and wife with dozen-plus children. Public expression of affection differed by culture and circumstance. In Viet Nam, endearment was a casualty of a prolonged war. Perhaps it was an Asian thing enlarging the western stereotype of the "inscrutable Asians."

Maï bought Toan's complicity with money. To his credit, he was about doing the right thing for his children. Asian men that failed to tend family dishonored themselves. He walked a narrow path when it came to saving face, showing dominance and meeting his obligation to their children.

American cash spent better than the Vietnamese piaster (*soon to become the North Vietnamese Dong*). Vietnamese paper money rapidly lost value. American dollars became dangerous to possess in a few months when the country consolidated under the rule of Hanoi.

Maï told Toan to avoid excessive haggling over price. Farmers fled south abandoning their crops to the NVA. She expected inflated prices if not shortages of sweet potatoes and rice. The invading armies lived off the land. NVA literally gobbled up excess produce from Western and Northern provinces as their supply lines fell behind.

Maï told Toan to pay the asked price as necessary for staple foods. He might have to pay twice that in half a week. (*Asians seldom pay the "asked price." Everything is a negotiation. In particular to North Americans, what often seems an offensive conversation is simply practiced barter.*)

Maï instructed Toan to buy construction materials when he returned to Sai Gon with the children and family belongings. In a Cantonese phrase that amounts to "beg, borrow or steal," she gave him money to re-enforce the house by whatever means he could find.

This was in the end of February when Sai Gon had less than a hundred days.

Her last message to Toan on his trip back to Sai Gon sent him into one of his darkest mood. Mai told him that the NVA were shelling loyalist communities to the north prior to moving their forces. The cruelty of NVA soldiers reached new levels. No civilian of any age or infirmity was spared of destruction.

The NVA were moving in "long rockets" as they called the 122mm Russian and Chinese weapons to terrorize civilian communities. The unguided weapons sizzled erratically overhead into villages hitting military and civilian targets at random. It was an act of terror directed at "soft targets" to minimize an uprising of the communities. He should plan his works on the house accordingly.

By Monday, April 22, 1975, Maï told him to reinforce the front gate and have the younger children form mud bricks at every opportunity. She told him to line the front and sides of the house with mud bricks wherever possible. She told him to put them up even soft. There was no time for proper drying. A "wet" brick was effective as a dry brick when it came to stopping shrapnel.

Hanoi had played it badly during the Tet offensive in 1968 expecting Sai Gon's neighborhoods to rise up to overcome an oppressive South Vietnamese government. They misread South Viet Nam wholesale. The uprisings never occurred. The Viet Cong fell apart in several months. By April 1968, they were no longer an effective fighting force.

During the offensive, VC killed civilians to quell uprising of communities sympathetic to South Viet Nam. In the city of Hue *(Roughly pronounced "Way," aka: Way City)*, a vicious slaughter of defenseless civilians stripped Hanoi of its "moral imperative." Over 4,000 city administrators, teacher, Buddhist monks, and local civilian directors answered the summons to collect in a stadium for a meeting. NVA and Viet Cong fired into the assembled masses there and acted similarly in other meeting areas. Some estimated that 6,500 hundred people voluntarily arrived at their execution as the TET Offensive of 1968 went into full bloom.

Many events during the 1968 TET offensive demonstrated how conflict over state and socialist ideal mutated into total war. The ruthlessness of North Viet Nam became obvious and intensified American military resolve for a short time. Combatants met in ambushes and assassinations in lieu of large massed battles. Maï's most productive times occurred from 1966 to 1972.

Hanoi believed the ethnic-Chinese Vietnamese posed one of the larger threats during the invasion of South Viet Nam. North Viet Nam expected citizens of the Cholon and most of the city to resist the invasion. They shelled and bombed the Cholon of Sai Gon in advance of taking South Viet Nam.

Bottom-line: Maï knew the NVA might shell, bomb and "rocket" Sai Gon neighborhoods as they entered the city. None of the rural housing structures protected families. Toan must reinforce the house against artillery. Her request imposed an impossible task.

With her instructions completed to Toan, Mai softened her demeanor. She shifted from the shocking appearance of the peasant commander to mother of her brood.

As the traffic moving south stalled, Maï approached each of her children to give each a word of comfort. She held back her tears giving each child a dry kiss on their foreheads and a smile telling them to obey their father and left them heading north in the ARVN jeep.

Loan later recalled thirty years later that she watched her mother for the first time transform from parent to some other creature of alien origin. The male driver in the jeep was silent and subservient. Maï was in charge.

Loan forever viewed her mother's roles as parent and commander in that moment as surreal. Her mother revealed herself as two people. It took decades to realize and understand she was the same person driven to adapt with the circumstances. Maï was a chameleon in the truest sense of the description. She would adapt as needed.

The older sons followed the Xe Lam with laden tricycle "trucks" over-flowing with family goods. Mostly, they carried cooking utensils and sleeping mats. The Xe Lam plowed a slow path in the throng for the older brothers pushing the carts behind. Chickens in bamboo cages fluttered and squawked as they wove among the crowds toward Sai Gon. Annoyed civilians begrudged the road for the Xe Lam and its caravan.

Loan watched her mother greeting her sons, handing the older boys something. Loan assumed it was American cash. She never saw her mother so animated as now. Maï was all instruction and control.

Years later, she learned the motive of that day. Something terribly went wrong north of Tay Ninh. The NVA moved in from the northwest massing to create another front heading toward Sai Gon. The NVA were on the move. South Viet Nam was on the run. To a little girl of six, it seemed as if all of Viet Nam was moving south. In fact, all of South Viet Nam was moving south. If they had a way to leave Asia, that would be their next move.

Toan's Mood Swing

Loan's father's scowling expression put off Loan's questions. She and two brothers rode into Sai Gon in silence. Her father cursed in Cantonese at anyone or anything.

Toan had to convert their one-story long narrow rural house on the fringes of Sai Gon into a bomb-resistant shelter. Handmade mud bricks worked if he had months to form, dry and stack the bricks. April was at the end of the "dry" season before the monsoon rains began. When the wet season begins, mud bricks finish slowly if at all.

Above all complaints of discomfort, Toan succumbed to his wife's directives. He was Maï's errand-boy shepherding their family back to their house in Sai Gon. Toan had lost face if to no one else, at least to himself. Toan lacked the intelligence to counter his wife's directives. She had all the connections to military actions. He knew she was right. He could not help but sulk for days.

Loan knew that she and all of her siblings would suffer for any infraction they made. Whether they made the infraction or not, Toan was going to be a terrible human being for at least a few days. Worst of all, the terrible human being was their father. They had to honor him and his manner of direction.

Near Tan Son Nhat Airport

Traffic thickened as they approached Sai Gon from the northeast. They entered the city on the main highway skirting Tan Son Nhat Airport and the American operating base.

American transports flew in and out of the American bases traveling east to Thailand and west to Guam or aircraft carriers stationed off of Vung Tau on the coast of the South China Sea. American military quietly removed sensitive communication equipment and ordnance lest the Vietnamese know the United States had given up hope for Viet Nam and attempt to kill Americans.

As Loan and her family plodded in the traffic to the Cholon in late February, the American transport aircraft mixed with commercial airlines heading to Thailand, Japan and Honk Kong overhead. The pace of aircraft appeared normal. Lumbering C-130 Hercules mixed in with C-141 Starlifter and smaller transport aircraft.

Before long, the United States air-lifted out Vietnamese they could reach. They left behind six-plus million Vietnamese that wanted to leave to preserve their future if not save their lives.

American Remainders - CIA

Most combatants of the American military returned home by late 1974. The United States maintained a cargo and defensive presence in Sai Gon to protect their embassy and CIA assets.

America retained intelligence operations to the last days of Sai Gon. Unfortunately, the CIA did little more than document the fall of South Viet Nam. The early sponsors of the Viet Nam War, liberal Democrats of the United States Senate and Congress, stripped the military ability to intervene beyond rescue of Americans.

Much as the CIA and the State Department struggled to negotiate a settlement between Hanoi and South Viet Nam, none of the efforts worked. By March 1975, Hanoi held all the cards. Sai Gon fell even as the CIA attempted to change the outcome.

There were also "grunt" Americans who had no choice but to coldly conduct their jobs. Despite their high regard for the Vietnamese, US marines were compelled to serve their positions or return home earlier than expected. They were evacuated by demand of their superiors.

More than a few military men left Sai Gon weeping for a populace of friends they had to leave behind to a fate that for many was caused by a capricious American politic.

Vietnamese easily spotted American CIA driving their Ford-made vehicles in the city. The strange looking white men in pressed white short-sleeve dress shirts and black slacks stood out among the people of Sai Gon. There was no mistaking them as Americans. They were tall, white, unpleasantly sweating and unable to well speak Vietnamese.

The salient feature of these men was their ignorance or perhaps their reticence of the hard fact of Viet Nam over the last decade. Since the end of WWII, Viet Nam had become an amalgam of issues, partly of political refuge and another part of the effort to secure its identity as a nation. Viet Nam represented the perpetual conflict between the Asian work-ethic and the infection of communal socialism invested by China. Everyone underestimated the ruthless of the murderous Chinese regime and its impact on North Viet Nam's conduct of the vanquished.

Vietnamese in South Viet Nam knew what the Americans seemed to ignore. China and Hanoi's passion to absorb South Viet Nam exceeded the resolve of the allies to sustain its independence. Hanoi could win now. They played the mercurial politics of America to exhaustion. Liberal Democrats voted America out of success and even an honorable withdrawal in Viet Nam.

The Vietnamese populace was left behind to "pay the tab" as it might be called. It was an awful price.

Russia and China sought American failure. The fall of South Viet Nam demonstrated the frailties of capitalism and free-market systems.

Viet Nam's collapse confirmed nothing. Out of desperation, many pro-Hanoi Vietnamese fled in the coming decade.

Viet Nam had become an arena where East met West and where political ideology was tested by strength of arms and resolve. It was a poor test but nevertheless, Hanoi won the day. It did not win the future for many Vietnamese.

As it was, the Central Intelligence Agency (CIA) documented the fall of South Viet Nam in its final role before fleeing the inferno that was Sai Gon April 30, 1975. The CIA under-predicted the capability of North Viet Nam and overestimated the durability of South Viet Nam. Sai Gon fell in six months instead of eighteen.

Sense of the City

The sense of the city changed. People were all business, unhappy and focused on something else.

Sai Gon swelled with refugees streaming south from Northern provinces and east from the western borders. Radio and television broadcasts provided limited information. Gossip and rumor filled in the unknowns.

Everyone speculated on the change in regime. Would it be much different? Opinions ran the gamut from business–as-usual to life threatening. Some speculated it was going to be a living nightmare.

Many citizens in leadership positions committed suicide by April 30, 1975 rather than face what they knew to be a cruel victor. Sai Gon prepared for a siege it could not sustain. The "open" city possessed limited means of isolation by the surrounding rivers. That isolation was useless if the military failed to defend the roads.

North Viet Nam's spies and collaborators infiltrated high levels in government and the military. Emboldened NVA cells emerged and assassinated key civilians as the armies approached.

Sai Gon fell badly. There was no real siege. There was only capitulation. Two decades of misery for nearly all of Viet Nam would follow. Sai Gon would be punished. By structural incompetence, all of Viet Nam fell into hell.

By February 1975, resourceful Vietnamese with American or Canadian connections departed the country on airline tickets to somewhere else. Many carried gold and American cash readily finding comfortable sanctuary in Asian communities in North America.

Devoid of the constraints of western morality, Asian prostitutes traded their exotic beauty and favors for access and migrated to North America. They arrived rich and became richer. Many naïve communities in the Midwest were unprepared for their commerce. Communities across America saw a proliferation of massage parlors that provide additional services not on the menu.

Cantonese-speaking Vietnamese had little trouble blending in to the Chinatowns of North America. Vietnamese-only speakers had more trouble. Many new Asian communities cropped up and grew throughout North America.

The general buzz: Get to Sai Gon. Then, get to America.

Arrival: Late February 1975

At sunset, Loan's family arrived in the neighborhood four miles southeast of the airport. The noise of the main roads faded as they rounded the curve rising to their permanent home in Sai Gon. Away from the hum of the center of the city, the semi-rural scenery established a sense of normalcy.

The crowded roads were significant. People had been traveling, fleeing in fact, from hundreds of kilometers to the north. They moved into Sai Gon and farther south.

The flood of people on the roads leading to Sai Gon was a symptom of a larger event. South Viet Nam was losing the battle of independence. Toan could dwell in his isolated and self-indulged world as he might. A collision with reality was inevitable.

Toan's demeanor shifted to the business of preparing the house for full occupancy and something ominous … attack. Per Maï's caution, he reinforced the structure and gate in case the neighborhood fell under fire. Sai Gon had not been struck by rockets for four years. Times were different now. The Americans left the fight reducing consequences for bad acts.

Construction work drained Toan's cash and imposed on his agenda with girlfriends. His mood migrated from occasional bad to permanently foul.

Toan reinforced the front gate of the house just before he was summoned to Tay Ninh to move the family back to Sai Gon. Maï told him it wasn't strong enough as she handed him more money for materials.

The city was flooded with refugees from the north. Anything not tied down disappeared at night if not during the day. Southeast Asia circa 1975 was in total distress and the mores of a disciplined Asian population was broken. The sense of desperation was palpable.

The drug trade in Cambodia and the war changed much. Gated enclosures and barbed wire on the top of scalable walls was relatively new to the Cholon. The front of homes had been open to where neighbors walked into other homes of friends pausing only to leave their sandals at the front. Houses as home to with three or four generations and multiple families always were always occupied by someone. Having someone there all the time was no longer a deterrent to theft. Front gates and entrances became closed if not locked most of the time.

Without street lights among houses lacking electricity, homes became targets for theft. Sunset meant a family member had to stand watch until sunrise. Gates and barricades became necessary to improve a restful night for the entire family.

Assignment Toan-Style

Toan assigned everyone down to six-year-old Loan specific tasks. If the job was unfamiliar and a son or daughter asked a question, out came the broom handle. Toan lacked patience of anything unsympathetic to his own interests. Despite poor instructions, he beat any child for their misunderstanding of a command he considered intuitively obvious.

Sometimes the punishment was a simple whack on a shoulder or the butt. Other times, he held a child's arm while he thrashed their backs repeatedly. The repeated strikes left the child's back bruised if not bloody.

He expected everyone to be in the house at a certain time. The concern might have been safety but more likely, he wanted them available for a chore. He hated tardiness. Late arrival guaranteed broom treatment.

To this day over three decades later in America, Loan has a wall clock set ten-minutes fast in every room. She is never late to anything and has words for anyone who is tardy.

The Sai Gon Rural House

Maï's family resettled themselves into the long narrow one-story house/ home/factory with a singular large room. It was enclosed with thatched bamboo walls and covered by a roof of coconut leaves supported by bamboo rafters. Western people might think the house was a barn.

Most of the rural houses were single story barn-like constructions. If the families prospered, a second story was added where the family dwelled leaving the first floor for commerce and livestock. To this day, there might be a factory on the first floor with two floors above loaded with six families spanning five generations.

Per the standards of the day, property taxes were assigned by the width of the front. Common property widths were five meters *(16 feet)*. The building ran front-to-back 40 meters *(130 feet)*.

The bamboo & thatch roof pitched at a 20 degree slope *(a 3:12 slope)* to shed rain without washing off the coconut leaf cover. The tie-poles typically five meters above the clay floor. There was no ceiling. Sunlight leaked through the thatch spotting the floor with light and thin beams of light in cooking smoke overhead.

The roof was easily constructed by necessity. It often had to be replaced frequently. Wood fires used in cooking often caught the roof on fire. A portion of the roof was permitted to burn out limited by "bucket-brigades." Neighbors aided in controlling the damage lest the entire neighborhood of closely packed houses go up in flames. Roof replacement followed immediately.

Corrugated metal roofing was a status symbol. Wealthier houses had red-brick walls plastered in concrete with a corrugated roof. Toan had money to do more for their home. Unfortunately, some of it went to girlfriends.

The narrow long house was gated in front with a small court-yard where Toan parked his Xe Lam next to bicycles and a shallow table and sitting mat. The rickety front entrance made of 8 centimeter (~3") and 12 centimeter (~4") diameter bamboo posts stood about 3 meters tall (9 feet) with strings of barbed wire on top.

Five meters of dirt road separated houses of similar construction facing each other. Some houses had walls common to others where mud-brick or red-brick was used. In semi-rural fringes of Sai Gon, empty five meter wide lots often separated houses with gardens or orchards.

The spacing established fire separation. As the city swelled with refugees, the voids filled in with hastily built housing of similar construction. As Sai Gon grew, the orderly layout gave way to the appearance of a shanty town as the Cholon accommodated friends and relatives with nowhere else to live. As the population swelled, fire separation disappeared.

Roads and Utilities

Roads in the neighborhood were dirt/clay with some laterite gravel mixed in on better streets. A string of flimsy power poles ran up the main road. Affluent neighbors and businesses had electricity and telephones. Electricity in this part of Sai Gon was a status symbol as much as a utility.

Erratic at best, power often went out either by fault or diversion when it was needed elsewhere. Electric power could be "assigned" as needed depending on the size of the bribe. Diversion of power still occurs when it is transferred elsewhere in Viet Nam.

MaI and Toan had neither electricity nor a phone. As it was, the electric service became increasingly erratic and phone service for Toan required a trip to the post-office or the kindness of the few neighbors that had service.

The neighbors that had a phone connection had worked for the South Vietnamese government and/or the Americans. With the evac-uation of the Americans, phone service for even the most influential citizens became increasingly unreliable. Sai Gon's "western" infrastructure began to fray after the United States had removed most its military support by mid-1974.

Mai's Visits to the House

Loan recalls a string of instructions from Toan that lasted for weeks. Her mother provided the only break in his diatribes on sloth and errant children. These interruptions failed to occur often enough to satisfy Loan. Her father could act like such a kuc *(Vietnamese: poop)* at these times.

Once everyone had settled in after moving back from Tay Ninh, Loan's mother continued her cycle of two and three day absences. Mai arrived unexpectedly seldom staying longer than a day, usually at sunset.

Loan learned to watch for her mother in the late afternoons. Any woman pushing a laden bicycle up the road excited her. At a distance, wearing the non la conical straw hat, black pajamas and sandals, Maï blended in as any peasant woman on the street. Maï relied on the anonymity of poverty.

Loan learned decades later that her mother had pushed that bicycle loaded down with rice and boxes a few hundred meters. She had been dropped off outside of the neighborhood by an ARVN jeep where she loaded up the bicycle and walked it to the house.

The loaded bicycle was a ruse. Everyone thought she traveled from Tay Ninh with a load of several hundred pounds strapped over the bicycle wheels. Maï encouraged the image of poverty and a marriage to a difficult husband.

Her bicycle was tied off on the back of the jeep. She sat in the back giving the appearance of a peasant woman getting a free ride. An ARVN driver and soldier sat in front with M-16s in their laps. They were Mai's chauffeur and body guard.

Maï seldom allowed them to drive up to the house in Sai Gon. This minimized neighbors witnessing her connection to the South Vietnamese army.

Her visits to the house, shrouded in mystery, differed only if Toan was home when she arrived. If he was off on one of his "errands," she spent time with the children checking on their needs and helping Loan's oldest sister prepare a meal before settling down at sunset. When he showed up, their business usually revolved to buying his silence with money and arguing with him about his spending habits.

Asian Men and Girlfriends

Ethnic-Chinese men are generally impervious to questions and instruction from women, particularly if the issue of conflict was about their girlfriends. The ancient roots of polygamist China persisted. Asian wives expected husbands to have girlfriends as often as not. If a man prospered, he had a good wife. If he had more than enough money, he had a wife and a number of girlfriends he could support.

Toan used to berate or strike her when she confronted him. Loan's oldest brothers in their twenties put a stop to that by beating him up a few months earlier. They threatened him with more punishment if he ever struck their mother. Yet, the verbal abuse continued.

After his older sons turned on him, Toan was outnumbered. He confined himself to preparing the house-hold for the larger population that had been living in Tay Ninh. Loan and her younger brothers made bricks of dried clay changing out wooden forms every other day as the bricks dried. This worked in the dryer winter climate and not so well during the monsoon that ran typically May to October.

The objective of his instructions was obvious to all but Loan. Toan prepared the household for trouble. Ho Chi Minh and Hanoi had refuted the division of Viet Nam at the 17th parallel for two decades. North Viet Nam continued its campaign despite horrendous losses. They figured correctly that time was on their side.

The cease-fire of 27 January 1973 enabled North Viet Nam to rebuild and re-arm. By 1974, it was well equipped to take South Viet Nam. In the same period, South Viet Nam was losing the strength to hold out. The American congress withdrew funding for the war. South Viet Nam lacked political leadership to manage its resources and it's military.

Politics or not, money drives every ability to wage a conflict. South Vietnamese operations began to hoard ammunition and weapons creating real and perceived shortages. They also depended on the Americans for too long. They did not adjust well to the American withdrawal.

South Viet Nam with the help of The United States prevailed over a number of conflicts including the notable Tet Offensive in 1968.

Infiltrated Viet Cong struck in approximately one hundred towns and cities throughout South Viet Nam on the eve the Chinese Lunar New Year, *(Vietnamese: Tết Nguyên Đán)* on January 30, 1968. *(The Vietnamese call the offensive, Tết mậu thân)*

South Viet Nam and with the help of allies, achieved a tactical victory. Sai Gon had enough resources to suppress the Viet Cong during the Tet Offensive in 1968 including full American support.

In the spring of 1975, South Viet Nam lacked enough of essentials to sustain itself. No American troops. No American air power. Plenty of armament. Poor political leadership.

The NVA uncovered caches of hoarded American weapons as they invaded South Viet Nam. Some of the hoarded American-made weapons fell on Sai Gon in the final days.

Ensconced in the Cholon

Toan, isolated in his self-absorbed affairs in the Cholon, expected repeated conflicts. Hanoi was relentless in its conquest of South Viet Nam. Yet, Toan figured they could somehow prevail as before. After all, South Viet Nam had remained independent for almost twenty years.

Born in China in the 1920s, he spoke and read Cantonese. He picked up some French from his earlier days in North Viet Nam before moving down to South Viet Nam in the early 1950s.

Toan refused to speak, or write Vietnamese. This removed him from half the stream of information available to Maï. Although not fluent in speaking it, she understood the southern and northern dialects of Vietnamese well enough.

Toan objected to embracing the local language. He refused wisdom expressed in other tongues. After he picked up French in the few years they lived in North Viet Nam, he witnessed the demise of the France's leadership in 1954. From then on, he wrapped himself in Cantonese and Chinese culture.

Toan discouraged his children from picking up Vietnamese. Yet, their years on the move north of Sai Gon exposed them to the language. Toan, alone, spoke only Cantonese using a few words in Vietnamese as fit his desires.

By 1975, seven years after the 1968 Tet Offensive, the situation in the south was starkly different. While a small contingent of Americans remained, America was out of the fight. Only the presence of the U.S. Navy off the eastern coast near Vung Tau posed a threat of retaliation in the event Americans working for the U.S. Embassy were threatened.

North Viet Nam had fully infiltrated the south with of thousands of NVA cells of insurgents throughout the cities and villages. The cells of the NVA prepared to enhance the chaos as Hanoi's main forces assaulted Sai Gon. Key individuals and their families were targeted and "neutralized" in advance of April 30, 1975.

The mechanics of the war had significantly changed from what worked in the 1960s. Shoulder-mounted missiles reduced effectiveness of helicopters and slow fixed-wing aircraft. American B-52s no longer operated in Viet Nam. The Russian-backed North Vietnamese Army was equipped to stage a conventional ground assault without threat of America air power.

Since the Tet Offensive, North Viet Nam conducted a steady propaganda campaign to confound South Vietnamese as to what side to defend. The corrupt government and regional administrators disillusioned and confused South Vietnamese loyalists.

South Viet Nam government's authority weakened on the fringes of the cities and in the villages. Hanoi whittled away and the resolve of the citizens with megaphones mounted on small vehicles. NVA infiltrators toured the outlying neighborhoods propagandizing the citizens in Vietnamese and Cantonese.

Toan was susceptible to misinformation peddled by megaphone prior to the fall of Sai Gon. The misinformation campaign worked. He was hobbled by fear.

The NVA were coming sooner than expected. In fact, they had already arrived. While Maï was working to defend South Viet Nam or make plans to flee, Toan was digging in to endure an inevitable NVA victory.

Toan prepared the house for calamity. It was late February 1975. War-related violence was nothing new. Sai Gon had been spared the scale of violence and atrocities visited upon other cities to the north.

The TET offensive of 1968 introduced Sai Gon to large scale violence. Yet the Viet Cong failed. The remainder of VC blended with the NVA. Over the next seven years, Hanoi had re-armed and steadily amassed its Soviet-equipped forces in the south.

The wisdom of the American CIA: South Viet Nam could hold out for more than a year, perhaps eighteen months after the final evacuation of American forces in 1974. It didn't last six months. In the spring of 1975, most of Sai Gon prepared for the worst. Only the ignorant including Loan was spared of dread and despair.

Preparations

Loan barely knew enough to dread anything beyond Toan's damn broom handle. Her despair took form in drudgery. Endless tasks started before dawn and ended at midnight. Her father reinforced everything in the house, more bamboo and bailing wire. Corrugated steel roofing was expensive if not scarce he added more fresh coconut leaves to the roof.

Toan lined the top of the courtyard wall with broken glass and a string of barbed wire to deter thieves if not invaders. He sealed high openings in the rear of the house used for ventilation, opening up one vent for the "latrine" after the older children complained of the stink.

Older brothers moved in four 55-gallon steel drums with American markings "acquired" by Maï. They filled the drums that had plastic liners with water from a sunken well-pit situated between the kitchen and the latrine. The poly-liners flavored the stored water. Unless boiled and spiced with lemons or limes, nobody used the water for purposes other than washing.

They positioned the drums against the east side of the house and repositioned the children's sleeping mats to the interior. Loan assumed the barrels were for cooking and bathing. Her brothers knew the water-barrels provided limited fire projection. The oldest brothers knew an American-made oil drum full of water could stop shrapnel, bomb blasts and bullets.

Her father's infrequent kindness surprised Loan at times. He gave her brothers a handful of piaster and told them to spend the rest of the day at the local open-air market a few blocks west. Toan and her older brothers told her they would join her and the younger children later. They never showed.

As agreed, the younger children returned to the house before sunset. Something had changed while they were at market.

They returned to the house to find her oldest brothers muddy and exhausted along with her father. Nothing in the house seemed out of the ordinary. Maybe more supports from the roof and a few more bricks, but nothing that justified exhaustion of three grown men.

Life's Basics

A rough cotton curtain separated the latrine from the open barn-like house. One corner held a water barrel, bucket, ladle, and what might have passed for a bath towel. A bath consisted of filling the bucket from the barrel and using that with the ladle for all bathing and manner of body maintenance.

Toilet paper was a western luxury. Vietnamese used the ladled unheated water to wash themselves of all manner of foulness. In the constant heat and humidity, the washing brought a pleasant comfort.

Drinking water came from a pot heated to boiling several times a day and then set to cool. Vietnamese struggled with contamination and disease in tropical temperatures that seldom fell below 21° C *(70° F.)*

Refrigeration required electricity. Both were decades away from common use. Operation of the electric service more than six hours a day constituted reliability. Few counted on electric service on the fringes of Sai Gon.

The day's meal required a visit to the open-air market a few blocks west of the house. Stalls 2 meters square covered by canvas awnings packed into a one-block area. Under the awnings, women wearing the conical non la sat on their heels as they peddled fruits, vegetables, chicken, fish and duck. Some stalls contained tubs filled with water or sea-water teaming with shrimp and crabs. Vendors hand pumped billows to aerate the tanks to keep their stocks in good condition for sale.

Perishable items sold quickly. Goat's milk and human milk potentially contaminated with tuberculosis sold by midday. Without refrigeration, it was thrown away after a few hours.

Boiled water left to cool was the safest drink, along with tea and Viet Nam's excellent coffee mixed with cocoa. Lemonade made from lemons and ground sugar cane was a treat, especially if the market had electricity to make ice. Nothing tasted better than ice-cold Vietnamese lemonade during the midday.

Concrete tiles set a few inches below the level of the floor defined the latrine. A small trench drained away to the side of the back of the house into an alley of sorts. Small holes covered with a wood platform formed squat toilets with a wooden cover to seal off the latrine. In a household population of fifteen people, the latrine was a "three-seater" with dividers made of translucent cotton stretched on a bamboo frame.

In prosperous times, a sack of white powder *(lime)* and a scoop sat beside the squat toilet. Stacks of fragrant lemon grass thrown in the latrine suppressed odors reasonably well. A section of the roof in the front and back of the house remained open for ventilation. On windy days, the interior of the house received a decent breeze blowing through.

When fly maggots became too numerous or the stench unbearable, a layer of dirt and lime was added to the trench. Once the latrine filled up, it was covered with clay soil and an adjacent latrine went into service. The latrines rotated on a regular schedule. The schedule changed according to the population of the house.

The three areas excavated for the latrine usually rotated in twelve to eighteen months. When they excavated the first latrine after a year, the human and cooking waste, lemon grass and clay layers had all broken down into odorless well-fertilized soil that nourished gardens on the east side of the house. Herbs, peppers, green onions, and tomatoes grew closer to the house to limit theft from wander refugees and less-scrupulous neighbors.

Quick growing sweet potatoes dominated the garden. Boiled sweet potatoes mixed with rice made up a large portion of Loan's diet. If a chicken meant for market went sickly, meat became a part of the meal. Loan's brothers occasionally accelerated the demise of a sickly chicken in order to have meat in their rice bowl.

Hygiene

Loan owned three pairs of clothing, pajama-like blouses and shorts along with one pair of sandals. Her mother provided her a non la, an iconic cone shaped hat made of rice-straw when she worked outside. Vietnamese in rural areas bathed outside behind the house with their clothes on using rain water or well water stored in a rusted oil drum.

The common Vietnamese soap was coarse and unscented. A bar of white American soap engraved with the word "Ivory" sat on a pedestal from time to time. Loan remembered the scent of the American soap as a mark of better times. *(Author's Note: To this day, she returns to Viet Nam with cases of American-made soap as gifts to her family.)*

The neighborhood was split between housing and small plots of farmland. The small trench that drained away the bathwater fertilized the garden and mango trees. Good soil was seldom wasted.

Loan considered her life as normal if not prosperous. She considered the growing number of homeless refugees as poor.

At times, her mother showed Loan cash otherwise hidden from her father. It required little cash for a Vietnamese husband to have a girlfriend or two. She kept Toan on a "short vine" as it were.

Mai reminded her children to ignore the urge to show money when they had any to spend. Errands to the local market required barter and/or cash with instructions on how to limit exposing more money than needed to complete the transaction.

Asians haggle over every purchase. ***Every purchase***. One hand holds only the money willing to be paid, not the asking price. Flashing wealth purchased no value in Asia unless soliciting politicians, prostitutes, drugs or assassins.

The American dollar went far. Consequently new wealth elicited curiosity. Where did it come from? During America's participation in the war, sudden riches implied earnings developed in relationships with the flood of "western" people that dwelled in Viet Nam for more than a decade.

At the height of involvement in 1969, America populated Viet Nam with half a million military and support personnel. South Korea, Britain, Australia and Canada provided smaller numbers. Similar numbers of Vietnamese and foreign contractors built, fed, and maintained the allied military presence. The military issued "script" to its personnel in order to avoid inflating the South Vietnamese economy with foreign currency. Yet, American dollars and British pounds were impossible to control as the cash left no trace of purchaser in most circumstances.

Spies and Foreigners

South Viet Nam and in particular Sai Gon was rife with spies. The census fluctuated as rural populations relocated to the cities for decades. A large number of Catholic Vietnamese in the north relocated to South Viet Nam in the 1950s, many of them to the Cholon districts where the population spoke Cantonese. By the spring of

1975 as NVA forces began the assault on South Viet Nam, Sai Gon was awash with strangers.

One instruction became a daily reminder: "The walls have Vietnamese ears." Loan's family spoke in Cantonese regarding family matters and particularly with or about her mother, Maï.

South Vietnamese made reference to Viet Cong in code. Use only "VC," never to use the full term. After the Tet Offensive in 1968, the NVA absorbed the decimated ranks of VC. The term Viet Cong is now used interchangeably for VC and NVA. *(Author's Note: In areas where Viet Cong operated heavily, English-speaking guests are instructed to avoid using certain words in full term to this day.)*

Americans, Canadians, British, French and Australians were "western people" or similar simplifications. "Westerners" were a constant target for wares and services with limited haggling skills. Community economy grew when a contingent of foreigners began operating nearby.

When a person was unfamiliar or untrustworthy, it became accepted practice to lie about the source of money. Responses about inheritance or a deceased relative, "family money" and other references deflected most questions for a time.

Toan and Mai suspected the appearance of any stranger in the Cholon as a VC spy scoping out the community. Families closed ranks and discouraged open conversations with non-family. Neighborhoods tightened security.

The battle for central Sai Gon in 1968 basically ended in two weeks, the fighting in the Cholon went on for a month. No living adult in 1968 forgot the terror of the VC death-squads that wiped out entire families.

The assassinations were retribution for supporting South Viet Nam's fight to remain independent of Hanoi. A husband or wife taking a job with Americans and South Viet Nam became a death sentence for the entire family should they become a target.

The VC objective was terror and disruption of South Viet Nam's society. The violence was nearly impossible to manage as the VC emerged from isolated cells that knew nothing of the network of other VC. Interrogation of captured assassins seldom yielded useful information about VC strength or location. Over American objections, South Viet Nam executed most all of its VC prisoners of war. As said before, few that traveled from North Viet Nam to fight in the south ever returned to Hanoi.

In the darkness of the house, Loan occasionally heard her mother argue with her father in hushed Cantonese. By mid-March, the unpleasant tension between her mother and father each evening grew well above whispers.

Mai always left house around midnight. At sun-rise, if Toan was in a better mood, the children assumed Mai had given him money.

Mid-April 1975, Sai Gon, Viet Nam

For days, Loan heard thunder that brought no rain. One of her brothers talked about smoke rising in the distance from a community 20 kilometers to the east known as Xuân Lộc (*"soon lock"*). They had ridden the Xe Lam with their father on an errand for their mother to Long Binh, less than 10 kilometers from Xuân Lộc. The thunder was artillery. South Viet Nam and Sai Gon made a stand at Xuân Lộc. It was the last "gate" to Sai Gon. When Xuân Lộc fell, Sai Gon had less than two weeks.

For another week, Sai Gon's refugee population swelled. Strangers roamed the neighborhoods looking for some place to settle. Anything not tied down was stolen. Fresh produce at the markets became scarce as Sai Gon residents and refugees hoarded anything that could be bought at inflated prices.

At one point in the third week, Toan filled the lined drums with water and covered them with steel lids. They stacked sacks of rice on top of the drums. Loan had seldom seen so much rice in the house. Toan estimated he had a year's worth of rice for twenty people. He muttered it might not be enough.

In the last week of April, close thunder turned out to be explosions as the non-combatant neighborhoods on the fringes of Sai Gon came under attack. The frequency narrowed and the concussions grew stronger until today when her father asked everyone to stay in the house. His older sons kept the gate closed on the compact courtyard that faced the narrow road.

The children gathered in the front of the house. They stood near their parents bed-matt perched a few inches above the clay-mud floor. Loan's father pulled back the rice-straw matt to reveal heavy twine that disappeared into the smooth clay surface of the floor. As he pulled on the twine, it split the mud producing a rough square 30" on a side. The twine pulled up a stained white nylon rope that formed a crude handle.

With a few tugs, the square rotated up, the opposite side cracking as the clay folded on itself. It was a hidden hatch over a deep hole.

He raised the closest edge as it pivoted on a bamboo and twine hinge revealing a dark square abyss. The hole penetrated a cavity beneath the rest of the bed platform. Her father lay on his stomach next to the hole to reach for something with his left arm. Then he moved to his hands and knees holding another rope attached to a thin bamboo ladder. He set it to rest on one side of the opening angling down under the bed mat.

Holding the top of the ladder with his left hand, Toan turned to Loan and pointed to her with his right hand, the index finger uncoiling and then waving her toward the hole. It was a gesture meaning move quickly. Then he grabbed the broom. Without hesitation, Loan moved around to where she could step onto the ladder.

He made the same gesture toward her older brother Quy motioning the two younger children to descend the bamboo ladder. They hesitated when another explosion rocked the neighborhood. He grabbed his infamous broom yelling, "Lot Hui!" *(Hide!)* He pointed to them and to the hole. "Lot Hui!"

All but the oldest sons were surprised to learn of a large cavity under the bedding at the front of the house. The wooden sides raised half a foot above the polished red-clay floor of the house. Most woven bed mattes were less than an inch tall. Their father frequently volunteered that he did that just in case a monsoon flood covered the floor of the house. It was a lie meant to divert curiosity. Toan had built a vault under his bed matt.

Since the last typhoon that hit Sai Gon in the 1960s, the neighborhood remained dry. Before the Americans had left Viet Nam, their "Seabees" cleared swampland to the south. Chronic neighborhood flooding ended. Toan's explanation of the unusual bed construction was hollow. Chinese culture dictated they respect their father's explanation.

Mai and Toan's children in the house ranging from six to nineteen, two girls and seven boys along with half-brothers squeezed into the darkness, standing on the tops of wood crates that covered the bottom of the pit. Heavy cardboard boxes piled up on opposite sides stopped inches below the bed platform. The platform rested on heavy timber poles that crossed the top. Light that bled from the entrance was now blocked by the older boys rendering the cavity pitch black. They packed into a three-foot wide slot running ten feet to the back of the pit, the older ones crouching to keep their heads from hitting the timbers. The smell of wet clay walls, damp cardboard and machine oil permeated the air, their rapid breathing the only sound in the cavity. No one spoke.

The slow rot of American plywood supporting the boxes produced a familiar hint of woody mildew. Another instruction from her father, Toan: "Rap Hui, Rap Hui." *(Vietnamese: Move back. Move back.)* The older children pressed in on the younger children in the steamy darkness. Toan climbed down and turned his back to the children. He groped something in a dark niche cut into the clay wall. A light flared as he ignited an American butane cigarette lighter touching the flame to the wick of a squat white candle. The western writing on the lighter read "Zippo." Some Vietnamese thought "zippo" was English for "matches."

The wick flamed blue at first then to an incandescent yellow as the wax began to burn. He set it on the top of the stack of boxes. He lit another candle off the first flame and set it on the other side. He then made a motion of his hand telling the children to stay where they were and climbed the ladder to wriggle through the opening. He disappeared as he instructed the older boys standing above them to keep everyone in the hole.

The children were panting now as the air soured and the sticky heat built up among them. As they waited for instruction, they heard something scraping on one side. It was the distinct sound of ceramic red brick sliding on brick on one side of the wall.

A crack of light appeared as Toan pulled an orange-red brick from the east side of the house. It was an air vent. Deeper in the pit, another opening appeared. Blue-white daylight bled into the dark cavity. The children moved instinctively to the openings to draw in fresh air.

Outside air leaked into the hold and reeked of burning vegetation, explosives and the distinctive smell of burning animal flesh. The smoke of burning wreckage lingered close to the ground. There was little wind.

Columns of white smoke rose from the houses, flames licked out of burning vehicles east of the house. Tires on burning vehicles sent up oily black smoke. Relief, at least visually, arrived at sunset. Darkness silenced most of the artillery. Artillery depended on spotters advising where to direct fire for effect. Darkness blinded both sides.

Sunrise on the 28th: New threats

Shelling and a few rockets resumed just before sunrise. Distant concussion resounded in all directions as the NVA bombarded the city indiscriminately. The explosions grew in number. The NVA made their final push into Sai Gon as the Army of the Republic of Viet Nam retreated and fell into disarray.

Cantonese and Vietnamese voices rose from the China-town neighborhood of Sai Gon as mortars and artillery once again fractured rural and city structures. In the lulls, neighbors called to neighbors from their hiding places asking for help.

The bombardment set many thatch roofs ablaze. Families under the burning roofing sorted between two choices of enduring the fires or leaving the house to be exposed in the streets.

Neighbors lacking heavy construction screamed as they could only stand by as their homes burned. The dilemma: remain in the flimsy construction now burning or run into the road or street with zero protection. Unprotected and unarmed, those that survived the initial bombardment had little protection.

Various instructions said the same thing. Run for cover to the northeast. Run away from North Vietnamese Army (NVA) closing in from the southeast. Few understood why Nguyên Xuân Loan' father ordered his children into the house. Explosions "walked" again into the city ahead of the NVA. The neighbors seeing this thought Toan was committing suicide and taking his children with him.

Cocky and bragging as Toan tended to be, he kept his underground vault secret from neighbors. He was not prophetic about the fall of Sai Gon. He had dug the cavity under the bed matt out of fear and avarice. Toan was afraid his wife's activities would be uncovered by Viet Cong spies that infiltrated the districts of the Cholon.

Short of a direct hit from an explosive, the reinforced pit could withstand some destruction. Toan wondered if anyone else built similar sanctuary.

NVA pickets moved into and through the burning neighborhood cautiously. The Cholon resistance never materialized. The infamous Viet Cong black pajama had been replaced by olive-green uniforms, the NVA moved in with wearing helmets in lieu of the conical straw hats. All carried the ubiquitous AK-47 with the iconic 30-round banana-clip.

The shattered remnants of the roof partially covered the bed matt. Toan shifted the thatched walls and coconut fronds to permit access to the opening of the hole. At the appropriate time, he could retreat into the hole and pull the cover over to wait out until the NVA moved into another part of the city.

Better to Spank Than Bury a Child

Loan wondered at the unexpected void in the red clay underneath the bed-matt for only a moment as she crowded in with her brothers in the hole in the ground. She indulged her curiosity soon enough. Now was the time to be still and invisible.

Her father was on the edge of berserk. Sweating and panting quietly in the south end of the hole, Loan recalled her mother's instructions to still her mind. Be ready to act smart. She began to understand that odd instruction.

Toan crowded in with them showing all manner of fear. Unlike decades before in North Viet Nam, he was on the receiving end of an artillery barrage.

He had witnessed appalling devastation near Hanoi in the early 1950s when the French reclaimed the city. It was unclear whether he worked for the French or was part of their army. Toan exhibited little military training. This was before he and Maï moved their family to South Viet Nam.

Toan flinched at unexpected sounds. He peered out one slit or another crawling over the top of his crouching children to gain a better view. Their house was on an elevated rise from east to west. Toan could only view the eastern approach, down the road as he called it, scanning the burning wreckage of flattened houses.

Nothing moved except for the roiling white and black smoke of burning wreckage. Their garden of sweet potatoes, peanuts and herbs appeared intact. The orchard was destroyed. In the midst of the far edge of the garden, an unexploded olive-drab iron bomb with a propeller fuse protruded from the ground. It was buried half into the earth.

As the bombs began to fall, he spared no child who hesitated when he gave them an instruction. Better to strike a disobedient child than to bury them.

As her eyes adjusted to the darkness, Loan realized there was a second hatch on her end. A plywood hatch above her with a bamboo ladder half imbedded in the wall. She tested the wood panel. It yielded a few inches. She pushed more and an edge of daylight appeared. Smaller than the first hatch, it was about half a meter square. The other end of the bed mat covered it. As her brothers and older sister faced the other opening, she tested the hatch again. It moved but stopped short of being fully open. The roof had collapsed on it.

She could smell burning coconut leaves. Part of the roof burned. It was new roof, too green to burn well.

Toan was preoccupied peering out the slits in the east wall. Loan's curiosity took over. When her father was preoccupied with something in the other end of the hole, she climbed out of the second hatch. One of her brothers, Anam, followed whispering to her to come back.

The youngest girl in a large family of mostly male siblings, her many brothers tried to manage her, protect her from harm. Much like her mother, she was independent of mind. Her boldness was often construed as recklessness. She ignored her brothers more than listened to them.

Her brothers and older sister constantly scolded her for disobeying them and her father. Obvious to all, she was Maï's daughter.

The collapsed roof had gaps in the coconut layers. Fortunately, the fresh leaves only smoldered.

Loan emerged from the gloom and stand amidst the coconut leaves to gaze through the shattered thatch walls. Anam, slightly larger than Loan, wriggled through the broken roof behind her.

As her eyes adjusted to the hazy sunlight, she could see in most directions. Anam was whispering to her pleading to come back inside. As he stood up next to her, he went silent as he viewed the destruction.

The neighborhood had been leveled. Smoke rose in every direction. The house on the west that took a direct hit was fully engulfed in flames. A three-wheel Xe Lam lay on its side burning, its tiny tires making thick black smoke. Explosions nearby, some muffled as mortars and artillery detonated inside another house or cracking sharply when going off on open ground.

Curiosity reigned. Loan and Anam stood silently gazing at the destruction in all directions. On their right, to the south, a mortar round exploded in an orchard 200 meters away. A few seconds later, another round detonated 150 meters away. More rounds "walked" toward them. Twelve year old Anam grabbed Loan and spun her back toward the hatch. She wanted to study the destruction rather than cower from it.

Concussions of near explosions buffeted her 35-pound body as she watched the next mortar round arc into the sky and then land in among the houses 100 meters to the south. The next rounds came in close. Anam shoved Loan into the gap to find the hatch. Loan found it under the leaves and climbed in head first. Anam squirmed through falling on top of her.

They heard her father screaming at them from inside, on the other end of the covered pit. The second round hit the latrine on the south end of the house. A few seconds later, the next mortar round landed on top of the front gate blowing out the glass of Toan's Xe Lam and mangled the bicycles. Rounds continued to explode to the north.

The dry coconut leaves on the shattered roof above the latrine burned. The fresher leaves on the remainder smoldered but failed to ignite.

Nearby shelling stopped a quarter hour later as a large engine could be over-heard over the clinking of metal tread. A NVA light-weight tank slowly rolled up Hóa Bình Street one block over. The first of hundreds of NVA soldiers had arrived following the tank, their AK-47s leveled at the businesses and homes that lined the only paved road in the districts. Platoons of tanks split off north and south into the adjoining neighborhoods. Many carried a megaphone to coerce the surviving population to come out.

The NVA that invaded Sai Gon was the "group of bad men" her father mentioned. The mystery: why did they kill defenseless civilians? District 11 of Sai Gon was all neighborhoods and small business. There were no military facilities in the area.

The Chinese-Vietnamese supported South Viet Nam and the Americans in operations against Hanoi. Their only crime was loyalty to South Viet Nam.

The slaughter of civilians was payback from Hanoi. Zealous forces attempting to take Sai Gon before Ho Chi Minh's birthday *(19 May)* had taken significant casualties. They treated ungrateful South Vietnamese roughly.

World opinion splits its view in regard to Hanoi's consolidation of North and South Viet Nam by force. Viet Cong and NVA believe in part that they invaded South Viet Nam to save South Vietnamese from themselves. April 30, 1975 became "Liberate Sai Gon Day."

Between April 30, 1975 and April 30, 1995, this political objective would kill over two million people and stress forty million to extremes. Those that could not live under those conditions fled. By best reckoning of a population in chaos, one third died in the South China Sea by error, natural events, or at the hands of pirates.

By 1985, 823,000 Vietnamese landed on American shores. Another 400,000 or so made it to at least six other countries including Thailand, Canada, Australia, Malaysia, France and Israel. Conservative estimates are that over two million fled the country.

Anecdotal information among Vietnamese in Viet Nam and expatriates: the number fleeing greatly exceeded two million. Records only indicate that maybe 1.4 million Vietnamese arrived somewhere else. What happened to the rest?

The loss of life in the South China Sea had become horrendous. With China's insistence, Viet Nam ceased severely prosecuting people who were caught escaping and developed the Orderly Departure Program or "ODP." By then, the worst of the horror had largely played out. Despite the program, the tragedy continued as untrusting Vietnamese fled although in smaller numbers.

Shredded Families April 29, 1975

During the shelling, the sound of NVA mortar tubes reached them moments before the arcing shells landed. The "fooom" of the mortar tube and the slow arc of the shell meant two things. NVA were close and something bad was in the air and headed for them. Mortars lob a weapon high in the air to fly over ramparts and walls. The weapons land on top of the target. Some were loaded with shrapnel. Other mortars were loaded with incendiary explosives. One killed people, the other burned neighborhoods. The NVA threw everything at the neighborhoods.

Her mother had instructed her children: "Don't watch in wonder as the shell lobs your way. Find cover." On top of the improvised shelter, Loan grabbed pieces of roofing for protection. By the grace of Buddha, it was just enough. Hot metal fragments imbedded in the coconut leaves, stopping short of the skin on her back.

Another mortar landed in the center of neighbor's house to the west, erupting in a flash blowing out the roof. The size of the explosion meant one thing. Another Vietnamese family met total disaster. They trying to hold things together and weave the gauntlet of life. The survivors, if any, now faced indelible tragedy.

Loan returned 20 years later to see another family in that location and recall the precise moment in 1975 when fortunes changed. Just as a bad car wreck transforms life views for the survivors in America, artillery amid neighborhoods transform generational opportunities. Life moved on despite the memories of loss.

Shrapnel from another explosion shredded the remainder of their roof. Pieces of metal and coconut leaves fell in around her. Anam scolded her for staying above ground as he stood up in the entrance with her.

Loan heard more mortar tubes send up rounds. The NVA were close, a city block or so away. Enemy advance teams launched the mortars in the next block or two as they move into the neighborhood.

Capitulation and Punishment

The attacks stopped when Sai Gon fell on April 30, 1975, only to be replaced by other forms of torture and destruction. One of Toan's brothers took Maï's advice to reach the U.S. Embassy or the barges with papers in hand and leave the country. He sealed up his house and left with his family too late in the process. The embassy was overwhelmed and the barges left before the NVA confiscated them. He returned to his locked up house a day later.

The new regime knew that he attempted to escape Sai Gon. He, his wife, and children were murdered in their home a week later. Toan, in his infinite wisdom, believed that would have been his family's outcome had they made for the barges.

The post-war punishment of South Viet Nam for being South Viet Nam drove millions of people to flee in the following years. I repeat a simple summary: by conservative estimates, over two million fled, a third of them died in the Vietnamese exodus between 1975 and 1984.

Sai Gon: Under New Management

The city went under martial law of the most egregious form. As survivors of Loan's neighborhood salvaged what they could, mend the injured and bury the dead, NVA soldiers set up local jurisdiction.

The new city regime regarded most everyone in Sai Gon as if they were rats. They commandeered personal possessions as needed to satisfy the NVA soldiers. Conquerors first in line for food, all others not of the NVA were expected to sort it out for themselves. Intact families had better opportunities; injured survivors had little chance of treatment. Some had no chance of survival.

The first event was marked by the arrival of a confiscated American-made bulldozer that excavated a bombed-out building one block north. The machine carved out a deep long pit.

Entire families had been wiped out to the point there was no one to help recognize the bodies or assemble body parts to bury the whole of a person. Literally at gunpoint, NVA soldiers spread through the neighborhood commanding everyone to remove the remains of dead Vietnamese neighbors and throw them into the newly excavated pit.

Loan remembers the large pile of bodies and body parts. Odd smells remind her of the honey-sweet-but-sickening smell of human flesh rotting in the tropical heat.

After excavating the pit for the mass burial, the bright-yellow bulldozer worked up and down the main east-west road shoving debris to the side. The NVA cleared the main road for a parade the next day, on May 1, 1975. It became Viet Nam's "May Day".

May Day to the Russian backers of North Viet Nam meant Russian Memorial Day, International Worker's Day. From then on, April 30, 1975 would be celebrated as "Unification Day" and Sai Gon eventually became Ho Chi Minh City by title. To most, it is still called Sai Gon.

The NVA and Hanoi had conquered Sai Gon and South Viet Nam to save the region from itself. The witless automatons that knew nothing else but what Hanoi had told them now began to strangle a thriving city and fertile region with a 365 day growing season into oblivion.

The most loyal and courageous soldiers of North Viet Nam received management positions over the conquered city. Former city administrators and support personnel were sent to the "re-education camps."

Some South Vietnamese committed suicide as the NVA invaded Sai Gon. There were allegedly 30,000 military personnel rounded up and never heard from again … disposition unknown.

In the case of managing Sai Gon, there was seldom an interview on technical or professional qualifications. Loyal party members and courageous combatants became the new administrators of one of the most productive regions of Southeast Asia. They strangled the region in a matter of months creating real famines. They added artificial famines for loyalists including the ethnic Chinese Vietnamese by denying rice and other staples of Asian diets.

Perspective on Competence

North Viet Nam indoctrinated young men and sent them toward Sai Gon to save South Viet Nam from itself and re-unify the country. Hanoi conscripted young men in their early teens from villages throughout the country. Armed with little more than an AK-47, meager rations of rice and a belly full of propaganda, many of the Viet Cong and the NVA died along the way to promotion.

If they went the distance and survived, the cadres of North Viet Nam ground forces graduated to the new ruling class of all Viet Nam. They had spent their formative years moving into South Viet Nam and fighting the ARVN and American forces. By age 25, some of them had been in the jungles and tunnels since they were 12.

Depending on the ferocity of combat, attrition in NVA command offered rapid career advancement. Capable unschooled soldiers quickly climbed Hanoi's "corporate ladder" so to speak. Careers often advanced quickly for NVA cadre. Their reward: a place in management of South Viet Nam thanks to the vision of "Father Ho."

Ho Chi Minh, "Father Ho," died September 19, 1969, six years before he could realize Viet Nam united under one flag. Sai Gon, the "Paris of Southeast Asia" became Ho Chi Minh City. The "City of Light" it was not. All went dark.

Former South Vietnamese administrators and business leaders that didn't leave Viet Nam hid out as rice farmers or committed suicide. The rest were removed to "re-education camps" where they were worked to death or held for years. South Viet Nam's military leadership was executed, either directly or through punishing work-gangs repairing the war damage created by both sides of the conflict. Some of those that survived were "re-educated" for decades.

Those that avoided the re-education camps by bribing officials have been perpetually punished by restriction from immigrating to this day. I know the offspring of these stranded men. They live in the United States unable to move their parents to America.

After April 30, 1975, who ran South Viet Nam? Who was available and qualified?

Answer: Those remarkable young unschooled indoctrinated men and women that fought well for the revolution. Party loyalty was credential number one and service to North Viet Nam was credential number two. Administrative and technical skills might have mattered as a weak third requirement for hire. Humanity wasn't on the list of necessary skills or attributes.

Hanoi's recipe for the future: Blend a strong dose of enduring North Vietnamese hatred of their former enemy, now all citizens of a united Viet Nam. Stir in ethnic bias and paranoia of an uprising by conquered loyalists. Add in a command economy salted with social unaccountability.

Traditional to Asian culture, seniority among strictly male management rules over general wisdom. Witless older men with all the correct political credentials operated unchallenged. Accountability and humanity became a casualty of the new regime.

As of May 1, 1975, Viet Nam entered the "dark ages." It took nearly a decade to restore a measure of sanity to the region and another decade to enable Viet Nam to make its way back into the present.

To extend the "Brain Surgeon Analogy," you are wheeled into the operating room and realize something is a bit off. The surgeon is blind and hates patients. And besides that, the last tool he used for any serious surgery was an AK-47 or an RPG.

The term "medieval" understates the atmosphere of the next decades of South Viet Nam. Is there any wonder why over two million Vietnamese fled Viet Nam? There is more on this.

Cholon Damage Control - May 1975

Damage control is an oxymoron. If you are getting damage, something is not in control. A more proper term is "damage limiting" or "damage minimization." Within the limited domain of the Cholon neighborhood, everything and everyone was damaged.

Every flimsy typical urban/rural house was flattened or damaged by the concussions of the bombs and mortars. Triage as it might be called sorted unidentifiable dead and parts of the dead to large excavated trenches. Standing families that could manage the grim task of respecting the remains of their lost members took the identifiable dead to hastily embalm them, bury them unprepared or cremate the remains.

This was nothing new to Loan and her family. They buried the few remains of Cường with the few remains of four others in a single grave outside of Tay Ninh in January.

As Toan Loan's father, predicted, the house collapsed on top of them as near explosions unraveled the flimsy structure. Fortunately, their coconut-frond roof did not fully catch fire.

Anam and Loan sought the sanctuary of Toan's secret hole in the ground as the last mortar rounds struck, Anam a bit more bloodied than Loan. Just as in a tornado, the debris in the chaos becomes as lethal as the initial destruction. He had taken some shrapnel. None of it was life threatening.

Toan among few had dug a hole in the ground to hide contraband. He hid cases of American C-Rations, French liquor, AK-47s and Chinese grenades. The hole in the ground protected them from the shells and bombs that destroyed other families in their homes. Loan's family among few had sufficient shelter. For once her father's selfishness saved the family from greater harm.

Loan recalled three decades later that Toan's egregious ways inadvertently help her and siblings survive. If she could say the term clearly, she would have called her father's behavior ironic.

The pit now sheltered his family as the NVA paid vengeance on the people it meant to save from western influence. Loan buried herself as deep into the clay floor as she could. Her brothers laid on top of her and her older sister, Maï. Her father peered now and then through a thin opening in the floor cover.

Explosions went off through the community. They flinched in response to the sounds and shock waves as they huddled in the hole in the ground. And then the shelling, mortars and bombs stopped. The first wave of chaos ended in abrupt silence.

Toan wept in the sultry darkness with his children huddled all around him. He knew of this before in Hanoi and before that in Shanghai during World War II. He hated the anticipated pain of the next level of chaos that was to come. But he wept mostly for himself and how he might endure the coming years. It is hard to know if he wept for his children. *(Author's Note: From what I can gather in our coffees in Sai Gon between 2009 and 2012, he did.)*

If Sai Gon waged a longer battle, Loan never saw it. South Viet Nam basically had lost the fight months before and only played a stopping game to give time for some of them to exit the country. Effective counter measures only stemmed the NVA tide that was invading South Viet Nam wholesale.

As Toan chided his children to lay low, he witnessed the neighborhood disintegrate, friends and neighbors died in senseless destruction. Toan had provided for himself and his children. He provided nothing for others. *(Author's Note: If not for his selfish acts, I would not share life with his daughter. I critique Toan with difficulty.)*

Shanghai Invasion

Maï was eleven years old at the time, Toan was fifteen years old in 1937 when the Japanese shelled and bombed Shanghai neighborhoods. They lived in neighboring villages outside of Shanghai and knew of the senseless destruction of civilian areas. The Japanese wrought destruction of non-combatants all along the eastern coast of China.

China fought back largely with small arms fire and limited artillery against a well-armed invasion with superior numbers of everything including an important aspect the defenders lacked: advanced aircraft.

In theory, the general ratio of casualties between equally armed combatants has a low defender-to-aggressor loss ratio. Often, the ratio is 1:2 or more. This does not include the loss of un-armed civilians who are "collateral damage".

Shanghai's defending force suffered the opposite. China's forces lost three times the Japanese numbers during the four months of The Battle of Shanghai.

The Battle of Shanghai was the opening of a series of battles that stalled Japanese incursion to inland China. China sacrificed ill-equipped troops and civilians to forestall Japan. It worked at a great price.

China's heroic fight for Shanghai bought time to relocate industrial production inland. Over-extended for a time, Japan was unable to sustain larger incursions to inland China beyond Shanghai. Japan occupied the Shanghai region until September 1945 but was unable to penetrate and occupy western China.

Significant to Toan and Mai's experience, as the war with Japan began to close, American Marines entered mainland China in 1945 to assist in the disarmament and removal of Japanese forces. As teenagers living through China's prolonged war with Japan, they heard of the aid of the Americans and the awesome might of the mysterious atomic weapons.

Unlike the French and British incursions of previous centuries, the Americans came, fought and left. Hanoi accused America of imperialism. Salient facts contradicted the propaganda. America gave of its blood and treasure and returned to America including the repatriation of its fallen soldiers. The only territory occupied by Americans during WWII is the real estate of grave yards in other countries.

Older Chinese populations grew to know this difference. They welcomed the American forces. From 1939 on, the "buzz" among Chinese peasants grew. The Americans did this or that. The arrival of the U.S. marines confirmed that the nightmare of Japan was over. And then, the Americans went home.

The brief exploits of American "voluntary" air force, the "Flying Tigers," led by General Claire Chennault in 1941 the early days of WWII were the stuff of legend. American's had been flying the "hump" over the Himalayas to supply arms and supplies to Chinese forces. Here and there, Americans trickled in before the war with Japan began in earnest in December 1941.

On April 18, 1942, American airplanes in a daring raid on Tokyo crash landed their B-25 bombers in China. It was a one-way on-the-edge mission to send a message to Japan flying high on its string of successes going back to the invasion of China.

To Asians of any politic in 1942, the American attack on Japan was a suicide mission. This was an unexpected event from a country of "decadent imperialists."

The American initiative led by a handful of "decadent imperial Americans" led to a conflict of perceptions. As in so much of Asia of the time, there was Asia and there was the rest of the world as an amorphous mass of "others" unless there was a significant civilization or politic that had an elevated advantage of intellect, industry or boldness/bravery/will-to-be.

Asians, and particularly Chinese, prided themselves on a stability of tradition going back five millennia. The Americans lacked a culture steeped in ancient tradition and were racially impure. They appeared undisciplined but inventive and reckless to a virtue. Even though their wealth alluded to spoiled character of low depth, they accomplished much.

American actions contradicted expectations. They came into to aid China in its fight against Japan. Far from home without the comforts of their culture, they fought in behalf of the Chinese and for three times the pay they received in other theatres of war. They risked much for profit. That fit well into the Chinese paradigm of risk and profit.

The Doolittle Raid became dramatized in a book and movie "Thirty Seconds over Tokyo." It became an iconic phrase of the daring of sixteen B-25 aircraft launched on a one-way flight.

Overall, the raid achieved its intended effect. Japan reacted to its vulnerability and shifted resources to homeland defense. The balls-all adventure raised morale in America as well as China. The Americans were coming. In China, they had already arrived.

Prior to "Thirty seconds over Tokyo," the stories of the Americans spread. The "Flying Tigers" boosted the morale of Chinese soldiers.

At the same time, the Japanese Navy sought to achieve an initial objective in the attack on Pearl Harbor. They meant to destroy America's aircraft carriers. Consequently, Japan committed its aircraft carriers against a tiny American outpost called Midway Island. It was a disaster for Japan crippling its ability to operate aircraft from its navy for the rest of the war.

Doolittle's bold raid on Japan made an invisible difference. It built a legacy in the minds of Asians who knew little else of America. Americans, despite their personal defects and low culture, were capable adversaries with the ability to surprise and come out on top.

The exploits of the Americans from the history of World War II to the present created an amalgam of expectations among Asians. They had returned to Viet Nam not as conquerors but as co-combatants in a cause of independence. Few South Vietnamese expected to become another colony of a western country.

NVA and Viet Cong promoted the opposite via indoctrination. America would essentially colonize South Viet Nam and eventually North Viet Nam. The story had mixed reviews and seldom took hold among the South Vietnamese caught in the middle.

The mystique of the American participation in Asian conflicts over the last 80 years persists to the present. Toan, as much as he cursed specific impressions of the Americans, wondered why Sai Gon could be left to suffer as happened on that horrible Tuesday.

Betrayal of Purpose

Toan wept silently at the repeat of events he experienced at the age of fifteen outside of Shanghai in 1937. Japanese aircraft rained bombs indiscriminately around the city and outlying villages. Virtually every village was bombed within a ten mile radius of Shanghai. Any building of significance was strafed or bombed. Factories, large shrines and warehouses were damaged if not leveled.

The thicker sections of red brick walls stood up to the concussions as the coconut roofing collapsed. Other homes caught fire. Motorized vehicles in the rubble burned. Oily black smoke rose from burning three-wheel trucks in the street. The dark smoke merged with white smoke of other fires throughout the city. The dust raised up by the artillery combined to create a haze that dimmed the sunlight. The ravaged neighborhood appeared as if at dusk. It was 10:00 AM in the morning on a cloudless day.

Toan wept as he hovered over his children in the sweltering heat of the hole in the ground. He wept knowing Viet Nam plunged into the dark ages. Civilization collapsed on Tuesday, April 29, 1975.

The miraculous marvelous spoiled-rotten amazing witless Americans weren't coming in to save the day. South Vietnamese were abandoned to their own purposes.

The tragedies enlarged in the ensuing days. Citizens of all manner and means, men and women of the Cholon committed suicide. Others disappeared in "extra-judicial executions." Whole families attempting to flee returned home to be caught and executed including one of Toan's brothers and family.

Nguyên Maï instructed Loan to shed tears for the fallen at her leisure. In the fight to survive, survive. Distraction and heart-felt emotions could be deadly. Indulge emotions when the luxury of time permits. Survive. Weep later.

Loan compressed in between her brothers stilled her heart and settled her mind waiting for the moment to crawl out of the hole. The beginning of bad days was now upon them.

Those Barges Have Sailed

As the city fell, Mai sorted among arrangements to transport for all the family to a barge that would take them to an American ship parked three miles east of the coastal town of Vung Tau. The US Navy had given her papers to make safe passage out of Viet Nam. She only had to get three dozen people to the docks on the Sai Gon River and sail into the unknown.

By mid-April, Maï knew that Hanoi marked her for destruction. She was unable to openly act. Assassins had moved into Sai Gon ahead of the NVA driving combatants such as her into hiding. Maï's public movements were restricted by threat to her family.

Maï's name was on the top of their "kill" list. Unwitting CIA operatives in Da Nang had not destroyed those documents and she was named in them. If the family did not make it to the American-chartered barges in the Sai Gon River, they could all be executed.

Loan's father did not know the full extent of this. It was a single instruction from his difficult wife. Get to the docks and find the Americans. Board the barge or ship. Tiring of his screaming tirades, Maï pleaded in her terse way.

"Do this one thing for the family. It may be all that we have left when Hanoi takes over. Move the family to the barges." Her pleas fell on deaf ears.

Toan's Perspective

Toan was unable to embrace the scope of disaster about to wash over South Viet Nam. Perhaps this was due to the fact that he and Maï had muddled through horror since their early days in southern China in the 1930s when Japan invaded Shanghai. If they didn't directly witness the atrocities of Japan, they knew of it through family and friends. Somehow, they waded through the horror and survived.

Times were tough and frightening but Toan and Maï managed to work through them. They adapted owing much to her father's and her resourcefulness in the 1940s. This was before an "iron curtain" descended upon communist-held East Germany creating a country with impenetrable borders and penalties of death imposed on anyone attempting to flee.

Toan was incapable of managing the move of family to the barges. What of his friends, his girlfriends, of having to manage life somewhere else than Viet Nam? He knew little and cared less of life outside of Asia. He might as well been asked to move everyone to the moon.

Toan's fears of moving to a truly alien world were understandable given some perspective. Toan's resistance takes on a reasonable view point. *(Author's Perspective: I have imagined someone asking my father to move our large family spread around the Albuquerque community to assemble at the airport and leave the formerly comfortable middle of the United States to relocate to a new home in Antarctica. He would have refused the concept from the beginning. He had a comfortable house in the city with many features of life he would lose by moving to Antarctica.)*

The United States Navy had a standing offer to move her mother and all of their family out of Viet Nam in reward for their service to America. It did not take into account the cultural issues of Chinese-Vietnamese and their concern for infirm family and deceased family. Who would watch over the graves of elders? The hesitance to flee Viet Nam delayed many. The selfishness of Asian male chauvinism killed many.

America's CIA originally estimated South Viet Nam could hold out for eighteen months starting in late-1974. It fell in less than six.

In the book *Decent Interval* by former CIA agent that was in Sai Gon down to its last days, Frank Snepp, he documented the situation well. Poor American decisions led to the early failure of South Viet Nam.

Frank Snepp's title is "tongue in cheek," the indecent abandonment of Viet Nam condemned many. It did not document the view from the Vietnamese who worked for the CIA and were stuck with their names on a hit list provided, of all things, from surviving documents uncovered in Da Nang. America had no end-game for their comrades in arms, the South Vietnamese. They anticipated events based on a number of errors, most of which that white Americans failed to fathom the complexity of Asians.

Old Asian ethics made the situation worse. No one refuted the wisdom of Chinese elders. Families lingered as authoritarian old men pondered the wisdom of fleeing. Americans misread Asian culture and politics.

Above all, Asians misread themselves and the cost of their intractability. Entire families suffered and died as a result.

South Viet Nam fell too soon to help people seeking a life in an open economy with basic freedoms. With the help of Russia and China, the Viet Nam War became The United States of America's first-ever loss.

Defeat isn't quite the right term here. America left the fight to let the Vietnamese to go it alone. It was euphemistically called the "Viet Namization" of the Viet Nam War. America through LBJ and Nixon inflated a war in a country and region it barely understood. In 1969 with over half a million American personnel in Viet Nam, the United States withdrew its support for reasons Vietnamese to this day cannot understand.

The tragedy: South Viet Nam, misunderstanding the mercurial politics (resolve) in America, placed their faith in the United States to help them remain independent of Hanoi. Four decades later, some of the surviving Vietnamese warriors do not yet know why America left.

(In the summer of 2012 in Ho Chi Minh City (Sai Gon), Vietnamese veterans asked me: "Why did America leave?")

It was more than that to the Vietnamese left with a country in total chaos. The hope created in the early 1960s by the United States disappointed an Asian nation addicted to the largesse of the most powerful economic engine of the world. America, with all of its magical skills and legends of its deeds in World War II, enthused and subsequently disappointed Southeast Asia.

Smart Vietnamese did not understand the mercurial aspects of America and its two-party system of politics. It did not fathom the blithering largesse of the ego-centric President Lyndon Baines Johnson, the impact of an assassinated John F. Kennedy or the tragic effects of Richard M. Nixon and Watergate. Most of all, it did not measure the emerging liberalism of America's Democratic Party that was capable of destroying futures of whole segments of people through its capricious largesse and consequences of their abundant ignorance of history.

The kingdom of Saudi Arabia offered to stay the disaster in the last weeks. Unfortunately, an untimely assassination spoiled the offer in the last months of Sai Gon. It might have bought some time. Inevitably, the support could delay but not prevent wholesale tragedy. In the end, $25 million of aid as South Viet Nam teetered on collapse might not have mattered.

The immense capability of America clashed with the unmovable resolution of an Asian ethic going back millennia. Western thinking, looming disaster and insufficient planning proved unpersuasive to win over ancient Asian culture. Many Vietnamese were doomed.

East Meets West Badly in Viet Nam

Much of the population at risk waited on the wisdom of stubborn men incapable of quickly making life saving decisions. The expedience of brash American arrogance bolstered by marvelous deadly technology clashed with the venerated traditions of Asian elders.

Ensuing cruelty of Hanoi's vengeful NVA cadre compelled intractable South Vietnamese to re-consider the wisdom of flight. Viet Nam's coastline became a porous barrier to intrepid Asians.

Quality of life for all Vietnamese fell as an incompetent core of victors drove the entire country into the dark ages. Over the next decade, many victors of the long war joined the losers in hazardous flight to other countries.

The new regime patrolled the coastline and initially killed refugees including would-be fugitives captured during secret preparations. Hanoi interned all captured escapees in the "re-education camps" until the Orderly Dispersal Program (ODP) started a decade later.

Mai was high on the "wanted list." Discovery meant death. Flight risked death. Flight also cost gold.

There was the high hurdle of cost. The going price for escape was 15 ounces of gold *($20,000/person in 2015)*. For several dozen immediate family members, 400 ounces was an impossible sum. She refused to consider leaving anyone behind. o one left.

Another option was buying or building a boat. Unfortunately, none of them knew anything about boats and sea travel. Except for two or Loan's brothers, no one knew how to swim. Over the next decade, these deficiencies proved no obstacle to desperate people.

By all appearances, the American participation forestalled inevitable North Viet Nam's consolidation with South Viet Nam. That "first domino" fell in 1975 and took several others with it. Cambodia and Laos fell into similar darkness. Corruption, cruelty and mass murder expanded to appalling dimensions west and north to the borders of Thailand and China.

Wandering warrior aspects of America's "limited war" bombed Cambodia gave additional excuse to the Khmer Rouge to rain chaos on the ancient civilization that was Cambodia. A toothless and witless kingdom capitulated to martial law that migrated into a communist dictatorship. It wiped out the national core of Cambodia's educated, skilled and caring citizens. Cambodia and Laos may never recover from their descent into darkness within in the next century.

Loan's Moment

Loan cowered as explosions shredded lives and the neighborhood. She shivered in the dimness below clouds of smoke, dust, and foulness of burning dead as whole families perished in the barrage. Improbable images of shaking skies and pieces of neighborhood flying upside down overhead visit her dreams to this day. Lesser chaos seldom disturbed her for the rest of her life.

Thus started her journey through improbable trials few could survive. She had no plan other than find a better way, to find an opening to a better life. Find that opening, to fresh air, to the light, perhaps a full stomach every few days … out to something better

Viet Nam's coastline was a barrier that eventually became a milestone. She survived despite the best advice of older people who failed to heed their own instruction. Loan crossed a number of coastlines and return to Viet Nam to everyone's surprise and amazement.

From April 30, 1975, the day celebrated by the revolutionary regime as the Fall of Sai Gon, the rise of Loan's story begins.

End of Section 1

SECTION TWO: JUNGLE COAST

June 1977, Late Afternoon
Western Coastal Jungle, Bataan Peninsula, Luzon, Philippines

N arrow face dogs probed the underbrush with their snouts. In open air, they raised or lowered their heads or moved them left and right to capture scents. The animals interrupted their panting to sample the air as they chased elusive odors. Strength of the scent in one direction or another gave them the track on their quarry.

The knee-high dogs had small pointed snouts that made their fangs seem over-large when exposed. They traveled in a loose pack number often more than a dozen. Their range of sizes and mottled tan coats indicated a mixture of breeds, the largest standing less than two feet at the shoulder, and weighing less than forty pounds. The dogs descended from Philippine pets that had gone feral a century ago.

The dogs moved down the jungle hillside toward the rugged shoreline. Lead dogs panted in the steamy heat breaking the silence with a low bark or yip to redirect the attention of younger dogs. Subtle changes in the yips of senior pack members meant everything from alerts to calling other dogs together.

On occasion, they lost the direction of the source when wind gusts parted jungle canopy and churned the air near the ground. Breezes mixed the aromas of rotten vegetation on the jungle floor with the perfumes of tropical flowers.

The pack became noisy when they lost the track. Low ranking dogs watched and listened to the alpha male to know direction of travel. The importance of the scent; the track of carrion was their lifeline.

The pack crossed the lost track as it deployed a rhythmic movement along the line of the lost trail. In a wilderness ballet, they shifted one from another. Each played its part to find the lost scent. They avoided clusters and spread out to cover more area, repeating practiced head actions, sniffing the air.

One dog picked up a trace and yipped to the others. As if on cue, the spread out pack-members gathered to the successful dog. They packed together behind the "nose" that had the scent.

A day-long storm kept the dogs down in their jungle lair. Unable to hunt in the wind and heavy rain, they had grown hungry. As the storm passed at midday, they smelled animal flesh turning ripe in the afternoon sun.

The pack slowed their movements as they emerged into lighter areas of the forest. Angled shafts of light split jungle interior otherwise locked in twilight. Even below a cloudless midday sun, the jungle floor remained dark.

The animals preferred dim surrounds; open sky alarmed them. Clearings and light exposed them to danger. Wariness, legacy knowledge, passed down from generation to generation from when they were domesticated animals when they were pet, servant and among some Filipino people, food. Older dogs knew the thunder-sound of guns that dropped a pack-member to the ground without a fight.

The pack's wariness included a natural regard for snakes, wild boars, macaques and small panthers. They also had a new competitor; hairless monkeys that traveled upright on hind legs. The hairless animals, new to this wilderness, acted odd, routing other carnivores from food they didn't eat.

The pack's numbers ran off boars and rats from carrion. Dogs took their due leaving the scraps to other scavengers. The boars, pigs, rats and flies consumed the rest.

Serpents were another matter; dogs, too small to endure a full dose of venom, avoided conflict with snakes. Boar's possessed tougher hide yielded less to snake bites; dogs deferred the issue of snakes to the wild pigs.

Macaques annoyed the dog's domain more than it threatened. The opportunistic omnivores consumed undefended food. The macaques traveled in troupes and ranged from six to several dozen or more.

Numbers implied strength. However, the dogs routed them with ease. The bothersome animals retreated to the trees to taunt the pack and posed no threat.

Macaques often foraged on the ground but moved into the trees when threatened. They lacked physical design to deal with packs of dogs. The arboreal animals possessed large teeth, agile hands, and advanced brains. However, the packs of witless dogs and powerful boars ran them off or killed them. Hapless monkeys made acceptable fare to the ground dwelling predators. Macaques could strip a defenseless carcass but they had easier but less delectable food options in the trees.

Jungle Shore

Similar to the macaques, the hairless monkeys also retreated to the trees at the first sign of dogs. However, this small group had become bold in recent days. What changed? The shy monkeys had become aggressive. Weak as they were, they no longer retreated in a fight over carrion.

Domain for large animals in the Bataan peninsula split among three realms, jungle floor, in the trees and the shoreline. The rugged coastline separated territory between sea and land creatures. Inland meant less-contested food. Shoreline where the three land domains met led to complications.

Ancient lava flows ran into the sea and broke up the coastline. There was no continuous beach. Constant wave action polished and wetted the rocky cliffs making climbing along the shoreline treacherous. Heavy rains and tremors loosened the mountain slopes and littered the cliffs with boulders and rock slides. Hard surfaces near the sea stay wet and treacherous. Each year, one or two careless members of the dog pack died among the boulders and crashing waves.

Only mammal flesh drew the wild dogs from their jungle sanctuary. The pack dwelled upland in the jungles and avoided the sea. Scavenging among the treacherous rocks was seldom worth the risk.

In the last eighteen months, this unforgiving seaside real estate rarely proved a productive place for food. However, something changed. Large numbers of bloated carcass began to appear on the jagged cliffs and in the boulders at water's edge.

Prevailing west winds blew off the South China Sea driving any-thing afloat into the shore. Large waves deposited debris and dead mammals along seventy miles (100 kilometers) of rugged coastline.

The west winds blended the smells of dead animals, sea-air, and aroma of jungle floor. A strong wind mixed and diluted the scents. Carrion became harder to locate.

Wind shifts forced the pack to spread out, enlarging their move-ments to recapture a thin scent trail. They expanded sensory swings back and forth suspending forward progress when the scent altogether disappeared. Then the pack waited for one dog or another to detect the track. A few barks hustled the pack toward the successful dog. The lead male accepted the track moving toward the source.

Low in the Philippine sky, the drooping position of the sun prod-ded the pack to hurry. Jungle animals knew the measure of the day by the change in light; daylight would soon fade to total darkness under the canopy. When night fell, there was absolute obscurity. Even a dog's keen vision failed. Outside of their lair, lone dogs were vulner-able to boars and small Philippine panthers. There was also the matter of dangerous ravines that split open the unforgiving terrain of Bataan.

Instinct and experience urged them to locate the meat soon or head back to the lair before night fell. Dogs had another concern besides locating the carrion on the shoreline before nightfall; they detected the scent of man-flesh, the naked tailless monkeys. The strange animals were upwind, perhaps near the carrion they sought.

Creatures unfamiliar to the Philippine peninsula showed up in jungle many months before. The unusual monkeys exhibited odd behavior; they protected carrion that washed into the shoreline. The strange thing was they didn't consume the dead animals they shielded. They only ran off the dogs, boars and rats seeking nourishment from the inert flesh on the shore.

The dogs expected to possess carrion on the shoreline unchal-lenged. The strange apes changed the situation.

Fourteen degrees north of the equator, the year-round growing season yielded constant bounties of fruit. Tropical vegetation sus-tained wide variety of animals. To a point, the fruit fed herbivores, ultimately feeding meat-eaters. However, an ecological ratio was out of balance, there were too many carnivores in Bataan.

The boars, dogs, rats and jungle cats competed for limited quantities of flesh. The carnivore population, decimated by the fighting forces during World War II, had returned. In the rugged Bataan coastline, the meat eaters in the 1970s had few predators other than themselves. The demand for animal flesh grew with their numbers. For all the bounty of jungle growth, shoreline carrion was hotly contested.

In the last year, abundant carrion was readily found on the western shoreline. The pack learned to patrol the shoreline after storms. A few days of bad weather on the South China Sea left the shoreline littered with bloated dead animals. A dogs' domesticated immune system had also gone feral; most any meat no matter the state of decay was appropriate fare.

This hunt marked territory in addition to being a contest over resources. The canines marked trees and rocks along the shoreline to forewarn if not intimidate competing packs. However, feral pigs and boars ignored the markings.

Wild swine competed with packs for shoreline carrion. Boars tended to travel alone and avoided dogs, however, when cornered; they could injure or kill full grown canines. Pigs traveled in numbers. Regardless, they yielded to larger numbers of dogs.

Macaques dominated the various troupes of monkeys defended their territory in the trees for arboreal fruit, insects and an occasional gecko or rat. They taunted dogs as matter of sport and showed little interest in the dead animals washing up on the shoreline.

Until now.

Up to recent times, the monkeys ignored the gift of easy meat on the shoreline. Unfamiliar alien apes contested dogs over the bounty with a curious distinction; they did not leave their scent on the carrion. When dogs ran across food previously denied, interfering alien monkeys did not consume the dead animals they defended. The diminutive apes challenged dogs for meat they did not eat.

Dogs acquired a new respect for the odd-looking alien monkeys standing on their hind legs. Small and few as they were, they held their ground. These odd creatures swung dangerous sticks and lifted hurtful rocks into the air. They did something else unexpected and unknown to denizens of a tropical jungle, the monkeys maintained fire in their ground lair. The dogs had lost their memory of fire; the illumination at night was as if the sun was on the earth at night. The fire introduced new scents as well, the aroma of cooked flesh of lizards and fish.

When encountered outside of their shelter, the unusual animals moved up into the trees. These monkeys planned ahead, storing food and stones in hollowed out limbs. They could remain for days in the trees able to eat and sleep in the branches and hurl rocks down on pack members.

They made high-pitched screams with their small-toothed mouths, delivered pain with hard flying objects. Unlike other simians, these cunning monkeys intruded the forested mountains of Bataan and violated the domain of the canine pack.

The long day of rain and wind rain ended; the hungry pack became restless. Their hunger motivated them to investigate the shore line and the alien monkeys if necessary. Up to now, the agile and nervous canines had faced two of these curious animals. Now, the pack had six strong seasoned adult males and a similar number of capable females. This would be the day dogs overwhelmed the strange competitors. This would assure that the abundant animal flesh showing up on the eastern edge of the South China Sea belonged to the pack.

The animals, a wild off-shoot of Malaysian Telemonian dogs, roamed the forests of Bataan on the western coast of the Philippine archipelago. They became feral and semi-social, hunting in groups, hailing back to the pack instincts of ancient wolf ancestors in another continent a million years before. Coming from Eurasian climates, they had migrated with the movements of mankind arriving in the Philippines fifty thousand years ago.

The Philippines descended into chaos three decades before as Japan brutalized the archipelago during World War II. Resistant farmers died by the thousands leaving farmland to languish. Their pets managed to survive among a collapsing civilization in 1941. Generations later, dogs returned to the wilderness with few instincts other than to avoid man.

Civilization in the Philippines collapsed in 1941; it was a desperate time. Filipino guerillas added anything to their diet Japanese soldiers had not already confiscated from the population. Asians, accustomed to dog meat, resorted to canine flesh to head off starvation.

Canine survivors in the wilderness rapidly developed a wariness of man. Contact with humanity meant destruction during WWII and beyond.

They had tan and white short-hair coats that wrapped a tight mus-
cled body of fifteen to twenty kilos. Their oversized ears and narrow
muzzle, open and non-threatening, obscured the fact they attacked
almost any single animal with their numbers. Packs of dogs threatened any animal smaller than the wild Indian elephants, larger boars
and man. Even then, a grown man was not a match for a motivated
and hungry pack. Filipino natives avoided packs of feral dogs.

Dogs knew of men and avoided contact with fishing villages dot-
ting the western Philippine coastline. Men captured or killed careless
pack members. Cautious tendencies bred into successive generations
enabling stronger groups of feral dogs to thrive. The packs lived
unmanaged and untamed on the frontier of civilization, as it was, of
the Philippine western coastline.

Dogs failed to treat the odd hairless monkeys as immature members of a human community. The size of the two creatures they had
encountered misled their instincts. They hunted an unfamiliar version
of man; they hunted and challenged young Vietnamese girls.

Vietnamese Girls

The pack competed with two young females lost from humankind in
another part of the world. The war in Viet Nam, subsequent collapse of
Sai Gon in 1975 and exodus of millions of Vietnamese pushed many
people into hostile wilderness throughout southern and Southeast Asia.

Many died of horrible misfortune as they made a desperate journey to a better life; some landed in unreceptive and untamed regions,
others passed out of Asia and ended up in other countries. As two-
million-plus people fled horrendous tragedy of South Viet Nam after
1975, it thrust upon many regions of southern Asia a population
struggling in the extreme to survive utter chaos.

The packs emerged from the chaos of WWII and thrived in the
isolation of western Bataan for decades. The aftermath of the end of
the Viet Nam War created a new situation for a tragedy of the Viet
Nam War and its aftermath. The calamity of refugees fleeing was
physically evident on the Philippine coast line. Broken boats along with
Vietnamese dead and dying washed ashore and rotted on the western
coastline of Bataan.

Dogs were hungry for meat. So were boars, feral pigs, panthers
and rats. Dogs dominated the top of the shallow food chain; they had

the numbers and social structure to take the bounty of the sea as they wished...until ten months ago. The new monkeys stood upright and carried tools; they showed up and disturbed the dogs' world.

Animals don't distinguish between sacred and essential where food is concerned. Meat is meat. There is no other ethic among the canine packs than survive.

The Vietnamese girls were not animals. Dead humans on the shoreline represented the last connection to a civilization they had lost. Preservation of their dignity was essential to their comfort of find their way out of jungle and back to Sai Gon. They would practice what they knew of life in Viet Nam in this wilderness as best they could. They would protect the Vietnamese bodies on the shoreline from predation. As best they could.

In the summer of 1977, human artifacts of man at war merged with raw nature on the Bataan coastline. The packs of wild dogs were competing with three young Vietnamese girls stranded in a jungle domain. It was the dog's jungle domain.

While dogs treated them as intruders, the girls thought they were still in a world of blood kin and ancestors. For all they knew, they had remained in Viet Nam. To them, these feral animals were a neighbor's pet turned bad. They expected better behavior of dogs. One of the girls suggested finding the owner of the pets and complain. After all, this was Viet Nam where manners and conduct were important.

Carrion

A new scent distracted dogs from the hunt, sniffing with their noses again low and high as they approached the shoreline, the underbrush and the trees thinned. The alpha male yipped, shifting his path, leading the pack to the new scent. The air blowing off the edge of the South China Sea had an unmistakable odor of dead mammals.

The dominant aroma was the sickly sweet stink of human flesh ripening in the afternoon sun. The stench alarmed the pack. Where there is death, they expected to confront predators competing for the meat.

The lead male warily crossed a ledge above a sloping pile of broken volcanic rocks and jumbled boulders. Others of higher rank in the pack joined him. In moments, a dozen dogs of several sizes with coats of varying colors and patterns crept out of jungle underbrush keeping a distance from the edge of the sea.

Bordering the Philippine jungle and the South China Sea, dogs stood twenty feet above churning water. Transition existed between jungle and sea in this region did not exist.

The dogs stood on a high ledge without a canopy of shading trees. Jungle was their home. South China Sea formed absolute boundary of a dogs' world. The sea meant death, going too far inland meant capture and death, the inhospitable mountains in between meant life.

Below them, the sea crashed into jagged shoreline chock-a-block with boulders piled against eroding cliffs. This rugged shoreline built up from prehistoric volcanic flows formed a sweeping crescent bay. Formerly part of the land, submerged boulders lurked at the foot of the cliffs and became exposed briefly in the troughs of large waves.

This area of Bataan lacked open beach. Large rocks and boulders from the mountain slopes littered ancient lava flows that intersected the sea at steep angles. Hapless land animals that fell into the sea could only swim along the shoreline in hope of finding an opening to the ledges above.

Lingering in water near the cliffs was often fatal; the turbulent surf dashed anything near the edge into the rocks. Creatures thrown up on the ledges by large waves more often fertilized the forest at the edge the sea.

These waters, rich in marine life, were tempting, dangerous and foreboding. Filipino fishermen rarely risked fishing in the treacherous shallows close to shore as the waters were seldom calm. Shattered fishing boats of less prudent captains littered the waters of the region.

Areas facing west toward Viet Nam had a six hundred mile fetch of open sea. The strongest prevailing winds on the South China Sea blew east. However, the monsoon seasons of Asia meant, as the word implied, big shifts of wind and moisture movement. The rocky coastline of this section of the Bataan was an anvil; the wind and waves, the hammer.

Bataan's western jungle coastline thrived on mayhem from the sea. Most plant life thrived only when set back ten meters or fifteen meters above the water. Storms and high winds frequently sent immense waves on top of the rocks poisoning topsoil if not washing it into the sea. Even then, waves broke over the high cliffs frequently depositing jetsam and flotsam including dead animals on top of high cliffs.

Steady streams of scavengers consumed the detritus. The animals in their afterlife fertilized the jungle ecology.

Coastal fishing villages dotted less mountainous shoreline tens of miles north and south of the region. People lived where the cliffs gave way to open beaches and milder terrain set back from the sea.

Any man or beast that made it to land on the rugged shoreline had little choice but to travel inland over the mountains. "Beach travel" was perilous in the extreme and they had no idea of how far they had to go. Rugged adults would have trouble. Going eastward and inland was their only choice.

The mountains, covered by prehistoric pyroclastic flows, possessed treacherous ravines and chasms. Tropical rains cut into loose volcanic deposits creating ravines a meter or two across and twenty meters or more deep. Ferns and vines often concealed the narrow openings. Bones of hapless animals littered the bottom of deeper ravines. The bones included those of hapless man who fell to their death or starved unable to climb out.

People who crashed landed here had two options to reach civilization, climb out to the east toward Manila or swim. As a people in 1977, most Asians who were not of fishing-families never learned to swim.

Most of the Asians making landfall that year were dead. They weren't Conquistadors invading a new land, they were refugees fleeing an old land. The few survivors eventually climbed the mountains to find civilization, as it was, in Manila. Along the way, human and animal bones mixed together at the bottom of many hidden ravines. For a time, the inland jungles of Bataan were fertilized by the aftermath of the fall of Sai Gon.

An hour from sunset, dogs became nervous. A bright yellow sun hung in a blue cloudless tropical sky above the flat horizon of a blue-green roiling sea. The low undiminished sun lit up the surface of the rough sea and produced a blinding glare.

Darkness fell quickly in the tropics; it also brought danger. Standing in the late afternoon sunlight on the western shore, the pack hurried to find carrion.

Dogs faced a stiff onshore wind laden with salt spray that stung their eyes and nasal passages. They squinted into the light and the wind to locate the sources of the stench. The jungle edge behind them blew about, wind moving palm and banana fronds wildly. Behind them rose the mountainous jungle and below them lay the irregular plain of a roiling sea.

Large rolling waves crashed into the rocks below spraying fans and jets of frothing water high on the shore. The on-shore winds whipped spray off the crests of waves and great splashes. Wetted rocks and ledges all along the shallow bay glistened in the low angle sunlight, adding to the afternoon glare.

Pursuit of mammal flesh proved intimidating. Only hunger for the meat kept them from dashing back into the sheltering jungle and away from the stink of salty ocean.

Dogs studied the roiling ocean for just a moment; the dangerous edge of their world held no utility for them. They had come this close to the water only because their noses led them here. Somewhere on this hazardous frontier, they had detected something of better worth; red meat. Their concern for the hairless monkeys could wait.

The alpha-male led the pack along the ledge, their heads rising high and then dropping low, scanning with brief pulsing sniffs for carrion on the shore. They looked for sea birds or vultures that might give away the location of the meat.

In the high wind, the carrion-feeders had trouble with the shifting air currents. In unfriendly weather, the scavenger birds were elsewhere, consuming easier prey. Another dog picked up the scent again and yipped to the others to follow. They moved north along the ledge overlooking the water.

Bounty on the sea-side ledge

The carcass of the animal lay on a ledge just above the large rocks that broke the waves. Had the carrion been lodged lower down in the boulders near the violent surf, it would have been out of reach. Even impulsive members of the pack avoided the ledges near the water; unpredictable waves often broke over the higher rocky surface washing hapless members into the sea.

The wild dogs, acceptable swimmers in fast-flowing rivers, avoided this churning water and uneven coastline. This edge of the South China Sea executed even the most durable creatures who carelessly embraced its violent nature.

The saw tooth shoreline remained unforgiving. Even when weather was calm and the sea still, the treacherous reputation among Filipino fishermen persisted; this was no-man's coastline. Westerly winds rising meant the jagged shore line loaded with cliffs and boulders became deadly to humans. The Filipino fisherman called this shoreline the dead-man's fishery. Fishing near shore was the folly of ambitious men. This bountiful shoreline took more than it gave.

The dog pack moved down to the edge and spotted the remains of the animal. Similar to many other animal remains that appeared on this coast in the last few months, the bloated creature was hairless except for its mane of long black hair. They found the creature head down, a conical straw hat attached to its body by a string.

The carcass, covered in a black cloth with exposed hairless flesh turning red emitted gases from internal decay forming in the skin and muscle. The animal had died a day before. The lower part of its back legs, partially mutilated by something in the sea or recently on the land, was partly missing. Likely suspects: land crabs, jungle rats, and scavenger birds.

The bloated female form of human rotted in its horizontal recline on the shore, dogs recognized the woman's body as an unspecific animal. To them, this became easy meat. Domestic dogs were loyal to the living. Humans that dominated their world and bred them for pets and servants lost alpha status when dogs went feral. Masters became food same as any animal.

These were jungle dogs; they owed their fidelity to pack and stomach. (*and maybe breeding rights later on*). The alpha male moved up to the foreleg of the woman that lay outstretched, sniffing around the limb. The odors, rancid in its nose, remained acceptable for consumption. The carcass would remain acceptable fare for another day.

It knew from the rank that the meat would be foul beyond usefulness before very long. The few crabs that made it up here would be joined by maggots and rats already working on the carcass. Dogs mastered the retching reflex, rats had evolved to ignore it.

The flesh would be sufficient for durable digestive systems if they moved quickly. The leader made the decision, this pack benefitted from this carcass today. Summer meant warmer seas and changing weather, now was the time to act.

Other dogs stayed back watching and sniffing as the lead male nipped at the woman's right forearm. Its strange limb had long toes without claws; it was similar to the forepaw of the monkeys they hunted. If this creature stood up right, they would have known the animal belonged to mankind. Prone, it was just another mammal. Dead but not over-ripe, the carcass was meat.

The bites elicited more stink, the creature remained dead and inoffensive. The dog bit hard into the flesh, shaking its head back and forth to separate meat from bone. He chewed on the tough drying flesh separating meat and skin from the limb. The pack watched the alpha male in appreciation; he determined what would be acceptable to them.

As the alpha male peeled away flesh from the forearm, other dogs took their cue and moved into to do the same. Half a dozen adults jostled around each other making a rough circle around the carcass. Dogs nipped at one another as they vied for position in the hierarchy of the pack.

The alpha allowed each dog in the pecking order of the pack to move to successive lesser places to feed. Younger dogs circled the group waiting for their turn. Sated adults of higher position yielded to lower rank to exploit the feast. In short order, this creature's flesh would feed the entire pack today.

A few minutes into feast, the alpha male backed away from the human corpse. He sniffed the air of something upwind, something familiar and threatening. This odd movement of the lead dog signaled other upper hierarchy dogs nearby to do the same. He backed out of the feeding circle to focus on the new scent; a large rock flew out of the blinding low sun into the pack hitting a lower ranked female in the back. The dog yelped spinning around growling, looking for its attacker. Out of the afternoon glare, more rocks flew into the circle of dogs. The feeding dogs scattered, a few rushing into the underbrush.

Above the wind and crash of the waves, they heard screams as the hail of projectiles pummeled the group, missing but landing close. Chunks of pumice and sandstone cracked about on the rocky surface. The noise startled the nervous animals. They reluctantly gave ground, barking out the universal canine message of distrust and curiosity, "What is it? What is it?" or "Stay away! Stay away!" until they returned with the standard bark: "What is it?"

The startled dogs strained to look up the shoreline into the sun hanging low above the horizon. Three hairless monkeys brandished large sticks and hurled rocks at them. They screamed at the pack, waving their forelegs above their heads, each carrying a long stick in a five-fingered hand.

The monkeys appeared to be charging them. This challenged the experience of the alpha male; the long-tailed macaques made threatening barks only from the security of the trees.

The unexpected attack stampeded younger dogs into the forest. The alpha male and two older dogs retreated a distance as if to defend the corpse. The girls pressed the challenge, the dogs retreated.

For months, there were only two that challenged the pack. Now, three animals confronted them. The hairless tail-less monkeys had become aggressive, rushing the pack of dogs. Their timidity was gone. The odd monkeys took action, moving closer, swinging the long sticks and throwing more rocks, barking and screeching at the animals brave enough to test them.

The alpha male had limited contact with the fishing villages, these creatures reminded him of man. The monkeys acted like half-sized humans. This unexpected behavior elicited curiosity in the dog. However, further study would wait; the pack was clearly ambushed and retreated out of surprise.

As far as the alpha-male expected, this meat belonged to the pack. However, the alien monkeys had twisted the situation around by throwing hurtful rocks and challenging dogs in their strange barks. Damaging objects landed on them. The pack of animals had been focusing on the hunt for easy food. They found themselves in ambush. The surprise attack of weaker animals routed a strong dog pack.

He was reluctant to give way to the strange animals but in the face of this onslaught, he chose flight. He yipped at the other dogs to follow as he headed for the forest; the remaining dogs yipped back in response as they turned and followed.

Feral dogs unaccustomed to man treated the young girls as another form of monkey. That could be their only measure. Somewhere in the evolution of wolves-that-became-dogs, the interaction modified dogs to respond to humans. However, there was no real memory of man.

Unlike other creatures living in the trees near the coastline, these monkeys stood and ran upright on hind legs without relying on their forelegs to prop them up. The common Philippine long-tailed macaque moved about with the use of its forelegs (arms) as forward support. The macaques relied on the trees for sanctuary, waiting out the occasional siege of dogs.

These terrible new marauding monkeys stood firmly on two feet freeing their forelegs (arms) and paws (hands) to manipulate harmful objects that hurt dogs. They were something apart from the long-tailed macaques. These monkeys delivered harm from a distance.

Except for their manes of long black hair, the monkeys' hairless bodies appeared weak. Their teeth were short with small incisors. Their bite could not harm. Thin and lacking great muscle, they ran slowly on spindly hind legs; unable to jump more than half their own height. Their over-sized heads made them ungainly.

What they lacked in strength, they compensated by using objects to extend their reach. They applied something unlike other animals; they had tools and more, they had weapons. They carried sticks and rocks delivering pain and damage from a distance.

These alien monkeys hurled rocks skyward to land on their ene-mies. They jabbed and swung large sticks; the motion of such an action appeared harmful, even deadly. Their barks were complicated and car-ried more information. They also revealed something dog packs had missed before; they now traveled in a pack of three.

Three hairless monkeys wielding sticks and rocks showed resolve. Initial hesitance and fear exhibited months before vanished when two became three.

Three bold monkeys over-powered a pack of a dozen dogs. They did so with weapons, cunning and guts. For the first time, the scrawny spindly animals that barely stood upright worked together as a pack. Shock and awe ruled the moment and this day.

The surprised dogs had few choices for the moment. They had to yield, give up the dead animal on the shore and seek the sanctuary of the jungle. Dogs ran into the underbrush and up into the jungle; the alpha-male paused on the ledge to study his attackers one last time and then he turned to join his pack inland. They retreated to the shadows and stopped, checking if the monkeys followed them into the gloom of the forest.

Dogs made their way silently up the mountain. They would eat rotten fruit and chew grass that night instead of meat. As a rule, domesticated dogs lose the association between wrong action and pain if the span of time is greater than three seconds. In essence, the dogs retreated for other reasons and would forget the lesson of dealing with the strange monkeys. They would repeat the conflict again. Such were the ways of dogs.

The pack thrives by the immediacy of the experiences of the alpha-male. It would learn little today that it could use tomorrow. It would repeat the mistake because the girls did not land enough harm to change the dogs "algorithm," if you will, on how it should change its behavior.

The three monkeys did not pursue the dogs into the jungle. Their interest: preserve the sanctity of the dead animal on the shore. The carcass of the woman was of their race, perhaps even of their kin.

Dogs bided their time in the jungle anticipating another time to strike. However the energies of conflict work between man and beast, the dogs sorted out to retire and fight another day.

Loan's View of the Dogs

One of the three girls studied the dogs' retreat into the jungle knowing them to stay away only when the girls defend the body. The other girls moved up to the woman's prone form, taking care to stay upwind of the partially mutilated body. Carrying long thick sticks and vine-wrapped satchels made of banana leaves strapped over one of their shoulders, they lacked clothing.

They were unashamedly naked. Two of the three were thin and darkly tanned with long black hair down to the middle of their backs. All of them were agile and confident for girls at such an age. They survived events that killed smart adults.

The oldest girl's body showed the early stages of womanly maturing (budding breasts and the hint of pubescent hair) but little else distinguished their ages. Their ages ranged from nine to thirteen.

Other than putting a handful of mint leaves to their nose or glancing at the forest to watch for the dog's return, they appeared to be emotionless about the dead woman. Quiet and expressionless, they motioned to each other to look at something or move about, speaking a few instructions to each other in Southern Vietnamese. They remained all business on a grim task; they had done this before.

Their movements resembled the conduct of older adolescents, not pre-pubescent girls. Having survived murderous misfortune; they had become adult more than their years suggested.

Animals had torn open the woman's right arm outstretched from her body, her diminutive hand curled into a rigid fist. The ragged opening, bloodless; her life's fluids had congealed the day before.

Dogs had spent effort on the woman's black blouse to access softer nourishing tissues underneath. The Vietnamese cotton clothing proved resilient; the sharp canines of the animals only managed to expose the skin of her back before they fled.

The darkened skin had a waxy appearance mottled with darker patches. The woman had long straight black hair splayed forward around her head by the waves. Long black hair confounded cutting teeth, forcing dogs to focus on other parts of the body. The pack had been ineffective; the woman's body remained well intact.

Holding her breath, the eleven-year-old Hué squatted down "Asian-style" on her heels by the woman's left shoulder and untied the conical rice-straw hat. The girl treasured the ubiquitous nón lá of Viet Nam, the ubiquitous "coolie hat." The hat lay near the woman's head. Hué set the hat aside to consider whether to take back to camp. They discussed taking the head cover. To their Asian thinking, the dead woman still owned it.

In another circumstance in distant parts part of the world in a different culture, survivors in a similar circumstance would have removed the woman's clothing to extend their chances of survival. However, this shoreline remained an extension of South East Asian culture. Even in the depths of chaos, Vietnamese girls required the consent and guidance of adults for any action with other adults.

Thúy at 13 would be regarded as a child. Status changed when she started menstruating. Their erratic diet and the stress of coping in the wilderness suppressed the development of a cycle. Thúy remained a child.

These immature females managed within the mores of their culture as dictated by their parents. They knew touching the woman's clothing meant disrespect. Respect, not revulsion, prevented them from taking anything from the woman.

The body decayed rapidly in the tropical heat and the sun. The dead woman's skin swelled almost visibly; the heat of the equatorial sun decay cooked the woman's internal organs. The corpse pulsed out an unbearable stench. Had they been able to get the stink of decay out of the clothing, the issue of dealing with the dead woman's ghosts remained.

Dogs worked on the body briefly; most of the Vietnamese woman's body remained intact. They observed the side of her head but avoided seeing her face.

Bad luck fell upon those looking upon dead people's faces outside of a proper ceremony. The older girls learned from their parents about what to do when confronted with dead elders. They knew the basics of what pleased and angered ghosts: (1) be respectful when viewing the face, (2) immediate family could touch the body of blood-kin and (3) don't trifle with the disappointment of ghosts.

The central theme of Asian culture is of strength of character, respect and honor. It has lasted them for over five thousand years enabling a sense of continuity at least that old. Chinese culture provided guidance and produced burden; the girls held to a specific discipline about death that at times disappointed their heart.

The female had been dead a day, maybe two. Curious about her time in the sea before she washed ashore, the answer remained beyond the forensic skills of pre-teen girls. Her body was returning to nature. Swollen tissues blotted out the definition of age.

Age was a curiosity on this shoreline. Of the hundreds of dead that washed ashore, few were adult, none was male. Besides Loan, few children washed ashore alive. Vietnamese women tended to be small; hard to tell if she was adult or child.

Important issues remained. There was the matter of ghosts.

According to the mores of their culture, the woman's ghost lingered near the remains. The girls honored their parents by being respectful to their elders, even deceased ones. Respect bought insurance against the wrath of spirits. The girls avoided a dead person's phantom whenever possible.

If the female had been poor or young, she might only have one ghost. However, if she had been powerful and bore many children in life, she might have many spirits intent on guiding her benefits in the afterlife. Simple instructions applied; don't mess with phantoms.

Thúy, at thirteen, as the oldest girl, decided for them as she constantly did, to avoid contact with bodies. The woman resided in Buddha's hands, regardless, her ghost might take vengeance on them if they acted improperly. Initially, Loan thought Thúy was an idiot. However, due to hierarchical respect and the fact that Thúy found her on the shore and decided she might be able to live, Loan gave her the benefit of her doubt.

They debated whether to take the woman's hat; Thúy insisted the woman would need something to wear in the afterlife. Huế and Loan believed the ghosts would be grateful her hat went to good use in this life.

Thúy ignored Huế's and Loan's arguments; other pressing issues required their attention. Sunset was imminent. The treacherous uneven ground of the coastline would become a bigger problem for them if they failed to get back to their camp before dark.

Huế, eleven years old and tallest of the three scanned underbrush and coastline for signs of dogs and other scavengers. She dreaded confronting the aggressive canines more than Thúy or Loan.

Huế was more emotional about carnage on the shoreline than the other girls. She loathed nature's treatment of dead Vietnamese. With so much easy flesh here, she knew the pack would return. However, it would be the next day. Both humans and dogs had to retreat to safety for the night. As the sun lowered in the sky, she knew that crabs would scuttle up the cliffs in search of protein. Long-tailed macaques would come down to the cliffs in search of crabs. The dogs would return later.

The woman's body fed the sea and the jungle in a few days.

Loan's Recovery

Loan, eight years old and the smallest of the three, had recovered well in the last few weeks. A month had lapsed since she washed ashore barely alive. Coming from strong stock of Chinese, the girl washed ashore, hair falling out from over a day of exposure to seawater. She landed otherwise intact and regained strength quickly.

The girls nursed their new companion back to the living. They actually expected her to die. To their surprise, she was up and capable of doing her part in days.

Loan deferred to the guidance of Thúy and Huế. However, she showed a current of strength and resolve. Age and respect had its place as long as it was better than intellect and adaptation. The older girls had yet to measure Loan.

Geographical Bliss

As the latest arrival, she believed as the others; she thought she had landed in some other region of Viet Nam. The older girls had some schooling before the fall of Sai Gon; however, they lacked a working sense of geography. They did not recall a mountainous region of Viet Nam that faced a western sea.

In most of Viet Nam, the sun rises on the sea and sets over land. On the Bataan coastline, the opposite occurs. The sun rises over land and sets on the sea.

This puzzled the girls. Theories abounded. Perhaps the world had turned around or the sun had begun to work in reverse. This could be the work of angry ghosts who were known to be small and petty about such things.

For various reasons, the adults on board the boats failed to tell them where they headed for another country. No one told the girls they had headed for America or that first landfall would be in the Philippine Archipelago.

Loan's employer told her their boat was taking the family she served to Sai Gon. It was a lie to calm Loan down in order to conceal their plan for escape from a community near Rach Ghia on the southern tip of Viet Nam.

The other girls knew they had been heading toward Manila in the Philippines. However, they believed Manila was another city in Viet Nam. The older girls would die over the next few years never to learn they were in another country six-hundred miles from home.

Loan would learn she was no longer in Viet Nam in 1982 when she ended up in a Catholic orphanage. Other than what she learned from her incredible mother and siblings, she had zero formal education. She could not write her own name until she was fourteen. She was not an idiot, she just didn't have any schooling. None. Zero. Nada.

By then, she had fifteen siblings in a fallen Sai Gon that believed she had died in mysterious circumstances. She became the "lost sister" to her family for eighteen years between 1977 and 1995.

Preparation for Life in Bataan

As Loan recovered quickly, she acquired better skills of foraging for food, firewood and banana leaves for shelter. As time allowed, they stored rocks in hollowed tree limbs in strategic locations along frequently used paths.

When dogs or boars were hungry, a Vietnamese girl weighing less than fifty pounds became tempting prey. In pairs or now as three, the girls never separated from each other; it improved their odds against the challenge with other mammals.

On occasion, one pack or another came after the girls. The three moved into the branches of one of their trees expecting to be there for a day or more. Few threats deterred hungry dogs. Rocks worked on occasion; it also entertained the girls as long as their stores of food and water held out.

Supplies in the trees included fruit, rain water cupped in elephant-ear leaves and banana leaves for cover at night. Large lizards known as water dragons tied with vine to the trees and the ubiquitous gecko fed them if supplies of apples and bananas ran low. With no way to contain them, crickets were consumed immediately. There was no value in eating dead crickets as they would vomit its nutritional value immediately.

Measure of Tragedy

As the girls built up resources, they gained more time to comb the shoreline for useful debris. The storms rolling in off the South China Sea broke the monotony of life on the jungle coastline; rough seas meant new things to find on shore.

Violent seas also meant more dead Vietnamese among the rocks on the shoreline. The few living that expired on the shoreline came from Viet Nam. One hundred percent of the dead were Vietnamese.

Put this in American perspective. Imagine being an American child born in Kalamazoo, Michigan and eventually becoming stranded on the wilderness that is Chicago. The Upper Peninsula and Lower Peninsula feuded over political and economic ideologies for decades. Things went badly for people of Kalamazoo and you are sent away to thrive in Chicago only to find that you barely survive disaster in the transit across Lake Michigan.

Every few days, you find bodies on the beaches of Chicago. All the dead and dying are from Michigan. Something in Michigan had gone terribly wrong compelling Michiganders to flee to Wisconsin and Illinois. Their miserable sea-craft weren't up to the task. What the cold waters of Lake Michigan failed to consume washed up on the beaches of Chicago.

As an eight-year old Michigander girl with zero education, you are left with the task of respecting the dead kin-of-Michigan on the barren shores of Chicago. Add this to the mix; you still believe you are in Michigan.

Philippine Reality

The numbers of dead on the shoreline depressed Loan. She had counted a dozen bodies since she arrived. The problem was more than just a few bodies of Vietnamese people had been washing ashore. The numbers dying in The South China Sea ran into hundreds per month.

A great river of humanity fled Viet Nam by any means possible. From walking to Thailand to escaping by unworthy sea craft, more than a third died in transit. Those that didn't starve to death or die at the hands of Thai and Vietnamese pirates drowned in the South China Sea.

In the end, Thúy and Huế waited until Loan strengthened enough to endure the grim truth. Vietnamese people had been dying in larger numbers. A month elapsed before the older girls told Loan that hundreds of bodies had washed ashore on this stretch of coastline over the last nine months. At times, the carnage became so dreadful, they moved their camp to avoid the horrendous smell.

The girls had to break the news to Loan at some point. After the big storm that just pasted, Thúy expected to see many bodies in the bay over the next few days. They might have to move their camp again. The sickly sweet stench of death had forced them to relocate the camp two days after they found Loan on the cliff.

A boat overloaded with refugees broke apart and sank somewhere near the coast two days before they discovered Loan. Some of the passengers on Loan's boat washed ashore in the same area. None but Loan survived.

Thúy and Huế knew in time, as human flesh rotted among the boulders, they had to move just to be able to breath. The artifacts of a world gone insane forced them to relocate camp dozens of time while the three girls were together.

They had come to know endless disaster. The shoreline where they camped would, in all probability, become rancid with dead humanity. The carnage became the larger cycle of their life on this rough coastline. The calamity started after the fall of Sai Gon on 30 April 1975 and would run for years.

The Providence of Buddha

Thúy told Loan she was had the providence of Buddha; she reminded Huế as well. Thúy believed there was something special in Loan and that Buddha watched over her. They knew the chances of landing on a rugged shoreline and surviving more than a few days. The three of them were the lucky ones. They were gifted to life under the generous hand of Buddha.

Each of the girls had beaten the odds and lived. The fact resided in the act; they stood alive and thrived in an inhospitable jungle. It meant Buddha had plans for them.

Thúy consoled the others with the benefice of Buddha. A magnificent idea emerged; Buddha guided their lives toward a better future. Thúy was full of wisdom from Buddha about their circumstance. Huế nodded in silent agreement. Loan wondered why thirteen-year-old Thúy was so full of water-buffalo dung.

Faith in Buddha provided few comforts to eight-year-old Loan. She only knew she had become stranded in an unknown region of Viet Nam with dead and dying Vietnamese littering the coastline. She arrived here by happenstance because she thought she had been heading, by way of boat, to return to her beloved mother in Sai Gon. Now, she was somewhere else in Viet Nam and had no clue how to find her way back to Sai Gon.

Something went terribly wrong. Buddha's hand or not, she was unhappy to be away from her mother.

The flotsam of great tragedy continued to drift into the rocks and boulders. Thúy and Huế had dealt with it for nine months and told Loan things were getting worse; the number of dead was growing. Numbers varied, regardless, evidence pointed to a steady increase of the frequency of sinkings and number of victims.

There were times when there were too many bodies in the water to count. Boats loaded with refugees that ran aground on this coastline ended up in the worst of situations. They had traveled six hundred miles to drown scant yards from dry land.

Parents with limited swimming skills could not suppress instincts to save their children. They struggled to save the children; the result, all died, dashed into the rocks or drowned in the shallows below the cliffs.

When the sea was calm *(seldom)*, the girls could still see the remnants of a large wooden boat submerged in the water. The fishing boat had run into the cliffs during the nighttime storm. People were still alive on the boat as it foundered helplessly in the roiling water. Thúy and Huė could hear them scream each time a large wave shoved the sinking boat into the face of the cliff.

They were fifty feet from land; it might as well have been a hundred miles out to sea. Nobody on board could swim. This section of the western Bataan coastline killed the strongest swimmers. Falling into the water was a death sentence.

Huge waves broke over the boat washing people into the water. Thúy and Huė had taken shelter under an overhanging cliff. They had wrapped themselves in banana leaves to stay warm in the driving rain. They were not far from the shoreline and left the safety of the trees only to stay out of the rain and maintain their fire. The dangerous animals hunkered down during the storms. The girls felt safer on the ground until the weather improved.

Over the howl of the wind and waves, they heard the sound of the boat crashing into the cliff. Loaded with people, the craft was blown into the bay during the night. After the first crack of the timbers hitting the cliff, Thúy stood up and crept toward the shore. In the blackness, she could creep only a few feet without losing her way. She had a sense of the cliff's edge based on the salt-spray blowing in her face. She dare not move closer to the edge.

Philippine coastal storms were often just rain and wind. There were no flashes of lightning to help her see what was going on in the churning waters below. Without moonlight, the girls were blind. Wherever they were located at nightfall, the girls remained until morning.

In the darkness, Thúy heard men shout, women scream, and children cry a few times after the boat first collided with the cliffs below. In minutes, the shouts, screams, and cries stopped. Over the howl of the wind and crash of the waves, she heard the crack of lumber against rock, but little else. She returned to where Huế was crouching, shivering from the rain. She felt around for the banana leaves and lay down with Huế re-wrapping the both of them.

She whispered out of habit (fear of attracting marauding animals) to Huế that there was little else to do until daylight. They laid there on the hard ground crying for whoever had landed in the violent bay. They had hoped for more company, adults, someone who could help them out of the wilderness. In the dark of night and a storm, they knew that no one would survive.

The morning meant grim discoveries. The wind and the waves drove on and somehow, they fell asleep.

At first light, Thúy was up. The rain had stopped, however the wind blew off the tops of monstrous waves. A horizontal driving salty mist wetted everything and stung her eyes.

The roar of the sea was deafening at times. To the girls it became background noise, part of the silence.

Huế peered down from the cliffs to see a large boat bent in half and on its side half-submerged. It had the high prow of a Vietnamese fishing boat. The blue hull sported a faded red trim. A single mast and boom bobbed in the water as waves rocked the hull. It was broken and empty.

A hundred people might have crossed the sea in a boat of that size. The deck of such a boat would have been carpeted with people. It had probably left the Mekong Delta, or coastal cities such as Vung Tau or Nah Trang up the coast.

Vietnamese constructed fishing vessels of this type for safer water ways in Viet Nam. Its timbers were insufficient for open expanses of the South China Sea. Most significant, the structure was never intended to carry thirty, forty or a hundred passengers.

Along the churning waters among the boulders below the cliffs, here and there were bodies, some naked, others partially clothed in black pants or blouses. All were Vietnamese. There were a few bodies atop the lower cliffs. None was moving and no one was standing.

Thúy and Huế checked on the bodies they could reach. Huế used put a feather under the nose to detect breathing. They did not understand taking a pulse and besides, they were forbidden to touch the dead.

Bodies lodged in the rocks and boulders below were beyond help. The bodies of the ones that drowned and sank would bloat and re-appear in the bay in a few days. The bodies re-appeared if something in the water didn't consume them.

Depending on the number of dead in the shoreline, Thúy and Huė relocated their camp inland or out of the prevailing wind somewhere up or down the shore. Location depended on the wind direction, difficulty of moving along the shoreline and the carnage.

Viet Nam's war involving America and South Viet Nam ended April 30, 1975. Any child older than four years would never forget the last days of a Sai Gon as Hanoi bombed civilians in non-military sections of the city. The bombing was payback to the South Vietnamese loyal to the South and supported the American allies. More than a month lapsed before most of the civilian chaos subsided.

The grind of the victors on South Viet Nam began in the summer of 1975. As South Vietnamese realized the scale and duration of the oppression, families began fleeing a year after the fall of Sai Gon. The older girls were part of the initial exodus in June 1976. Their knowledge of anything of the world ended there. From July 1976, Vietnamese tragedy grew. Thúy and Huė miraculously survived land fall nine month before Loan arrived. They would die in different accidents in the next 24 months. They would never know more of Viet Nam than what they knew in June 1976.

Of the three girls, Loan had the least formal education; she had none. At the age of eight and misinformed by the family that fled a month before, Loan added little to their knowledge of the conditions at home. She knew that the famine was worse; she had been a servant in exchange for rice for her siblings in Sai Gon. By design, she knew nothing else.

Over-informed children inadvertently betrayed their families in the government inquisitions that followed the fall of Sai Gon. Anybody who served the South Vietnamese government and/or the Americans in any capacity instantly became ignorant cooks, farmers, fishermen, and taxi drivers. Adults destroyed incriminating records of anything and converted American money to gold or hid and destroyed the evidence. Adults practiced stories with their friends and children attempting to supplant their memories with invented identities, careers and parents, aunts and uncles that never existed.

They gleaned a few truths from their families as civilization collapsed.

- Sai Gon good, Hanoi bad.
- Hmong good.
- Mountain people (Montagnard) good.
- Americans good. But never praise Americans in public.
- All else bad.
- Listen well, talk little.
- Above all, clean your rice bowl (if you had any rice).
- Waste nothing.

The girls knew one other thing with any certainty: Thousands of Vietnamese were fleeing. Many of them were dying on the Philippine coastline which they thought was another part of Viet Nam.

Thúy and Huế had lost all of their family. Loan had lost the family she served along with connection to her parents and siblings in Sai Gon. They had no news and no adult to help them cope with each grim discovery that occurred almost daily.

Tragedy had become a universal constant in Southeast Asia of 1977. Girls in the budding spring of their lives dealt with one horror after another. They woke up with one grim question each morning: "What struggle and horror do I face today?"

Buddha in the Wilderness

Loan's mother and Buddha (the "teacher") alone prepared Loan for the wilderness. As a nine-year-old girl with zero formal education and stranded on a rugged jungle coastline, her future was in doubt. She believed she was still in Viet Nam having no knowledge of geography of near regions. To her the world was flat, warm, wet and full of threats.

From birth in the fall of 1968, Loan was constantly on the move from village to hamlet and then to another village unable to attend school. Her mother spent resources for education on her brothers if they dwelled in a community longer than a few months. As a female in an ethnic Chinese-Vietnamese family, her education was secondary to her brothers. She had never been to school. Not even one day.

If she grew up healthy, she had most of the assets needed by an Asian female. She could bear and nurture children and tend to her husband.

Her mother provided her only education and that was seldom. As the youngest of a dozen children and a girl, Loan shared her mother's spare attention with everyone else. She drew what knowledge she could from her aunts and siblings. It was too dangerous to ask non-family or trust in the gossip of neighbors.

Loan learned to exploit her mother's time by volunteering for any task where they could work together. Preparing a meal gave her the best un-interrupted moments squatting alongside "Ama" and asking her about the world. Knowing little else, she often asked mother about Buddha. Her mother responded best to those questions and explained the world in the "eight-fold path".

The eight-fold path to enlightenment was central to Buddhist meditation. The teachings were simple and instructive. Her mother reminded Loan to focus on obtaining right positions in her mind and activities.

She was compelled to seek right view, right resolve, right speech, right action, right livelihood, right effort, right mindfulness and right concentration. That was all fine and good when she was rested, fed and secure; difficult to remember when hungry and threatened by wilderness.

Buddhist priests, Christian friends, and psychologists years later would speculate on her miraculous survival. A common thread was that God had plans for her. However, many adults would speculate that Loan's ignorance might have been part of her hidden strength. She resisted dwelling on how bad she had it.

She was eight-years old, ignorant, and misinformed. She believed she was in Viet Nam hoping to find her way back to Sai Gon. The three of them believed they just hadn't traveled inland far enough to find a road or a village to help them.

She was naked in an inaccessible jungle with two older girls that exhibited some reckless tendencies. While grateful for their aid to her when she washed ashore in a fragile condition, she marveled more about their survival than her own. The girls were near-idiots.

She deferred to thirteen-year-old Thúy decisions out of Asian respect for age. That would be temporary as the older girl's judgment proved faulty.

Hué was impulsive sorting decisions emotionally. Loan decided early to rethink poorly conceived plans of the older girls. It was about right mindfulness and right respect.

Loan, dealt a bad hand in life, resisted self-pity. Yes, things were bad. Enough said and it didn't bear repeating. From her mother's teachings, the next moment was about maintaining a right view.

If she could survive to the next day, she knew she would take that gift of life and improve her opportunities. It was about right resolve, right action and right effort.

Loan's hidden strength was the example of her mother. The tireless woman endured much with few rewards. She provided for her large family and community avoiding personal indulgences.

Ever the entrepreneur, Loan's mother operated a dozen small industries in the household turning seeming refuse into saleable product. As soon as Loan could walk, (circa 1969), she worked at one task or another working alongside her older brothers and sisters. Nguyên Xuân Loan became accustomed to working on any task, no matter how menial or how large, from dawn to dusk and almost from birth.

Loan missed her mother. Maï had been progenitor, provider, teacher, and mentor.

Her brothers and sister were more co-workers than family. She was always the "little-sister" to her siblings. When she traveled at the age of seven to serve a prominent Communist family as "nanny" in exchange for 200 kilos of rice, she did so in place of her older sister who was not as strong. Loan did so because she knew she would eat better. She became "ambitious little-sister".

Loan's father was a difficult self-indulging man; Toan came from relative wealth and prestige in Shanghai, China prior to the invasion of the Japanese. World War II over-turned the social order in China and sent entrepreneurial China into exile.

She would later refer to him as a jerk in Cantonese parlance. Loan gave her father tacit respect as a matter of Chinese culture, nothing more. She favored her mother in appearance, intelligence, and willfulness.

Her mother had been essential in her life. Not just in Loan's life, her mother proved essential in a number of Vietnamese citizens and a few US Navy SEALS. That is for some later discussion in this remarkable story of strength and perseverance.

Regardless, Loan was stranded in another country 600 miles from Sai Gon. She had no way to know whether her family knew where she was or if she was even alive. The fact was that no one in Sai Gon had a clue as to what happened to Loan.

Mystery, fear, grief and disappointment danced together every day in Southeast Asia 1977. An eight-year old Vietnamese girl naked and nearly alone in a Philippine jungle and her large family hanging on to life in medieval Viet Nam knew the dance of chaos. Loan clung to the love of her mother and the teachings of Buddha. That would have to suffice.

Jungle Resolve and Deliverance From Idiots

Unable to mend the physical and emotional connection with her mother, isolated by six-hundred miles and a treacherous sea, Loan focused on the day-to-day demands of survival. Many people of all walks of life have speculated years later how she survived. It is apparent that she avoided impractical expectations.

As she would later explain, expectations have nothing to do with the future. The future shows up unaffected by hopes and dreams. It can change only due to prior action. Otherwise, the future is just the present postponed.

Smart actions now mattered. She prayed to Buddha for guidance of the moment, little more. She also prayed for deliverance from idiots.

In most any circumstance, Loan seldom attached blame upon others as long as she could act independent of the actions of fools. The population of her universe had shrunk from tens of thousands to three human beings in the isolated Bataan mountainside for dozens of months ahead. If she listened too much to the older girls, she would die.

Thúy and Huê helped Loan survive after a difficult landing. However, it did not take Loan long to realize the older girls were more lucky than smart. Before long, she wondered if she could have survived without them.

Loan was often amazed the girls survived the jungle as long as they did. Within two months, she began to redirect their purpose threatening them with striking out on her own. Loan allowed Thúy to make errors of judgment in order to test her sense of reality as long as the decision couldn't kill Huê and herself. She kept a mental log of Thúy's errors for later argument.

Thúy and Huê were survivors of total chaos thinking like rich girls in central Sai Gon. Thúy grew up in richer circumstances and maintained expectations of a better life and appropriate treatment of girls. Her father was well connected in Sai Gon and was openly rich by Vietnamese standards. He flaunted his success which led to the family flight by boat. Her entire family drowned on that coastline ten months ago.

Huė, two years younger, followed Asian culture and Thúy. Thúy, with budding breasts and thin black pubic hair growing in her armpits and above her "coo-che" marked her as the closest female in their group that fit the description of "elder."

Thúy demanded respect and subservience of Huė and subsequent expectations flowed to Loan. Thúy was obviously the eldest of the three. Huė and Le, entirely devoid of body hair, could not refuse. Such was the way of hierarchical Asian culture.

Age mattered in Asian culture. Artifacts of being older than younger mattered more among young people. Pubic hair established differences, girls who had it were more senior than those who didn't.

Huė made the mistake of allowing Thúy to think for both of them too long. Thúy arrogance would get her killed first leaving Huė puzzled by her faith in elders. Loan mourned the loss of a companion but that turned to anger at Thúy. Thúy believed her own words too much.

The habituation of thought and culture would eventually kill Huė leaving Loan by herself for many months. Again, Loan mourned the loss of another companion. As before, Loan became angry with Huė because she believed in her own wisdom as she was the oldest of the two girls. She would not listen to the quiet thoughtful Loan and at a critical moment, Huė's lapse of attention to her companion's cautions would kill her.

Loan had learned a basic thing from her mother than ran through most of her thoughts as she negotiated the wilderness. She knew to think out each action in advance.

Thinking out each action in advance

Carefully consider in advance the choice between sleeping in a tree during a storm versus hiding on the ground. The human mind has the power to anticipate, use it. Figuring out something when the storm is pounding overhead creates unnecessary risk and deployment of resources.

Similarly, weigh the value of spending precious daylight protecting dead Vietnamese from wild animals versus harvesting food. The animals that desire your nutritious flesh lack the same agenda. When you are dead, your special attention to honor of the culture dies too. Big Rule: Don't die.

Loan knew something Thúy and Huė did not seem to understand. Culture depends on the point of view who survives alone among all the dead. Great ideas and culture is meaningless if all the bearers of great historical wisdom are dead.

The three girls were all that remained of Chinese culture, transplanted to the Bataan coastline. If all the rest of the world had ended and it depended on these three immature human females to resurrect humanity, it depended on them to survive.

The coin of trade was cultural purity versus leaving one vestigial component, a single survivor, capable of multiplying the philosophy of a society exiled into the Philippine jungle. In short, to hell with Chinese tradition and culture. Among the three girls, Loan had become agnostic to Asian mores. Her focus shifted to those damn dogs and how to kill them.

Damn Dogs

Boars and dogs appeared threatening as the girls learned to test their resolve. Weighing less than fifty pounds, the girls intimidated most animals in the Philippine jungles as needed with guile and surprise. Loan introduced them to a level of boldness that at times became amusing. For the first time in many months, Thúy and Huė laughed as Loan introduced them to "out of the box" thinking about dealing with the damn dogs.

There was simple math for survival. Loan had the formula of wit, guile and guts. Loan was prepared to live by that formula. In simpler terms, Loan believed in being the first to act with most threats.

In another world thirty years later, she learned the term "pro-active" in her own way. In the jungle, this meant she must meet the threat rather than wait for it. Unfortunately, Thúy and Huė seldom shared the same view. In Asian culture, age determined intelligence. Loan, the youngest was therefore the least smart.

Each event had to be considered, thought out, and planned. Action required thought in advance. They knew they could last several days in the trees when stranded by packs of dogs. Duration depended on stores of food, however, the canine siege didn't last long if they had a larger supply of rocks.

More rocks meant less need for stored food and water. Loan advocated storing more rocks in the trees than fruit and lizards. One of her compelling arguments; it could be more fun when the pack of dogs besieged them in the trees. For the first time since Thúy and Huẻ hand landed on the coastline, they laughed at the thought of having fun in the trees as the dogs waited to kill and consume them. The laughter of three girls contemplating the demise of the dogs was a new sound in the jungle.

Life in the jungle was moment-to-moment and day to day. Indulgences of dreams wasted mental and material resources. As it was, there was plenty of time to dream between sunset and sunrise.

In idle moments, they dreamed of another life in a faraway place that was very different. They knew of the talk of America, their parents talked about the Americans. They considered the strange people dominated with the white race and their round eyes and pale skin, weird with freckles and the red, blond, brown, and curly hair. In their own way, the girls all thought that the American soldiers were handsome, large as they were compared to Asian men. Most of the Americans disappeared largely by the time Thúy was eight, around 1973. She remembered seeing them in Sai Gon in the restaurants, driving around in cars and flying overhead in helicopters. The abundance of America was portrayed by all the aircraft they possessed.

The Americans were over-sized humanity. America was populated by many races, they called it a "melting pot." They were vulnerable and invincible at the same time. Everyone called the Americans naïve wealthy idiots with nothing else to do but fight in Asia.

The girls knew little else. The Americans were bold and rich. They invented the modern world, spaceships, television, telephones, and movies. America was the land of opportunity. All of the rest of the world knew this.

In Bataan, survival depended on deferring wishes and focusing on the moment. The girls survived by luck and circumstance. They had thin chance to build a bigger expectation; they survived so far because they were resourceful and lucky. They also had to resist dwelling on their circumstances too much. Self-pity led to depression; it bled off right action and right effort.

At quiet moments, usually when at sunset when their activities ceased in the darkness, they would discuss among themselves asking the same questions repeatedly: "Why this way? Why Now? Why Us?" They had no answers, the questions usually led to them retiring to wrap up in banana leaves for the long black night, often quietly crying until they fell asleep.

Politics were beyond Loan's knowledge. She only knew, as her mother explained, that life in Viet Nam was doomed to misery after the Americans left.

Her mother seemed to understand the Americans well; she respected them. When she spoke of America and their role in Viet Nam, her tone was reverent. Few were the times she saw her mother's eyes well up in tears. When she spoke of the Americans, it was in quiet tones, her head turned away.

The record of the Americans and her mother's work with them during the war was another story in itself. Loan would not learn the full extent of her mother's role in the war for decades.

Loan was the victim of circumstance beyond her control. Just as she was in the South China Sea, she was afloat across two days at the mercy and benevolence of Buddha. Vietnamese Catholics, Baptists, and Buddhists fled a dangerous Viet Nam to uncertain outcome. Many of them died in the South China Sea as they escaped knowing little more than find a way to the free countries. It was a simple mantra: Find a way out. Find a way to America.

Duty to the Dead and Fear of Ghosts

In the meantime, the girls on the shoreline were compelled to do something for the dead. Loan wanted to do something for the bodies; cover, bury or cremate them per her limited experience with deceased family. However, Asian culture prohibited the girls from doing much more than run off marauding animals.

Touching the dead remained off limits. Burying them in the rocky soil inland was unlikely; they lacked familial authority, soft soil, and tools. They only came out on this shoreline search when all of their daily tasks had been sufficient to spare precious daylight hours for this solemn duty.

Per Asian mores, the girls would only lay a hand on a family or companion that had died. Touching someone else's departed summoned trifling mischief or worse from malicious spirits, coastal life proved hard enough without ghosts.

They had enough trouble with dogs and the other animals; however, they knew the rules of conduct that avoided ghosts. They did what their resources allowed for the dead when they had the wherewithal to do so. However, their fear of ghosts and banshees limited their involvement with the dead on the Philippine coastline.

Thúy, Huế and Loan laid down banana leaves next to the woman's body. They removed some small apples from one of their satchels and placed the fruit on the center. Placing the palms of their hands together in front of their face, they bowed to the body and then to the fruit, telling Buddha in Vietnamese to take their gift of food to the woman in her afterlife. They made the traditional wish of prosperity, happiness, and joyful days.

Loan repeated the phrase in Cantonese, just in case the woman might be ethnic Chinese and had trouble understanding the others' Vietnamese. The older girls nodded in appreciation; Loan easily spoke a Chinese language. Huế and Thúy spoke Vietnamese with some halting use of their native Cantonese. They appreciated the opportunity for a useful communication to another Asian of unknown languages.

Thúy gently placed the nón lá back on the woman's head careful to avoid physical contact with her body. She reconnected the hat's chin band to the string on the woman's blouse. If the conical hat remained on the beach after a week, they would retrieve it; Buddha, the benevolent teacher, would provide.

Loan stood by with Thúy and Huế in these ceremonies rolling her eyes and cursing Thúy. Take the damn hat. It doesn't matter. The ghosts are ghosts, they can't pick up a the hat. Her disgust with Thúy grew.

Thúy motioned on the younger girls pointing up the beach toward the setting sun. Time to head back to their camp became obvious. Each avoided calling their camp home; all of this circumstance on the jungle coast had to be temporary. When they found a Vietnamese village, this ordeal would end.

Huế and Loan wanted to rest a few minutes. Thúy, as relentless leader, always avoided traveling the treacherous shoreline in the dark. She lacked tolerance for Huế's lazy streak and improvised. She told them dogs would be bolder today after two days of rain. They would be hungry. Hunger for easy flesh on the beach would bolster their courage against the girls. She told her companions they might be a dogs' next meal; Huê and Loan looked hard at Thúy to determine if she lied.

Thúy stared back with an indecipherable expression. The bluff worked, Huê helped Loan find some better throwing stones as they prepared to head up the shoreline in the waning sunlight.

Loan arranged a mental note to herself to avoid this strip of shoreline for a week or more. This permitted nature to have its way with the body out of her view. The remains would soon cease to give the impression of a human being, turning into scattered bones or disappear altogether. The sea might reclaim the corpse or animals would drag it into the jungle, disposing of the awful stench. Time and wilderness would remove most of the sad evidence soon enough. However, some artifacts of the woman's end might remain. Dogs had little use for conical straw hats; she hoped the nón lá could be recovered.

Regardless, the woman's banshee would likely torture dogs and rats feeding on her body. It was a problem for dogs and rats to manage.

The girls picked up their long sticks and added a few rocks to their banana-leave satchels for ammunition. Huê handed Loan some of her rocks to Loan to carry with her, telling her to work on her accuracy. Few of Loan's throws landed well; she would hone her rock throwing skills.

Thúy, as always, led them uphill as they left the woman's body. The setting sun, hovering above the horizon of the South China Seas urged. The yellow orange orb filled the surface of the roiling sea with sparkling points of light off the waves. Abandoning the body on the shore proved hard; however, they had no choice, the dark jungle would take them in minutes if they lingered tool long.

The girls said little as they picked their path along the rocky ledges. They alternately scanned for storm debris in the rocks along the water and checked the edge of the jungle for animals. The bad weather had lasted for two days; a number of things washed ashore they might be able to use. At next daylight, they might return.

The girls had done their duty to the dead for that day.

Indian Casino on I-25 North of Albuquerque, New Mexico

The definition for "jungle" is mixed and large. It implies wilderness, fertility and danger depending on how it is used. The term "jungle" implies tropical circumstances with 46 degrees of latitude straddling the equator. However, the original meanings of wilderness and danger can apply to wherever that exists. It can be in the Congo, Brazilian forests, Philippine coastlines or even in Albuquerque, New Mexico.

The "Boys" searched for her car, meandering through the light snow falling from a velvet-black sky. Their anger, amplified by drugs and liquor, climbed with their frustration. In the empty casino parking lots, her car should be easy to find.

One of them recalled how employees usually parked near the service entrance on busy nights to make more room for patrons. They determined the Asian bitch might park her car near the service entrance.

Ian steered the dark car as he told Bjorn to use algebra more often. Hardly a mathematician, he often talked about applying algebra in his thinking, his words meant to impress the slot-machine-ladies in the casino. "Doing the algeeber," Ian said, unable to spell the word or add two digit numbers in his head, made decisions easier. Ian figured she'd park where other employees would park on such a busy night. The solution required higher math.

If the girls bought his fake-out line, he figured it must be a right thing to say. This time, his 'math' connected the dots. Ian's amorphous logic yielded quirky results, however, this happened to be the right answer. He and his dim partner had driven to the correct parking lot.

Ian and Bjorn had to sort among the dwindling number of vehicles in the south parking lot for her car. Bjorn remembered from his conversations with her; she drove a new sport utility vehicle; a 2004 Honda Pilot. Bjorn recalled, "That Chink chic had money to own a new SUV."

"Yeah," Ian responded. "Do you remember what color it is? Lots of those SUVs look the same. Hard to tell in this light."

Ian and Bjorn sorted among their memory of the card dealer's comments for clues leading them to her vehicle. She had told them about Chinese culture in her banter as she dealt the cards. In her rough English thickly loaded with an Asian accent, she elaborated on her birth in the year of the dog. She explained the Asian zodiac with twelve animal signs slotted in the lunar months similar to western astrology.

She joked with them about being a dog. Her simulated dog-bark amused patrons as it resembled the sound of a large hiccup. Loan was not good at imitating the sound of dogs barking.

Ian, more curious of the two, asked her if she knew their astrological animals based on date of their birth. "You born in the year of the peccary." She told him with a grin. "You born in 1971, that your sign."

She told him the truth; the creature is a South American cousin of the boar. The Asian sign traded animals from boar to pig. Ian was born in the year of the pig.

Ian believed the name insulting. Loan intended to shock them; however, the barb went over Ian's head. He had never heard of an animal with such an earthy name. He thought it a mangled term for his manhood.

Similarly, she told Bjorn his birth put him in the year of the dik-dik, a diminutive deer-like animal in Africa and distant cousin to the horse. Similar to Ian, Bjorn objected to the name of his sign.

She added both astrological signs signified female gender; Asian culture developed this over five thousand years. She admonished them to avoid trifling with an ancient culture. They could only change the time of their birth through a lie, however, ancient gods of the zodiac would know. Don't mess with the Asian zodiac unless you burn in hell, she would tell them.

Loan modified her dealer-banter as required based on the tips of the players. Few could sort between facts and fictions. Her mangled English enhanced her comments on inappropriate behavior. Loan was a hoot.

If the players were not tipping, she mildly abused them. Her caustic "charm" worked in reverse; it was counter-intuitive. Most men and some women enjoyed her personality. Her cash tips were among the highest of the card dealers.

The humor of these comments escaped the "movie boys" as they were known in the casino. Ian and Bjorn didn't know the actual appearance of their animal signs. Consequently, they developed a perverted image of how their birth signs, the peccary and the dik-dik, might appear.

The petit blackjack dealer told them these altered factoids with firm conviction. Ian, and Bjorn mulled over their unfortunate luck with Asian birth signs. It became the point of an endless series of jabs between "Ian-the-peccary" and "Bjorn-the-dik-dik."

Year of the Dog

Through various discussions, they recalled her sign: the dog. This had special meaning to her as her mother was also born under the sign of the dog.

Unfortunately for Loan, the "movie boys," found a Honda Pilot in the south end of the parking lot. Unsure whether it hers, they examined the vehicle.

A "Scooby-Do" cartoon playing card dangled from the rear-view mirror; two bobble-head dogs stood sentry on the dashboard. The vehicle's owner liked dogs. Ian applied more of his "algeeber" summing the observations. This had to be Loan's car. They had found the bitch's car.

Her witchy foreign ways had made their life untenable. They found her property. She would pay.

They parked beside the bronze-tan sports-utility-vehicle (SUV) to wait for her to clock out of her shift and leave the casino. To improve their patience; they passed back and forth a large bottle, also known as a "handle," 1.75 liters of dark Kentucky bourbon. Each swig of the smoky liquid improved their acceptance of the slow passage of time. Enlarging intoxication withered some lingering doubts about the wisdom of their exploit.

They hurtled in alcohol-numbed slow motion toward an indelible lesson. They verged on rewriting guidelines on whom to assault when seeking money and parking lot romance.

In a few days, they would update their intelligence on acceptable victims, all from the comfort of a jail cell. Foreign-born women of undetermined willfulness moved to the top of their growing list of poor choices. The lesson in short, don't mess with pissed-off Vietnamese women.

Fifteen minutes earlier, Ian and Bjorn had left the Indian casino at the insistence of the tribal police. Their sorry situation emerged as they drove off property; they had little gas and no money. That Asian card dealer drained them of their cash.

Remaining solutions dwindled without gas and money early Saturday morning on a casino parking lot north of Albuquerque. At 4:00 AM on a winter night with security guards assuming they had left the casino for the night, one option remained: return and assault the Asian she-devil.

Their strategy: tap the probable resources from a small ethnic-Chinese Vietnamese woman getting off work in half an hour. They knew she had cash. Some of it had been, per their poor reckoning, acquired a few hours earlier. They gambled. They lost. However, it was still their money.

Asians did everything in cash when they could. She had to have cash; they paid her in chips when they were winning. She put the chips in her "toll box," a small black box clipped to the side of the play table. The casino in turn processed the toll box taking out 38% for the government.

They hatched their strategy to acquire gas money and possibly some parking lot romance. They were drunk, broke, horny, and out of options. Ian executed a lurching turn on the access road leading to Interstate 25. At 3:40 AM, he was driving on an Interstate service road the wrong way.

As travel on most roads ran both ways, the access road also led back to the casino. Ian steered them back to recover their evening's losses.

Since they had just been directed by tribal police to leave the property by a northerly exit, they entered the casino parking lot access further south of the property. The thinly-monitored and inconvenient south access was poorly illuminated and managed. Customers parked on the north, closest access from the highway.

They deduced security cameras scanned parking areas closer to the casino. Consequently, they assumed the boundary around the outer perimeter of the casino was less guarded. The studied assessment came from experience; they scored on crack-cocaine purchased outside the perimeter of casino property.

Many people involved in illicit business knew the south parking lots went overlooked. They acquired drugs without trouble as long as they stayed off-property. Per history, Ian's "algeeber" fired on all pistons. Frankly, Ian had no pistons. They were on the long side of stupid.

In addition to gambling, drugs, consumer-sex, and other social transgressions, all compromises of American morality were available at a price in or near any large casino. No casino in the USA was immune. None.

The churches and moralists were right to object to casinos in their communities. Despite the facts of an enlarged depravity, the objectors to casinos lost out to the power of richer purses who lobbied politicians and regulators. Indian casinos became isolated islands of depravity with a marginal immunity from prosecution.

The biggest downloaders of porn come from suppressed communities. The Islamic countries download more porn than anyone else. America is less repressed but the issues of gambling persist. Except for Nevada and a few other communities, gambling is outlawed unless sanctioned by the Native-American nations. It has become the big comeuppance of the tribes.

During the promotion of gambling enterprises, so much was going to state education and social needs of the tribe. As Indian casinos blossomed like desert flowers after a summer rain, potential revenue split. Thanks to weasel words in the authorization, few if any tribes delivered the revenue, as promoted, to the state. Screw the blue-eyed devil of the "Americans," the tribe did as it could by proxy and judicial sanction.

By design, illegal and illicit acts occurred off tribal property. Activities on neighboring properties became another issue. The tribe alleviated liability by renting parking surface on their boundaries. As long as it did not affect public relations and customer counts, unfortunate events occurring off-property became someone else's problem.

The tribe's blind-eye policy failed to consider an event on the fringe parking lot affecting a high-producing dealer that delivered tens of millions per year in revenue to the tribe. Good card-table dealers had a following of patrons, particularly wealthy gamblers. They were hard to train and even harder to replace in the robust economy of 2004.

Two men intended to rob and rape the little Asian card-dealer and perhaps take her car if it had gas on that winter night in Albuquerque. It was the least she could do for them.

Casino management tended to neglect the southern boundary parking lot. They rented the surface for customer overflow during robust times. Intoxicated self-impoverished men intent on payback changed security strategy for personnel and patron by 16 February 2004.

Ian and Bjorn eased their vehicle through vacant outer parking lots. They drunkenly meandered across empty parking spaces, searching for her car. The dark low-slung car with dark windows rolled slowly through pools of blue-white light under the gaze of security cameras mounted lower on the poles. Bjorn suspected some of the cameras were "scarecrows," dummy cameras with glowing red lights to make him think he was being watched.

Security personnel nearing the end the graveyard shift focused dwindling attention spans on the open tables and unoccupied slot machines. Sleepy casino personnel watch dozens of monitors at a time. Some of the screens remained fixed on a scene, other monitors rotated through an array of cameras. The casino floor had fixed cameras, the parking lot views changed every five seconds among four cameras.

Near the perimeter of the casino, security could move some of the cameras on a joystick in their security console as needed. At the entrances, they had the ability to zoom in on patrons approaching and leaving the facility. Most of that security resource was exercised on female figures and cleavage. Beyond those attentions, anything moving quickly drew their focus. Slow-moving people and cars tended to be ignored.

Security might have noticed the car had it been moving faster. Intense activity betrayed purpose. Criminal intent showed up on closed-circuit-camera; illicit activity betrayed itself with faster-than-normal movement and furtive glances. Their dark windows and slow movement worked.

Up to now, the boys were in no rush. They had to wait out when Loan got off work. The slow meandering vehicle moved under the gaze of intermittent cameras without notice. Guards checking the monitors seemed more interested in whether the projected big snow was about to start.

Crystalline snow fell out of the blackness. The flakes created airy cones of floating white sparkles as the frozen precipitation drifted below the parking lot lighting. Snow sparkled in blue-white metal halide illumination. The sub-freezing precipitation, more ice than snow, created an awesome display in the harsh parking lighting.

The casino spaced the metal-halide lighting fixtures on forty foot poles close together to minimize gaps in the lighting. Color security cameras worked better with the blue-white light than the dusky yellow light.

Off-property lighting used high pressure sodium lighting on shorter poles giving a mottled, dark and dirty look to the outer parking lots. Casino personnel hated to park under the yellowish lighting at night. Light meters recorded adequate light levels; in contrast to the other lighting, perimeter parking areas in the yellow light looked dark.

The tribe refitted casino parking lot lighting with thousand-watt blue-white illumination on tall poles to improve security in the fall of 2003. Recent economic swings in New Mexico fostered muggings of casino patrons. Better lighting was considered a deterrent to crime. Better lighting made better video recordings improving the actuality of taking a criminal off the street before committing the next crime.

Land owners managing overflow parking areas were slow to improve lighting; they went the cheapest route. High-pressure sodium fixtures cost less to operate; the lamps burned out less often. Unfortunately, the yellowish lighting reduced closed-circuit camera resolution. The illumination muted blue and green tones.

Security personnel had trouble distinguishing one car from another under sodium lighting. In some cases, the light blurred facial features. Graveyard security shifts posted frequent complaints about the south parking lot off-property illumination. Casino management assumed security personnel were making excuses for missing a few muggings in the last year.

Light snow began falling after midnight. Any flat unobstructed surface remained clear; the thin snow accumulated on grass and in the leeward side of anything taller than six inches. There was no significant accumulation. Ian's low-slung 1998 dark-blue Chevy Impala stirred up spinning wisps of snow as it motored slowly through open areas of the parking lot.

Ian and Bjorn, already buzzed up on alternate hits of crack cocaine and bourbon, negotiated between the few cars on the lot. They consumed whisky on empty stomachs; the liquor joined a host of intoxicants and stimulants.

They had chugged Long Island Teas just before the casino security guards escorted them out to their car. The liquor simmered in their blood and adjusted their intelligence. Additional drugs and alcohol expanded their indignation. That Asian she-devil was going to have to pay.

They sorely missed their money. They lost three thousand dollars on the blackjack table. By 2:00 AM, they were up two thousand dollars on top of the movie-sales revenue. Within hours, they were penniless.

They settled on one culprit responsible for their financial dilemma. An Asian she-devil of a blackjack dealer shook them down. The devil had a name: Ms. Nguyên Xuân Loan.

Ian and Bjorn's stupidity exceeded historical norms this night. In most bad events, circumstances were never their fault. They were an oppressed minority; the world conspired against them.

They had doubled the money they made from selling pirated movies to slot-machine players. They doubled their profit on their luck and brilliance at blackjack.

They surrendered all their money to the casino. This is to say, they burned off all of their money and access to any resources.

There were no credit or debit cards, no bank account, and no collateral. With the exception of some coins on the floor of their car, they were broke.

Dealer insult multiplied the injury. They were just playing with Loan, talking "trash" to her. They viewed the banter as fun when their stake grew.

Nguyën Xuän Loan knew men and how to talk to them. She had grown up with a dozen siblings, most of them brothers along with a self-centered and difficult father back in Viet Nam. She understood men perhaps better than most men understand themselves. She had the advantage of being Chinese; she could be stoic or unflinchingly direct.

She thrilled or castrated men with a few words. Patrons assumed too much when they heard her rough English and appreciated her Marilyn Monroe figure. Many men assumed Loan stupid and easy. She played that "life-card" as she called it well. She made most of her income on tips from men's unfulfilled desires and penchant for earthy entertainment.

Loan thought like a man. She preferred them as a partner in life but finding a suitable mate had its conflicts.

She envied a man's world for its simplicity and directness. After her ordeal in the Philippines and landing in America in 1984, she wished she had been born male. As an Asian male, life would have been easier. That truth was also evident in America.

Loan's commentary and cussing confounded Ian and Bjorn. Their efforts to charm her and turn the luck of their cards went to nothing. The hands went as cold as her heart. She broke their play.

She was merciless. The diminutive Asian bitch, the devil herself, was going to have to pay.

Ian and Bjorn sorted out how they would achieve payback; however, current events eluded their dimmed sense of caution. They made fatal errors earlier in the evening at the slot machines. Women rejected their advances. It was all on video tape.

They were pitting their manly resources to exploit a defenseless female casino employee in an illuminated casino parking lot covered by security cameras. Yes, some of the cameras were fake. However, enough were real and the 24-hour rolling tapes tracked them well enough.

The "Movie-Boys" crystallized their error by making a scene at a well-monitored and video-recorded blackjack table. It was Loan's table and they had moved table-to-table with her. On camera, they had practically stalked her for hours. A final outburst by Bjorn sent the pair out of casino, escorted by tribal security.

Important critical information eluded higher brain functions. They had already convicted themselves before they acted. Any remaining intelligence between the men slipped out of the end of a bottle of Kentucky whiskey.

Bjorn nursed the large bottle of Jack Daniels bourbon and handed the uncapped bottle to Ian. Ian took a long swig from the bottle and handed it back; they were sharing eighty-proof bourbon: there was no need for concern about infectious germs.

Ian parked the Impala askew to the Honda, the front of each car several feet apart with the rear of the vehicles separated by five feet. He shut off the engine to save what was left of their fuel and sat back in the seat slurring, "Thish" shouldn't take long, thash Asian bissh has to go home soon, man." He paused as he gulped, "Soon!" Bjorn nodded silently taking a longer swig from the bottle.

3:50 AM, Saturday, 15 February 2004

The two men parked their car letting the engine idle for a few minutes to heat up the interior after which they shut it off to save precious gasoline. They mulled over their final bet of the evening; the woman had some cash and a new car. They had yet to determine whether she would be there with sufficient cash to get them home. However, they knew she'd be there with a useful car with more gas than their own.

Useful cash or not, a car with a quarter-tank of gas was more than they had that night. They figured she was the kind of person who avoided driving a car on empty. That would be just like that Asian bitches to operate that way, cautious and all that Chink tight-ass behavior. All cash, no credit, painful people to deal with on the downside.

The light snow was drifting down on to the windshield and hood of the car melting as it made contact with the warm metal and glass. The men's alcohol-loaded metabolism and the car's engine were heating up the vehicle in a New Mexico parking lot. On a cold winter night, from an infrared satellite image of Albuquerque, they would see a warm vehicle next to a cold vehicle in the middle of an empty parking lot. The image, if nothing else, spoke "ambush".

A small Asian woman in the New Mexico winter would notice the fact of thermal differentiation between the two vehicles. She wore two sweaters in summer and hated the cold winters of America. Her car had sat out all day and all night in sub-freezing weather. The mugger's car was warm and frost-free. In her best Asian-English, only an "idi-odit-dit-dit" would miss this difference.

Valentines and Casino Life (as it were)

It was 3:50 AM on Saturday, February 15, 2004, in the parking lot of an Indian casino north of Albuquerque, New Mexico just off the northbound service road of Interstate 25. Starting earlier during Friday evening, it was Friday, February 14, 2004, Valentine's Day. The occasion drew a large crowd to the casino. Little else says love to a casino like risking money in front of a hot date; poor players played bigger on Valentine's Day deploying the devil-may-care attitude of high-roller "wannabees" to their intended mates. The casino shifted its slot machines accordingly; they reduced the payout on slot machines. Valentine's night got busy and the slot-machine payout crashed. It took more than a few hours for the customers to figure their luck had turned cold on the slot machines. This sucked down customer cash pushing some of the players toward their ATM machines and the card tables.

The "movie-boys" as they were known by security made good on the best of times after starting their movie distribution business when the casino opened in 2002. Neither individual was a rocket scientist. However, they had become smart business-guys, unrestrained by copyright laws and professional ethics. By their morals, whatever they did was legal until they were caught, so they believed. Selling low-quality copies of first-run movies was an acceptable service to the community. There was a steady demand rising among an indiscriminate clientele of fuzzy reproductions of someone else's movie.

Ian and Bjorn's Casino-Based Movie-Distribution Business

The two men had worked out a system. They malingered in the casino moving from one bank of slot machines to another, playing the gambling equipment slowly at minimum investment. Their intent was about marketing their wares; winning at slot machines was an added bonus, losing money at slot machines was a minor marketing risk.

They used the slot machine action to strike up conversations with other players. In a matter of minutes of the start of conversation with other players, they'd switch the topic and make their sales pitch; they reached in their coats and pull out sleeves of CDs with various popular movie titles handwritten on them. Some of the titles were horribly misspelled. Regardless, the other slot machine players got the general idea; pirated copies of first-run movies at discount prices. The illicit copies of first-run movies were on hand within days of the release of the movie; legitimate full-quality CD copies of the movies would be available in a few months. These boys had low-quality CD copies right now. In behalf of an impatient and indiscriminate world, the movie-boys met demand for low-quality reproductions at low cost.

These large (overweight) men wore winter NFL jackets inside the casino, which fit in well enough in February in mid-state New Mexico. The odd thing, they kept wearing their jackets inside the heated building. It was a functional issue; the jackets carried an array of movie CD's without looking too bulky (for an NFL jacket). Ian wore a tan Fedora with a white band, maybe as a matter of style but since few men wore hats anymore, he looked more like an odd pimp with his bloated NFL jacket and the Fedora. He was the leader of the pack of two, and the "pimp" hat substantiated that leadership. Bjorn followed where Ian went.

They would work over one bank of slot machines as casino activity picked up. Then they moved from one section to another and back to the same place they started. As the patrons turned over throughout the night, they recycled their sales pattern systematically. They covered most of the slot machines in four to five hours. If the potential customer was an attractive woman, they even tried to set up a date or a rendezvous in their achieved Impala in the parking lot.

Oddly enough, they managed to have some parking lot romance, rarely with sober women. This prose is too kind; they only scored with drunken women. It usually turned out to be a one-event "romance" after the women sobered up and realized what they had done that night. What happens in an Indian Casino stays there; it's too embarrassing to brag on. This was New Mexico, 2004. The Albuquerque Chamber of Commerce was not about to put out a promotion on this issue with a flyer, "New Mexico Casinos: Where ugly drunks get another chance to fuck."

"Romantic" situations were at times stressful distractions. The "movie boys" had to choose between sex and sales during a good business night. They had gonads in lieu of "stop-nads"; their physical liaisons usually won out over the CD marketing program. Their return margins were low but their personal standards were lower, especially when a woman's interests were akin to their own. If anyone wanted to swear off sex, the images of these guys doin' the wimin in the back seat of the Capris would suffice. Romeo and Juliet it was not.

Regardless, the pirated-movie-moguls felt like their life was acceptably normal through the benefits of their enterprise and the Indian casino, they had money, position and romance. For them, life was good enough to stay with their ad hoc enterprise. If it worked, work at it, so they thought to stay with their enterprise and expand it best as they could. They could barely spell their own names. However, give them credit of the doubt; they had expectations of larger enterprise. They were realizing an American dream of independent business.

Blatant theft, as an entrepreneurial criterion, made it seem like they were doing good business. In 2004, the United States economy was flush with money and loose personal standards. The movie boys did well. Virtually any Indian casino in middle America did well.

When Ian and Bjorn made sufficient funds or the sales activity slowed down, they would go up to one of the casino bars and order some drinks. They pitched their CDs to anyone they thought a likely candidate for pirated movies. When their net sale was up more than four hundred dollars, they scored some cocaine or crack outside casino property. This was south of the casino in a parking lot leased, not owned, by the casino. The boys smoked or inhaled their purchase in their tricked-out low-slung dark blue 1998 Chevy Impala. If the night went well, one of them slept in back. The other slept in the front seat. The only un-cool thing about the Impala was that it had a bench seat in front. However, it made a better bed than bucket seats and a fricking stick-shift console in the middle.

Otherwise, when too exhausted or in need of a shower, they used their aunt's house to sleep in south Albuquerque. They would time their "re-charging" cycle sleeping over at her house during her grave-yard shift as a nurse at local hospital. Otherwise, a bottle of cologne extended their hygiene issues. They returned to the casino lit up, high as kites and reeking of Jade East. They would restart the same sales cycle with a new load of chemically induced confidence and stinking of old men from the 1970s.

On a good night and when they had enough money, they'd go to one of the blackjack tables and expand their "treasury" on the card games. They usually lost more than half the time. If their losses occurred early in the evening, and if they were still sufficiently sober, they attempted to rebuild their income. They often hit on some of the same customers they had visited a few hours before. This usually made them pests and all it took was one customer complaint to draw the attention of security.

Casino security frequently caught them hustling the slot-machine players. They escorted the two out on the justification that it was illegal to sell pirated movies. The casinos had to maintain standards, even low ones. However, and more importantly, CD sales were distracting cash that should otherwise be thrown into slot machines or converted to chips at the game tables. Casino management justified that it was better to throw money on slot machines than poor-quality movies.

The movie-boys waited for a shift change in security personnel. Usually in less than a few hours, they'd be back on the property working over the slot machine players for new sales. Funny enough, if the first night's slot-players were still there, they would buy identical movies from the boys often twice on the same day. It is hard to imagine their thoughts when they played the copies of a movie with miss-spelled titles sorting out how they now had two low-quality copies of a first run movie.

The quality of the movies: terrible - just really terrible quality. Ian and Bjorn made their initial copy in the back of a first-run movie theater with a medium quality camcorder on the last day's showing on a weeknight. They sat motionless holding the camera on a crude stand they could sneak in under their jackets. They often brought members in their family to sit beside them as buffer to isolate their "endeavor" from discovery. A few dollars donated to a pimply-faced high school kid acting as late night theater manager sealed the deal as required.

They had sufficient computer skills to make copies of the movies and polished the production by scrawling the movie title on the CD, two out of three times misspelling the movie title. The spelling was absolutely awful. Oddly enough, the illiterate scrawl made the bad copy of the movie more valuable as a joke to show someone unfamiliar with pirated movies.

Regardless of the crudeness and illegality of their product, these wizards of modern enterprise squeezed out a reasonable living, telling anyone who asked that they were in the movie distribution industry. It was the truth. They had copies of movies and they distributed. The pirated product was junk. However, they told the truth.

The boys depended on turnover of naive customers in order to have a viable and perpetual clientele. Indian casinos in New Mexico made a perfect market for their business. Drunken slot-machine players betting limited resources on hopes of walking away wealthy made ideal customers for poor quality copies.

When they were sufficiently sober on the casino property, they seemed harmless. They had become semi-fixtures of casino action on weekends as they wandered around the slot machines looking for their next sale. Casino security knew exactly who and what they were and on average, they harassed the "movie-boys" infrequently. As it was, the "movie-boys" would end up putting their earnings back into the casino. Despite their bluster as big-time movie distributors and about their prowess at playing blackjack and "Texas hold-em," they were poor gamblers. Similar to their spelling of movie titles, their gambling skills sucked.

Loan's Blackjack Table

That night, the "movie-boys" played blackjack on a five-dollar table with a fifty-dollar limit. A personable woman they knew as Loan operated the table in that first thirty-minute interval. Ian and Bjorn filled out the last two seats of the blackjack table.

Loan was an attractive young Asian in her early thirties. When she was "dolled up" standing five-foot-three in her three-inch-plus heels and black tuxedo, she passed for early twenties. She had a disarming smile and lively personality that often kept her table full of players.

Her Marilyn Monroe figure elicited questions, usually from Asian women, on whether she padded her hips and buttocks. Her curves were natural although Loan had a breast augmentation in 2003. Cleavage increased tips on the playing tables *(at least for women)*.

Ian and Bjorn knew her well enough; she was spirited. She gave better than she got turning customer trash-talk into outrageous rebuke.

A pit boss manages the dealers and interaction with players. They usually characterized their day based on whether Loan worked a blackjack or poker table on their station. Loan made the pit boss's shift interesting. They learned to expect anything.

Loan kept to herself avoiding trouble when possible; however it seemed to find her. Loan's Asian "exotic-ness" and her rough English gave her an unusual appeal among the various card dealers.

Gamblers, alcohol and sex appeal mixed poorly at times. On occasion, players got stupid.

Loan bantered with the customer by blending her rough English peppered with the occasional expletive to amuse and shock as fit the moment and the player. A dealer's main mission was to accurately manage the chips in and out of their tray. Loan's math was impeccable; it had to be. Three money errors on a table game ended a dealer's career at that casino. Five money errors ended a dealer's career in any casino.

While Loan manipulated cards and money perfectly, the other side of the table varied in quality and class. Drugs and alcohol seldom improved the interaction between dealer and customer. The problem enlarged with Loan because of the stereotypes attached to small Asian women with thick accents. A woman born in "Nam" with rough English had to be ignorant and dim...and easy.

When a customer played the "stupid-card" and expletives flew, Loan responded in kind. The pit boss's job: prevent Loan's table from getting too interesting.

She learned English, her fourth language, in New York as an orphaned teenager. Consequently, she picked up the habit of cussing in English when she was annoyed or having difficulty making a point. Fluent in her native Cantonese and South Vietnamese, she picked up Filipino Spanish in a Manila orphanage.

A few dozen words in English required some translation. She confused the use of certain groups of words such as "for" and "to." Combinations of letters in some words dropped a consonant; "dudes" became "doos," "virgin" became "version" and so on. She resorted to certain slang terms if it was easier to understand than a proper term.

Most expletives, however, came through loud and clear. Cuss words were not used in the course of polite conversation and not immediately in harsh moments. The "Brooklyn" words started when someone insisted on their "rightness" because they suffered at the hands of a stupid Asian dealer. Unclear as Loan's English might be at times. Stupid she was not.

Loan usually gave customers two chances to mend their words if not their thinking; the third event drew the harsh words. In Christian parlance, Loan turned the other cheek. Then she nuked them.

This happened more often to Loan largely because she was a small Chinese woman that has difficulty with some of her pronunciation. Strangers, particularly white and black women, often treat her as dim. This happened frequently, often in public setting where a store clerk or service person erred and assumed the Asian woman with fractured English was responsible for the service-persons error.

Then the fur flies. Loan's teenage daughter learned to explained away to anyone within ear-shot that her mother suffered from "Turret's syndrome." Turret's syndrome generally identifies a randomness in the brain where people do odd things unexpectedly. The most well-known symptom is random and unexpected cussing.

Good in math, Loan's handling of cards and payout of chips was flawless. Customers challenged her on one issue or another stood corrected every time. Still, challenges arose.

The pit boss on duty kept an eye on Loan more than other dealers. The pit boss's attention served another purpose; he or she might collect another one of those "Loan Stories" to be traded at the next break among the staff in the employees' cafeteria.

The movie-boys were stoned and drunk by that late hour staggering a bit as they walked up to her table. Loan greeted them as she often did, "Whazzz up doos?" her English thick with a Chinese-Vietnamese accent, unable to fully close off the end of a word such as the word 'dude.' The "movie-boys" responded in kind, "Whazzz up Miss China Doll?" Her response was a smile that lit up the room.

Loan's disarming manner did not work with everyone. The mild standoff between Asians and other minorities was evident. A "managed peace" existed between Loan and the movie-boys.

The exact source of animosities is hard to pinpoint. It may stem from the perceptions of the "haves" and "have-nots." It is fundamentally impossible to mark any of the Vietnamese as "haves" when they came to North America in the late 1970s and throughout the 1980s with nothing but the clothes on their back.

After South Viet Nam's collapsed, the Asian refugees came to America in harrowing flights to freedom. They had been brutalized by North Viet Nam. Most of them landed in America broke and traumatized. Many lost family and friends in the final days of a free South Viet Nam. As Viet Nam plunged into chaos and dysfunction, they ended up with little choice; struggle under a punishing communist regime or face a horrific exodus across The South China Sea or west to Thailand.

Vietnamese Expectations

Vietnamese refugees adjusted to life in North America in six months and began to prosper usually in less than two years. They came from a world that worked fourteen hours a day seven days a week, taking off only for Tet, the Chinese New Year.

America's five-day forty-hour work week was easy. With so much extra time, many took second and third jobs. Accustomed to two or more families living together, they often pooled their resources to acquire homes, vehicles and businesses.

Asian refugees lived frugally while adjusting to the abundance of the western world. First generation immigrants assimilated as best they could, learning the language while retaining their culture and traditions as much as possible. They worked hard to rebuild a life as Americans and Canadians.

The racial stereotype about education was based on the truth; Asian children rose notably to the top of scholastics in the communities that adopted them. By the end of the 1980s, they competed with native-born Americans for scholarships. Many of them began small businesses working with the system and in some cases working the system.

Asians avoided one part of the American system: welfare. While they accepted the aid of family and Christian organizations to start their life in America, they considered use of food stamps dishonorable. American welfare was a sure way to lose "face" among peers. The temptation to accept American food stamps was huge for a people deprived of country and comfort. A huge percentage of Vietnamese refused to exploit American welfare. *(Author's Note: I know this personally and exactly as Loan asked me to cash in her welfare "chits." I could not. She was too embarrassed to do so herself. As long as she could stand and move and work and think, she could not take welfare and "save-face.")*

People stranded in the lower strata of American society tended to resent Asians. The differences showed up in racially loaded dialogue from time to time. The antagonism went both ways, Asian men openly questioned Asian women who dated or married other races, or even different Asian sub-types. Ethnic Chinese tended to identify themselves as different from the local people of the country whether they were from Malaysia, Thailand or Viet Nam.

Ian and Bjorn typified the American melting pot; they were a blend of races. White, Black, American Indian perhaps with a little Hispanic thrown in, they were comfortable mixing with anyone. Class, however, was another issue. They had lots of class but it was mostly low.

Getting along with people was a necessity of the movie-boy business. They sold their pirated movies to anyone. Yet, they mildly resented the Asians that swarmed North America in the early 1980s.

"Where did all the Asians come from so suddenly?" was the common question among Ian and Bjorn's crowd. Albuquerque, like so many other cities and communities across North America, accommodated the refugees through Christian organizations and State Department assistance. Idle military bases became Americanization facilities for Vietnamese refugees. Asian Districts cropped up in cities with virtually no Asian populations a few years before; existing China Towns grew.

Ian and Bjorn joked of the Asian Invasion with Loan. She was open to the conversation. However, jokes and ribbing concealed a simmering conflict.

There were frequent comments about the "dang Asians" that moved up as soon as they landed in the United States. They went from grunts doing anything menial to bosses and business owners seemingly in just a few years. Residual issues festered with Ian and Bjorn that night as the Asian princess seduced them into draining their night's earnings.

Ian and Bjorn settled in the number five and six seats on the left side of the blackjack table, each throwing two one-hundred dollar bills on the table. Loan dragged a felt-tip "money-pen" on each bill to check for counterfeit bills then stuffed the bills into a bank slot in the table. The pit-boss logged in Ian and Bjorn's cash transferred into chips.

Loan converted each bill into a stack of chips. She counted out thirty-nine red $5 chips, four white $1 chips, and a couple of fifty-cent pieces for the fifty-cent-per-hand ante that covered the moral obligation of some obscure education fund for the State of New Mexico. Indian casinos promoted a funding scheme in a number of states where card-dealer antes and percentage of the slot income went to education, etc. Just as in all gambling, it was a variable reward system, even for the State of New Mexico.

She set five red chips in a line of four short stacks using her fingers to meter out each $25 and laying one stack of five so the overhead security cameras could "see" the stacks. Without turning her head too far, she called out "Two hundred." For Ian, then "Two Hundred" for Bjorn. The pit boss acknowledged the conversion and logged the transaction on a computer tablet near the table to the left of Loan.

Six people now played the table. Two gray-hair white men with weathered faces and wearing cowboy hats sat on the left. Two Vietnamese women working with a dwindling set of chips sat on the right side of the table.

They waited for Loan to deal out the cards after the new arrivals acquired their chips. The girls attempted to speak to Loan in

Vietnamese. House rules required players to speak English at the table during card play. Loan only responded to them in English admonishing them to do the same.

The taller of the two, Ian, put out a ten dollar bet; Bjorn bet twenty dollars. Bjorn made a circular motion over the chips for good luck as Loan dealt out the first two cards.

Players tipped dealers on winning hands. Either way the cards played, the blackjack dealers did their job; however, if the player won big, they'd get a tip. If the hand went for the house, dealers still kept their job. Since most of the dealer's typical income came from tips, it was advisable to avoid crushing a player.

Skilled blackjack dealers could manage the players to improve their tips but only during crowded hours before 2 AM on the weekend. After that, the security cameras and the pit boss ran the players' options for "managed" house losses. The house usually recovered losses by keeping the players at the table. Smart players left the table early when they were ahead.

The turn of cards excited potential gambling addicts. Black jack played quickly. Fortunes could rise quickly when the cards were hot. The table could break a player's stash in minutes when the table was cold.

The movie boys drew blackjack on their first hand of play. Loan drew a ten and a four busting her hand with a face card. To some gamblers, hot cards at the start might be an omen best ignored.

The first series of cards went well for Ian and Bjorn. They doubled down on occasion and won. Luck enhanced with cocaine and liquor pumped their confidence.

Good gamblers manage their losses when the cards go cold and know that when they're lucky that it is usually only that: luck. Six-deck blackjack works for the house; it reduces the player's ability to track (count) the card play. When the cards are good, they're considered to be "hot." When the cards go cold, there are few options but reduce the bet or leave the table.

The relationship between a card dealer and a player often made a difference in the "take" of the house. Savvy personable dealers stirred up conversation in order to engage the players to stay and play a few more hands when they should have left the table. More than a few men had played at Loan's table in an attempt to court her. A few others hung around to see if she was going to light up on someone acting badly.

Ian and Bjorn started with a strong series of hot cards. They lacked the discipline to quit when they were ahead. They improved the situation with liquor.

They ordered drinks feeling cocky tipping the waitress ten dollars for two watered-down bourbon and Cokes. Each frowned at the weak drinks; this was beneath their standards. Their buzz was slipping. They needed something stronger and ordered Long Island Teas.

These were a couple of too-cool dudes out on the town kicking butt and taking names. The Asian princess had improved their luck. They talked trash to Loan who handed it back to them in spades.

Loan knew how to talk to men at any level. Her outrageous commentary delighted the men; however, it had a mixed review with some women.

The Asian women at her table played out the last of their chips and left the table. The casino population was thinning out; most of the card tables were empty. This left it to leaving the game to Loan, the old white cowboys and the movie boys.

Ian and Bjorn decided as the dealers changed tables every thirty minutes, they would move with Loan to her next table. They figured in their clouded logic that a Chinese woman brought them good fortune. Besides that, unlike most Asians they knew, this woman had a full figure. They had lady luck and the view wasn't bad.

They made their vote by tipping Loan five-dollar chips when they benefited from a good turn of cards. In hindsight view of their impeding financial status, they would need those five and ten dollar tips in order to avoid unwise decisions later.

It was "un-cool" to win without tipping. For the players there for a social moment among strangers, they tipped the dealer on a good hand. The tip made no sense whatsoever as it generated no outcome other than good will between customer and dealer.

Tipping the dealer for a good play of cards to influence the next hand and if it a tip changed the shuffle. However, as they blackjacked, these men strived to maintain appearances.

Most gamblers pick a table and stay with it working with each dealer change on whatever schedule the casino maintains. Part of that rotation kept the dealers sharp on their management of the cards.

However, it was also about separating the relationship between dealers and customers.

Casinos anticipated collusion between dealers and customers. A dealer in cahoots with a player intentionally gives up hands. The player wins more and splits the take off-property with the dealer.

In Texas Hold' Em, card handling reveals the card as it is dealt. A particular player guesses at the hand's the advantage on the house and modifies bets accordingly minimizing losses and expanding wins. Black jack relies on the strategy of how cards add to 21. The dealer sticks on 17 and when a dealer draws 21, black jack, all players lose.

Security cameras, rules of play, handling procedures along with automatic shuffling and card dispensing reduced the abuse. However, floor management missed inappropriate alliance on occasion. They depended on routine dealer movement to reduce the opportunity for theft. A dealer that errs more than three times has to find another job.

Ian and Bjorn had established a mystic relationship with their China Doll as they called Loan. They moved with her shift to another table to hold their luck.

One other procedure is the management of the movement of numbers of chips. The casino required the customer to convert a number of smaller value chips into fewer larger value chips. The dealer converted the chips and called out to the pit boss "Color out!" to let him know of the conversion and that a player was leaving the table.

This drew the attention of the casino of player movement. It was routine.

As quickly as they were up hundreds of dollars each, Ian and Bjorn's luck turned. Their cards went cold.

Their tempers heated up from stoned to mildly warm after a series of bad hands. They played against the dealer and Loan's card hands outgunned the combined value of their cards. Adding quickly to 21 was also a bit of a challenge, particularly if they accumulated a series of low-value cards. They blew some good hands by under-estimating the card totals, drawing another card when they were showing 16 and 17. Their low math skills and the Long Island Teas unraveled their winnings. Loan could have given the tally of their cards but once they were ahead, the house admonished her if she helped the players with their math.

Hands of their cards, totals of nineteen and twenty, collided with the dealer's twenty and blackjacks drawn by the house; in this case played as Loan's cards. With the security cameras and bit boss focused on the only table with players at that late hour, Loan was just and only a handler of the cards. She shuffled a few times and the cards were further mixed by the card shuffling machine. She knew how to modify the shuffle to Ian and Bjorn's benefit when the casino's attention was spread out on the dealer tables. However, under the watchful eye of the empty casino, she could do little for them. It was up to Ian and Bjorn to manage their luck.

The over-exercised gambler's truth is that losers not winners build casinos. The key to gambling is don't. Short of that rule, leave when ahead, leave sooner when down. Playing longer to get even with the casino only makes more money for the casino.

Many players going for the next big win or attempt to recover their losses more often than not donate more to the "house." Ian and Bjorn gave up winning hands via their inability to add some combination of cards. The Long Island Teas, they had already downed several of them on the way up, failed to improve their judgment of the odds. Without a full table of players at the table playing 6-deck blackjack, they were playing on dumb luck. And it was now bad dumb luck.

Within an hour, Ian and Bjorn were down eight hundred dollars draining away all the money they had made earlier that night. They complained to Loan that she was busting them. She refuted the charged counseling them, "You are drunk, movie-boys. Stop playing if (the) blackjack sucks (goes bad)."

They complained again loudly after Loan drew blackjack. She repeated the same comments adding, "You stupid or what? I canna do anythin' about card luck. I'm just dealah'."

One of the pit bosses, an older swarthy Italian-American with a mane of silver-gray hair by the name of Vinnie heard Loan lighting up on the surly customers. Part of the mission of the pit boss on this shift was to keep this particular dealer from verbally wailing on obnoxious customers.

Loan was one of the casino's best producers keeping the customer playing when they should have taken their winnings home. However, she could be a handful when something annoyed her. Loan never started a fight but the casino was frequently afraid she might finish it.

Loan had a following of high-rollers, as big-stakes gamblers were called that like to play at her table. At certain times of the week, she dealt black jack and Texas Hold-Em poker in the high-roller rooms, depending on the traffic of wealthy gamblers. Players had to acquire at least one thousand dollars in chips to walk in the room; many of them would acquire ten and twenty thousand dollars in chips, gambling hundreds and thousands of dollars on each hand. Oil rig operators and roughnecks from northern New Mexico oil and gas fields rubbed elbows with doctors and lawyers in the room; a few of them pitching to Loan for a date or even her hand in marriage.

Loan's Private Life

Widowed eight years before, she remained unmarried caring for her two children. She socialized very little with customers outside the casino, more as a matter to elicit tips and gifts. She was lonely for the company of a man but her last relationship with a handsome Hispanic man soured when he became addicted to drugs.

Loan moved to Albuquerque as a matter of personal safety and the fact that Indian gaming was growing in New Mexico with the highest potential income for card dealers in the United States. Dealers didn't share tips in New Mexico as they did in Las Vegas. Glamorous Las Vegas was less profitable for good dealers.

Depending on the romance pressures from customers, she selectively wore a wedding band to minimize distraction and maximize tips. Men tipped female dealers better than they tipped male dealers, particularly if the women sported a nice figure, a pretty smile and the potential for romance.

Loan had an additional advantage; she knew how to talk to men peppering her banter with shocking epithets in her thickly accented English along with a mixture of gangsta slang. The humor of her occasional mangled words in English grew by the delay in understanding of what she had just said; it punched up her punch lines. She used her exotic-ness to her advantage. Dumbass old white men with some gambling cash in hand lined up just to hear Loan talk.

Security personnel had cameras trained on the table and microphones listening into the conversation. They heard something at Loan's table and studied the gamblers. Most of the time they'd be laughing but on occasion, Loan laid into a customer using two hands to hold the cards, touching someone else's chips or smoking a cigar at her table. The pit boss wore an earpiece and received voice messages from security personnel to check in on her table and see if something was getting out of hand. If the customer was out of line, the pit boss interceded as gently as possible to keep the play going.

Communicating with Loan had become an art form. Her managers used a combination of words, facial expressions and gestures to sort out an issue at the gaming table. In order to maintain visual contact with the chip tray, card dealers cannot look away from their table. A pit boss might say something and gesture, "What the "F" is going on?" at the same time. A dim pit boss operated at a loss with Loan. She told them directly to remove a bad player from the table using her rough English laced with colorful metaphors. She cussed out errant players and dim pit-bosses as needed. "Get the "blank" "blank" off my table "you blank-blank-idi-di-di-iot." usually in a pitched accented stemming from her Asian languages.

Security personnel, mostly men, enjoyed the moment. The tables all had microphones listening to dealers and players. A shrill series of epithets rising up from the table microphones meant someone agitated Loan. They switched cameras to her table as allowed and sat back to watch the show calling down the pit bosses that something was up on Loan's table.

Again.

High rollers were treated with a bit more latitude. However, they were generally better mannered when compared to players in the main area known as the "lobby." Regardless, if the card play went "south" with the "Asian Goddess" as she was occasionally labeled, the pit-boss heard about it early from the security boys watching and listening to the card tables.

Gambling attracted every strata of society. Welfare "credit cards" worked as well as debit and credit cards. Welfare Mommas spent long mornings at the penny slot machines, gambling with government largesse until the public found out.

In 2010, California learned that 1.9 billion dollars of public aid money went through automatic teller machines in Indian Casinos. Women with half a dozen children of half a dozen fathers were playing the penny slot machines on government credit cards. Loan deeply resented this behavior and often called them out when they waddled through the casino lobby to gamble their welfare money. Security personnel heard her calling out the welfare mothers from her table. Loan told the pit boss that she was joking with the woman as if the woman was an old friend. Security had no idea what to do. The situation didn't blow up so they let it go.

People would spend their last nickel hoping for a turn in the luck and resort to pan handling, theft or prostitution in the parking lots. Casino security constantly monitored the parking areas to at least control the begging and theft. Patrons could not be victimized or annoyed. Security was all about keeping the patrons comfortable and secure.

Others of limited means tried to expand their resources on a hot streak. Casinos adjusted the return of the slot machines electronically raising and lowering the probabilities of payouts. They adjusted the odds to allow them to win just enough to keep playing and posting the infrequent big winners on the displays and marquees. By dimes, nickels and quarters, the casinos entertained and drain the masses of their treasure.

Management was minimally concerned about the low-spend customer's relationship to the casino or the "house" as it was called. The impoverished gambler added to the bottom line. They they genuinely strived to prevent gambling addicts from destroying their lives but often at a level the customer hovered just above zero. A washed out gambling addict spent no money. Besides that, victims of gambling addiction made for bad publicity and hurt the casinos in the long term.

Casino management focused on minimizing the casino's legal exposure and maximizing the take of the house. High rollers and penny players alike could have bad days and take it out on the dealers and the casino. Loan worked for the casino for eighteen months and there were already half a dozen Loan-stories about a customer getting surly with her as their cards went cold.

Other dealers took the abuse calling in the pit boss when it the customer passed through some threshold of decorum. Loan seldom waited for a slow-to-act pit-boss to intervene at her table; a few customers that didn't manage the direction of their exhaled cigarette smoke often ended up with their cigarette in their drink. Casino personnel asked cigar smokers to play at another table if they had to light up anywhere near Loan.

Casinos became the last bastion of public places that permitted smoking indoors, but not at Loan's table. Unless the fat white man smoking the cigar was tipping her 20% a hand to play at her table, cigars were forbidden.

Loan produced great income for the casino. Her card-dealing skills gave her latitude. However, there were house liabilities if she strayed too far out of their comfort zone.

She had good manners and conducted herself well. There was just something about Nguyên Xuân Loan that elicited inappropriate treatment from strangers. Alcohol, drugs and gambling affected a player's mood and mixed poorly with jerks and buttheads. Personal judgment was variable. Loan, a smart diminutive Asian with a thick Chinese accent and seemingly fearless intolerance for fools expanded the potential for trouble.

Many Americans unwittingly treated Vietnamese refugees as second-rate human beings at the outset of their arrival. Loan was no exception. Maybe it was carry over from the fact that Viet Nam was the first war America "lost." South Viet Nam lost the war after America withdrew. Regardless, it was a region of the world most Americans would rather forget. According to US records, over 820,000 Vietnamese took refuge in America in the first ten years after the fall of Sai Gon.

Ignorant people misread the small woman with thickly accented English as an ignorant foreigner bleeding American largesse. It was as if the social equation added up for small foreign-born women with some difficulty with English; they had to be stupid. In addition, they had to be on welfare. For Loan, the assumption of dependence on the government insulted her. It insulted her to the extreme.

In addition, she had been a Buddhist all of her life and ultra conservative in her politics living in a largely Christian community. When people made the mistake of suggesting she change her religion or support liberal politicians, the fur (and expletives) flew. She considered it rude and offensive to volunteered unsolicited advice. Repeat offenses were met with rough language. A physical attack was met with a blistering reprisal.

A few female employees made the mistake of attempting to exploit or rob Loan. Two weeks earlier, Loan caught a large white woman dealer breaking into her locker. Two weeks later, the woman still had some visible bruises on her arms and face.

It was caught on camera and women security monitored female-only areas of the casino. The event lasted less than ten seconds.

Management admonished Loan for pulverizing the woman after she lashed out at Loan in front of the open locker. Her first swing struck Loan's face in a glancing blow on the cheek. For Loan, that was all it took. In seconds, she had landed a series of blows with hands, feet and knees on the large woman. By the time women security entered the employee locker area, they found the white woman dealer slumped on the floor underneath Loan's open locker. Loan was standing over her body calmly adjusting her makeup.

Casino management put the errant dealer on notice and management re-assigned her shift to keep the two from working the same hours. This proved difficult for the woman as Loan often worked across shifts when the Casino was busy or short-handed. Loan's work hours made life impossible for the other dealer. She eventually found another job.

Security and management often discussed what to do with Loan. She did not look for confrontation; trouble found her. Her appeal to the gamblers was also her curse; it drew envy and jealousy from less successful dealers.

In 2004, it was said that even an ugly female dealer could earn over one hundred thousand dollars a year in tips. Loan earned over twice that amount. The casino grossed over fifteen million a year on Loan's card tables.

Loan's charm had collected a number of admiring men who gave up untold thousands to play at her table and draw out her rough exotic charm. Some of the wealthy elite of central New Mexico asked repeatedly for a date. The single mother of two always declined, accepting at most gifts or dinner in one of the casino restaurants on her break. Many women dealers would have jumped at any of the offers that Loan turned down.

The few women that got close to Loan asked her why she turned down the wealthy men she flirted with as she dealt the cards, took their money and stole their hearts. Loan only answered with a shrug. When pressed, Loan responded "Nun yer biness, bisshh!" That nosey woman never got that close to Loan again.

The pit boss on the card tables and security carried one-way radios with an ear-piece that traveled down and tucked inside their shirt.

Security on the camera detail could talk to them individually. Unless they carried two-way handsets, they couldn't respond to questions from the camera and listening stations. However, with Loan, just in case, the casino required two-way communication with the pit boss at all times.

With near regularity, customers got stupid with Loan. Management attention spans lapsed. Security on cameras and table microphones failed to follow a customer's wayward conversation. A terse voice came in through their ear-bud that the conversation at Loan's table was going south. It was a code phrase that a customer had just crossed an invisible boundary and was about to get a double-barrel epithet or worse, a black eye or cigar stuffed down their throat.

On several occasions, smokers thought they were being cute by blowing smoke at Loan. Blowing cigarette and cigar smoke deliberately at a person is, technically, a form of battery. The cameras and microphones overhead always recorded each table with security personnel scanning the arrays of monitors. Often as not, as the last chip landed in the chip tray, Loan reached over taking the patron's drink and dousing him in the face.

Security escorted sputtering angry players out of the casino with the threat of filing charges. The pit bosses chided Loan uselessly; she was within her rights. The casinos made arrangements with the offended patron and furloughed Loan for a day with pay. The pay meant nothing as 90% of her income came from tips.

Typical inflammatory topics were any form of unsolicited volunteered advice, excessive nosey questions about Loan's life and liberal political arguments. Zealous Christian gamblers (oxymoronic?) made the mistake of proselytizing; liberals of any label made the same mistake. Her English was acceptable to a careful listener, perhaps a bit rough-hewn; however, the "f" and "mf" words came through loud and clear.

Some of the customers enjoyed the Asian woman's earthy retorts and sought her black jack and poker table to watch her "go." She had a handful of admirers, mostly older white men who enjoyed her unpredictable replies and tipped accordingly. A couple of patrons encouraged unsuspecting players into making the wrong comment to the dealer. A ticket to a better fight could not be bought; instigator and victim both received a memorable moment. For some mysterious reasons yet to be sorted out by government studies, lawsuits never ensued. Loan appeared to know the boundary of objection in a litigious society such as America.

More than few asked her out to which she largely refused unless they paid in cash and shopping trips to the local mall. They got little else from this exchange than her company and her gratitude. She had a mysterious reputation for endearing and disappointing a throng of wealthy men.

A widower from a marriage to an engineer that was killed on a project, Loan still wore a wedding band from time to time to keep suitors guessing but as much as anything to reduce their requests for a date. Her husband had died eight years before and she had difficulty establishing acceptable relationships after he died.

Loan had become a workaholic trying to maintain a single-parent household with two young children. She strived to have the American dream even if her life was a nightmare.

There was an endless line of suitors, which explained some of her difficulty with female casino employees; she had a number of men wanting to be with her and she kept them at a distance. More than a few of the women resented Loan and made a scene with her on occasion. Those issues would resurface in an event later that night.

Few knew whether she had limits if a situation truly got out of hand. Most employees heard of Loan; she was by all appearances, fearless. Every few weeks, another "Loan Story" circulated in the dealer break room.

"Don't mess with that Asian." Became the standard advice. Loan had yet to give a customer a black eye. Something about her that communicated that potential. Management believed when, not if, Loan struck a customer, they probably had it coming.

Big Vinnie

Big Vinnie knew much of the story Loan's difficult life in Viet Nam as Sai Gon fell to North Viet Nam. He heard pieces about her incredible journey to America prior to meeting her in New Mexico.

He met her a few months after Loan's husband was killed in a construction accident in Grand Island, Nebraska. She had moved to

Louisiana to stay with her husband's mother. She came to the casino with her sister and by chance, met one of Vinnie's mentors when he worked for the casinos in Nevada.

Vinnie was "old-guard," a soldier of the mob from Las Vegas. He heard of Loan through the brotherhood from Richard B.. Richard was high up in the organization in the early days of Las Vegas. As management of Las Vegas casinos moved from eastern mobsters to Wall Street, Richard and Vinnie found other means of plying their skills. Richard was the general manager of a Louisiana casino when he first met Loan watching play on a roulette table.

It's a long story to be dealt with later. Leave it to say, Richard took an interest in Loan. He was thirty-two years older. Had he been younger and in better health, he would have married her. By all measures, as bad and good as Richard was, Loan would have married him too.

Instead, he took her along with her young children under wing, so to speak, training her as a dealer and "Americanized" her as much as possible. Up to then, she was still very much an Asian stranded in a foreign country. She was smart and tough. Richard trained her. He made her smarter and tougher.

However, as intelligent as Richard was, he could only push Loan so far. He eventually gave up hope on making a life with her. His health was failing and much as it broke his heart to think it, she was a young woman who needed to have a younger man in her life. Regardless, he was in love with her and would do anything to help her.

When a good dealer job came up in New Mexico as the Indian casinos developed, "Uncle Richard" introduced Loan to Vinnie. Richard warned Vinnie as he complemented Loan. "She's got great manners, a big heart, and style, Vinnie. Only one thing. Don't piss her off."

Richard was deadly serious. It was no joke. Richard was more afraid for his partners than for Loan, she was similar to a ticking time-bomb, near as Richard ever knew. His advice was about protecting his buddies. Loan could take care of herself. Richard and his boys knew all too well how Loan could react.

Vinnie remembered Richard's caution when he relocated to Albuquerque and ran into Loan. Richard told Vinnie to handle Loan "like managing a grenade with the pin pulled half-way out." Vinnie advised other managers, "She's tougher than just about anyone I've ever met."

This advice came from an Italian American that, as a seven-year old boy, killed a man in defense of his mother. Young Richard drove a fork into his mother's abusive boyfriend's neck as the man was beating her. Growing up in a rough part of New Jersey in the 1940s, Richard knew exactly what he was doing. He knew that a sharp object driven in to a vital artery in the neck would kill the man. This would be the only death by his own hands; however, it was not the last by his direction.

Richard participated in a series of violent events as a young man in Las Vegas in the 1960s as a seasoned soldier of the Las Vegas mob. Regardless of his difficult upbringing and his association with ruthless people, he cautioned everyone in contact with Loan to steer clear of her temper. Richard would tell everyone connected with her that her diminutive stature and rough English made her, at times, appear ignorant and vulnerable. Richard summed it up simply, "Underestimate her at your own risk."

Bad Cards

Vinnie watched Loan's table, left only to the Asian blackjack dealer and the "movie boys," Ian and Bjorn. Their treasure skated off through poor choices as well as a series of bad hands. Their body language revealed the rising tension between them and Loan. They rose out of their seats, leaning into the blackjack table waiting for the next card. They were straining to realize an overdue recovery from their mounting losses flinching with each busted play. Enthusiasm with a good hand withered as they calculated their losses. They drained a couple of Long Island Teas as cash slipped into the casino's vault.

Ian and Bjorn turned on the charm with her, asking her to make it easier on them. She ignored their requests, most of the other blackjack and poker tables were empty at this late hour, and the pit boss along with the security cameras had little else to watch. When a dealer draws seventeen, they have to hold on their own hand. At selected moments, she helped the boys, breaking her own cards when she drew anything below seventeen. Under the eyes and ears of the pit boss, the security cameras, and microphones, she could only play the cards as they came from the deck.

Their tempers rose with each losing hand and swallow of liquor. At one point, Ian lost another hand and yelled at Loan, "Come on bitch! You're raping me!" Bjorn winced as Vinnie motioned to them to settle down or he'd have to close out their play. Ian apologized raising his hands up to the pit boss, "Sorry, sorry, sorry, sorry. I'll be good," as he drained his third Long Island Tea.

Foolishly, they kept playing with another hand going their way only to lose the next two or three hands against the dealer and the house. By 2:30 AM, they had lost everything they made from the pirated-movie sales that night and were digging into the money they brought with them earlier that evening. They had lost their "build" for the night.

They improved their gambling strategy doubling down on their bets to accelerate their recovery. A bad plan combined with worse timing.

Their strategy worked half way; they doubled the rate of their losses and the casino recovered the rest of their money. After a long string of losing hands, Bjorn finally lost it, turning on Loan, "You fucking bitch! You killin' us whore!" At that point the pit boss motioned to the tribe's security staff. Another customer had joined the table a few minutes earlier, shrugging at the commotion as if was part of the floor show. He looked at Loan who just smiled as the tribal police escorted Ian and Bjorn from the casino lobby.

"Betta luck nex' tym', doos." Loan advised them, once again not able to enunciate the word "dude." Ian and Bjorn just glared at her as the casino's security people guided them from the casino floor toward the parking lot.

At 3:30 AM the two men, in their puffy NFL jackets, Ian leading the way wearing his fedora, went out into the winter night. Light snow fell out of the dark sky. Although they were quite drunk, their crack-induced euphoria had faded. They lost the money they intended to spend on another hit with the "rocks." They badly desired chemical therapy.

They had been up and climbing into success a few hours before. Now, they practically, really and truly, were going to have to walk home. They lacked enough gas money for the drive back into Albuquerque. Their only source of income, the casino slot-machine customer, was unavailable.

They thought about walking up to the few patrons that were entering or leaving the casino at 3:30 AM. However, the security cameras picked them up getting out of the car. The tribal police came back out and escorted them back to their vehicle.

Ian and Bjorn asked for gas money to which the security smiled back, "Not a chance buddy, leave. Leave now and don't return."

"Red," the head security man, a heavy set Native American everyone called by that name, asked them to leave the premises. He told them that if they returned that night, they would be arrested as trespassers. They wrote this out on a pad and gave the men the notice. What "Red" said was gospel. He was a blend of full-blood tribesmen, the direct descendant of Arapaho and Navajo warriors. Educated a bit before the bottle took him for a trip or two, he also knew the law. The written notice with a carbon copy made the Tribe's threat official.

The boys had lost their humorous tone. They closed off the conversation with a couple of "F Us" to spice up the conflict. The tribal police stared at them, stoic, knowing that a reaction bought another reaction. At most, they smiled back at the epithet.

This situation could get ugly. This wasn't about man versus man in a a street fight. This was about getting the inebriated men off the property at the least possible impact to other customers. Let them flare and verbally abuse security personnel, just get them into their means of transportation and off-property.

They boys sat heavily into their car and Ian started the engine. The tribal police waited for them to drive out of the parking lot before heading back into the casino. As they watched the red taillights of the Chevy enter the service road, they headed to the warmth of the casino. It was a bad night to be that drunk and headed back into town.

Casino security contemplated whether to notify New Mexico highway patrol about those two. However, it was a struggle whether to notify police about errant casino patrons; the local churches had protested enough about the sin of the Indian casinos. Security decided against the notification; Ian and Bjorn were off property already.

These men were doped up and drunk nearly out of their minds and on the road. They would let the state of New Mexico sort it out in that cold winter night.

Ian and Bjorn depleted copies of the better movies. They'd have to give away the selections they had but only if they had access to the casino. Between the two of them, they had less than a dollar in change. The gas gauge needle was pegged on "E."

Ian guessed they had less than half a gallon of gas, just enough to get to a fuel pump somewhere south on I-25. They were out of reasonable choices. It was time to sort among unreasonable options.

They were rolling up big for the night and now they were stuck in their car with a dollar in change. The snow was picking up; the forecast was for three to four inches. They had a thirty-minute drive to Ian's apartment and two minutes worth of gasoline. A four inch snow would foul up their plans. Bjorn, tall and thin, hated the cold weather. Waiting out a snowstorm would be torture.

Ian was at the wheel with Bjorn on the passenger side as they aimlessly motored along the service road headed toward the south entrance ramp on Interstate 25. They had to go north to go south back to Albuquerque burning more fuel. They might have enough gas to make it to the next exit on the interstate that lacked a gas station. What was the point of getting out on the highway?

Bjorn took out a large bottle of Jack Daniels from under his seat unscrewing the metal cap and taking a drink as they approached the interstate. He spoke about how bad their luck had turned. They both concluded it was the saucy Chinese woman, Loan, who brought them down.

They figured she could have helped, at least broke a few of her own deals. She controlled the cards. All they needed was some gas money. They had given her thirty or forty dollars in tips when they won. She worked a long day; she probably had a couple of hundred dollars in tips in her dealer's toll box.

They knew of the men that wanted to date her. She was stingy with her tight body. The idea that was simmering in both of their heads merged into Ian's basic summary, "She owes us, Bjorn."

As they neared the entrance ramp to the interstate highway, Bjorn popped up from his seat, "Ian, I think I know what she drives, man. It's like a Honda car, a SUV Honda car."

"A Pilot," Ian chimed in. "She drives a light color Honda Pilot, man. She's proud of bein' able to buy a new Honda car. That car is $45K plus man and the bitch has a new one. That slant-eyed snake has cash, dude."

"Asians always carry cash, man," Bjorn stated, pausing, and then with certainty said, "Loan will have some cash on her tonight. She's been working since noon yesterday. She'll have some cash." Bjorn added in hissing, "And she owes us, Ian. She owes us."

"Yeah, Asians always have cash on 'em. We'll have to strip her down to find it you know. Shame we have to do dat dude." Ian added as he slowed but not quite enough and pulled a screeching lurching gawdawful U-turn in the highway service road, the Chevy fishtailing as they straightened out. Bjorn slowly nodded to Ian's last comment; they were heading back to the casino.

Parking Lot Ambush *(and romance)*

They figured she'd be coming out of the casino around 4:00 AM after her over-due replacement showed up. They knew she often worked over-time to cover a shortage of dealers. It seemed like she was always working long shifts. She mentioned that night while the boys were winning that she expected to be out of there by 3:00 AM. The night before was Valentine's Day and some of the dealers blew off their schedule failing to show up on time, if at all.

The casino relied on Loan to cover dealer shortages. She was one of the highest earning dealers in central New Mexico and her long hours and holiday hours were legendary. Unlike anyone else, she could work up to thirty hours straight and only complain that she was hungry to get the pit boss to bring her some food. The casino could count on Nguyen Xuan Loan; the Asian work-machine always came through in the pinch. Always.

As usual, late shift was later than expected, and it was 3:45 AM, by the time she was relieved and allowed to head for her locker and a thirty-minute drive home. She debated between waiting in line to have her tips in her toll box counted or go home and deal with it on the next shift.

Loan decided to leave her tips in her locker. She had started her shift early at 1:00 PM the day before working on her feet for over fifteen hours. Valentine's Day landing on Saturday night swelled the number of gamblers, and it had been an unusually busy Saturday going into Sunday morning.

She was exhausted. Loan felt like she could barely stagger to the parking lot to find her car. She centered her mind on the task of just getting home.

She bundled up not bothering to change out of her tuxedo uniform still wearing her dealer's apron. It was late night and four hours from dawn. She loaded her uniform with the usual precautions, a high voltage Czech-made stun-gun inside her dealer's apron and placed some "off-the-table" tips in cash inside her bra on top of her left saline-enhanced breast. It was true that Asians carried cash. However, it was less known that they carried money in other places than their purses and wallets.

Steal a wallet or a purse and that is theft. Take cash from inside that bra becomes a sexual assault and possibly, attempted rape. Liability is a two-way street better understood by the transplanted Asian than the American. Touch her money or her breasts and you die.

She stepped out of the locker room wearing a maroon woolen cap and a heavy red winter coat leaving by the south employee entrance of the casino. It was shortly after 4:00 AM as she made her way in the light falling snow. The crystalline snow had only just begun to accumulate on the cold pavement.

Due to the previous day's Valentine's activity, she was forced to park on the outer lots of the casino in an area that was leased with fewer light poles and security cameras. It was a long walk from the casino to her vehicle. She began to shiver.

Growing up near the equator, she hated cold weather. She remembered with some fondness of the heat of the tropics; she had not quite adjusted to cold weather in America even after twenty years of living in temperate regions. Yet, she adored the beauty of the light snow that drifted into the parking lot lighting, coming out of a featureless black sky. It was nature's art at a price, beauty in exchange for living in such harsh conditions where the world became cold half of the year.

As she trundled across the parking lot, her thoughts were a mixture of amusement at the light snow and the resentment of the fingers of cold penetrating her layers of clothing and outer coat. She spotted her car on the far south lot almost by itself. A low-slung dark sedan was the only other car in the lot and it was parked somewhat askew next to her Honda.

The arrangement of parked cars would have passed her muster but this dark sedan triggered some instincts from her jungle experience. Something was amiss; something was wrong.

Bataan Peninsula, 1980, month and day unknown

The coldest weather Loan experienced as a child growing up in the tropics came during monsoon season in the Philippines. Seventy degrees Fahrenheit, the typical lowest annual temperature on the tropical coastline of the Bataan Peninsula in the Philippine, rose higher inland. The weather was perpetually warm to hot.

Rain came often and hard. A slow moving front stemming from the monsoonal flows from the west sustained rainfall for days. In order to preserve her clothing until she eventually reconnected to civilization, Loan was always naked and exposed to the elements. Constant wetting from rain drained vital heat from her body. She always wrapped herself in banana leaves to insulate from the heat-draining rains and challenge intruding insects.

She wondered if the towering clouds reached into the heavens to bring such coldness down into the jungle. Her wonderment bordered on meteorological wisdom. Ignorant of thermodynamics, regardless, she figured she needed to stay out of the rain to keep warm.

Loan's banana-leaf shelter leaked during heavier rains. She huddled in the carved out hollow of a large mabolo (kamagong) tree limb wrapped in layers of banana leaves. If she stayed out of drips of water working through her shelter roof, she stayed warm.

Rain delivered one blessing, it kept marauding animals in the jungle canopy hunkered down. Monkeys were the worst offenders as she was in their territory. Her stores of fruit and water were fair game to the macaques.

During the heavy rains, the warm-blooded mammals conserved their strength huddled together in large trees. Loan envied their togetherness, grooming each other, keeping each other company as the rains soaked every crevice and crack in the wilderness.

The rain cooled down the cold-blooded reptiles, making them lethargic, easy prey. Yet, tropical deluges confounded the scents and tracks of prey and hunter. Chaos took a break; jungle life waited out the rains to resume precarious life the next dry day.

Monsoon rains meant Loan achieved the best sleep a twelve-year old Vietnamese girl could expect, sleeping in the broad upper branches of the mabolo tree. Storms and constant rain meant she had unmolested time to improve her rest, her strength and her mind for making it to the next moment and to the next day.

Life resumed at an above-normal pace after the days of rain ended. Hunger drove packs of wild dogs and couplets of boars out in the undergrowth looking for meat. Reptilian blood warmed, lizards and snakes resumed their tasks. Insects took wing. Insect predators such as birds, bats and larger insects also retook the air in search of food and/or mates.

Loan's encounters with boars occurred at unpredictable intervals. The dogs, however, appeared to have a schedule showing up roughly every five days or immediately after a prolonged rain.

One pack of dogs remembered her and sought her out when prey was scarce. Perhaps they viewed her as an odd singular hairless monkey without a protective troupe. She always stayed near the shore lacking human companions after Huė died. Regardless, after the long rains, the pack of dogs forgot previous lessons and showed up at the base of her tree at first light.

They had learned the distinctive scent of a man-child. Loan resorted as necessary to relieving herself at the base of other trees. She could not mark the tree trunks as high as the male dogs; however, she improvised. She crouched on her heels on a low branch upwind of the trunk. She doused the tree from ten feet or more. "Let's see the dogs top that!" she often thought to herself. She was aware that her scent changed with the days ignorant of puberty and the changes in her body.

That worked well enough, the dogs stalked a deserted nest. However, she could not help climbing the trees leaving the scent of her skin oil on the bark. The animals eventually found her current tree-nest.

The dogs, evil creatures that deserved death, also became a source of sport. She rose quietly at first light and checked the ground for sign of a pack of dogs. The impatient animals forgot the time before and waited under the branch that held her nest. They lay on the ground somewhat clustered together, panting in the steamy early morning heat.

Loan re-introduced herself by bombarding the best-available canine with a large rock from her arboreal stockpile. Her aim improved over time and achieved a fifty-percent success rate before she found civilization.

Had she been able to store larger stones in the trees, she might have even killed one. She would have cooked it and lived like a princess for a few days.

She had one chance as the pack scattered after the first strike. Loan delighted with a direct hit of a three-pound rock thudding into flesh and bone. The high-pitched shriek of the battered dog sent startled birds and bats to the air. Pack members on their feet barked in all direction, other dogs barked in confusion as they fanned out from the offending tree. The dogs focused on the base of the tree as if it had dropped the missile. The dogs were smart but not fully so.

This amused Loan. The dogs acted as if the tree dropped the rocks. She giggled if not laughed when she imagined what the dogs must think of such dangerous trees. Curse those trees!

The noise of her laughter often surprised her. It had been months since Loan had talked to anyone or heard anyone's voice, including hers. She would eventually lose (temporarily) the easy practice of talking. She attempted to suppress her laughter as it gave her presence away to the angry dogs.

The resilient dogs took up positions out from under the canopy of the tree, waiting for her to climb down. With Thúy and Huê, she would have dropped to the ground and driven the pack into the jungle. Huê's good throwing arm found its mark more than half the time. The pulverized dogs always yielded ground and lost interest.

Alone, she assumed they could take her down and rip open her throat. The pack did this to unfortunate macaques isolated from larger trees. The macaques were half her size and went down easily if more than a few dogs were involved. She imagined the dogs shredding her body in the same manner. The thought made her shudder.

Until the pack became too frustrated to linger, she stayed in the tree often for several days. As her aim improved, they stayed farther away and soon lost interest. Before long, she hoped the dogs would show up to provide her some amusement.

Marauding Wildlife

Troupes of macaques, a small panther and the spiders were her other problem when she remained in the upper branches of the trees. The arboreal macaques, roughly as large as her, treated her like a hairless competitor for the mabolo tree's succulent fruit. The small panther she actually thought was an overgrown cat prowled around her but was too small to be a threat. In a standoff in the trees, Loan made a few visual threats and yelled at the dusky colored animal. She learned never to take her eyes off the cats; as long as she faced them, she faced them down. The cats moved off with sufficient threat.

Spiders were another matter.

Spitting Spiders

The largest of the spiders were an insidious threat; any creature they could immobilize was a meal. Many were small, quiet, sneaky and toxic.

From Loan's description, her worst enemy was probably an overgrown cousin of the scytodes pallidus, a ground dwelling arachnid that hid in leaves and spit a glue-like toxic silk. The poisonous ground dwellers had bodies the size of her fist with long legs spanning six to seven inches.

The spiders were aggressive. They lunged at almost anything that tripped sensory silk strands strung out in front of their ground lair. Unlike jumping spiders, their vision was poorly equipped. If the initial ambush failed, smart prey became the hunter of the spitting spider.

While the spider could kill rodents and sicken small lemurs, young monkeys and the larger macaques could climb out of danger. Larger mammals had sufficiently large bodies to absorb the poisons of the spider without permanent harm. However, any creature weighting more than ten pounds was sick for days. Immobilized, Loan became vulnerable to other threats. The spider could kill her indirectly by giving other creatures a better chance of taking her down.

When she encountered a spider's lair on the ground, Loan's preferred option was to lure them out of hiding, dodge their lunge and flatten them with a stick. They were quick to ambush but strangely clumsy. Once they lost the advantage of surprise, the spider usually scuttled for cover.

Of all of the threats she faced in the jungles, Loan dedicated herself to eradicate the spiders. The spitting spiders had to die.

The spiders, while ground dwellers, could creep along and become intimate with other creatures that slept on the ground or in the trees. Its bite was sickening if not deadly and Loan made it her mission to reduce their numbers. The spitting spiders had to die.

Loneliness, of all, the hardest challenge

By the beginning of the third year of life in the jungle, she had assumed this was her entire future; she believed she would be alone for the rest of her life.

Three years in the coastal jungle, she knew everything necessary to survive; however, she struggled to endure loneliness. In the sixteenth month, Thúy died falling into a deep ravine. In the twenty-forth month, Huế died from a head injury. Thereafter, eleven-year old Loan spent fifteen months without human contact. Alone from humanity, she found ways to enrich her day.

Companionship has variable definitions; lacking human champions, Loan found new purpose and company. Routine has variable definitions; nature has its routine. The sun rises and sets as earth spins and orbits the sun with predictable precision. Nature follows the larger cycle, life works with the dark and light hours and the shifts in seasons where that matters.

Loan rose with the sun and rested in the dark. That was nature's cycle and she worked with it. Life became routine, predictable, perhaps even boring. She was largely powerless at night; however, she had choices on what to do with the light of each day.

She almost welcomed intermittent threats from nature. It broke up her day.

Sticks, Stones and First Actions.

Loan seldom went anywhere without a long pointed stick, rocks wrapped in a belt made from banana leaves and fruit. Anyone else would call the stick a spear; however, Loan never used it in that manner. It was just "the stick" in her mind, not a projectile.

The stick managed the spiders and the wild boars, the rocks sorted packs of wild dogs. The fruit gave her energy when she became treed by a pack of dogs, often for days. She stocked water in large "elephant ear" leaves among her "strategic" tree nests." Slaking thirst was no longer a problem.

The weapons bought time enough time to find a good tree. She might be there for a while. Left handed, she swung the stick in her right hand while she threw the rocks with her left. She hissed and yelled, swinging and jabbing the stick, reaching into satchel for another rock.

The motions, screaming and flying rocks confounded the pack having never seen a monkey act like that. They kept their distance and more, they often ran for cover.

Loan thought of the moment of confrontation with a threat as a "first action," a moment when a person moves from inaction to making threats on many levels and confusing the enemy, all in split seconds. She deployed actions that confused the foe and other actions to threaten them if not strike them. Motions and noise, shock and awe, came into play.

She remembered her mother's stories of the war; about being the "firstest with the mostest," something she learned from the Americans she served up until they had to leave. Her mother had told her that in conflict, it would be Loan's mind and body over other-mind and other-body. No matter what the foe, first action was essential. Dictate the encounter. Own the fight.

Her mother told her about the first action in a conflict and the likely second action when odds are against her. Strike first and large. Second, if the numbers are against you, run like hell for heaven, into one of her strategically stocked trees.

In the jungle, Loan was always outnumbered on the ground. In the air, six feet or more above the ground, the odds were about even for Loan. On a good day, the aerial jungle was at a disadvantage.

Luck favors the prepared. Loan had over a dozen trees along the coastline stocked with rocks, pointed long sticks (spears), fruit and perhaps a vine-bound water-lizard. She had water stored in banana leaves everywhere.

Loan only hurt the dogs and boars. The wooden point on her stick could not penetrate a boar's hide; however, the soft skinned dogs kept their distance. Neither she nor the boars and dogs could readily kill one another. It was a stand-off, she didn't pursue them and they learned to find other prey. Neither one would feed the other.

Without those tools, she would have died alone in the jungle. By the time she left the jungle at the age of twelve and rejoined humanity, the habit of carrying a defensive weapon was ingrained in her. Always have a stick or a rock or a weapon-de-jour ready.

Loan had something else in her arsenal. She had developed a sense of unseen danger. She could detect a threat through subliminal clues, even while asleep. Living in the trees in those years had transformed a child's mind that could sleep and still wake at the instant of a threat, of something creeping through the branches toward her.

Spider Sports

Spitting spiders were the only creature that successfully penetrated Loan's best defenses. Shortly after Hué died, despite her best preparations, some poisonous thing crept under Loan's banana-leaf blanket and bit her on the top of her right foot. It left a calling card; a small wad of toxic silk.

Loan became terribly sick lingering for what she thought was near death for a day. She was unable to eat and her body hurt too much to move. To a westerner, it sounded no worse than a really bad college hangover. She worried that the macaques a panther would make bolder actions against her. The effects of the poison ebbed after the second day.

As she recovered her strength, Loan decided to go on the offensive. For any creature with more than four limbs, spitting spiders appeared to be at the top of the annoying-creature food chain. The spiders proved most threatening, moving quietly and unseen, with silent toxic vomit. It proved to be her biggest hazard. The spiders had to die.

Loan's mother imparted much wisdom to Loan as they labored together. She seldom understood her mother's comments but set them to memory. Cantonese was their familial language; her mother imparted kernels of wisdom in Cantonese.

"Attack from a position of seeming weakness." stuck in Loan's mind. Another curious statement that seemed obvious and witless at the time: "To remain in the living is the choice of those still alive. If you think, you live. You have a choice to make. The dead do not."

Asians, famously inscrutable to the west, were frequently obscure to themselves. Her mother passed these sayings to Loan as they labored at one task or another, just as her venerable father passed them to Mai. Mai was the warrior-daughter of Huang. It was only natural that she pass on those leasons to her warrior-daughter, Loan.

Mai told Loan the sayings would become clear at the right time. At random moments, the sayings took meaning as she struggled to the next day.

Several decades would pass before Loan's mother could elaborate. However, Loan inspired those two esoteric instructions. Her survival became example of the lesson.

From then on, after completing her basic chores of storing more water, trapping a lizard and adding a few rocks to the her cache, she spent the rest of the daylight hours hunting the large spitting spiders of Bataan. Sport may be the application of survival converted into a seemingly harmless game. For Loan, an uneducated girl stranded alone in an unyielding wilderness, sport had become the practice of surviving in an unforgiving tropical jungle.

Sensory Spider Silks

Loan learned the likely structure of a spitting spider's ambush site. Loose leaves and debris across an open area in the underbrush predicted a likely spider lair. The vision-impaired spiders needed a crutch; spider-silk stretched across the animal trail worked well enough. Large insects, rats and other animals took the easier trail rather than forge their own.

After recognizing the trigger threads of a spider's lair, Loan beckoned the spiders by plucking their prey-detectors, the silky strands stretched across the animal path. Feathers and slim blades of grass worked best, dragged gently across the tell-tale silk, simulating an insect.

Unable to ignore instinct, the near-sighted creatures lunged at the spot where their sensory silk vibrated. Eight eyes scanned the area for movement of insects, infrared signatures of a mammal or outline of something it could identify.

Loan dispatched the arachnids with a single whack of the stick. She insured the kill by driving the point into the body and flinging it into the brush. The contest occurred in silence as neither Loan nor the spider made a sound.

It was business as usual on the jungle-covered slopes of the Bataan..

After Loan's bad spider bite, thirteen months passed before Loan found her way to civilization. Her departure was probably a good event for the ecology of the region. Loan was running out of spiders to kill.

The macaques had learned to give the odd hairless competitor space. She no longer waited to be harassed by the marauding troupes. She launched into a noisy whirling dervish of taunts and threats. Loan had become a singular alpha male, yelling fearlessly back at them, swinging wood and hurling rocks. The lone she-ape with the long black hair was more than they could handle.

The boars and wild dogs learned to give the small human distance in most instances. Her fearlessness and weapons out-matched them. They tired quickly of facing the long stick and flying rocks in order to bring the creature down.

Her fifty pounds presented only marginal benefit to the pack. The human female would feed them for a few days; there was easier prey to be had. Her message was simple and constant: "Eat something else. I am too much trouble."

Smarter men might have learned from the lessons of the wild pigs and dogs of Bataan. They could have learned from the macaques that a single naked immature human female that wielded sticks and hurled rocks could hold off a troupe of ten monkeys, each equal to her size with twice her strength. She had something the animals barely understood but respected; she wielded dangerous tools of pain. She used a stick and the stones. The hairless she-ape in the trees was quick with superior technology. She was even better with guile and deception.

Misfortune eventually took the lives of Thúy and Huė before they could find their way out of the Philippine jungle. Loan, alone, prevailed and made it out of the wilderness to Manila and then to America.

The invader of the wild dog's domain rejoined human civilization after thirty nine months in the jungle; taking with her lessons of survival. Twenty four years later, two males of her species misjudged her capabilities based on her gender, her size and rough English. Similar to dogs and macaques, they made similar errors of judgment. They made this mistake on a winter night on the other side of the world north of a desert city in a temperate climate. They made this mistake in Albuquerque, New Mexico.

4:00 AM, Alburquerque - Approaching The Vehicles

As Loan approached her light bronze 2004 Honda Pilot, she noticed in the otherwise empty parking lot, an older model dark blue Chevy Impala parked askew to the left of her SUV. Fussy about precision, Loan parked in the center of the parking space respecting the space on either side of her car in the designated parking spot. Parking correctly meant less body damage from some butthead's car door dinging the side of her car.

The jerk driving the Chevy parked poorly, more than ten degrees skew of the yellow lines delineating the parking slot. The right front of the Impala almost touched the left front of her Honda. The rear of the Impala was part way into another parking spot on the left. Jerk drivers!

She recognized fogged up windows. Her own car windows were clear. The Impala windows were hazed on the inside by moisture condensing on the inside of the cold glass.

Something else caught her notice; snow was melting on the top of that low-slung white-trash car. The night air temperature was well below freezing. The thin film of snow on her Honda Pilot blew off the hood, un-sticking and un-melted. Her car had been sitting out in the cold all night such that the snow neither melted nor stuck to her car.

In the low light level of the outer perimeter parking lot, she could see two forms in the front seat of the Chevy. Whoever was in there, they had been sitting in the car and running the heater for a while; the moisture in their exhales and farts fogged the inside of glass.

At 4:00 AM on winter night, in an otherwise empty parking lot, this was odd. It was also alarming.

The other car was warm, melting the thin snowfall as it fell on top of the vehicle. Those people had been in that car for time enough to warm the top of the car to melt the snow. That fact caught Loan's attention; in this wide empty perimeter parking-lot, why was this car position askew and next to hers? Why was it warm and fogged right next to her car?

The older model low-slung Chevy Impala, "tricked-out" with odd looking thin tires on gaudy chrome rims rode low on the pavement. The tires and flashy rims were worth more than the whole vehicle. She hated driving behind that type of car; it had to slow down for speed bumps to avoid making sparks from the low-slung steel frame scraping on concrete.

Low life people, she thought, drive cars like that. She had seen this car before; she tried to recall who she knew drove such a white-trash piece of crap. Her mind was fogged as well; it had been a long day.

After what had been a long session working over fifteen hours on her feet, she had already put the table-incident with Ian and Bjorn out of her mind. They were semi-fixtures of the casino landscape plying their elicit copies of movies and getting loaded on whatever gave the best buzz.

Ian and Bjorn were mostly harmless near-idiots but she rarely placed idiots in the category of people who do deliberate personal harm. She actually liked talking to them. They tipped her well enough when it was necessary to impress someone else. They broke up the monotony of regular players particularly when they were buzzed up on something.

Tired and looking forward to getting home and warm, Loan failed to recall who drove a car like that. It seemed important to know. Who owned that car?

Despite her exhaustion, her jungle-honed senses lit up. She felt the prickle of sensing something out of place. It was 4:00 AM and there were few cars in the parking lot but there was this overly-warm dark white-trash vehicle next to hers with what appeared to be two large people (men) sitting in the front.

Still, she failed to recall who this might be in the car next to her Honda. The parking lot was practically empty. She had walked halfway across the large parking lot without seeing another car.

Loan walked out in the open with this Chevy Impala, her Honda SUV and two unknown men in the front seat of the familiar-but-not-familiar vehicle. She felt the bow going taught before the arrow was loosed. She felt the fatal click of the landmine as if her foot had stumbled on its trigger.

Normally, she parked up near the casino employee entrance. The Valentine's Day crowd the day before had forced her to park farther from the casino than she preferred.

She was clearly alone in the wide expanse of a remote parking area. Correct that thought. She had company as it was, the two men in that low-slung Chevy. She walked slower than normal, working out in her mind what she must do next if the situation evolved to something unpleasant.

In Loan's haste to leave, she failed to put on her gloves. She buried her hands in her coat pockets. In the emerging circumstance, she thought better of getting out the gloves. She might need the dexterity of glove-less hands.

Loan was unsure if the people in the car could see her approach given how fogged up the windows in the Chevy had become. The figures in the car looked like large people, probably at least a couple of men in the car. She could make out a little motion of one of them, his head moving as if drinking something.

Could they see her through the rear-view mirror with a fogged back window? Maybe. Maybe not.

The occupants could track her in the side mirrors if they could see out of their windows. However, there was no evidence they had tried to clear the windows from inside. She might have time to get inside her car and lock the doors before they realized she was out here on this open parking lot.

Her sense of danger rose in her blood as she called the sensation of adrenaline as she neared her car. In lieu of panic, she organized the sequence of what had to happen next to exit the parking lot unharmed.

She was uncertain of safety, which was her equivalent way of saying she now sensed danger. She sized up her best defense. Get in the car and drive off. If she could get into her car and secure the doors, she'd run like hell.

If she could not drive off unmolested, she would go to Plan B. She hated Plan B. The outcome could be so variable in Plan B. The worst outcome: she would be raped, mutilated, robbed and dead on a fricking snow-blown parking lot in New Mexico. Who could recommend Plan B?

She had been here before, stranded, surrounded, in the Philippine jungle. Animals on the left of her, insects on the right. The awful weather above and the treacherous sea below. All conspired to kill her. Philippines, Schmilippines; Should New Mexico be any different? Civilization only concealed and postponed the wilderness. Predation remained. There is always a threat.

Events in the next seconds depended on whether the two men in the car were waiting for her. Was she a target or was this a random event making her a target of opportunity? Were these just some low-life dudes who happened to park next to her car at 4:00 AM in a snow-storm? Were they hapless and harmless? Was this just a benign coincidence?

A mild peace flashed through her mind; her perpetual curiosity amused her. The answers would soon arrive. She looked forward to the round the next bend, to dodge a hail of arrows. This was a good day to die as the American Indians told it. Her mother told her it differently: be curious about the bad that might come so you can embrace it and deal with it.

It was easier to say: "It is a good day to die." Acceptance of the condition is essential to managing fear.

Fear is the domain of the incurious. Mai's one sentence lectures hailed down from April 1975 as Sai Gon fell into chaos. Loan became curious about the outcome of the moment.

Left handed, she pulled out her car-keys in her right hand. She held the keys in her shivering fingers as she approached her car, moving between the vehicles. Still holding the key and the door lock fob, she pressed the unlocking button, the Honda flashing its fog lamps and the dome light coming on indicating the car-fob had unlatched the driver side door. As she did this, she unzipped the top of her coat down far enough to expose the top half of her tuxedo/apron giving access to the cummerbund at her belly. With her left hand, as she used her right hand to lift the door handle of her car door, she reached down into the cummerbund of her tuxedo and grabbed the plastic handle, feeling for the switches. She flipped the activation switch to prepare the canister of chemical-mace to discharge along with 200,000 volts of electricity.

In Filipino jungle parlance, Loan put a stick in her right hand. She had just now encountered a "stick" situation where she needed to whack a threat.

Tucked in her cummerbund was her stick; a piece of east-European technology capable of delivering 200,000 volts to an attacker's nervous system. In addition, the device sprayed an aggravating pepper solution into sensitive tissue. It spit annoying toxins and overwhelmed the nervous system with huge discomfort. The flood of pain receptors firing all at once literally numbed the mind of the recipient.

Loan stood less than five feet tall but wore three-inch high satin-black block-high-heels matching her black tuxedo. The leather and rubber soles made a "klocking" sound as she walked. She wore two layers of black socks to keep her feet warm as she stood and dealt the cards. She might be 5'-2" if she stood upright and held her breath.

Regardless of the vertical compensation of her shoes, her one-hundred pound frame appeared small next to her car. She had to climb up and into the driver's seat of the Honda SUV.

Loan would have her back to her these unknown people far too long. She would be defenseless for precious seconds.

She tried to modify her step to reduce the sound of her shoes without much success. Regardless, she moved to her door transferring her keys to her left hand. In a few more steps, she grabbed the door handle relieved to know it was unlocked. As she swung open her door, she used her right hand inside her cummerbund to switch the device to full activation. To young ears, a high pitched sound could be heard. It was the whining pitch of charging transistors ramping up the voltage by a factor of 25,000. The capacitors whined rapidly into silence in a split second. The device had two fresh nine-volt batteries. Most stun guns use a single battery; this had two and could spray a stream of stinging mace fifteen feet.

She could no longer hear the whine of the electronics. The batteries were fresh. She knew it was fully charged. Her stun gun was now charged to match her jungle-honed senses.

Some bad thing in a dark place was coiled up and about to strike her. She knew this moment many times between the age of nine and twelve. Two decades later, she returned to the jungle in the middle of an Albuquerque parking lot on a winter night.

This was now America, the land of the brave. Few were braver than Loan. She was the anti-victim. She was the conqueror of death and destruction.

Few men can know what it is to be a woman caught up in an attack. Men can be mugged and robbed. Yet, we cannot be readily robbed and raped in life-changing ways that women experience. It is one thing to take our wallet, it another thing to violate our body and compromise our future as un-violated mates. The violence of man upon woman leaves many marks to which men seldom can relate.

For Loan, who had been cornered and attacked by all manners of creatures including Thai pirates on a boat. Rape was another form of attack by an animal. It would be one more wound that had to heal in order to live and thrive another day.

She understood assault. Regardless, she had no intention of making it easy on her attackers.

The Chevy Impala was parked crookedly in the parking spot with almost no space between the fronts of the cars and about five feet between the rear bumpers of the two vehicles. As she swung open her door, the passenger side of the Chevy opened, the drunken man emerged from inside.

The light breeze carried the smells of the car's interior. He reeked of bourbon and cigarette smoke as stepped out behind her, closing his car door. A voice inside the car called out to the exiting passenger, "Grab her."

The man in the driver's side of the Impala fumbled with his door handle working to exit the car as the first man moved up behind Loan as she was about to step up into her car. If she settled into the driver's seat, she would be unable to defend herself with her right hand and start the car in the same motion. The man could keep her from shutting the door and the other man would be out of the car. She was cornered.

She had trained using the stun gun in her right hand maintaining balance with the left hand. If she couldn't shut the door, she had to stay on her feet. The man stood more than six feet and 220 pounds, he would be strong. He could block the door and yank her out of the seat.

Trying to move into the driver's seat limited her options. She needed to know what he intended to do and did the only thing left to her; Loan paused in the doorway. Her life-saving pause probably lasted two seconds.

The first man staggered as he moved up behind her and leaned down to grasp her hips. His hands fumbled as he felt through her heavy coat to locate her waistline.

Physical contact between people, no matter how minor, can be construed as battery. Bjorn's unsolicited grip on Loan's hips became assault as he slurred, "C'mere bissh!"

Contact changed the situation from impersonal conflict at the blackjack table to assault. The man's occasional sexual liaisons in the backseat of the Impala were a matter of record with security personnel. The men were broke and out of gas on a winter night. Their intentions might have been benign, however, grabbing a lone woman's hips as she was headed home after work irrevocably altered the event.

Loan was a young woman formed of tough Chinese stock and tested literally in the wilderness. She knew little of a safe life through most of her childhood. She witnessed the fall of Sai Gon in April

1975 and the brutalization and murder of ethnic Chinese that backed South Viet Nam. Her life cataloged the tragedy of Viet Nam and a Vietnamese exodus across the globe where one in three of the millions that fled died in the flight to freedom. An incident in a casino parking lot added one more event to the list of life's assault on her wellbeing.

Bjorn grasped the hips of a young woman who had lost count of the chaotic events in her life. Loan had been to hell and back and could take down the devil. Her presence of mind, a firm stance on the ground and free use of both hands were her only hope in the next few seconds.

Her Honda Pilot was false sanctuary now. She dropped the car keys in her left hand and fingered the triggers on the stun gun in her right hand as she paused at the door.

Her car dwarfed Loan; most of her body was in shadow. Bjorn staggered, almost running into Loan. He stopped short of bumping into her and placed his gloveless hands on her hips. He murmured something about her owing him.

Bjorn had to lean down to hold her putting him out of balance lurching into the door. He shuffled forward hunched over, pushing Loan toward the hinges of the open car door. Her head came up the level of the side mirror, he couldn't see precisely what she was holding. She showed no reaction and said nothing.

As he leaned over to get a better grip through her coat, to his sodden surprise, she crouched down low, her coat riding up in his hands. She turned on the ball of her right foot rotating clockwise out of his grasp. She moved to his right and then behind him, still in a crouching position. She faced him looking up, her back to the passenger door.

Surprised by her unexpected movement at first down and then to his right side, he turned his head to see her roll off to his right. "Shiiitt!" he exclaimed as he rotated moved his right leg toward her putting most of his weight on his left foot. If he hadn't been leaning on the Honda door, he'd have fallen backward. Bjorn managed to shift his weigh and took two steps to face her.

She was crouched down, her eyes looking rotated up looking through her eyebrows, her head level. Her left hand was in front of her for balance, her right hand held a long black object. Bjorn's first thought

261

she was going to hit him with her flashlight. She was coiled up with her head at the level of his knees. He'd have to bend down to grab her.

Before he could say anything, Loan, still in the crouching position, stepped into him on her right foot. She jabbed her right hand upward, rising up out her crouch, sliding the black object along his chest and into the underside of his chin as she fumbled with the trigger.

Just before she raised her hand, she squeezed the first trigger on the spray, the hissing mist laced with a stinging solution spewed from two gold-plated prongs. A wetting solution of 10% cayenne pepper soaked his chin and neck.

Bjorn felt the wetness. Mace! The little bitch has mace.

Loan drove the prongs into his neck and squeezed the second trigger. Normally, a two-inch blue-white electrical discharge arced between the prongs accompanied by a crackling sound. The arc didn't happen; Bjorn's wetted neck completed the circuit. Two-hundred thousand volts fled the windings and capacitors and landed in his nervous system.

The energy discharged into his body looking for a place to rest. The amplifying circuit trying to refill the capacitors continued to discharge as long as Loan held down the black trigger. She stood up to press the device into him for two seconds.

Two nine-volt alkaline batteries inside the device fed industrial grade transistors that amplified the voltage into capacitors that held the charge. The trigger released the high voltage at non-lethal amperage *(under 50 milliamperes)*. The voltage, high enough to cross the air between the prongs with a crackling sound, needed a place to rest. On a body, the electric energy fires muscles and pain receptors. It stuns the target temporarily. Recipients of the discharge say it is the worst four seconds of their life.

The combination of the pepper spray wetting his skin enabled the Czechoslovakian-made Scorpy 200 stun gun to deliver the high voltage low-amperage jolt into and throughout his body.

He had been turning to track her, his back facing the front hood of the Impala. He tried to follow what she was doing and regain his balance. Clear of the Honda's door, he teetered on his heels.

She had driven the gun into his neck, adding some backward force fully discharging the gun's temporary charge. The foreign electricity ignited his muscle neurons and pain receptors.

Bjorn he uttered an expletive toward the woman, "Hey mother fuhhh…." the electric charge suspended orderly control of his body. Leg muscles fired chaotically. Bjorn's muscle spasms exacerbated his imbalance. With a flinch, his leg muscles hurled him backwards. Bjorn landed unconscious on the front glass of the low-slung Chevy and slumped onto the hood.

As Ian was stumbling out of the driver's side of the car, Bjorn's two hundred and twenty pounds fell backward on top of the hood shaking the car sideways on its tricked-out suspension. The car rocked, nearly knocking the drunken driver to the pavement.

Ian straightened up, wavering, having chugged 80-proof bourbon for the last half hour. He had been sitting in a stuffy vehicle augmenting a fading crack-cocaine high with a new buzz on straight liquor. Bjorn had jumped out of the car leaving Ian to fumble with his door handle. As Bjorn moved through the door, he told Ian, "The little China girl is here!" and exited the car.

As Ian finally found the door handle, the Impala lurched side-ways. He nearly fell to out of the door. Ian turned around to see Bjorn lay on his back on the hood of the Chevy. A question bubbled up in Ian's mind, "What the heck was Bjorn doing? He was supposed to grab the card dealer." Ian stood up on wobbly legs and lurched toward the back of the car. In a few unsteady strides, he rounded the back of the car. Loan's car door was open. She wasn't in the driver's seat and Bjorn's legs dangled off the front hood of the car.

Another thought flashed him into some clarity, "Bjorn could be such a jerk goofing around like that." He muttered that "Bjorn was going to scratch the hood paint doing that crap."

Ian stopped at the right rear of the cars and tried to make sense of the scene. Bjorn's lower legs draped over the right front of the hood. The Honda driver's door stood open, the dome light revealed empty front seats. Light snow drifted into the shadows made by the mix of blue-white lighting and yellow and the positon of the cars. The missing item was the blackjack dealer. Where did she go?

"Bjorn! Bjorn! Where'd the bitch go?" He staggered toward Bjorn.

Light poles to the left of the cars left a deep shadow between the vehicles. As Ian moved up beside the rear wheel well of the Impala, he picked movement in his peripheral vision almost at his feet.

He looked around for the blackjack dealer failing to see Loan crouched below him in the shadows. She was looking up at him as she squatted Asian-style on her heels, leaning against the rear wheel-well of the Impala. Angry with Bjorn's inexplicable behavior, he reached down to grab her cussing at her, bjorn and the whole situation.

Immediate Action

Loan knew this place and moment. She stood alone, outnumbered and lightly defended against certain threat of uncertain intent. The first man had grabbed her; he lay stunned on the hood of the Impala. Another man staggered toward her from the other side of the Chevy. She crouched down and moved deeper in the shadow of rear of the Impala.

At this hour, she believed theft, rape and worse possibilities populated their intentions.

Again, Loan knew this place and moment. Available help sat minutes away. She believed she had only seconds to change the outcome.

She had been here countless times since she was eight years old. Simple choices changed exposure to harm. Go to work or stay home, leave work early or work through the night, drive home now or drive home on snow-packed roads; each choice meant a different outcome.

She cursed her own situation; she had literally walked into it. She had considered waiting out the night, sleeping in the break room until sunrise. Developing snow emptied the casino; it motivated her to go home before it the roads became impossible.

Sound decisions depend on sufficient information. A snow storm was moving in. It was Sunday. She could sleep in with the kids.

The incident in the casino an hour before was over. It had been a busy and crazy night. Security had escorted the inebriated men to their car and watched them leave the property. Nothing added up to alarm Loan.

Chaos was always near. It lurked under the façade of civilization and thrived on assumption and misinformation. Loan knew this better than anyone.

This was a moment requiring immediate action. There would be a time to contemplate the situation if she survived. Her only means to survival; act fast, strike often and move away. The moment Bjorn grabbed her replaced discussion with defense. Defense in the wilderness meant strike out, reposition, strike again and repeat the process and then find sanctuary.

She neutralized the first assault and repositioned herself for the next assault. She briefly considered whether she had time to get into her car. She had dropped her car keys on the pavement as she lashed at Bjorn. The second man was out of his car and coming around the trunk. Without the keys, she could lock herself in the Honda but then what? Did those men have weapons? Guns?

The jungle was everywhere. In the Philippines or in New Mexico, wilderness permeated everywhere.

When a creature has something another creature wants, bad things happen. It wasn't personal; it was just the way of the world.

Loan viewed chaos as a series of successive undesirable events. Survival depended on interrupting the succession and determine a different outcome.

Yet, badness happens more than once. Luck favors the prepared. Strike back and then move into position for the next attack. Strike again and then prepare for the next. The rule of the jungle (1) Outplay the predator and (2) Neutralize the situation and most of all, (3) Find sanctuary.

Loan knew of only a few stories from her mother during the Viet Nam War. Her mother had told of something called "immediate action," a term Nguyên Maï learned from American soldiers. It meant acting quickly with many blows all at once. Maï told Loan that immediate action had saved her life more than once during the war. Surprise, overwhelm and flee.

Ian had been leaning over to aid a compromised sense of balance. He loomed over her before he realized she squatted below him. He muttered something reaching down to grab her.

Loan uncoiled. Her right hand shot up as she rose up from her crouch. His hands missed her head grabbing at the back of her coat. She drove the hissing pepper spray into his face. The spray produced a jet of fluid over fifteen feet. At point blank range, the jet penetrated his nostrils and struck his eyes. The pepper lit up the ultra-sensitive tissues in his head creating instant crushing pain.

Ian towered over Loan able to grab her in a bear hug. However, his hands were needed elsewhere as his eyes and nasal passages were on fire. Blinded, he shrieked trying to cover his eyes. He wavered over her holding his face.

Loan stood up against the Impala off to Ian's left as he groped his face and flailed. He cursed at her as she moved the stun gun near the side of his face. The recharged mechanism threw out a small blue-white crackling arc as she pressed it to his left jaw.

The horrific burning in his eyes and nose stopped. Ian grunted as he collapsed. Loan held down the trigger keeping the stun gun prongs in contact with Ian's flesh as he jerked and slumped to the right.

Ian fell forward with his hands on his face. He hit the pavement, the only sound made from the rustling of his bulky jacket. He was stunned. He was still conscious but unable to move.

Stun guns immobilize and confuse; the longer the discharge, the longer the duration of immobility and confusion. In a typical situation, a stunned man recovers some mobility in a few minutes as the muscles reabsorb lactic acid built up in the tissues by the electric discharge. This enables an intended victim to get out of danger. There isn't much literature on repeated discharges and the effects of alcohol.

Loan managed a full discharge on each man. They would be down for five minutes. The effects of the pepper spray would last for an hour. As Ian lay groaning on the pavement, Loan walked to the front of the car where Bjorn's dangling legs began to move. Loan leaned over the hood and pressed the gun's prongs into his neck and held down the trigger. His body quivered as motor and sensory nerves fired.

She removed the prongs from his neck and let the capacitors recharge. She repeated the process. After four discharges on his neck, Loan grabbed Bjorn's left forearm and yanked him roughly off the hood of the Impala. He slumped to the pavement laying half across Ian. She returned to Ian and applied four discharges to the back of his neck. His body quivered as over-loaded neurons fired away.

The numbing effects of the liquor enhanced the disabling capabilities of the stun gun. It was also late; the movie-boys needed some sleep.

Ian lay next to the right passenger door. Bjorn sprawled over Ian. The repeated shocks to their bodies had rendered them unconscious.

Two minutes had passed since she had opened her car door. It is likely to suppose that Loan, similar to anyone in her situation, might act in one of several ways. She might have driven to the front of the casino to summon help. The men weren't dead, they'd revive eventually. Her danger would return. Security should know about this.

It never occurred to Loan to flee the scene. They messed with her; time to mess with them back. She wanted the movie-boys to stay down.

She went over to her car and found her car keys and placed them in her coat pocket. She began to shut her door but thought better of it and left it open. She still held the stun gun in her right hand.

She studied the two men on the pavement and returned to Bjorn. His blinking eyes stared at the night sky, snow falling on his face. Loan calmly pressed the prongs against Bjorn's neck and held the trigger down one more time. Then she moved over to Ian and applied a similar charge to the back of his neck.

She heard a strange sound coming from Ian. Faced down on the pavement, the last jolt made him incontinent. The Long Island Teas and Kentucky Bourbon had worked through his kidneys; Ian pissed his pants. Warm vapor fogged from his midsection.

She turned off the stun gun and wrapped it in the instructions that came with the device and put it in another pocket of her coat.

Loan noticed the cold now. She put her gloves on and buttoned up her coat.

She could see Bjorn's breath fog above his open mouth; she knew she hadn't killed him. Ian's breath fogged in the night air as well. Damn the luck.

She stood back and assessed what she had before her: two stunned assailants. It was then that she realized they were the movie-boys that had been giving her grief over their losses at blackjack. It was that bastard Ian and his buddy, Bjorn. She thought casino security had run them off half an hour ago.

By what the parking lot cameras would later show, she appeared in control. If the security cameras could have captured more detail, it would have shown she was shaking. Not from fear but from anger. She was a bit angry, made worse since the casino security should be coming out.

She looked down at Bjorn who lay half on his side partially on top of Ian. She positioned herself to one side and kicked him in the groin. Then she kicked him in the back and kidneys several times. Then she repositioned herself with Ian and a few blows in the same manner.

She grabbed the top edge of the Chevy Impala and used it to steady herself as she stood up first on Ian in her three-inch block high heels. Loan proceeded to jump up and down on him and then repeated the process jumping up and down on Bjorn. Almost in recital as she jumped in down, she cursed them in cadence as she tenderized their hulking frames.

They were stunned, perhaps semi-conscious from the liquor. They moaned and grunted but could make no protest. One brief jolt from a fully charged stun gun such as she had would immobilize a two-hundred pound man for five minutes; a series of discharges discharge could disable him for an hour. Each had received five long jolts; the "movie boys" would be out past sunrise. Their weird bruises lasted a month.

She jumped up and down on their bodies as best as she could manage. This this turned out to be difficult work. It's not easy thing, wearing high heel shoes and jumping up and down on top of large inert men.

Loan became winded. It also concerned her that she might hurt herself by twisting an ankle. She stepped off Bjorn's chest. Breathing heavily, she scanned the parking lot for anybody she could summon. She looked out across the empty parking lot with light snow drifting down through the cones of snow-delineated parking lot lighting and spotted movement outside the south entrance to the casino.

Three men walked slowly out of the casino unaware of what had just happened, headed toward one of the few other cars nearby in the empty parking lot. She had expected security cameras to have been closely watching. The commotion should have alerted someone inside the casino that something bad was going on in the south parking lot, even so, it had only been a few minutes since Bjorn first went flying backward across the hood of the Chevy Impala. It was 4:05 AM and the crack graveyard shift in the security department missed the big event of the evening.

Security cameras often worked on a continuous recording loop recording more than 24 hours at reduced of "frames" per second. The cameras recorded much of the activity in jerky action.

She was now out of breath. However, she had enough air in her lungs for one more task. Nguyên Xuân Loan screamed for help.

Somewhere out there in New Mexico in mid-February 2004, there were two large men who probably bare some scars and lingering persisting bruises made by the three-inch block heels of a woman's dress shoe. Did they know she jumped up and down on their inert bodies while they lay stunned between parked cars on a winter night?

Had they been conscious during their comeuppance, they would have felt their eyes and nasal passages burning, inflamed from pepper spray. As it was, their expressionless faces reeked of the pungent pepper spray while their bodies became tenderized by the target of their ambition. A seemingly defenseless woman less than half their size, jumping up and down with the weight of small her body concentrated through the small contact point of platform heels, brutalizing Ian and Bjorn.

Their necks ended up with had half a dozen pairs of dark red marks made from repeated high voltage discharges from the prongs of a stun gun. As mentioned before, one discharge could immobilize a two-hundred pound man for a few minutes at least; they both had received five prolonged hits. They were unconscious for hours. Their bodies ached for days.

The movie-boys were released from jail a few years later in late summer of 2006. They continue to this writing with their illicit trade of selling pirated movies to casino customers. By evidence of the spelling on the labels on their copies of movies, prison time failed to improve their literacy and attention to detail. Unless someone reads this book to them or they interrogate a security guard at the casino on duty that night, they are probably unaware of exactly what happened that night.

Loan's Call for Help

Three men leaving the casino wove toward their vehicles to head home just after 4:05 AM. There were few cars in the parking lot that night. Over by an older Chevy and a Honda SUV, they heard a woman scream for help. They might have been brave or drunk. Regardless, they ran to the screaming woman. As light snow fell, the men in full alarm ran toward the woman, unsure what to expect as they rose to gallantry. They ran to meet the undeniable call of a woman in distress. This happened in middle-America where men are men and do what they can for young women in distress.

As they neared the two vehicles, an incongruous scene unfolded. As they approached, a small Asian woman with a thick Chinese accent waved them over to her. She was standing between a low-slung Chevy Impala and a taller Honda SUV, yelling and motioning to them for help. One of the men recognized her as one of the blackjack dealers from the casino. She was standing over two motionless forms lying on the cold pavement.

In between the cars were two large men laid out on the paving; the young woman was yelling something about being attacked by these two men. The young woman, who tended to confuse tense of past and present verbs, was talking about something that had already passed using words as if the event was still in progress. The first man on the scene recognized the young woman.

He assumed large men are reluctant to lie down on cold snowy parking lots for no apparent reason; he figured out the scene for what it was. He asked her the first question that came to his mind sorting limited details that she was Asian.

"Lady, what kind of Kung Foo do you know?"

She ignored the question telling him that men were going to "rae me," as she put it. As the other men caught up with the first man on the scene, looking down at the inert Ian and Bjorn and then to her, the second man asked her: "Rae you? What do you mean rae you?"

Exasperated, Loan resorted to communicate as best she could convey in the consonants she could manage more clearly. "They try rob and fuck me!"

Point well made. A bit crude. Regardless, well made.

The man said to the others that joined him. "She says these men attacked her and were going to rob and rape her." This was Middle America and the other two men responded by cursing and looking around to see what next should be done to the sons-of-bitches. God certainly favors the passions of red-necks.

A couple up on the top of the entrance to the casino saw some of the commotion and mentioned it to a door attendant in the entrance of the casino. He used his security radio to call the main office security folks and word of an incident in the south parking lot quickly spread.

Apparently, it had involved the Asian card dealer and two of the customers that were escorted out half an hour earlier. Within a minute, security got word to the casino's night manager. Like a blood rush, the word flowed out that someone had attacked a casino dealer in the south parking lot. The sluggish activity on the early morning casino floor shifted to a frenzy.

Others, patrons and customers alike heard about the alarm going through the casino, came out of the casino and ran up to the small crowd forming around the two vehicles. As people walked up, the first man that asked about Loan's training in martial arts became an impromptu spokesman about the situation. As each person or group approached the crowd, he would turn to them and said to them, "They tried to rob and rape her." That was the word that went out to the casino. Some men in the parking lot tried to rob and rape the Asian card dealer. They tried to rob and rape Nguyên Xuân Loan.

By then, the ever alert grave-yard shift crew of the casinos crack security team saw the commotion on the parking lot cameras. In short order, the word went out that Nguyên Xuân Loan, the difficult-at-times-to-manage Vietnamese blackjack and poker dealer had been assaulted in the parking lot.

Loan was a favorite of the security team managing the cameras and microphones. She broke up the monotony of endless hours of tracking dealer and patron activities. When they heard about rather than caught the action, they began playing back the camera and microphone recordings and storing them on new VHS tapes. They cursed their luck that the event occurred out on the south perimeter; camera resolution was going to be lousy.

Word of the attack flew throughout the casino. Anyone on break or who was free to leave his or her post ran out and into the winter cold of the south parking lot.

The alarm went out wildly; Loan had been attacked in the parking lot by two large men, the drunken movie-guys. The answers elicited more questions. "Those guys? Those over-sized imbeciles attacked Loan? They're knocked out? Loan "Kung Foo-ed 'em!"

As the details of the story improved, it was passed around that Loan was doing okay but the men were knocked out cold on the ground. Loan's okay but the men are dead. No. Not dead, just knocked out. Loan knocked those men down!

Loan had enemies among some of the female personnel in the casino and those still on duty that night ran out into the parking lot to see if the Asian bitch got her comeuppance that night. They were disappointed to find that the situation went another way; it went crazily a whole other way. Diminutive Loan took down some big doped-up dudes.

Throughout the casino, the comments ran the gamut between fiction and truth. What the holy heck just happened out there? More importantly, how in the world did this ignorant Vietnamese ill-tempered woman take these men down? How in the world could a woman, one-fifth the weight of those two men anticipate, fight off an attack, and then kick their backsides wholesale? How?

On 15 February 2004, the 4:25 AM revelations among the employees and casino were electric. Casino operations shifted down as the employees ran out into the winter night to see to Loan's welfare. Or as some of the women dealers had hoped, Loan would be in a bad way.

By rules of procedure in a casino, any disruption is a cause to stop the slot-machine play. The central computer system that tracked the slots locked up the games; bank after bank of slot machines locked up, even in mid-play. Slot machine players could do little else but sit and wait. Floor managers told those with money in the machines to wait. Other gamblers that had their winnings left the floor to see what was going on out in the parking lot.

The poker and blackjack tables were empty, the dealers stranded tending over their trays of chips. Security teams had to retrieve the chips before a dealer was permitted to leave their table. Pit bosses watched over the dealers and the floor managers watched over the pit bosses. As the story about Nguyên Loan spread, they were locking down all the chip trays. For the first time in five years since the casino had opened, gambling stopped. The entire casino shut down to see what had happened out in the parking lot that night.

Albuquerque Police

By 4:28 AM, after security learned that two men were unconscious on a more-or-less public parking lot, the casino summoned the Albuquerque police. They arrived to trade jurisdictional issue with the tribe. This particular tribe lacked jail facilities for incidents like this; turning to the City of Albuquerque or the county to take these men off their hands. The incident actually occurred on rented land not directly owned by the tribe.

The city police showed up to see the crowd around the cars and the two inert bodies lying on the pavement. People crowded around Loan; they reluctantly parted for the approaching officers. Loan's crowd had been asking her to tell them what happened, patting her on the back and talking about the incident, marveling at the two large unconscious forms in between the two cars. The contrast between the size of Loan and her assailants added to the buzz among the growing crowd. She said nothing to anyone about the stun gun.

When the county sheriff and the Albuquerque City police arrived at the scene, they recorded the scene and the position of the inert bodies of the men on graphed sketch pads. This took a few minutes.

The situation recorded well enough since no one died, they worked to get the inert men into the back of squad cars. One of the officers downwind of the situation advised that they needed to put cover the seats with plastic to keep one incontinent man from stinking up his squad car.

Lacking conscious perpetrators, the police could only interview the one participant that could talk: the intended victim, Loan or Loan Xuân Nguyên as it showed on her driver's license. Her first name was easy enough. He wasn't sure how to say her middle or last name with the odd marks above some of the vowels.

They speculated on how much information they might be able to get from her; foreign-born Asians in New Mexico were usually reluctant witnesses to a crime. They had experience with Hmong and Vietnamese in some street gangs issues, the police natural expectation was more Hmong issues.

Maybe it was something about their country of origin; Vietnamese had a mild distrust for civil authority such as it was in Viet Nam. Expatriates of Southeast Asia expected police to be corrupt. Trusting authority in America was often a hard sell.

The crime situation was upside down. Two large men attack a small woman in the early morning hours of a winter night on a casino parking lot. One hundred percent of the time, if the victim is female, there will be with full certainty a brutalized or dead woman. There are always ugly civil issues to sort.

Instead, two large men reeking of cigarettes, bourbon, and urine lay on cold pavement; knocked unconscious. Their cloths were in disarray, as if they had fallen from the black winter sky. They had yet to learn that Loan gave herself a workout jumping up and down on top of them. Little was obvious even to a seasoned policeman. From the looks of the men, it would be hours before the police could interview them.

Albuquerque Police Matters

At the center of the crowd in between the two cars were the still forms of two large men in bulky NFL jackets. The men were inert, unconscious, but alive, bourbon-sodden breath condensing from their mouths, foul vapor steaming from one man's urine-soaked pants. Some people dressed in dark suits and parkas stood off to one side talking to a young Asian woman dressed up in a tuxedo and wearing a red woolen hat, a long red coat, and gloves, shivering in the winter night.

Two of the tribal police spotted the city policemen walking toward them. One of the officers motioned to them to move off to one side; they stepped back from the crowd to talk outside of everyone's hearing.

The first policeman asked "What do you know about what happened here? The second policeman interrupted the first. "Has an ambulance been called for those men lying on the ground?

One of the tribal policemen, a heavy set older man with a short black pony-tail who answered to the nickname "Red," explained as he pointed at the bodies, "The men attacked one of our employees. She used mace and a stun gun on them. The mace is built into the stun-gun. She zapped them at least a couple of times. Both of them have some marks on their necks."

The Albuquerque officers nodded as the casino police officer continued, "They were in the casino playing at her blackjack table for hours. They caused a scene and we have it on the main camera over her blackjack table. We know they were drinking heavily and might be stoned on something else. We escorted them to their vehicle, which was parked closer to the casino than it is now. We know they left the property around 3:30 AM."

The Albuquerque officers asked about hospitalization of the inert men on the pavement. Red responded, "They're probably out of danger but they should be examined when you get them to the county jail. It's your call if you think they need to be taken to the hospital."

The Albuquerque officers said little making notes on a report form. Red added, "A half-empty 'handle' of bourbon in the front seat of the Impala might explain some of their boldness. Hard to know beyond that. We suspect the men were building up their courage for the assault with that. Near as we can tell, they're out from prolonged contact with her stun-gun."

The City police officer responded, "We'll check them out in a minute. Did your security cameras record this?" Red nodded to both questions and the City police officer asked, "Give us a short summary."

The casino security personnel anticipated the question about the security cameras. They immediately told staff to back up the relevant video camera tapes and make two copies for the Albuquerque police. The second Tribal policeman stepped up handing the policeman two VHS tapes, one marked with a black and white printed label "Casino, 2-15-2004, Loan Nguyen's Table, 2:00 AM," and the other tape marked "South Parking Lot Camera 12, 2-15-2004, 2:30 AM to 4:30 AM."

"This is a copy of the last few hours from one of our casino cameras on her blackjack tables. These men followed her tables as she shifted each thirty minutes. The other tape is from the parking lot camera. The detail is rough but clear enough. It's consistent with the card dealer's statement," pointing at the woman at the center of the crowd.

Red continued, "Those two men were buzzed up on something more than alcohol. We see them up here hustling CD-movies to the patrons. We run them off if they annoy the customers. They're usually harmless, annoying the customers at most. Sometimes they play blackjack and we have them on tape playing at her table from a few hours ago." He interrupted the conversation as he handed the Albuquerque police the VHS video tapes.

The officer continued: "They were apparently stoked up on something, playing poorly. They lost some money and cussed her out. She handled them okay but at one point about an hour ago, the pit-boss had them removed from her table. The parking lot security reported they had to escort them to their car to make sure they left the property. They made a fuss so our security made them leave the property around 3:30 AM. Again, we're fairly sure they left the property."

Officer Pratt asked them "It's not hard to see that they're still here."

Red shrugged, "This is someone else's land. We just rent the surface for parking. Security staff said they saw them drive off the main property and were last seen on the access ramp to I-25." Red paused and then added, "We have signs posted on the entrances to the over-flow parking advising customers that the casino is not responsible for theft or damage. The signs are on every light pole and parking lot entrance."

Red became defensive, "Obviously, they returned after we saw them take the access road. Our security cameras have coverage close to the buildings. We can't watch the perimeters as it is some other dude's property. Besides that, tribal property ends at the service road. Beyond that, its New Mexico's issue."

"So what happened out here?" the second city cop asked, "Were there any direct witnesses? What's on the parking lot camera recording?"

Red settled down, "No one appears to have actually witnessed it, you know, actually seen it happen. But the in-close cameras showed it well enough; it shows her walking up between the two cars. It shows her unlocking the door. The Chevy's passenger side opened up as she was getting into the Honda. The first man at or near the front of the car stepped out and he appears to grab her from behind. His body blocked the camera's view of her but in the next few seconds, she's moved around him and his body flies backward across the hood of Impala. He fell backward on top of the hood of the Chevy as the driver's door was opening. The man on the car's front hood didn't move after that.

Red paused to think about it, "As quick as the guy is laid out on the hood, she crouched down and moved to the rear of the Impala. She stayed crouched down in the shadows as the other man is moving toward the back of the car. We can hardly see her in the shadows. She squats down on her heels like the Asians do, she is not standing up."

"The driver seemed to stagger as he was almost on top of her. He's standing almost on top of Miss Loan. For some reason, he paused there with the first guy lying on the hood, not moving. The next thing we see is her whipping around low to the ground and driving her right hand into his body. He fell instantly."

The second city officer interrupted Red, "What's your camera interval?"

Red responded, "I think we're on at least 10 frames a second. It might be more than that."

"Loan stepped out of the way as the guy fell forward." Red added with something of a grin, "Then she leaned over him and stuck the stun gun on his neck what looks to be four or five times."

The Albuquerque officers winced. They knew what a stun gun charge felt like, they had all been required to take a "taser" shot in order to be qualified to use it in the line of duty.

Red noticed the Albuquerque officer's reaction. "It gets better."

He described how she went over to the man on the hood of the Impala and gave him three or four more charges on the neck. "After that, she drags him off the hood where he fell to the pavement."

"Is she running from the scene or calling for help?"

Red responded, "Not that we can tell. This is all inside of a minute or two."

"She put the gun away and this is what the most interesting part is. She kicks the men a couple of times and then steps up on them holding the top of the Chevy to steady her. Then she jumps up and down on them a bit."

Officer Pratt glances over at Loan noting she was wearing four-inch wearing platform heels. That had to hurt a conscious man.

Red adds one more thing, "She appears to be tiring after maybe ten seconds of this. That's when we see her yelling for help. Then some patrons came running to the scene and we got our first notice of trouble."

"How long did this take?" Officer Pratt asked.

"It took less than five minutes, really, maybe less than two minutes. We can time it by the number of frames on the camera." the second tribal officer responded.

"Jesus! She zapped 'em two or three times?" The police officers flinched again at the thought of a stun gun being used, glancing over nearly in unison at the Chinese woman. She was hardly five feet tall and these inert men appeared to be roughly six feet two, one of them maybe six feet four and at least twice her weight. Officer Pratt turned back to the tribal policemen, "Then what?"

Red added, "Some of the casino customers starting running up to the scene. We received a call from someone's cell phone about the same time the guards watching the security cameras noticed that something had happened in the south parking lot.

Another tribal police officer added, "No one touched the two men. We left them as we found them."

"When did all this exactly happen? What time on the clock did it begin?"

"It just happened. It's been fifteen, maybe twenty minutes ago, around 4:00 AM according to the tapes. We can check the time stamps."

Sergeant Pratt motioned to another City police officer, handing him the two VHS tapes. "Take these inside the casino and play them back, play the parking lot unit first and report back to me. Let's do this quickly, it's cold and we're going to have to do something about the two gentlemen lying there on the pavement." He instructed another policeman to make out a report and get someone to record the scene. He instructed his officers to make a decision to move the men into the back of a squad car or call an ambulance to move them.

He motioned everyone to walk towards the cars and the shivering blackjack dealer standing a few feet away from the two inert bodies. He turned to Red and asked, "Is she rattled too much to talk to us?

Red shrugged, "Miss Loan? She seems okay. She's just cold out here. She hates cold weather."

The second policeman had out a clipboard with a pen. "What do I call her, Miss Loan or Miss Win? Can you spell that?"

Red: "Nguyen. N-G-U-Y-E-N. It is pronounced 'When.'" He repeated it, "'When.' Her first name is Loan. 'L-O-A-N,'" pronounced much like you see it." She has a middle name but I can't pronounce it. X-U-A-N, pronounced 'Shwoan' or 'Soon,' something like that. It doesn't sound like it is spelled."

"What kind of name is that? Japanese or Vietnamese?" He asked the tribal police officer.

"Vietnam. Nguyen is a common Vietnamese name, like Smith or Jones in America. We have a dozen Asian immigrants working here with that last name," Red responded.

The crowd opened up to let the police officer approach the woman. The police officer's six-foot plus frame loomed over the Asian woman. "Ms. Nguyên? I'm Sergeant Pratt with the City of Albuquerque Police Department. Are you okay to talk?" Noting her shaking, he added "There's no reason to be afraid."

"I'm not afraid." She said without emotion. "I'm cold."

He nodded noticing her shivering, hunched over in her coat. She shivered painfully. "I know its cold outside. We will make this quick as we can, Miss Nguyên. I just need to get some information from you. Do you have your driver's license? I also need to see that stun gun of yours?"

"Am I going jail, off'r?" she asked, her English in a thick Asian accent crunched the word officer. She had her driver's license ready to hand to him. She produced the stun gun out of her jacket with a folded piece of paper attached to the long handle by a red rubber band. She was shivering as she gave him the weapon.

"I don't think so Ms. Nguyên. If everything is as it seems, the casino people will help you file the complaint on these men." He found himself instinctively talking slower and louder than normal, a speech tendency he had when talking to people who mangled English.

His eyes went wide; it was a big stun gun. She handed him a Czechoslovakian device with a dual trigger for mace and electric discharge from the same prongs. It required two 9-volt batteries to charge the capacitors and release the pepper spray. This stun-gun carried a big charge.

This mail-order stun gun required training in order for a civilian to carry one. Placed on the right part of the body, it could hurt someone. On the elderly or children, it could even kill.

"Do you have the paperwork for this stun-gun Miss Nguyên?"

"Right there, on the hand'r of the gun, off'r," she quipped. "I went to schoolen to use that."

He paused on the word "schoolen." "Which police station held school for this? The one on 56th street?" he asked, assuming it would be one of the self-defense classes taught by off-duty policemen. It was one of the areas of the city where some Vietnamese had settled or at least there where small specialty grocery stores catering to Asian customers. Overall, they had become good citizens, just difficult to carry a conversation with them.

"Near the Southeast Station." She responded.

Southeast station slightly surprised him; wealthier part of town. Maybe she had a wealthy husband. If so, how'd she have to be working out here for the casino? He thought to check her left hand to see if she wore a wedding ring but she had put gloves on by then, her arms folded and she hunched slighting trying to stay warm.

"Are you single or married?"

"No, sing'r. Not married," giving him short direct answers. *She's cold out here*, he thought. He figured they could get better answers inside the casino.

"We'll get the rest of the detail inside the casino in just a minute." Two of the policeman picked up the first unconscious man at the front of the Impala and carried him, putting him in the back of a police car. They laid him face down on some large plastic trash bags and pulled his arms behind his back where they handcuffed him with plastic zip-ties.

Tribal policeman carried the second man to another city police car and restrained him in the same manner, with zip-ties, face down in the back seat. This face-down maneuver was done in the event they vomited on the way to the police station. They reeked of bourbon and cigarettes indicating a chance of throwing up in their "sleep." They didn't want a citizen choking on his own vomit on the way to the police station. More important, they did not want these guys stinking up their car.

"Miss Nguyên, you didn't leave much for us to do here. Let's go inside where we can warm up and get the rest of the details." He guided her away from the vehicles and toward the casino. She had to take two steps to his one as they walked back to the casino. The officer shortened his stride slowing down to make it easier for her to keep pace.

Her steps emphasized how small she was compared to the two hulking men laid out cold in the back of the squad cars. She seemed child-like, direct, simple, and almost defenseless now as compared to what he would see on the security camera tapes. The large contrast between the attackers and victim amused Officer Pratt; this situation was completely upside down.

The crowd dispersed as the police officers and the blackjack dealer went into the casino and over to an empty snack bar where they could sit down and review the details of the attack. The casino was returning to normal with the few employees on break standing off to the side waiting to see what the policeman was going to do with Loan.

A couple of women co-workers on the fringes hoping that Loan was in trouble went back to work, sullen in view that Loan turned out to be better than okay. They would later learn the story was true, that Loan took her attackers down in less than a minute expanding the semi-legend of her toughness in the casino. The word went out with new emphasis, "Don't mess with Loan."

As they sat down, the policeman with the security camera tapes came up and told Officer Pratt that the camera recordings backed up the story they had heard so far. The two men had assaulted, or rather attempted to assault the blackjack dealer in the parking lot. At minimum, it looked like attempted theft but one of them had grabbed her, it could have been attempted rape as well. It was obviously an assault. The men never had a chance to demonstrate their romantic interests. Regardless, one of them had clearly grabbed her from behind before she knocked him on top of the front hood of the Impala. By all appearances, it was an assault that went badly for the perp.

The officers studied the casino recording at her table where they had audio as well as good color images of the table play. Nothing seemed out of the ordinary other than the two men appeared intoxicated. It looked like they lost more than a few thousand dollars to the casino by the time casino security removed them from the property.

The money, although not a big sum, was enough to establish a motive for the assault. They talked some trash with the blackjack dealer. She apparently took guff from no one.

The movie-boys had a minor record of parking lot romance with women patrons. The liaisons were noted from time to time in the security logs. It was seamy activity between consenting adults in a low-life situation but not something the casino prosecuted. Money might even have changed hands which invariably turned back in tribal coffers if the woman was sustaining a gambling addiction.

The only issue that might be argued (vainly) in this was whether Loan had enticed the men to her car to add to her income. Given the long line of wealthy but unhappy suitors for Loan's charms, the argument lacked legs. As with most Asian commerce, it is always "Cash up front." These men were broke.

Flirting with customers was part of the ploy of blackjack dealers to improve their tips. As for using her for some impromptu romance in the parking lot, they misread the target of their ambush. Loan apparently defended herself after they made first contact with her. As was always the case, she didn't look for a fight. There was little dispute she could finish it.

Another city police officer came up and asked what to do with the perpetrators' car as it still had the keys in the ignition. Officer Pratt told them to lock it up and take the keys to the tribal officer in charge. It was up to the casino to have the vehicle towed off the rented parking-lot property. The 1998 Chevy Impala was the tribe's problem in an assault issue. After a few days, the tribe had the car impounded.

One of the casino managers of the dealers came up to the officer and Miss Nguyên. When they called him and he learned it involved Loan Nguyên, he immediately threw on some clothes and drove to the casino. He wanted to avoid leaving the situation with Loan to the tribal security; it was for protection of the security as much as anything else. It was now about 5:00 AM. "My name is Bruno Vitoli." The sixty-something heavy set Italian-American said to officer, shaking his hand. He looked at her and shook his head, grinning, "What'd she do this time?"

The officer was unaware of the long pseudo-father-daughter relationship between the two and tried to assure Bruno that Miss Nguyên was the intended victim, not the perpetrator of a crime.

Mr. Vitoli nodded his head, "I heard about most of it on the drive over here. Those men picked the wrong dealer from what I hear." He looked down at her as she sat quietly at the table, her coat and gloves still on trying to warm up, "You doin' okay?" She nodded and then he turned to the officer, "I'll let you do your report. I'll be up at my office if you need me." As he walked off toward the management office, Bruno was grinning, shaking his head; just another moment in the life of managing or at least attempting to manage the Asian princess.

Sergeant Pratt sat down and took out his report book. "I'll keep this brief for now but if we need more information later, can you come down to our station?" She nodded yes. "Before I start, can I ask you a personal question?" She motioned him to continue, watching him. "Are you Vietnamese?"

"Chinese Vietnamese, Yes." she replied.

"Where do come from?" he started.

"Shreveport, Louisiana."

"No, before Shreveport? Where did you come from?"

"Grand Island, Nebraska. Before that, I lived Long Island, New York."

"Miss Nguyên, let me start over. Where were you born?"

"Viet Nam. Sai Gon, Viet Nam. Now it's called Ho Chi Minh City," she replied. He mused about the simple direct answers without much elaboration, typical Asian-immigrant dialogue. Getting details could take a while.

Chinese-Vietnamese, he thought to himself. She looked like she could be in her mid-twenties but she was thirty-three according to her driver's license. Asians age well. Sergeant Pratt could rarely judge a women's age. It was even harder to judge the age of an Asian woman. He was single himself, he contemplated what it would be like to date a pretty young Asian like this. Regardless of his musings, he stayed on point and did his job.

He asked her if she was a US citizen. She shook her head and then he asked if she had her green card. She reached into the inside left side of her coat. She pulled out a laminated card showing a darkly tanned Asian teenager. In the photograph, Loan had the dark skin of someone who had spent over three years in the Philippine jungle. It hardly looked like her; the picture was taken in 1984. She gave it to him.

Loan had a permanent residence green card going back to an application in 1982 filed in Manila, Philippines by a Catholic organization. She had been in the United States since 1983, over twenty years. There was high likelihood that she was a Vietnamese boat-person, part of the refugees from communist Viet Nam that started arriving in the late 1970s. She would probably have experienced some very difficult times.

Her taking down two large men made more sense now resurrecting a recent rule among minorities that had moved into the area: "Don't mess with the boat-people."

He filled out more of the police report for a few minutes. She was silent watching him write down information about the incident.

"Miss Nguyên. The men are unconscious. I will not be able to get both sides of the story until they come to and we can talk to them. The casino is filing a complaint of assault on them. Do you want to file a complaint as well?

"Will I go jail?"

Sergeant Pratt laughed at the question for the second time. Grinning now as he was piecing together who she was, "No, Miss Nguyên. You are not going to jail. However, those men will end up in jail or with a record at least. The casino is filing a complaint and we have the incident on video tape. You don't have to file a complaint unless you want to."

"I think about it?" She seemed small and defenseless now; like a little kid. She acted as if the incident hadn't happened or was nothing more than dumping over a pitcher of water on the family dinner table.

"Yes. Think about it. In the meantime, may I ask you a question?" Loan nodded.

"Where'd you get that stun gun?" Sergeant asked with a grin.

"A friend ordered it to me." Loan had trouble between using "to" and "for" in conversation. She added, "He was worried about being safe in parking space." Loan paused. "Then I had policeman show me how use it. I went schoolen three times. I have papers for gun and schoolen."

"Yes. I know." Officer Pratt remembered he still had the device in his jacket pocket. He pulled it out and handed it back to her. "That's a powerful stun gun. It has the pepper-spray and one of the more powerful charges in the industry. I don't see many people carry one like this. It's the first time I've seen one used by a civilian."

She sat quietly as he over-explained something that was obvious. He changed the subject, "Can you tell us about what happened tonight?"

She was anything but indirect, "The bastards tried rae me. I got pissed. I knocked them out."

"Rae me"? the officer asked. "Explain please."

"You know, rae me, put me down in the parking lot and rae me."

"Rape you?" he asked beginning to catch on to some of her difficulties with English. "They were going to rape you?"

She nodded, "Yes, they grabbed me and were going to rae me and the mother f.., the doos were going to take my mawnie. They talked some crap at my table. I just blew what they say off. But the doos tried to take my mawnie and rae me."

He was sure they were going for her money; it was late shift with dealers going home with cash tips. The men were otherwise probably too stoned to pull off a rape but it would be hard to know what they were planning when they grabbed her. They were unable to carry off their attack. They clearly assaulted her. However, their ability to "get it up" and rape her was speculative.

The other guy came out of the car might not have had intention and it would have to wait on what they say when they're conscious. He actually didn't touch her but the first man did. Based on "on-camera" recordings, these guys were going to jail. This was an open and shut case based on assault.

Mugging was relatively uncommon in this part of New Mexico, except at the Indian Casinos were people tended to have cash, particularly someone who hit a good run on the slot machines and was going home with more than the usual money in their wallet. Security actively patrolled the parking lots attempting to avoid events like what had happened tonight.

Protecting casino patrons was job number one for exterior security personnel. Assaults on patrons is always a problem. *(Author's note: In 2013 and 2014, one of the biggest problems in Atlantic City was mugging of customers walking to and from the casinos. The muggers went after the customers mostly likely to have cash which usually meant Asians and then white people. It has resulted in driving off the well-cashed gambling clientele to other casinos in neighboring states. This has resulted in a large decline in Atlantic City's casino industry and is generally not reported in the media.)*

The casino made the mistake of mixing patron and dealer parking together. The incident forced them to remedy the situation immediately.

"Where'd you learn to move like that, Miss Nguyên?"

"The policeman shows me. It wasn't a fight off'r Pratt, I was defending. I went to schoolen two week ago. I learn to defend. I defended."

Officer Pratt nodded. Yes, she was defending. She defended the hell out of those two men.

"But you already had them down on the ground. You could have driven off. But you stayed. Anyone else would have run, you didn't. Why?"

"Bastards pissed me off. They broke, out of money, they wanted my tips. They touched me, grabbed me. I kick their ass. End of story." she said matter-of-fact.

"Yes you did, Miss Nguyên. Yes you did." Shaking his head, thinking to himself "This was one tough woman." It was getting late and he'd have to write up his report before the end of his shift. He looked at her address; she lived in an upper-class side of Albuquerque, a nice neighborhood. She had a twenty-minute drive ahead of her; it was late with light snow falling. The snow was heavier in Albuquerque.

"I'll be back in touch with you later this week." After getting her address and phone numbers, he handed her a card with his name, badge number and contact numbers. "Do you have family here, Miss Nguyên? Will you be okay to go home tonight?"

"Yes. Thank you off'r Pratt, my sister and her husband live with me. I'r is fine." She stood up and held out her hand to shake his. He shook her hand. Now she was all business. She was composed, calm, and matter-of-fact about everything.

Had she been from America, she would have been in a hospital or a morgue. She was in fact going home, by herself, acting as if she had done little more than fix a flat tire. He had little doubt she could do that as well.

This woman had been attacked by two men twice her size and they were now on their way to being processed to holding cells and then to court and then to prison. Probably an open-and-shut case and all without an officer of the law, not even the security guards involved in the initial event.

Officer Pratt amused himself with the thoughts the two men would have in a couple of hours when they regained consciousness in a jail cell. They'd be curious about the aches and odd square-shaped bruises on their bodies, the marks on their neck, the irritation in their eyes. Something in their plans had gone terribly wrong.

But as their memories go of that night, that is about it. Had they been conscious, they would recall several more high voltage jolts to the neck, repeated kicks to their groin, chest and back, uncounted blows from 100 pounds of an indignant blackjack dealer jumping up and down on their inert bodies as many times as she could until she ran out of breath. It was merciful that unconsciousness came to Ian and Bjorn when it did.

The Drive Home

The snow was falling now, covering the parking lot, sanitizing the landscape into a gentle whiteness. The darkness of the parking lot changed as the whitened surface lightened up the surroundings. Bruno Vitoli escorted Nguyên Xuan Loan to her car, chiding her in a joking way about making such a fuss. The casino resumed normal operations and released lock down on the slot machines and resetting the game tables with dealers and their trays of chips.

It was 6:00 AM. Loan headed home. There was a new "Loan story" to tell among the morning shift employees at the Indian casino. The story went out even larger from the resentful co-workers: "Don't "f" with the Asian bitch." The local Buddhist priests heard the story the next day and by late in the afternoon, most of the Vietnamese community heard the news.

As she settled into the driver's seat of her 2004 Honda Pilot, she smiled at the bobble-head dogs mounted on the top of the dashboard and the "Scooby-Doo" printed card hanging from the rear-view mirror. These were gifts from her mother. Few knew about Loan's mother, Nguyên Mai, ill from failing kidneys at the age of seventy-eight, living in the Cholon of Sai Gon. It was from Nguyên Mai that Nguyên Loan drew her strength and fearlessness. If it had been Loan's mother in that situation tonight, those men would have been dead.

Loan drove slowly out of the parking lot stirring up eddies of drifting snow. The sun would be up in an hour, the darkness of the night a memory. The City of Albuquerque county holding cells had two new occupants, headed for country lockup and then to prison for the next thirty months. The Indian casino on I-25 formed a new security policy with employees parking in a secured area. The casino scrutinized surly gamblers a bit more for a time at the poker and blackjack tables; tolerance for drunken and abusive players tightened.

Loan entered the on-ramp of I-25 heading south toward Albu-querque. The snow reminded her of how foreign America could be to someone who grew up in tropical Southeast Asia. She debated whether she could return and recapture her lost childhood; Viet Nam had improved greatly in the last decade. However, she had two children born in America. America was her adoptive home and her children were American citizens. She was not a citizen but it was time she changed that.

As she drove home in the large flakes of drifting snow, she thought about her mother in Sai Gon. She missed her. It was time to return home, see her, and tell her of the two men that had attacked her.

Loan already knew what her mother would ask of her. Why did she let those men live?

It was hard for Loan to explain to her mother about America. It was the richest country. Americans could and did everything. They even went into the heavens and landed on the moon. They seem-ingly invented everything. They were also made up of everyone in the world, mixed with white, brown, yellow, red, and black people.

While they were smart, the Americans could also be stupid at the same time. In America, it was the land of the rule of law and the benefit of the doubt. Their laws protected their people from problems that eluded Vietnamese in Communist Viet Nam.

In Viet Nam, as Mai had explained to Loan after they re-united. The police are corrupt. The only justice upon whom the Vietnamese could rely was in cash. They paid to have the police take care of their problems or stay out of their way. However, when it came to a person's welfare in Viet Nam, immediate action just as Loan had performed in the jungles, was necessary to survive in many circumstances in mod-ern Viet Nam.

In the United States, people expected the police and the courts to serve justice according to the rule of law. Buying policeman was considered scandalous, it was inappropriate and illegal. Loan's mother understood some of this. Yet, she had difficulty understanding that a fair police was rarely a perfect police. Loan would have to explain to Mai that bad people act when they think the police cannot adequately intervene. Justice is slow in any country, it is ponderous and inaccu-rate and often inept in the best of conditions.

In the perfect America, Loan still had to protect herself in the interval between bad people and a reactive police. Loan had to carry weapons in America to cover the gap between the crime and the intervention. Bigger thefts moved slowly, robbery and rape of a young woman in a parking lot happened in mere minutes.

The variation of circumstance of victims required that some had to act just to preserve a chance of remaining alive. Small Asian women with rough English were forced to defend their welfare differently, even in the over-sized benevolent environment of New Mexico in the United States of America of 2004.

Thinking of her mother's life and now her own, the jungle was everywhere. She made plans to return to Sai Gon as soon as possible to spend more time with her mother.

End of Section Two

Notice to Employees:

One of the south entrances otherwise known as the employee's door of an Indian casino in February 2005 displayed an array of cork bulletin boards. Neat government work notices, car-pooling rosters, notes, business cards and ragged notes competed for attention. Similar bulletin boards repeated official notices mixed in with ad hoc social and entrepreneurial announcements.

Centered prominently among the bulletin boards, a 12" by 18" cherry red frame displayed a photograph of an Asian woman in her dealer's black tuxedo. Her broad smile and black hair trimmed to accent her Chinese jaw line gave a china-doll appearance. The exotic and attractive woman's photo drew more than casual glances.

A placard in crisp Times New Roman font congratulated her bravery and strength. In smaller font, the placard described how she defended herself when two customers attacked her early on a Sunday morning, 15 February 2004.

Author's Note:

On a slow night, I parked in close to the casino in the employee parking area as it was closer to the facility.

I had to walk fewer steps on a winter night and entered through the employee entrance.

I noticed the framed picture a number of times.

On February 19, 2015, I played blackjack at a table and recognized the card-dealer from her picture and recalled the description of her conduct from a year before.

It was a quiet night and the tables weren't that busy.

As she dealt the cards, I asked Loan about the picture and her story that night. And so it began.

SECTION THREE: FLIGHT

Nắm chặt Nắm chặt *(Vietnamese: Hold on! Hold on!)*
Anh's Last Instruction, Late March 1977

"Loan!" Anh shouted at the girl, "Hold on to something!" She clarified her instruction, "Grab anything that floats. Hold it, Loan! Hold on to something!" Anh shrieked her instructions over the howl of the wind and the crash of the waves on the port railing. Her voice competed with the screams of the crowd sliding on the listing deck. The dissolving Vietnamese fishing-turned-refugee vessel tilted to port. Standing upright on the wet working-deck became increasingly difficult. Each large wave pitched the tilt another increment into an impossible angle.

Eight-year-old Loan stared at Anh a few feet away focused on her new instruction. The most she could make out amid the cacophony of shouts and screams: "Loan! Grab something that floats!" She made out one other message from Anh. It was shorthand for the previous instruction, "Nắm chặt! Nắm chặt!" (*Vietnamese:"Hold on! Hold on!"*)

Second Day on the South China Sea

The weather behaved well most of the day. By mid-afternoon, favorable southwesterly winds shifted from blowing the stern to port (*From the rear to their left*). Waves built on three-foot southeasterly swells in the afternoon, the top-heavy boat riding with the roll of the sea. The boat ran a generally eastward heading for most of two days, riding swells flowing to the southeast. The transit west-to-east had been harmonious with the weather and mood of the South China Sea.

Erratic winter monsoon usually ends in March making for qui-
eter seas for a month or two. Key word in that description is that
Asian monsoons depended on many factors spread over 9% of the
earth's surface. Colder winters over mainland Asia prolong the winter
monsoon. Warmer late winters change the dynamics from China to
northern Australia.

Winter conditions over mainland China dominated Indochina's
monsoons as immense land mass in temperate weather zones generated high atmospheric pressure. Nature seeks a balance and the
monsoons are the effect of shifting energies between the atmosphere
and the seas.

High winter pressurization of the atmosphere in one place responds
by filling a relative low-pressure area in another. The bath-water warm
tropical areas of the South China Sea fuels wet and dry cycles in South
Viet Nam enabling a year-round growing season.

Weather in the eastern side of The South China Sea can be different from weather on the west side of the body of water. Mid-afternoon
heating of the Philippine archipelago often made nonsense of weather
forecasts projected for regions 600 miles to the west.

The wind shifted from the northeast across the portside of the
boat. By mid-afternoon, the wind rose. Gusts animated the grey-
green stucco of the seascape with chop and white caps.

By late afternoon, the wind whipped spray off the crests of the
growing waves. The spray dried in mid-air leaving behind tiny crys-
tals of salt that gave the wind a stinging bite on exposed skin. The
overloaded boat plowed through the backs of rising swells, slowing as
motion changed from forward to hesitant and oscillating. New waves
on top of the swells ran faster than the over-loaded vessel. Some of the
waves began to wash over the stern and port railing.

As sea conditions changed, the ad hoc crew debated whether to
stay on course for the Philippines or ride out the storm by turning
into the wind. They were close to the Philippine coastline and desperate to find the entrance to Manila Bay or Subic Bay farther north.

The bilge pump labored to eject water coming over the stern.
Continued travel eastward guaranteed to overwhelm the pump.
Worse yet, the weight of bilge water compounded stresses within the
vessel's structure.

The crew attempted to turn the high prow toward the wind to reduce risk of flooding the vessel. Thai pirates broke the steering connection to most of the rudder the night before. The brutalized survivors struggled to manage the boat which wandered in broad circles throughout the night into the third full day.

In addition to killing the pilot and the original crew, they killed several of the male passengers and raped every female older than Loan. Small for her age, Loan was spared. Unfortunately, she witnessed the systematic violation of every older female including Anh. Two older women that resisted were thrown in the water. Unable to swim, they floundered briefly and sank below the surface.

Turning a top-heavy riverboat on a downwind heading is risky in heavy seas. Yet, changing course presented fewer risks than flooding from the stern.

An older Vietnamese man assumed the role of pilot. Like every adult male, his right ear was missing. The pirates carried off the severed ears as trophies. Dried blood stained the right side of his neck and shoulder.

The pilot throttled the engine to slow the lumbering fishing boat before turning counter-clockwise into the troughs, face the wind, and slice the swells. The rolling motion changed to buffeting as the boat plowed into oncoming waves. Sprays of seawater wetted the bow and portside passengers.

The boat sliced into a trough and split the oncoming wave, sprays exploding to the sides of the prow. The bilge pump stayed ahead of the water coming down from the deck. If the waves remained constant, they only had to wait out the change in weather before resuming course.

The Boat and Its Crew

The young crew, drafted with five ounces of gold and a ticket out of Viet Nam, knew little about managing a large boat in open seas. They had operated close to shore and the channels in the Mekong Delta.

It is not known who owned the boat and whether the owner was among the boat's manifest. If anyone had asked who owned the boat, they would not be told in case the boat was captured and returned to Viet Nam.

The waves were the largest they had ever seen in open water. They debated on the speed to apply as the waves grew.

The crew managed smaller fishing boats within sight of the shore. Few of them had piloted a shallow-draft boat of this size. The ten-ton passenger manifest carpeting the work deck made the boat top heavy. Unlike inert cargo, the human load could move about the deck and shift the stresses in the structure.

None of the crew had ventured out in the South China Sea more than a few miles from Viet Nam's eastern shore. Similar to all the passengers, none of the crew knew how to swim.

As they traveled west, southwesterly prevailing winds blew across a fetch of 600 miles towards the Philippine coastline. The waves could only build.

The lives of the remaining ninety passengers depended on an untrained crew piloting a patched-up riverboat in open seas. While the first day fared well enough, toward late afternoon, they saw other fishing boats in the distance. Then a larger boat loomed on the horizon heading toward them.

Besides freighters working back and forth between Korea, Taiwan and Japan to ports of call to the South, the two boats of concern were Vietnamese patrol boats and pirates. Once 12 miles out from shore, Vietnamese government had no legitimate claim on citizens beyond the international limit. The passengers concern turned to Thailand's ruthless and brutal pirates.

As the wind shifted and the seas rose, the crew argued whether to strike the waves head on or run at an angle. They headed into the waves at an angle as best they could estimate. The residual swells flowed from winds blown on a different day. Fresh waves arose on a new vector in the change of weather that afternoon. Choppy surface waves rode tops of the swells.

The chop and wind-blown spray confused the crew's sense of actual movement of the sea. The boat headed directly into larger waves. If the waves became much larger, a few degrees one way or another changed nothing of the outcome. The boat would come apart differently but just the same, it would come apart.

They successfully turned into the wind without incident. The bilge pump stayed ahead of the sea coming over the gunwales and prow. The crew consulted each other about whether the boat should ride better at different speeds. They revved the diesel engine adding an increment of speed to the vessel. The boat worked well enough, they moved against the waves to stay somewhat in place. They planned to resume their eastward travel after the wind shifted and the waves settled down.

The boat muddled through the waves. Passengers hunkered down low in the deck minimizing stinging sea spray and the seesaw motion of the boat. After thirty minutes of plowing into the waves, most passengers believed the boat was running well.

To starboard, to their right, the conical top of a Philippine mountain peaked now and then above the rough horizon. They were close to landfall. Hopes rose as the mountain top came into view and dimmed as they had to turn into the wind.

Hidden in the spray, chop, and swells, an unusually large wave struck the bow. It exploded above the prow and washed over the port gunwales.

The vessel shook. Passengers lurched forward as the boat suddenly slowed before regaining speed.

Many of the passengers and all the crew heard snapping sounds beneath the working deck. New sounds emerged from below where timber ground against timber as if two ends of a broken bone tore against another.

East of shipping lanes, within sight of a jungle-covered Philippine mountaintop and an hour from nightfall, the ship's skeleton began to fail. One crack in the structure followed another. Inadequate bracing secured to rotten timbers gave way. Interdependent ribs and planks failed in cascade.

Against reality, some hoped the noises below were an anomaly. As odd sounds continued under the deck, adults hearing the complaints of the structure realized they might be doomed.

Screams pierced the air as another large wave jarred the boat. The wave shook the boat down to its over-stressed timbers. The impact twisted the deck telegraphing bigger strain in the hull's framework. Deck planking popped loose as the boat bent in the middle.

Essential timbers simultaneously failed, warping the hull. Caulked seams separated below the water line, squirting seawater in a dozen places. The bilge pump again strained to keep up.

Two of the crew organized the men to assist the flagging capability of the bilge pump. They formed a bucket detail, bailing water out of a low part of the boat's hull. The first big wave jarred the boat interrupting their bucket brigade. Some returned to being passengers.

Individual concern for their families on the deck took precedence over activities that might have improved the fate of the entire vessel. Regardless, the crew rallied an insufficient few to stay with the task. They finally coerced more men to make the manual bailing effort work. By that time, the bilge flooded up around the base of the diesel engine.

Another large wave squarely struck the hull knocking anyone on their feet to the deck and on top of other passengers. Structure below deck broke noisily.

The noise of the water slamming the old hull and dull crack of fragile wood snapping under the deck broke discipline and command. The sound of failing timber under the deck might have been a fluke after the first wave. The cracking noises caused by the second wave converted denial into panic.

The sound of breaking structure preceded instructions from everyone to everyone else. Loud commands turned into yells. Mothers ordered frantically to their children. Leaderless men commanded anyone able to hear them. A furious cacophonous mixture of Southern Vietnamese and Cantonese oddly mixed with English expletives rose from the deck.

Asian languages sound angry to western ears. The passengers sounded as if rioting on the crowded deck. It was a mixture of panic and anger directed at the inept crew.

Unmistakable cries of many small children, sensing the shift in demeanor of the crowded deck, understanding the disturbing eruption of angst amidst an already tense afternoon, began to cry. The noisy crowd would go silent in a matter of minutes.

Anh flashed a look of fright at her friend's daughter, Nguyên Maï's youngest child, Nguyên Xuân Loan, who served her as babysitter, only in servitude. Yet, Anh cared for Loan as family.

Anh urgently needed to tell Loan much. The remainder of their lives might be measured in minutes. Anh had run out of time to correct some vital details of this voyage. She lied to Loan on essential facts about their destination and the overall purpose of the trip.

Anh planned to tell Loan the truth about the voyage once circumstances improved. She needed to arm Loan with more information than just the facts. Loan had never attended school. She barely knew the difference between Sai Gon and everywhere else. Loan knew only of Viet Nam as an undefined place seemingly without end. Anh's miscalculation ultimately cost Loan eighteen years of a vital part of her life ... connection with her mother, Nguyên Maï.

In the thirteen months of Loan's servitude, Anh regarded the girl as nearly as she cherished her own children. Unfortunately, Anh expressed her regard toward Loan in limited ways.

She wanted Loan to feel accepted and comforted in their home. Loan was in fact the youngest daughter of the remarkable Maï. Yet, Anh restricted familial treatment toward her friend's daughter because Loan was there in servitude. Being of different blood meant Loan was not of their family. Anh denied Loan a broader range of emotional acceptance she provided her own children.

Anh, like many traditional Asian mothers of Chinese culture disciplined their children to suppress unwanted display of emotions. Chinese mothers, as an extension of the male-dominated family, disallowed whining and minimally tolerated crying. The frequent reminder was a stinging slap of a hardwood stick on soft young palms to remind young Asians: maintain composure. Punishment that elicited crying drew additional punishment. More crying drew more punishment and so on. Asian children quickly learned to suppress emotional display by the age of four. They became substantially in control of their public selves by the age of seven.

Every child in the household learned to restrain emotional displays early in life. Frivolous emotional outbursts were intolerable. Two to six (or more) families spanning three to four generations often lived under the same roof throughout Asia. Crowded living conditions required personal discipline. It was necessary to preserve sanity.

Loan accepted the discipline. It was no different from life at home. Loan honored her mother and her difficult father by directing proper attention and action toward and in behalf of her elders.

As panic took over the passengers, Loan could only watch her mistress without expression, publicly emotionless, waiting for direction. Inside, Loan's sense of panic made her want to scream. She wanted to reject the situation but to what end as the boat fell into trouble?

Chaos descended upon this boat and dutiful Loan stood by for the next instruction. She froze in fear as she attempted to remain responsive to her surrogate mother.

Anh was effectively Loan's mother in this circumstance. Without Anh, Loan was isolated and stranded in a horrific moment. Anh was Loan's only link back to Sai Gon and Nguyên Maï.

Unfortunately, Anh became totally preoccupied and unavailable to comfort Loan. The eight-year-old girl understood her need was secondary to the moment. As a singular human being in a disaster, she struggled between obligation and survival. Without instruction, she could only stand there and choke back fear and panic.

Loan stood by attentive to next instruction if only to keep her mind off horrific reality of the moment. Seawater squirted up through the deck planking in miniature geysers and waves broke over the prow. Everyone and everything seemed to go into motion. Nothing was still. She was soaking wet from the warm sea yet she shivered.

The boat and its passengers were becoming one with the sea.

If only she had something to do as the passengers on the deck turned to riot. The ad hoc crew had lost control as everyone fought to escape destruction.

When the instruction came, Loan prepared to carry it out to the best of her ability. The girl had become adept at avoiding the sting of that damn hard stick on her palms. She knew Anh carried it with her. She obeyed. As the passengers descended into panic and the boat disintegrated, Loan delayed sorting her alternatives which were two, (1) assist Anh or (2) do nothing but wait for instruction.

The horror unfolding before her gripped her in full panic. She knew little else to do but wait for instruction. She waited for advice.

Monday, Two Days Earlier

Two days before, Anh and her husband, Lam, weighed the risk of storms on the open sea versus remaining in Viet Nam. A month before the summer monsoon season arrived, the weather could turn deadly out on The South China Sea in a matter of hours. It was impossible to know the weather more than a few hours in advance.

Viet Nam's new regime was in disarray focused on subduing a hostile population. Propaganda replaced news and weather forecasts on state-owned radio and television stations. Independent information from Thailand AM stations focused on the travel conditions in Cambodia and Laos for future refugees from Viet Nam.

AM transmission depended on bouncing the signal off the upper atmosphere and concealing antennas from discovery. Combined with intermittent electric power, reliable outside news was thin when available.

Long-wave radio stations in the Philippines provided similar information to Vietnamese who possessed forbidden HAM radio equipment. American radio out of Subic Bay provided the best information for those who understood English. Most Vietnamese refugees knew Hmong, Cantonese and Vietnamese.

In actuality, Viet Nam's ability to provide useful weather information ended with the fall of Sai Gon two years before. Viet Nam's technical infrastructure such as weather forecasting went full medieval. Sparse weather stations installed by South Viet Nam and the Americans ceased operating through equipment failure and shortage of technical personnel. Most weather analysis and prediction during the Viet Nam War and up until 1975 depended on American satellite imagery and aircraft.

Weather monitoring equipment left behind by Americans around air-traffic sites fell into disrepair. Power interruptions disrupted weather readings and radar, when it was working, reached out less than a hundred miles off Viet Nam's eastern coastline.

Someone had to assimilate radar telemetry and atmospheric measurements in order to report weather conditions and forecasts. This was essential due to the erratic nature of the monsoons.

The revolutionary government gutted previous South Vietnamese leadership and technical capability. Those who had not been executed or imprisoned disappeared. Hanoi promoted NVA cadre to repopulate civil functions regardless of education, experience, temperament and accountability.

Vietnamese weather forecasts, such as they were in the 1970s, became guesswork reinforced by superstition. Assumptions of weather on the west side of The South China Sea were meaningless near the Philippines.

The United States operated out of Subic Bay and Clark Air Force base. Unfortunately, the weather-related information was isolated to military interests and not shared with civilian Viet Nam after April 30, 1975.

Viet Nam's revolutionary government severed diplomatic ties with western interests. The Philippines cooperated with the United

States and other western countries in facilitating refugees to safety but much of that would not be in place until 1980. Viet Nam similarly cut ties to the Philippines.

The refugee program "Frequent Wind" depended in part on Philippines assistance to Vietnamese refugees. Viet Nam conducted minimal communication such that vital maritime information on weather conditions ceased to exist on the eastern side of the South China Sea.

Hazards Grow for Anh and Lam

The chance of discovery of Anh and Lam's escape plans changed for the worse. Key people who knew anything significant about Lam's clandestine activities during the war recently went missing. After the fall of Sai Gon on April 30, 1975, disappearances often meant the revolutionary government had arrested someone. Officials usually moved "detainees" into "re-education" camps. If worse, missing citizens sat in a prison facing interrogation if not summary execution.

The new regime worked lists of enemies of the state. Many of the names on the list came from records the American CIA failed to destroy in the spring of 1975. The list included loyalists of South Viet Nam or served the Americans.

Those who could went into hiding, changed identities, and made up fictitious histories. Lam had worked up the ranks of the North Vietnamese Army in the final days of South Viet Nam. Loyal cadres received positions of authority as reward for service. NVA leadership appointed Lam as an administrator near Rac Ghia on the southern tip of Viet Nam.

Lam's wife, Anh, was a native of the Cholon in Sai Gon who had re-invented her birthplace to Tay Ninh. They insulated themselves from the chaos of Viet Nam in their new identities. Unfortunately, Lam's old name and career was on one of those lists the CIA failed to destroy. Worse, color Polaroid photographs of Lam in 1968 remained clear enough if someone in Hanoi connected the faded image nine years later.

Truth became toxic in Viet Nam. Lam worked as an agent within and against the Viet Cong. Lam's work for the Americans created a dangerous legacy after April 30, 1975. He had worked for the CIA in the Phoenix program that recruited Vietnamese in the American-managed counter-insurgency program.

The counter-insurgency program had varying degrees of success. In the process between 1966 and 1972, it produced mountains of documents on operations and Vietnamese personnel it employed. After the program was turned over to South Viet Nam, the CIA continued to monitor the program without direct involvement of American advisors. The legacy of the program: Phoenix operatives were at risk after Hanoi consolidated the country. Those that didn't commit suicide went into hiding or escaped Viet Nam.

Up until Lam learned that the Viet Cong seized others that knew his variable loyalties, he believed there was more time to plan and provide for his family's escape from Viet Nam. Unfortunately, details of his disloyalty resided in the heads of prisoners of the regime.

In addition, their escape plans remained a secret for only so long. Certain preparations such as selling off possessions or property in exchange for gold were impossible to conceal over time. People the world over like to gossip. Vietnamese were no exception.

Real and artificial starvation stressed entire communities throughout South Viet Nam. Consequently, secrets traded readily for a few kilos of rice. It became increasingly difficult to trust anyone.

If they hesitated for even a few days, Lam believed events became bad. The chaos that had ravaged South Viet Nam's loyalists (anti-communist) population for two years closed in on them.

Lam had prepared well for the possibility of discovery. Sudden interest in gold in the village drew unwanted attention. He had steadily accumulated over 200 ounces of gold in Sai Gon. It was more than enough for passage for each of his family of six and ease of transition in another country.

Lam could only buy his freedom with gold. Smugglers refused to trade in Vietnamese đồng. American dollars were contraband.

Payments in advance were forfeit if a passenger canceled. It was a difficult thing fleeing a country and older Vietnamese at the last minute returned to the hell that was Viet Nam leaving behind life savings and any hope of a reasonable existence.

It took years to amass that much gold for another escape attempt assuming he was alive and free. If he remained in Viet Nam, he believed Hanoi will imprison him in days and kill him within a week. The amount of time he had left depended on which of the damnable CIA documents ended up in the hands of Hanoi in May 1975.

CIA

America's CIA failed to destroy files containing the names of their Vietnamese agents fighting as counter-insurgents. These agents were essentially spies and mercenaries neutralizing Viet Cong assets and personnel. The United States developed the program to reverse the increase in Viet Cong activities throughout South Viet Nam.

North Viet Nam recognized early that direct military action with South Viet Nam and the American forces could be costly in the extreme. The Viet Cong insurgency worked the fringes of South Viet Nam's cities and communities. They hid by day and fought at night, preferring hit-and-run and ambush to open confrontation.

The Viet Cong literally worked underground and out-of-sight. Approximately after 1965, North Viet Nam avoided head-to-head battles with South Viet Nam and American forces and resorted to guerillas warfare. Wisely, North Vietnamese only fought from positions of ambush. It was effective as the Americans favored open confrontation to exploit their technological advantage.

The only efficient counter measure for South Viet Nam and its allies, the United States, Britain, Australia and South Korea: fight them with individuals and small numbers of highly-trained fighting forces. The individuals varied from spies recruited or planted among Viet Cong cadre to soliciting the intelligence of villages, hamlets, and citizens who traded goods and services with VC.

At the height of the program, there were over twenty thousand Phoenix agents throughout South Viet Nam. As the war enlarged in the mid-1960s, the CIA operated throughout Viet Nam, recruiting Vietnamese to unravel and neutralize the tactics of the Viet Cong.

A particular challenge was sorting among Vietnamese to find dedicated and trustworthy combatants and spies. One arena was Special Forces work where they paired Vietnamese with American military. The CIA depended on reports of capable South Vietnamese soldiers. Ambitious soldiers went on a list of reliable candidates for inclusion in the Phoenix program.

They recruited Lam from an American small navy boat with a crew of three Americans and three Vietnamese. The boat was a Navy LCM-6 or "Mike Boat."

The navy converted the boat, known as a mini-battleship to serve US Navy SEALs for direct combat capability. They deployed the shallow-draft boat to support attacks on Viet Cong from the rivers, performing "snatch and grab" missions. It worked well as a platform for insertion of Special Forces teams into an area and retrieving them after the mission.

Lam had volunteered for the duty after his father died in Viet Cong action against an inland village near the coastal city of Kien Giang. Americans noted he was particularly bold in various operations in the Mekong Delta. After a few months, Americans spoke to him about a different means of warfare where he could be more effective. For Lam, the job had another appeal. It paid better.

The Americans paid better than the South Vietnamese Navy. It also enabled him to engage the Viet Cong on a new level of "payback."

The Americans and ARVN "repackaged" his identity to confuse if not erase his military record and provide him with credentials to work as a "policeman" for a village chieftain. He moved into a rural community where he could be drafted into the Viet Cong. It took three weeks before he was tested and drafted into a VC cell south of Sai Gon.

From there, he passed on what he knew to a chain of contacts. Those contacts fed the information to South Vietnamese and American "handlers" assigned to gather information.

One of Lam's contacts was an ethnic-Chinese Vietnamese woman who sold recycled medical supplies among her numerous enterprises. Reluctantly, she sold her supplies to the Viet Cong who otherwise would confiscate her supplies if she didn't barter with them.

The Chinese-Vietnamese woman nursed a virulent hatred of communism. She dealt with the VC only as commerce as she otherwise killed all that she knew. She fled its appalling cruelty from Southern China two decades before. Her name was Nguyën Mai.

The counter-insurgency program was large and directly supported by the CIA. It coordinated the intelligence gathering and "search-and-destroy" planning that the South Vietnamese and American forces utilized to attack the Viet Cong. It had varying success relying on small numbers of agents operating independently throughout South Viet Nam.

The program achieved a significant level of success by frustrating the Viet Cong's ability to operate in theater. Secret cells of VC disappeared without a trace. VC weapons, bunkers and stores of food ended up on the black market or in the hands of enemy military.

Following the principals of war first penned by Sun Tzu, a famous Chinese general who wrote "The Art of War" around 500 B.C., the Viet Cong were effective. Success changed when they were challenged on their own level of warfare. The counter-insurgency program prevented the VC and NVA from realizing larger goals throughout South Viet Nam up to 1972.

Phoenix

The Americans called the counter-insurgency program "Phoenix." Vietnamese knew it as Chiến dịch Phụng Hoàng, which translated to feng huang, the Chinese name for phoenix. Phoenix employed tens of thousands of Vietnamese to track and neutralize the Viet Cong and NVA. Information fed in from the network of South Viet Nam's counter-insurgency forces (spies and assassins) led to the intelligence that NVA and Viet Cong were building up within and around Sai Gon for what appeared to be a broad offensive.

Phoenix produced captured documents that spelled out the time and locations the offensive began. The Americans and South Vietnamese believed the intelligence and repositioned forces. Yet, they did not figure the offensive to be so large.

Despite underestimation of the scale of the offensive, South Vietnamese and American forces exploited the information to reposition forces around Sai Gon in late 1967 and early 1968. The new positions proved provident. South Viet Nam massed its resources well for the surprise attack that was no longer a surprise.

Just as the information acquired by Phoenix declared, Hanoi's Viet Cong struck on the eve of TET betrayed a mutually acknowledged cease-fire. They launched hundreds of attacks on January 30, 1968. VC attacked everything from local neighborhoods and the US Embassy in Sai Gon to military bases south of the De-Militarized Zone (DMZ).

Viet Cong massacred an estimated 5,000 *(estimates range from 2,800 to 6,500)* civilians in the city of Hue and assassinated village chieftains throughout South Viet Nam. Despite the atrocities, redeployed ARVN and American units shredded NVA and Viet Cong in Sai Gon and a number of communities.

The TET Offensive was a tactical failure for North Viet Nam. ARVN and Americans rendered entire VC networks inoperative. Hanoi lost the moral high ground as it slaughtered innocent civilians by the thousands. South Vietnamese forces successfully anticipated the offensive well enough to avoid a military disaster thanks in large part to intelligence acquired by the Phoenix operations.

The Americans kept detailed records on their Phoenix agents. Operations were numerous and sometimes large achieving high numbers of VC casualties. They captured "charlie" when they could in deeper "snatch-and-grab" operations. In many cases, they killed 100% of Viet Cong cells and destroyed caches of weapons and supplies.

Most captures and interrogation led to nothing as most VC cells were ignorant by design. Prisoners of war had little value and when turned over to the South Vietnamese and South Korean forces never returned to North Viet Nam.

In turn, the Viet Cong killed anyone who was working for the Americans. From 1966 and in each year, isolated Viet Cong death squads operated primarily in Sai Gon and a few of the larger cities in the north. They killed anyone who worked with the Americans. The hit was not limited to the agent. They wiped out entire families connected to the operative.

Phoenix became increasingly effective. It was precisely the strategy in war to neutralize insurgents. It worked. But it was politically repulsive to Americans growing weary of the war.

Regardless, Viet Cong were desperate to prevent anyone from working with the Americans. The terror program of the NVA enlarged.

Phoenix was well organized. In the process of its evolution, the CIA generated mountains of documents that tracked its agents and their operations. It created warehouses full of damning evidence in Sai Gon and CIA field offices.

CIA documents presented a large "hit list" for the Viet Cong should those files fall into enemy hands. American CIA staff knew the threat any of their agent information posed to Vietnamese. Many operatives literally staked their lives on a sustainable and independent Viet Nam south of the 17th parallel.

Unfortunately, key wilderness positions well north of Sai Gon became South Viet Nam's thin front line when Hanoi began its push south in 1975. Inconsistent channels of authority further compromised South Viet Nam's defensive assets. Similar to the political escalation of America's involvement in Viet Nam, Sai Gon politicians comingled their personal ambition with management of the military. It was recipe for chaos.

The CIA maintained Phoenix documents in field offices in Da Nang and in smaller operational offices. Not to worry, the CIA had projected a collapse of South Viet Nam perhaps eighteen months out from estimates made in the fall of 1974. There was time enough to destroy the records should the time come. So they thought.

Fall 1974

The CIA's initial estimate: South Viet Nam could hold out for a year, maybe two operating alone. Sai Gon fell in less than six months.

Starting with the quick losses of armies and cities to the north, The CIA left behind vital information that threatened the lives of tens of thousands of Vietnamese. The agency destroyed some of the documents but not enough. By May 1975, Hanoi possessed a sizeable detailed record of their worst enemy, the counter insurgents of Phoenix.

Sunday, 1977

Word in Sai Gon was that Hanoi had tentatively connected someone similar to Lam's description as an infiltrator of the Viet Cong cadre and rose in the ranks of the NVA. They searched for someone described in the infamous "Phoenix files" seized in the spring of 1975.

Many families had members on both sides of Viet Nam's "revolutionary" war as Hanoi called it. In Asia, family issues dominated priorities more than political or state agendas. Significant intelligence often passed between North Viet Nam and South Viet Nam through familial connections. Sisters informed brothers and cousins traded intelligence if not by phone by bicycle and motorcycle messaging. Sons told fathers who passed information to uncles and aunts.

This was true for Lam and Anh as well. After Hanoi consolidated the country under one flag, the victors switched to wholesale effort to suppress the counter-revolutionary undercurrents.

The appalling death toll from suicides, extra-judicial executions, and imprisonment raised the stakes among families formerly split along political lines. State information became one of the remedies that led to horrendous suppression policies that fragmented if not destroyed families.

New state curiosity about a particular family member in Hanoi or Sai Gon ignited a network of family communication. After April 1975 and among family members on opposite sides of the conflict, a family member at risk dissolved many former political hostilities. They snitched among themselves to save family members.

Family notified family about sudden government interest in one or more of their kin. Questions in Sai Gon became notice that mechanically notified the farthest village or hamlet where family resided. Rac Ghia was a day's travel from Sai Gon by motorcycle or three days by train and bus. Fuel was rationed to the point that car travel had to be authorized. Black market fuel stolen from government depots was the only means of making unauthorized travel.

No one trusted the erratic telephone system when it worked. Everyone believed the state routinely read the mail.

A young cousin from the Sai Gon area showed up unannounced to see Lam a week before. She traveled on a motor scooter to stretch her ration of gasoline. While she greeted the children, she was all business talking to Lam and Anh in whispers. It seemed odd to Loan but she thought little of the behavior at the time. Her world had been erratic since she was born.

Lam's cousin stayed with them for the evening and returned to Sai Gon early the next morning. She was been exhausted by such a short stay, yet she left in a hurry to return to Sai Gon lest her absence be noticed. Even by Loan's measure, Lam's cousin made a very odd visit.

Mood Change

Loan noticed a significant change in Lam and Anh's mood the day his cousin returned to Sai Gon. Anh's demeanor with her and the children became harsh. Her warm sense of humor disappeared.

Lam left the house early and returned late for the next few days. The parents left Loan to manage the children seldom interacting with her for the next week other than to instruct her with new tasks such as preparing food wrapped bundled in banana leaves or collecting the children's clothes into rice sacks as if planning to travel.

The family routine had changed. Years later when Loan reflected on the mood change, she realized the family was preparing to flee.

As in any conflict, spies and double agents operated during the war. Sai Gon was rife with spies. NVA and Viet Cong infiltrated The South Vietnamese Army and government. In turn, South Viet Nam and Phoenix infiltrated the Viet Cong and NVA. Although the war ended in name on April 30, 1975, the combatants continued to spy on each other.

Lam was uncertain of what Hanoi exactly knew about him but as occurred so often in Viet Nam, he had blood relatives in high places. Distant family advised him of increasing scrutiny.

Hanoi curiosity seldom meant anything good. Lam often considered rumors of interest as a deliberate leak to flush fugitives out into the open. It was easier to learn about a person's attitude by forcing them to deny something. Hanoi suspected everyone of deception.

Lam knew this: Hanoi had become smart about Vietnamese agents of America's CIA. Recently, they began interrogating people about Lam's history and activities during the war. Some of Lam's cadre formerly on CIA payroll had "disappeared."

The Viet Cong cum civil administrators were following up on some Vietnamese "civilians" Lam knew had changed their identities. Two of them became rice farmers and relocated to a hamlet east of Sai Gon. Out of necessity, former combatants broke off contact with friends and family to protect all sides of the relationship.

One of them had drafted Lam into Phoenix. The broader documents captured from a CIA field office described someone fitting a description of a resident from Sai Gon similar to Lam. If they had a photograph, it was at least ten years old. One problem among Asians is that they aged well and appeared the same for decades. Poor as it was, Lam grew out his facial hair. He made a miserable image of a young Ho Chi Minh. Anh laughed at his image often. It was a poor disguise.

During the war, Lam fed useless information to Hanoi and vital information to Phoenix liaisons between 1967 and 1972. Much of his concern lay in what the CIA recorded about him.

If the worst were so, Lam's duplicitous activities were in writing. At minimum, his misdeeds imprisoned his wife. They expected their children to be orphaned. Lam would die.

As a ranking police captain in a fishing village south of the western coastal city of Rac Ghia, Viet Nam, Lam made his share of enemies. Position provided larger rations of rice and gasoline. His had an envious position many sought.

Lam wrangled position on the merits of a ghostly resume. Based on the war-time merit system, Lam shoved aside politically worthier men immediately after Sai Gon fell.

Some of those nursing resentment from two years before rose to high position within the regime. They looked forward to returning the favor to Lam.

Lam rose above them by exploiting his "war record" as it were. He kept his history vague, legitimized by assuming the accomplishments of VC cadre killed during the war. Lam took credit for actions of a wiped-out Viet Cong component. Lam insinuated his role in the event. There was no other soldier left alive in the VC unit to contradict his story.

American combatants wore "dog-tags" to identify their remains after a battle. This included their blood-type, race and in some cases, their religion. This was not so for North Vietnamese soldiers.

Hundreds of thousands of Vietnamese were interred without identity. Vietnamese combatants often beheaded fallen enemy during the war and left the bodies to rot in the jungle. Thousands of nameless and headless dead littered South Viet Nam during the war.

Lam feigned false modesty. It was more real than false. He did not kill anyone on either side. In truth, he seldom fired a weapon for the remainder of the war, let alone act as a real combatant.

Lam was a total fake. *(Author's Note: To this day, I have not learned of his real name even though his mother was still living in Sai Gon in my last trip there in 2012. It is hazardous to ask too much about such things in Sai Gon to this day.)*

Lam exploited Hanoi's blind spots. Being a reasonably good liar, he utilized names and associations blending in the details of his "war record." North Viet Nam's losses between 1962 and 1975 were estimated at nearly two million casualties. By design, VC and NVA isolated one cell from another to reduce intelligence gathering by South Viet Nam's intelligence units. In the event of capture and interrogation, one soldier knew little of other forces in the field.

In the carnage of the Tet Offensive of 1968, the Viet Cong was effectively crushed as a fighting force. VC platoons perished to a man and left gaps in the network of isolated cells. Lam patched up the missing history with a few fictions stitched together by his acquired deeds. Dead cadre could not argue otherwise.

Lam exploited the revolutionary government's tendency to promote first among party revolutionaries and soldiers based on participation in the war. He demonstrated legitimate management capabilities.

He only had to wait out Hanoi's experiments in civil management for the next opportunity. He moved up the ranks as incapable men fell off the "communist corporate ladder."

Government incompetence enabled him to worm his way into a higher local position with fabricated stories of valor during the war. It was his word against voices of the dead.

For a time, Lam's deceptions worked. He was good at being a total fake.

Former NVA cadre dedicated themselves to reigning in a hostile population. Hanoi color-coded maps of every home and business in the cities and villages based on who was pro-Hanoi or pro-Sai Gon at the war's end. Between forced and voluntary relocations and unknown numbers of people hiding or living under a new identity, sorting the population loyalties constantly tasked the regime. Viet Nam's society went feral and the economy went feudal for decades.

In the chaos of the first few years, Lam's fictitious war record stood unchallenged. Regardless, Hanoi sorted among CIA records and interrogations of Vietnamese interred in the re-education camps.

Hanoi established the re-education camps at first telling civilians the internment might last a few weeks. As the population proved resentful and intractable, the internment stretched to months and years. The regime held many in order to glean information on fugitives in hiding.

Many that didn't die of starvation or forced labor languished in the camps for years. For the price of an extra ration of rice or lighter work load, individuals gave up sensitive information about one person or another. The government relentlessly wove together a complex picture of who was still at large.

Through a process of elimination in the fullest use of that term, the regime turned its gaze on "revolutionary loyalists" for hidden fugitives. Everyone was suspect including the administrators of the new regime.

Identity change and lying became essential to survival after April 1975. Former city bureaucrats always drove a taxi or washed toilets. Former Sai Gon policemen "managed" water buffalo or worked in the rice paddies all their life. A few served in the NVA in an obscure series of campaigns. Any anonymous job became desirable.

South Vietnamese destroyed photographs, letters, diplomas, war medals and any other incriminating identification. Loan's family destroyed letters of authorization from the United States along with every photograph of family preceding 1975. They changed names on titles to property as necessary using a cousin to hold the property.

Eventually, the regime examined people with "difficult-to-confirm" histories. War wounds elicited questions on where and how the injury occurred. Claims of heroic war records backfired when the government sought detail. Many veterans practiced stories of a different life. Amnesia became pandemic.

Hanoi compiled lists of people such as Lam where all supporting witnesses died in the war. It took time but time was Hanoi's asset, they had little else but time to prosecute the guilty.

Without an agency of relief, extra-judicial imprisonment and executions dominated life in the first years of the new Viet Nam. Bribes paid in ounces of gold provided the only remedy. Bribes only worked with persons of lesser interest in payback for the war. Bribes to stay out of the re-education camps had consequences decades later preventing would-be-immigrants from leaving the country. That condition persists to this day.

Hanoi paid attention to complaints from pro-revolutionary citizens. On suspicion alone, the regime removed civilians from circulation and "stored" them for later interrogation.

A disgruntled neighbor's complaint to authorities could solicit Hanoi's attention. Lam's fictitious claims might fail intense scrutiny. Without rules of evidence, Lam's enemies could own him. He only had to slip a little to slit a lot.

Lam used family connections and guile to gain a position as chief of police. What passed for local civil authority was little more than officials for sale at a price. The appointment assured larger rations of rice, an income, and other benefits including a better house for family.

Communist authority added income and privilege. Police corruption was expected. A few ounces of gold redirected Lam's attention away from a misdeed. Yet, there were limits to bribes if the resentment fueled suspicion.

Lam lied, bluffed, and paid his way to the best position he could hope to have after the fall of Sai Gon. The rice allotment was good as gold. He and Anh traded authority and rice for things the erratic currency could not buy.

In the new Viet Nam, a ranking police officer made a decent career among former NVA and Viet Cong soldiers. It paid well enough and required little work in a culture that habitually labors fourteen hours a day seven days a week. Thanks to the regime, the police barely kept the peace.

Wealthier citizens purchased civil authority. Politicians sold police position to the highest bidder. One citizen could put another in jail by paying the police to do so. The second citizen stayed out of jail by paying more than the first. That practice continues to this day.

The new regime extorted neighborhoods and entire communities throughout Viet Nam for protection by the police. Payment assured less trouble from, well, the police. In addition, solely the Viet Cong and NVA cadre populated the police. It was the spoils of war.

Lam offended more than a few veterans suspicious of his claims. Lam's deeds were unproven but peppered with enough detail to keep his detractors from proving otherwise.

Former-military believed they deserved the position and benefits. The benefits inflated envy and resentment. Any small event could upset Lam into trouble with Hanoi.

Lam and Anh acquired a better home with galvanized corrugated roof, wood walls, erratic electricity, and running water. The father of the family that owned this house had prospered through dealings with the Americans. The regime confiscated the property and interred the father in one of the re-education camps. His family fled into the wilderness. No one knew if the man was still alive.

VC confiscated the house and the distributed the man's holdings to Lam including two 1972-vintage Honda motorcycles. Lam and

Anh received an allotment of rice. Reliable access to rice was a as a significant bonus as Viet Nam's economy disintegrated after 1975.

The Vietnamese đồng lost most of its value in a series of devaluations. Gold and food became the unofficial coin of real commerce. The new wealth enabled Anh to seek domestic help such as hiring a young girl from a friend's family in Sai Gon to tend to their four small children. She paid Nguyên Maï for a year's service of her youngest daughter in 200 kilos *(440 pounds)* of rice.

Lam held high office, a fine home, food and the ability to afford domestic help. In South Viet Nam post-fall of Sai Gon 1975, Lam and Anh had won the equivalent of the lottery. Unfortunately, it was a fragile accomplishment in a country that had been in some form of warfare for decades.

Resentment and suspicion threatened Lam and his family. His enemies saw to that.

Two hundred kilos of rice that brought the girl from Sai Gon to help Anh enlightened wagging tongues. Rhac Ghia by the creaky rail system, Sai Gon was a three-day journey. Neighbors took notice of the luxury of domestic help sent from Sai Gon.

Viet Nam was destitute and hungry. Lam's fortune was fair game to former VC. Many waited for him to stumble. Lam's high position and his life verged on a cliff. And he ran out of time.

It was difficult to conceal aborted escape attempts. If they returned to the village, an empty house and sold-off luxuries provided condemning evidence to higher authorities.

In the meantime, Hanoi diligently prosecuted impostors. The government checked on everyone repeatedly to confirm they were who they were. They tallied prisoners, suicides and extra-judicial executions. Where did the rest of the guilty go?

Former NVA and Viet Cong examined Lam's background a bit deeper. Without a hint of disloyalty, they searched for more information on his background. They sorted Anh's history to see if it connected with any of the names within the CIA's Phoenix program. Every citizen was a suspect. No one was immune.

Existence in the re-education camps was marginally worse than the disintegrated quality of life for Vietnamese on the losing side. Those who escaped with the Americans as the United States withdrew its support of South Viet Nam dodged real calamity. Those left behind coped amid varieties of Hell.

South Vietnamese, particularly the hill and central people, Montagnard and Hmong along with the ethnic-Chinese were trapped in the unstitching civilian fabric of post-war Viet Nam. They bid their time and watched for an opportunity to escape.

When they openly worked against Hanoi including any North Vietnamese Army (NVA), the Viet Cong (VC) or the Peoples Army of North Viet Nam (PAVN), they were forced to hide. Hiding in another identity was difficult for Montagnard and to a lesser extent Hmong. Those two groups appeared different than Vietnamese and Sino-Vietnamese. The ethnic purges were appalling.

The balance of the population that blended in assumed a new identity, moved to another community or lived on the run. Lam and Anh hid in plain sight.

Loyalists that vocally objected to Hanoi had to run, go to the re-education camps or as often happened as Sai Gon fell on April 30, 1975, committed suicide. Community leaders from elected officials to village chieftains that weren't summarily executed saved the last bullet for themselves. Thousands of Vietnamese used over-dosed on medications and jumped off building tops and church steeples to avoid torture.

Hanoi's success surprised everyone on both sides. When Sai Gon and the South Vietnamese armies collapsed in the spring of 1975, the communist regime was unprepared to manage and assimilate a hostile population and the "rice bowl" of the country.

It took time for the bureaucratic machinery of Hanoi to secure its hold on an uncooperative southern population. The government also had to overcome some distinctions in Vietnamese spoken in the North and South.

Many assumed new identities as rice farmers and peddlers after the fall of Sai Gon in 1975. Gaps in civilian records and identities across Viet Nam in 1975 allowed many to reappear under new names and occupations. Couples faked divorces or assumed new names in marriage ceremonies that never occurred. Families moved from place to place shifting their names as needed and rotated brief stays with siblings and cousins.

The language differences, obfuscation and movement and shifting population confounded administrative capabilities of the new regime for a time. Unfortunately, America's CIA created the best records ever kept in Viet Nam. The detailed descriptions and photographs alone condemned many.

With the exception of the remnants of French colonials and the influx of Russians, Viet Nam's population remained entirely Asian. The population varied in blood, culture, and attitude as did any ethnic assembly.

Ethnic Chinese were culturally distinct from the mixtures of other people including the dominant native group, the Kinh (Viet) people to the blend of French and Asians that resulted from the French colonial days. Montagnard and Hmong populated middle Viet Nam who like the ethnic Chinese tended to resist socialist dogma and backed the politics that permitted them to hold on to the fruits of their considerable ambition and labor.

Naturally, they gravitated toward an open capitalistic society and toward the influences of the west, particularly the French, British, and the United States. The Montagnard *(thuong, Degar mountain)* people of mid-Viet Nam, backed South Viet Nam wholesale and were at risk of extermination by Hanoi. *(i.e. Đắk Sơn Massacre, c 1967 et al.)*

The regime assembled re-education camps to suppress uprising of the population rife with small arms and ammunition. "Re-education" was a thin euphemism for revenge and concentration. The camps interred anyone capable of fomenting resistance or revolt. Hanoi imprisoned South Vietnamese leadership *(Of those they didn't exterminate outright)* for years keeping them out of circulation.

The atheist state also persecuted Christian Vietnamese and in particular, Catholic Vietnamese discouraging faith in anything but the principals of the state. During state celebrations, officials told children to pray to "Uncle Ho" (Ho Chi Minh) in lieu of Jesus or God. April 30 became a state holiday in which candy is handed to children only when they expressed appreciations of Uncle Ho.

In the process of wearing down the citizens, they used the captive population of the camps to locate fugitives. The camps operated tortuous interrogation intent on breaking or converting anyone who worked against the Viet Cong and the PAVN forces during the war. Now and then, Hanoi worked out useful leads of someone. Missing sections of the Phoenix files filled in as the regime mapped out names, gossip and spurious accusations.

Finding a name for capture encountered a problem unique to Viet Nam. Many people have the same first and last names. Many don't have middle names.

The ancient feudal system of Viet Nam created entire communities that had adopted the same sir name as their King of the empire. Viet Cong had to sort out who exactly was the enemy of one to two among a crowd with the same full name. The common name Nguyên *(pronounced "when" or "win")* was pervasive There might be hundreds of people with the same full name beginning with the surname Nguyën. *(Author's Note: Over 33% of Viet Nam has the family name Nguyên. The "most common last name" in the Los Angeles phonebook is Nguyên, surpassing Smith.*

VC and PAVN heavily infiltrated all levels in South Viet Nam's government and military. During the 1960s, allied military complained that it was difficult to tell the difference between friend and foe. For the new regime, it was also difficult to distinguish minor threat from sworn enemy by names alone, especially among some of the communities.

Hanoi incarcerated South Vietnamese on vocal objection, lack of compliance, and complaints from egregious neighbors. The regime faced the main obstacle to rounding up people on Hanoi's villain's list … a population unwilling to become informants.

The ethnic Chinese were especially adept at denial and obfuscation. They spoke Cantonese as well as Vietnamese feigning language barriers. Family chose last names as well as first names for children. Some of Loan's brothers had different last names even though they were all of the same blood.

Securing national consolidation took time and coercion. Regardless, Hanoi systematically narrowed down who should be "re-educated" varying tactics between "carrots and sticks." Over time, they resorted to more stick than carrot. Regardless, this gave time to many prospective victims to hide or prepare to flee.

Hundreds of thousands of North Vietnamese died as they fought to unify the country under one rule. They in turn killed and maimed hundreds of thousands of South Vietnamese civilians who simply wanted to be left alone. The characteristics of independence and self-reliance were in conflict with the expectations of totalitarian hard-liners in Hanoi. North Viet Nam persecuted people that demonstrated any resistance. The most salient of these groups were the Montagnard, Hmong and the ethnic-Chinese *(Sino-Vietnamese)*. They made up a significant percentage of refugees in the following decade.

Finding and punishing Hanoi's enemies became a grinding relentless process. Western organizations petitioned Viet Nam to end the witch hunt. As a result, Viet Nam cut ties with western economies eliminating significant communication and commerce. In the absence of expanding productive industries, the Viet Cong needed something to do.

Communist Viet Nam's Bounty

Hanoi was victorious. By reasoning, that righteous victory funded future needs. North Viet Nam won. South Viet Nam lost. More important: America lost.

The new Viet Nam, the ideal communist model of a self-sustaining, self-reliant economy, could restore and improve itself without doing anything special to curry outside assistance.

As a consequence of Viet Nam's self-reliance, no one did anything special. All powerful consolidated Viet Nam fell to pieces.

Hanoi boasted they had beaten the wealthiest and the most powerful country in the world. In fact, they had beaten the southern half of what was formerly their own country. They beat the southern half running up unnecessary civilian death toll before April 30, 1975.

There was no military reason to kill the civilians as they did in the final months before and the years after. South Vietnamese wanted to be left alone to seek their own destiny apart from parasitic socialism known as communism. South Viet Nam avoided prosecuting a war with strategies that united the north under an open democracy.

South Viet Nam and the United States refrained from prosecuting the war north of the 17th parallel with large troop assaults. It relied on air strikes on strategic sites around Hanoi and mining harbors to reduce flow of arms from Russia. The porous western borders along Laos and Cambodia known as "The Fence" enabled a portion of the Ho Chi Minh trail to operate with impunity for most of the war.

By fighting a limited war as a holding action against North Viet Nam, South Viet Nam assured inevitable failure. When in a war, one side has to convince the other to fight no more. South Viet Nam never made the case by itself. It never carried the war to Hanoi. *(Author's Note: Hanoi's urban population was never directly bombed despite Hanoi's war propaganda and the declarations of Jane Fonda.)*

America, for many reasons already covered in numerous studies, documents and books, abandoned Viet Nam. Many Americans believed America should have stayed out of Viet Nam in the first place. Unfortunately, once there, America postponed and exacerbated what may have been inevitable, the fall of a freedom-seeking people to a brutal regime. The totalitarian communist state had designs on suppressing irrepressible under-currents of capitalism and self-reliance. It was an ideological battle ground during the Cold War.

South Viet Nam attracted industrious people in the region. It has been and continues to be a non-static economy in a non-stagnant population in a non-isolated region. Hanoi eventually had to rethink its plan to exploit an errant population centered in Sai Gon.

Gold and cash dominate Asian economies. The golden rule they know is the one most non-capitalists deny: The one with the gold *(and the ambition, and the will and the cash)* writes the rules.

Conquerors may come and go. Cash makes kings in Asia.

Communism fully subsidized by China and Russia sustained North Viet Nam in its conquest of South Viet Nam. By itself, Hanoi could achieve nothing without subsidy from the communist bloc. As it is, it remains mostly an ideal in South Viet Nam.

Once South Viet Nam tasted the economic engine of North America, an addiction to a way of life took hold. Capitalism remained in South Viet Nam in a muted state after April 30, 1975. It took hold of South Viet Nam in the decades to come barely hidden under a communist veneer.

Ho Chi Minh City rose out of the chaos in name only. It remains Sai Gon to most everyone. Commerce took over two decades to restore. In the meantime, South Viet Nam struggled through virtual and actual hell as Hanoi mangled what it didn't understand: South Viet Nam.

As it was, North Viet Nam lacked abilities to manage the entire country. They refuted ties to the rest of the world believing they became a powerful self-sustaining communist state.

Ideals alone cannot clothe, shelter, and feed the people. Viet Nam went bankrupt in the first year and fully destitute in three. The currency became one of the most devalued monies in the world. With the collapse of the Zimbabwe currency, Vietnamese currency is now the most devalued world-wide. At times, it has relied on the influx of expatriate contributions to family remaining in Viet Nam.

North Viet Nam socialized the economy relocating urban populations and killing off dissidents by the tens of thousands. With many international ties severed for decades, Hanoi remained largely immune to criticism.

Citizens fended for themselves. Some had to fend more than others. Hanoi persecuted the ethnic-Chinese in Sai Gon with a form of artificial starvation and material confiscation. Unable to purchase gasoline for vehicles and food for their families, many sought desperate remedy.

Many were unable to operate their businesses as before it at all. If and until the new government ceased harassing them, life in Sai Gon was hell. In the meantime, the new regime had time to locate, persecute, and punish their enemies. There was little else to do but chase down the former enemy, punish, convert, and/or kill them.

Once the new regime had rounded up the obvious suspects, they started on the next tier of candidates. They worked on the next and the next and Lam's identity eventually surfaced. His name was in one of those fourth or fifth waves of investigations. Depending on assessment (torture), Hanoi either re-educated or killed him. Lam would die in the "re-education" camps if he was even interred there. There are no public records of deaths in the "managed" re-educations camps.

The remnants of civilization slipped away. He and Anh had their family to consider. Being on a list of "possible" antagonists eventually reduced his access to food allotments. Lam's condition had few chances of improving, once the VC painted him with the color of disloyalty to Hanoi, life of any quality was over.

Abandoned Allies, Abandoned Friends

North Viet Nam became economically barren beginning with immense wartime losses during the 1968 Tet Offensive. The Viet Cong (VC) losses rendered their forces ineffectual and operated in name only. The North Vietnamese Army (NVA) absorbed its remaining cadre.

Modern-day Vietnamese lump references to the NVA and VC into one term, VC or Viet Cong. No one refers to the NVA as anything but VC. Americans referred to them as "Victor Charlie" in radio transmission parlance. It became shortened to "Charlie" which is now a term of reference in Viet Nam.

Even with the backing of Russia, the attrition of years of high losses of North Vietnamese personnel and resources rendered the war a stalemate. It might have resulted in a permanent North Viet Nam and South Viet Nam similar to Korea. To Vietnamese expatriates, they distinguish North Viet Nam and South Viet Nam as the Vietnamese language idioms also distinguish north and south.

US media contributed to the withering of public support in America. Nightly news reporter Walter Cronkite, in one ill-spoken televised report, unsettled the viewpoint of a besieged American president and mangled public perception. In his misguided ignorance of the circumstances of NVA and Viet Cong, Cronkite stated that the war in Viet Nam was unwinnable.

Cronkite volunteered an answer to an unspoken question: Which Viet Nam War was unwinnable? Was America in the war over independence of South Viet Nam from North Viet Nam? Or was America in the war for unification of Viet Nam under a democracy?

The Viet Nam War was many things. It was largely a socio-economic feud fueled by economic and class envy between North and South. It was also a four-decade long series of conflicts peppered with political and ethnic hatred that ranged from Southern China to most of Southeast Asia.

The perception that the war in Viet Nam was beyond winning enlarged despite the fact that North Viet Nam was on the verge of settling for a divided Viet Nam. Unclear objectives of the war bled Allied patience tiring of the mounting losses without a clear end in sight.

Few Americans including the politicians understood the complexities of Southeast Asia. Some version of the conflict was winnable to a stalemate, it just was not the one Americans understood they were supporting.

North Viet Nam exploited diplomacy to obtain cease-fires that permitted the NVA to recover, recruit, and rearm. Politicians and diplomats hampered US military conduct of the war with rules of engagement *(ROEs)* and restricted arenas of combat. Americans operated with guidelines that gave sanctuary to the NVA forces in Laos and Cambodia. *(Americans referred to actions west of Viet Nam as "across the fence" or similar terms.)*

American allies were less restricted. South Korean forces exacerbated the American politics by seldom giving quarter to surrendering NVA. A string of South Korean massacres of NVA topped by America's Mai Lai Massacre further changed American attitudes. Ignoring the Viet Cong massacre of civilians topped by an estimated 6,500 civilians slain in the City of Hue during the 1968 Tet Offensive, American support withered.

Hanoi outlasted American impatience. It was South Viet Nam and America's fight to lose and they lost it by choice.

The United States chose to give up the fight for South Viet Nam just when North Viet Nam teetered on collapse. Additional pressure could have forced Hanoi to sue for resolution. The only question after a time was whether North Viet Nam was capable of honoring an agreement for longer than the time to reposition their forces for the next violation.

The United States inarguably had the strength to conclude that war. Unfortunately, it lacked the resolve. It gave up on a war and an ally that had nearly achieved "permanent" independence south of the 17th parallel. Subsequently, the disorderly manner of America's exit from Viet Nam abandoned hundreds of thousands of allied Vietnamese that had risked their future with Sai Gon leadership.

The hammered leadership (and troops and munitions and monies) of the north took heart in the American withdrawal. By 1973, Hanoi rebuilt its forces and shocked the world in the speed of its success by April 30, 1975. Sai Gon fell quickly. Hundreds of thousands of vulnerable Vietnamese remained behind waiting to be evacuated by an impotent USA.

Millions more contended with a living hell that was South Viet Nam for two decades following 1975. The collapse of South Viet Nam changed the future for many thousands of Montagnard, Hmong, Kinh and ethnic-Chinese Vietnamese trapped on the wrong side of the war's conclusion.

The withdrawal of United States support by 1974 left an inadequate and compromised South Vietnamese government to hold the line. The un-desired loss of American support of South Viet Nam, the most economically powerful country in the world with the largest military capability in the world, devastated an entire region of Indochina including Laos and Cambodia.

The exit of American support stranded capable South Vietnamese military. The exit was further compromised by a conflicted government structure. South Viet Nam's corruptible government was heavily infiltrated with spies enabling Hanoi to know where to apply political pressure. By early 1975, South Viet Nam was ill-prepared to resist ruthless battalions of battle-hardened North Vietnamese and National Liberation Front *(Viet Cong such as they were)* forces.

The only restraint PAVN and VC showed was in suppressing fire on helicopters and fixed-wing aircraft shuttling Americans and Vietnamese out of the country in the final days. That restraint was strategic more than charitable in order to prevent the Americans from re-engaging U.S. military to protect their own countrymen.

This final American withdrawal occurred as South Vietnamese forces collapsed with surprising speed. This emboldened the coarser aspects of PAVN and VC forces figuring there was little consequence to their actions.

As a harbinger of brutality to come, NVA artillery shelled non-military areas of the city, particularly in the ethnic-Chinese neighborhoods in Sai Gon. Entire blocks of semi-urban neighborhoods were leveled, leaving an untold death-toll of non-combatants. This was similar to the death tolls of fleeing civilians as the NVA and Viet Cong began their march to the south and from the west. The rape of South Viet Nam only just began.

All this eventually resulted in setting the tone for life in South Viet Nam for loyalists and allies to the Americans. The conditions created the largest ad hoc seaborne exodus from a nation in the history of the world, an exodus that crossed a large sea, past many coastlines and through unfriendly countries, all populated with ruthless and inarguably evil people. While the extent of the exodus was unpredictable, American and other allied officials were well aware of the horrors that awaited Vietnamese stranded in Viet Nam.

American intelligence knew what the sloppy withdrawal had done to South Viet Nam. As the last helicopters headed out to sea, hundreds of politicians, intelligence agents and military knew the price stranded Vietnamese might pay.

The United States continued the program that enabled all of the Americans and some of the Vietnamese to escape by April 30, 1975. The United States, Canada, Australia, Great Britain, France and Israel assisted virtually any Vietnamese that made it out of the country to Thailand, Hong Kong, the Philippine Archipelago and the rest of Malaysia.

They only had to reach a location where they could receive aid and sanctuary. Reaching any location was easier said than done.

The US Operation: "Frequent Wind"

North Vietnamese retribution for failed escape attempts was deadly. In many instances, the new regime summarily killed entire families repatriated to Viet Nam. At minimum, the father or both parents went into re-education and the remainder of the family was re-located to rural "Northern Economic Zones" (NEZs) to rebuild agriculture to feed the nation.

The United States and other western countries extended the "Frequent Wind" program set up to evacuate South Vietnamese. The very act of aid exacerbated the treatment of Vietnamese caught in escape attempts.

Entire communities of refugees arrived in a number of countries including Thailand, Cambodia and islands throughout the Philippines and Malaysia. The United Nations proved competent in providing aid for the refugee camps and processed the political refugees to accommodating countries. Most went to the United States and Canada.

The refugee's challenge was getting out of the country safely. The nearest useful landfall was 600 miles to the east over tropical seas populated with natural and human hazards.

Viet Nam's new regime could barely stem the tide of humanity leaving its coastlines. Hanoi spent vital resources on retribution and repression of the population. It also engaged in conflicts with China and Cambodia further distracting civil re-construction. Once an overloaded boat of Vietnamese traveled beyond the generally regarded 12-mile boundary of Viet Nam's "waters," Hanoi lacked the resources to retrieve refugees.

The mounting death toll of its people in the South China Sea was fractionally reported. The remoteness of Southeast Asia and large expanse sea concealed a horrendous human tragedy. Thousands of Vietnamese, in their bid for freedom and a better life, died each month.

Starting in the spring of 1976, one year after the fall of Sai Gon, fishing villages along the western coast of the Philippine island-archipelago witnessed alarming numbers of bloated human remains washing ashore. There was little identification on the remains to reveal they were all Vietnamese. They were seeing only the bodies that came ashore along four hundred miles of the western Philippine coastline facing Viet Nam.

The dead washing ashore on the Philippine coastline represented a fraction of refugees consumed by the vast expanse of the South China Sea. Large numbers of fleeing Vietnamese perished out of sight of the rest of the world.

More Rocks, More Hard Places

Even if Lam and his family were able to slip back into their house and resume normal appearances, basic quality of life deteriorated. The country verged on famine. The quasi-capitalist economy of the south disappeared. Communist politics determined how foods were distributed.

This meant non-socialist entrepreneurial citizens of Viet Nam stood last in position for resource allotments. When there was any issue of who was deserving of a scarce food allotment, Hmong, Montagnard, and Sino-Vietnamese stood last in the receiving line.

In fact, they weren't in line to receive anything at all. Hmong, Montagnard, and Chinese ethnicity generally meant they were also likely backers of South Viet Nam and American forces during the war. This pushed them to the tail end of food allocation. If the food shortages continued to worsen, a dishonored Lam and his family could starve.

Lam and Anh faced confiscation of everything. Their above-average home with a galvanized-iron corrugated roof and wooden walls was sacrifice. Hanoi redistributed their possessions to deserving Viet Cong officers.

One or both of their precious Honda 250cc motorcycles would be "acquired," their belongings "re-assigned" as needed to satisfy state purposes. In short, Lam and Anh's quality of life was over.

There was no agency of relief. Viet Nam, circa 1977, had ended any pretense of legal due process. Without the help of the Americans or some other agency of relief, their life was forfeit.

It was also only a matter of time before Anh's role in support of the South Vietnamese and particularly the American forces might surface. Anh was one of Nguyên Maï's networks of informants for the CIA during the war. She knew the price that Maï had paid for helping the US forces neutralize Viet Cong cadre between 1966 and 1972.

Anh relied on the tightness of ethnic-Chinese culture to maintain her anonymity. Unfortunately, she knew, secrets traded well for food and leniency in the "re-education" camps. Information about her might earn an extra helping of rice and less time clearing land mines.

Landmine: Viet Cong Payback

One hour north of Sai Gon near the city of Tay Ninh, Nguyên Maï stood inside her thatch-covered house talking to her oldest daughter, May. The house occupied a six-hectare *(12 acres)* plot of jungle/farmland she owned. Several dozen farmers rented the remainder of similar plots of adjacent farms. They had moved to Tay Ninh from Cau Tre in 1973 and had stayed there longer than in any other location for the past nine years.

The Viet Cong had presumed Maï to be dead after they had ambushed her and husband Toan in Cau Tre in 1972. She reduced her exposure to risk moving generally every four to six months according to the hazard her counter-insurgency activity created for her family. She moved to another location based on feel of the situation and her effectiveness. Lingering in a community made little sense after she exhausted her base of contacts within a VC cell. She also thought it was better to relocate on a regular basis to reduce her identity. Hanoi knew that Vietnamese people like her were neutralizing VC cells throughout South Viet Nam.

Maï moved from Sai Gon to Kien Giang on the coast in 1966, leaving there in 1967 to settle in Phu Thu in 1968. She resettled in Phú Dinh where the VC ambushed Toan and her. Other operatives came in and helped her move to Xom Dat in 1970 and the Khu 2 in 1971. From there, she move to Cau Tre in 1972 and finally to Tay Ninh in 1973.

Maï planned to move back to Sai Gon in 1974 except for the fact that her husband had impregnated another woman during his many dalliances in Sai Gon on this or that excuse. His charm was his curse. For reasons inexplicable to western culture, Maï did little more than object to his behavior by dwelling elsewhere.

South Viet Nam's economy withered as America reduced personnel. Lam once again was unable to support his addiction to women and its predictable outcome. This was Lam's sixth bastard child. He could barely support himself. Once again he failed to support the impoverished girlfriend and her son.

Old-culture Asian marriages tolerated a wide range of a husband's extramarital activities. It was different for wives. Go figure the inexplicable Asian attitude that any blood was treated as full blood. Maï accepted the baby as child number sixteen wet nursing as she could.

Mai raised the boy as her own with no distinction between a child of her blood and a bastard child from her husband's wanderings. The child was half-blood to her children. Yet, another bastard child was more than enough. With her resources, she maintained all of her children under her care in Tay Ninh an hour northwest of Sai Gon. She left Toan to his own devices in Sai Gon. It was punishment enough. He barely maintained his own circumstances without infusion of Maï's money. Toan was her seventeenth child in a way, the worst of the lot.

As she drew the line on Toan's dalliances, she refused to move back to Sai Gon at the end of 1974. She wanted little to do with the whoring bastard even if that meant living at an inconvenient distance from other family. This kept Maï in one place until she figured out an alternative to returning Sai Gon. The pause violated one of her rules of survival as an operative for the CIA's Phoenix program. She stayed in one place near Tay Ninh for more than four months. In fact she resided there for more than a year.

Maï had considered her next options as the Americans made final preparations to turn South Viet Nam loose to manage its future. American contacts had paid her well. Unfortunately, the counter-insurgency program wound down and became front-managed by South Viet Nam.

The Americans were still in Viet Nam as observers of the end of South Viet Nam. It was January 23, 1975. The Paris Peace Accords had strangled American involvement to provide advice without material support. Advice is not instruction or command.

Maï's days of guiding US Navy SEALs in search-and-destroy missions ended in 1972. South Viet Nam's counter-insurgency became ineffective. VC cells under the guidance of the NVA thrived and expanded throughout South Viet Nam.

Corrupt and incompetent Sai Gon politicians over-managed the military command system. This devastated the capability of South Viet Nam to manage and defend against a concerted invasion by North Viet Nam. Hanoi pumped up by increasing Russian support and disregard for the restrictions of the peace accords moved troops and supplies with impunity along the western side of the Cambodian and Laotian borders.

Maï's network of Vietnamese connections working for the CIA passed information that South Viet Nam's military positions far to the north were functionally compromised. She was unable to verify this through Sai Gon's censored press.

America's CIA contacts were interested only in new information that affected their field offices. They shared minimal national information with their former Vietnamese agents. The peace accords hamstrung the support of the United States. Americans went silent leaving Maï isolated and afraid of the future.

She knew one thing well. Hanoi would violate the agreement as soon as their forces were in position to strike south. North Viet Nam had broken every agreement and promise to date. How can the Paris Peace Accords accomplish anything toward peace? It was a tragic joke on South Viet Nam.

Maï knew North Vietnamese forces were pushing through northern regions virtually unopposed in some areas and meeting disorganized South Vietnamese resistance in others. Formerly durable positions to the north were now porous and the eastern boundary collapsed. Without intervention by the Americans, Maï believed South Viet Nam was doomed.

Maï contemplated the need to spend her resources on another move of the family until the course of South Viet Nam improved. Their money dried up. Direct military support disappeared. It was obvious to her that the current leadership of America was abandoning South Viet Nam. The American men she had come to know and adore during the counter-insurgency would not have done that. Yet, she did not fully understand how American politics worked. She only knew that the favorable wind at her back, the American involvement, was gone.

Unused military capabilities remained but that diminished over time. The American dollar had transformed South Viet Nam's economy for over a decade. Its absence created an economic vacuum.

An infusion of American money and arms was necessary to avoid a dark future. South Viet Nam's political talk was merely that. There was little on which to depend.

Maï nursed her resources. Viet Nam's "Boom Time" was over. She mulled these thoughts over repeatedly as she spoke with her daughter about the upcoming celebration of the Chinese New Year in the next week.

In a field next to Maï's that had been harvested a week before, five of her children worked through soil collecting over-looked peanuts hidden in the dirt. The field was being prepared for a spring crop. She planned to plant sweet potatoes in the newly turned field.

Sweet potatoes, second to rice as a staple group in Vietnamese diet, harvested quickly. Son number three supervised the upcoming planting.

Sixteen-year old number three son, Nguyên Cûông, kept up with the pace of a noisy Korean tractor. An old farmer drove the tractor, similar to a power tiller with a seat, as it dragged a large iron rake. The simple farm tool had stiff iron tines that penetrated the soft field, unearthing up to a foot of dark-red pungent soil. Cûông along with three young children from other families raced each other to collect the peanuts missed in an earlier harvest.

The children bent over busily picking through the overturned earth, racing each other to sort peanuts from the clumps of dirt. They stayed close to the back of the iron rake as the tractor crept along in low gear, digging deep to turn over the soil in ten neat rows from a foot below the field. The noisy two-piston diesel engine popped every now and then as unburned fuel ignited in the muffler producing small clouds of dark smoke. The backfire sounded like a loud fire-cracker and often made the kids laugh at the random surprise.

At intervals, each child ran from the tractor carrying a bulging sack of peanuts, unload it at a strategic point in the field into a larger sack, and return to the tractor. Four of Nguyên Maï's other children were either picking out peanuts on their own or tending the larger sack. This included Maï's youngest child, six-year old daughter, Nguyên Xuân Loan, who was twenty meters to one side of the tractor. Loan, too young to allow working near the plowing rake, guarded a large burlap sack filling with peanuts.

Her older brothers delivered the peanuts sporadically. Cûờng and three of his younger brothers worked in other parts of the field unloading smaller sacks into the big one from time to time. Loan occupied herself digging through the exposed soil near the big sack, finding peanuts others missed. Some of her discoveries ended up in her stomach.

Her brothers trusted Loan to protect their treasure from children of other families that might raid the big sack. The brothers knew that the diminutive youngest sister could face down any marauder, buying them time to foil the raid by other children. She was the small tough little sister. They counted on her to protect their hoard.

This harvest was important to the entire family of fourteen or so. The population in the house varied depending on who stayed there and who returned to Sai Gon. The peanuts became part of the food for the Chinese New Year celebration next week. Tet was the only holiday of the year in which many Asians stopped working their usual fourteen hours every day of the year. Every family did what it could to put on a good feast for the three to seven days they celebrated the New Year. They cooked peanuts and mixed it in soup and roasted it with mint, garlic, and cilantro. They threw in pork, dried fish and wrung a chicken for the occasion. It was a feast worthy of their biggest holiday.

Loan bent over the exposed earth picking up the muddy peanut shells when the plow's ten sets of iron tines hung up on something. Sub-surface rocks and remainders of tree stumps were rare in this flood plain. The tractor engine loaded as the farmer gave opened the throttle to overcome the drag of the rake.

The sub-surface object emitted a loud click. The farmer on the plow recognized the sound in his last living moment. He had no time left to express a curse.

The tractor, the farmer, Maï's third son and the three younger children

No. 2 Son's Grave including the farmer and three other children, about an hour north of Saigon. (2/13/2002)

disintegrated in a deafening eruption from beneath the surface. A geyser of brown dirt, machine parts, and red mist exploded into the hazy blue-white sky.

The explosion ejected soil, machine and body parts up and outward from where a tractor and five defenseless human beings last stood. Tumbling rubber tires flamed and diesel fuel burned producing oily black smoke in an expanding dark cloud.

The concussion from the blast knocked Loan down as chunks of soil, metal shards, and bloody fragments of flesh rained down around her. Iron and tissue fell from the sky making thumping sounds in the upturned soil.

Typical of people near an explosion, they seldom remember hearing it. Either too stunned by the concussion or some other mechanics of a shockwave, they remember something else. Loan only remembered the rude shove. The rolling wave of compressed air planted her face down into the soft dirt.

Her first fleeting thought it was one of her damn brothers playing too rough. Then she heard the sound of objects hitting the field around her. Something much worse than her brothers' playful abuse occurred ... one of them had just disappeared.

The concussion knocked Loan's nine-year old brother, Quy, son number nine, on his back in another part of the field, pelted by stinging sand and soft debris but otherwise unharmed. The small boy stood up to see the long iron rake and a remnant of the tractor frame falling back into the field ten meters away. He looked around for his brother near the tractor and the others following the machine. He realized the hard truth instantly.

Quy's stunned senses cleared knowing he had to do something. Running toward the site of the explosion helped no one near the tractor. He turned from the direction of the new crater and ran for the thatch-covered shed that was home. Quy ran to the house yelling to his mother that something terrible had happened to brother number three.

Maï was inside the farmhouse with her oldest daughter. She had stepped out to take a break and look over the field. To her left, Cûóng along with the children worked in the upturned soil behind the small tractor. Then they disappeared.

The concussion from a hundred yards away punched her chest knocking the wind out of her. She and daughter, May, staggered for a moment against the thatched side of the house.

They shook off their disorientation. Long moments passed as Maï looked at May's questioning expression. She heard one of her children yelling for her. Quy sprinted across field running to the house yelling for his mother. He ran in yelling for her, "Ama, *(mother)*, Ama, Cûõng! Cûõng!" He willed himself to tell the hard truth. "Ama! ... In the field." "Something happened to Cûõng!"

Maï and her daughter headed for the doorway as Quy came running up. She heard her son calling as she emerged into the sunlight. A column of black roiling smoke rose into the hazy noon sky from the center of the field. Dirt and dry vegetation stirred up from the field by the shock wave left a dusty haze that lingered around the field.

A fragment of the tractor frame and engine tumbled off to one side of the crater after traveling in the air for a few seconds bouncing to rest on its side. Mai and her daughter looked for the children and the old farmer. They were nowhere to be seen: the old man, three children, and her man-child son had disappeared. Fragments of flesh and bone plopped into the field.

Mai ran haltingly out into the field looking for her children. She looked for son number three. As she approached the crater, the size of the rising column of black smoke and spreading cloud of dust revealed the size of the explosive.

Knowledge from too many experiences tugged at her racing heart. Her logical mind computed that this was too large to be an anti-personnel weapon. This was something much bigger, less random. Her mind replaced cold facts with a mother's emotions. One of her children had disappeared.

She scanned the field. Six-year old Loan picked herself up from the ground twenty meters away from the crater. Half a dozen children and young adults in other parts of the field stood up from the dirt. Quy was already counted. She could see thirteen-year-old Hua and ten-year-old Anam farther out in the field, running toward the crater.

Mai counted her kids denying Quy's declaration, approaching the crater and the chunk of ragged iron that had been a working engine block moments before. The raw size of the crater, the cloud of dust and column of smoke computed large unforgiving destruction. Anyone close died. Her stomach tightened. Her heart exploded in her chest. Nguyên Cûông a most earnest child and son number three, was missing. The farmer and three children that ran with the tractor were missing. All were missing.

Pieces of smoking debris radiated out from the crater. Iron parts do not smoke like that, only flesh. Most of the debris was human.

Mai had witnessed landmine carnage before. She knew the worst of what big land mines could do. She had used them against her enemy to great effectiveness. Landmines were cold, impartial, and remote destroyers.

A tank mine had been deployed in this farmland against her defenseless family. Her run toward the crater faltered as new information converted fear into certainty. Certainty converted to heartbreak and shock. Maï screamed as her legs gave way. She collapsed to the ground.

The tractor set off a Viet Cong tank mine buried deep in the ground to focus its energy upward into a heavy vehicle. Its arming mechanism failed to trigger with the mere weight of people and farm animals.

It was a tank mine. This mechanism required the weight of a heavy vehicle to detonate. This enabled the device to do the most damage to a hardened iron machine directly above.

This mine sat in indefensible open farmland removed from traveled roads lacking military significance to either side of the war. ARVN vehicles had little reason to pass through this field on the way to somewhere else. As appropriate placement of tank land mines go in the tank land mine business, this field was a poor choice to intercept tanks.

Therefore, it was a cowardly payback to an uncooperative farming community. The only military objective of this land mine was a farm tractor. Nguyên Maï came to no other conclusion.

She did not own a tractor. Her neighbor did. She hired the old man him to prep the land for a new crop of sweet potatoes. He was a good neighbor. He freely plowed the land considering that Nguyên Maï had asked him to do so. She accepted none of his generosity. She paid him a fair price to plow her field. She knew there were unpicked peanuts in the field. She could not know there was a waiting tank mine in the ground.

Maï's community of small farmers, many of them refugees from devastated villages from the north, refused to divide their produce with the Viet Cong without compensation. The VC had been terrorizing unwilling farming communities for a decade, killing and maiming tens of thousands of non-combatants. The civilians made easy targets in a porous tropical country covered in jungles. VC operated with impunity throughout South Viet Nam until the counter-insurgency program was developed. Little did they know, they settled on top of one of the largest concentration of VC forces in the country in the community outside of Tay Ninh.

Few of the community immediately suspected that the land mine was revenge heaped upon Nguyên Maï for her service to South Viet Nam and the American CIA. The Viet Cong delivered their message much as it had throughout the country, bend to their will or pay the consequences. Specifically to Maï, the VC message said "Confront us and we will pay you back ten-fold."

As it had been in the past decade, proof of the perpetrators and intent proved elusive. Maï was living in Tay Ninh because her father had given her that land. Her activities against the VC had ended. She moved there out of convenience.

Tay Ninh may have been one of her mission sites. It had also become a place of refuge from an inappropriate husband. At least that story worked as part of her cover as she moved from village to hamlet to town over the last nine years.

Nguyën Mai lived out her next thirty-one years without enjoying the celebration of Tet. The hideous deeds of the Viet Cong that day permanently dimmed her enjoyment of her most cherished holiday for the rest of her days.

Luck shined on Maï and the twelve children with her in Tay Ninh except for Cuä. They were physically unharmed. The brutality and the terror left a wound of the heart that remained unhealed to the end of her days. Loan remembers that moment to this very day.

Anh, like so many of the secret cadre of Vietnamese operatives for the CIA, heard of Mai's tragic loss of Cuä. She was surprised to hear Mai stayed in Tay Ninh for so long. Everyone that knew Mai was aware she rarely dwelled in the same place more than six months. Even after the VC believed they had killed Mai, she seldom rested and moved as a matter of habit to stay a step or two ahead of the VC's posse.

As it was in Tay Ninh, three of her sons had some regular schooling. All in all, Maï made the mistake of dwelling in Tay Ninh too long. Hanoi caught up with her.

Anh did what she could for Maï who was struggling to just feed and house a dozen children. With so many mouths to feed, a proper funeral and grave marker was simply beyond Maï's means. The farmer and other children's family were in similar circumstances.

There was one more complication. Separate burial of one or another of the victims was impossible.

The horrific explosion created a field of macabre debris and vaporized the remainder into smoke and air. The accumulated body parts weighed less than a third of their original mass in life. Furthermore, it was impossible to be certain of which part belonged to another. Assembly of one body exclusive of commingled parts of another was beyond technological resources of the day. Four grief stricken families elected to inter the remains in a single grave, collecting the grisly pieces of family in a shallow trench on one corner of Maï's field.

Days later, they found some body parts including Cau's head. As if nature had become sympathetic to their loss, a stray dog had brought his head to Maï's porch a few days after the explosion. It was a grisly revelation.

After sorting among the discoverable remains, the families exhumed the first grave and created a more suitable burial site. They buried what they recovered of Cûông, the farmer and the 3 children in a single new grave.

The grisly event concluded with four grieving families wetting the rough grave with their tears. This sadness and grief exceed the capability of text. Words cannot encompass a pain this deep.

Placing a proper marker challenged these impoverished Buddhist. In Chinese culture, marking and attending the graves of family is a large and persistent obligation. Ancestral worship may explain why so many ethnic-Chinese Vietnamese remained in Asia when they could have escaped to another country.

Anh and others who knew Maï contributed to the red pumice markers where she buried her son and the four others. Before her passing in the fall of 2006, Maï requested burial next to the grave of the five lost on 23 January 1975. Two hours northwest of Sai Gon, Maï lies buried adjacent to the pumice markers so she may watch over son number three through eternity. PICTURE of Grave

Compared to Maï's record against the VC, Anh's own efforts against the Viet Cong were inconspicuous. Where Maï had fully penetrated the Viet Cong network with devastating achievement, Anh had marginal success. She was limited to reporting VC movement and coercion of farming communities near Kien Giang on the coast. Regardless, Anh's participation with CIA and South Vietnamese army units was enough to condemn her. The Viet Cong would penetrate her deceptions. If she remained in Rac Ghia, she would be discovered.

The re-education camp interrogations of allies were bound to expose Lam. Hanoi unraveled his self-constructed story of loyalty to the revolution and sacrifice.

The Viet Cong collected key people and tortured them. Lam knew he was disliked well enough. He could not secure everyone's silence.

Worse for Lam, he exploited his position in the final days of Sai Gon to sell off some property in which the title was clearly what someone else claimed. In short, Lam defrauded another family with mixed political loyalties.

He was able to insulate himself from disgruntled Chinese families that unwisely invested with him. Unfortunately, Kien Giang was too close to Sai Gon. They would find him and deal with him in their own way. Regardless, Lam had emerging problems with the regime of Viet Nam.

Other distortions as a VC comrade unraveled. His deceit as a real estate sales representative on property outside of his control gained on him.

Death from two foes is still death. He had to leave.

Few outside the prisons expected those inside to conceal their secrets under forced labor, depravation and torture. Hanoi knew that many of the enemy had fled Viet Nam with the United States evacuation.

The speed of North Viet Nam's success surprised themselves as well as South Viet Nam. Had South Viet Nam fell more slowly, more Vietnamese could have fled.

They knew many of the South Vietnamese loyalists were unable to escape with the Americans. The country was theirs and time was now on their side.

Hanoi became hell bent on finding the traitorous allies of the Americans. They would have their revenge.

The new life-math for Lam and Anh: they faced imprisonment and/or death and sacrificed their children to unknowns. It was unbearable algebra.

There had been only bad and worsening news about anything in the future. Life in Viet Nam meant misery, deepening sorrow and death. Their only options: flee now or hide to escape later. They had no other options.

Once Lam and Anh had made the commitment to escape Viet Nam, the ample evidence of home abandonment left behind became incriminating. Abandoned homes cropped up throughout South Viet Nam as a steady exodus began in June of 1975. Empty homes became clear indication on land that South Vietnamese loyalists had taken to the sea.

The trick for the refugees: maintain normal appearances to the last moment. Lest a neighbor report them to the former Viet Cong who served as "officers of the peace," faking compliance and loyalty to the revolution meant survival.

Deteriorating conditions everywhere created desperate individuals among family and friends willing to sell out a neighbor to buy better days in their lives. As so many other ethnic Chinese caught up in Viet Nam's new politics concluded, there was little good in life left for them in this beloved fertile country. Everything good decayed.

All this added up to make the exodus decision painfully simple the night they locked up their grand but now empty house and stepped out into that dark street, risk storms and pirates on the South China Sea or certainly suffer and probably die in re-educations camps.

One Problem: Nguyên Xuân Loan

What to do with Nguyên Xuân Loan? For Loan, in servitude to the family, she had limited say in the matter of escape. Viet Nam's chaos that affected her own family affected adults that ran her present state in life.

One evening close to sunset, without warning, Anh and Lam thrust into Loan's hands a wad of blue bills—new regime money—đồng—Vietnamese cash. It was enough Vietnamese money to enable her to make her way back to Sai Gon and then some.

Loan had made the trip on the rickety railway transportation system three times. At eight years of age, she became a veteran of what was left of the railroads after the fall of Sai Gon. To a little girl of 1977 Viet Nam, the decision to stay with a family that fed her well or take a rickety rail system back to a Sai Gon whose new regime withheld rice from the ethnic-Chinese was easy. Stay with the family in the Kien Giang province and eat well.

They had prepared a satchel with her clothes and another with sticky-rice and sweet potatoes and said that Maï wanted Loan to return to Sai Gon. It was a barefaced lie. Maï was in hiding near Sai Gon, the phone and mail service went medieval. It took two weeks to trade two pieces of mail in cities 100 miles apart. And that was so it could coordinate a phone call at a precise date and time a week later.

Outside of mail, neither family had other means of communication. It took a month for a cycle of letters between Sai Gon and Rac Ghia. To set up a phone call between postal stations, they still had to use the mail.

Loan was in the hands of trusted friends. The mail system had been poor to insufficient. Plans changed so quickly, there was no time to advise Maï that her daughter returned to Sai Gon. Vietnamese mail posed another risk. The regime read everyone's mail with impunity. Privacy disappeared with the fall of South Viet Nam.

Anh and Lam could say little to Loan without jeopardizing their plans.

Loan could not figure there was enough time for an exchange of mail between Rac Ghia and Sai Gon. She had just returned to Kien Giang province less than two weeks before. Regardless of what she thought, she avoided confronting Anh and Lam with her concept of their contradictions. Eight-year old Vietnamese girls rarely challenge parents or surrogate parents without fear of stinging reminders to keep their station. In short, Loan needed to shut up and take instruction.

For Loan, breaking with tradition was an uncommon aspect of her character. She rejected the story wholesale and resented the imposition of silence and respect. A young Asian girl's option: everything is negotiable.

Anh knew it was improper to send Nguyên Loan back to Sai Gon in such an abrupt and dishonorable manner. Unfortunately, their life and perhaps existence was about to collapse. Her choices were miserably few.

Hanoi locked millions of people out of normal commerce. If they protested, they became imprisoned for the slightest accusation of support for the former government of South Viet Nam. Hanoi operated in fear that loyalists might foment a revolt. They repressed a hostile population in every way.

Anh believed that Nguyên Loan could avoid danger. Loan would reconnect with her mother with Buddha's guidance. Maï should understand and forgive their lack of manners.

Lam and Anh planned to find a way to help Maï and Loan once they rebuilt their life in America. For all their dreams of a better life in this fertile land, their realized their hopes died and their lives were in jeopardy. They had to leave now.

Anh expected to seek forgiveness for bad manners later.

Lam traded his motorcycles, bicycles, rice cooker, propane stove and the few pieces of remaining furniture for gold minted in thin plates. It was the only payment for passage on the boat along with the remainder of the increasingly devalued Vietnamese đồng. They were fortunate to be able to post money and wares up for passage by themselves but it wiped out most of what they had accumulated.

Risky passage in Viet Nam 1977 was expensive. The one-way fare for 600 miles on an open deck fishing boat to the Philippines for the seven of them cost roughly $180,000 in 2015 money.

Lam and Anh carried the remainder of their funds: US dollars, jewelry and a few plates of gold sewn into their clothes. The American dollars had value in Manila and the jewelry and gold spent everywhere throughout Malaysia. The American money gave a toe-hold in the next country.

Asians Don't Swim

Neither Lam nor Anh, similar to most Vietnamese and for that matter most Asians, could swim. Swimming was an uncommon skill throughout Asia. Europeans and Americans grew up with recreational water activities making swimming an essential skill. Swimming was a luxury in Asia, the asset of leisurely people. Why learn to swim when there was little time to enjoy the skill? Asians do not swim because it is a waste of time.

Lam and Anh contemplated the hazard the weight of the gold and jewelry. He had served on a boat in the Mekong Delta alongside American navy that chided him about wearing a life preserver. The weight of the precious metals in his clothing negated his minimal swimming skills. Sinking boats meant he and his family drowned with their precious gold.

The insane decision to travel across a wide stretch of open sea in over-crowded sub-standard watercraft without safety equipment tested belief. Besides the threat to non-swimming passengers if the boat sank, Viet Nam's government imprisoned captured refugees. If they avoided execution, they were imprisoned in the re-education camps.

Over two million fled Viet Nam by risky sea craft between 1975 and 1989. Doubtless, they had compelling reasons to flee.

Burn versus Jump off the Country

Desperate plans made sense in contrast to what actually happened to people's lives in the country. When people in the top of a burning high-rise building face burning or jumping to their death, they always jump. 100% guaranteed choice. Burn or jump?

Choice No. 1. Jump.

Choice No. 2. Jump.

Choice No. 3. Jump.

When they have a choice, few people chose to burn. Viet Nam circa 1977 was a lost country on fire. Lam, Anh, and several million others were jumping off the country.

Eight-year old Loan believed she was returning to Sai Gon by boat. She wasn't fleeing, she was going home. She had unwittingly decided to stay with Lam, Anh and their four children.

Loan believed in what Anh told her. She was excited to return to Sai Gon. Disregard the fact that it was officially Ho Chi Minh City. Ethnic-Chinese missed the memo, so to speak. It was still Sai Gon to them.

Loan's belief in return to Sai Gon and to her loving mother was misplaced. Anh sold Loan a ticket to hell.

South China Sea Pirates

A boat sinking in the South China Sea was among several primary risks for refugees. Thai, Vietnamese, and Cambodian pirates knew that the ethnic Chinese among the Vietnamese tended to be more prosperous, frugal, and worthy targets unable to complain to authorities about crimes committed against them.

Thieves relied on that segment of the refugees to carry gold, jewels and cash on them. Refugees made the escape as much as possible to avoid capture by patrol boats and detection by pirates.

Refugees made ideal victims. First, most boat people were rarely armed. Second, government authorities were seldom aware of who was leaving and when. If they heard of another boat heading east, they knew it to be a one-way trip. Hanoi's main concern: they missed the chance to punish another enemy of the state.

Initially, foreign ports-of-call and hapless fishing villages throughout Malaysia were unaware that a crowd of Vietnamese were coming across the sea. Of the numbers that made it ashore, alive or dead, receiving countries were unable to determine what percentage were making across successfully. As far as the pirates were concerned, when the victim is unknown, unreported and at the bottom of the sea, they (the pirates) committed no crime.

Any pirate on the high seas dreams of an era when the victims are abundant, anonymous, the country of origin lacks disclosure and the sea hides all evidence of their evil. Such a pirate's golden era occurred on the South China Sea between 1976 and 1989. In fact, the crimes of pirates continue to 2015 and probably beyond.

Thai, Cambodian and Vietnamese pirates worked over the boat people at will. They raided the refugee boats with impunity, boarding the boats, taking their money and food, often killing the men, always raping and brutalizing the women and girls.

Bereft of husbands, brothers, food and water, the women and girls were left to starve or die of dehydration. Rendering the boat inoperative and puncturing the hull completed the horror.

The pirates brutalized all the passengers in one form or another. Pirates competed with starvation and bad weather for the title as the worst culprit in the Vietnamese boat people tragedy.

The pirates exploited and destroyed a large segment of helpless desperate people fleeing a virtual hell that was Viet Nam. They or their descendants operate to this day.

Tragically, most of the pirates got away with their crimes. Thailand in particular prosecuted a handful of events where acts of gang robbery, rape and murder were confirmed in their territorial waters.

Those evil people and their descendants prospered on the plight of the Vietnamese. They and their descendants of appalling evil live unpunished among the people of Southeast Asia today.

Statistics of accommodating countries tell some of the scale of the story. Over two million people fled the country by boat. One third never made it. Over six hundred thousand missing refugees have yet to show up anywhere in the world. Indisputable skeletal evidence is strewn across the bottom of the South China Sea and the Gulf of Thailand. *(Author' Note: If providence grants a selfish desire, I would turn into an angel of death and slay those pirates and all their male heirs so their seed will end on this earth. I would make all the females of their spawn infertile as well. Their kind deserves oblivion.)*

Vietnamese Boat-People Statistics

Facts are annoying things. The six or seven countries that accepted political refugees or "asylum-seekers" are among the few public details available that measured the scale of the exodus. Unfortunately, they tally arrivals, not departures. By conservative estimates, 2.3 million people fled, 1.2 million landed and were logged in somewhere else in half a dozen accepting nations. Do the math. Question: what happened to the 600,000-plus who failed to arrive somewhere?

In some communities in Viet Nam, popular opinion is that over four million fled and two million people perished in the flight to freedom. Given what Vietnamese witnessed, it is possible.

Unfortunately, the full measure of the tragedy escapes confirmation. Viet Nam offers little public detail having censured internet search engines of condemning information.

The scale of the Vietnamese flight to freedom staggers the beat of the heart and defies eyes to remain dry. Every time I try to get better numbers, a no-answer is the answer. Viet Nam will not speak of this travesty and has sanitized any record of it on the internet.

Information gleaned from interviews of refugees and refugee-arrival statistics in other countries provide the only measure. It is difficult to gauge the number who actually died fleeing the country between 1975 and 1989. Viet Nam has not publicly conducted or published a census of disappearances since April 30, 1975. Again, Viet Nam's internet sanitizes objectionable history from search engines.

Forced re-locations, people in hiding, voluntary re-locations, and actual escape added to the number killed starting from April 30, 1975 in extra-judiciary executions, mass suicides and death from abuse in the re-education camps. Hundreds of thousands of North Vietnamese moved into South Viet Nam residing in abandoned or previously confiscated property further complicating assessments. Conservative estimates place the over-all death toll in the first four years after the Fall of Sai Gon at nearly one million people. The number may be short by 100%.

Estimates in Asia can only be guesses. From what has been uncovered and roughly estimated, at the very least of the numbers, over 600,000 died in the South China Sea. A rule of thumb in chaotic situations in Asia: take the number you know and multiply by three.

The smallest assessment is horrendous. Three times that numbs the mind and crushes the heart into tears.

Check this against the concept of putting out a few butterfly nets in a hurricane. Merchant ships, American naval surface ships and submarines intercepted refugees in need. That might have totaled in all to a thousand boats with populations that ran between 5 to 125 people. Multiply that by the 99% that American ships and other navies did not intercept. The number is staggering and similar to the claims, if not in scale, at least in proportion to the number of native Vietnamese.

There is one un-disputed fact. Hundreds of thousands died in the South China Sea. People who could not swim risked a dangerous sea in lieu of remaining in Viet Nam. Ask this: Why?

A slow boat with reasonable engine capability crossed the stretch of water to the Philippine coastline easily in two to three days in fair weather. It could make landfall in a sheltered harbor in the Philippines.

Unfavorable weather added a few days to the transit across the South China Sea. Bad weather ended the voyage without a landing. This was before the start of the monsoon season and without the complication of Thai pirates.

The South China Sea is perpetually warm enabling hair-trigger weather situations where calm conditions change to rough in hours. It only took an errant wind between the Philippines and the Himalayas to stir up trouble on the South China Sea. Storms happened anytime of the year but worsened from summer through to October.

Refugee Transporting

Refugee shipment as an enterprise had a few flaws in the business plan. Even though a successful trip paid well, people who owned and piloted the boats took large risk. One voyage with twenty to a hundred passengers paid fifteen ounces of gold per passenger. That sum of money retired an enterprising individual in the Philippines or Malaysia.

One ugly issue: retirement to a life of ease required survival. Many boat operators perished with their clientele. The circumstances of transporting refugees varied widely, chocked full of pitfalls and deadly risks.

First flaw in the enterprise: the endeavor lacked repeat customers as the trip was one way. Round-trip customers ceased to exist after the fall of Sai Gon.

Second, it was illegal. The downside to ferrying refugees to other countries: captured owners and crew go to prison with the refugees. Third, pirates, murderers, and rapists plied the sea with impunity. Fourth, storms and less-than seaworthy boats posed a final set of problems. The boats sank and all the occupants drowned.

343

In the conflict between storm and Vietnamese boat-people on the South China Sea, bet on the storm. With flimsy boats, the storm wins.

The price of passage was high. Usually more than most anyone of that day could manage. Guarantees were often hollow or non-existent. Payment of fifteen ounces of gold per passenger only guaranteed somebody was paid. Actual escape to America turned out to be optional.

South Viet Nam new management: Thugs known as the Viet Cong or higher levels with the NVA. Their management credential: They were Viet Cong or perhaps NVA. Hanoi conscripted many from villages in their early teens in the 1960s and early 1970s. Their education developed on the Ho Chi Minh trail or in a tunnel north of Sai Gon. Stripped of their familial connection, their new patriarch was Father Ho Chi Minh and their VC cadre.

Civic management became the equivalent of hiring the maintenance man to perform heart surgery. The justification that any man is acceptable as an expert on heart surgery is over-extended because the only qualification is that he is a member of the tribe. This tribe was the Viet Cong and NVA. Hanoi promoted brave soldiers to management because their managerial skills were based on, well, they were loyal soldiers and still among the living.

Viet Nam 1975 became a brutal new country with low standards. Those standards declined for more than a decade.

The Viet Cong was very good at looking the other way if it involved a civil dispute, particularly if the dispute involved ethnic Chinese as victims. Ruthless entrepreneurs took payment without necessity of providing goods or service.

Viet Nam 1975 lacked an agency of relief, especially for the persecuted ethnic Chinese of South Viet Nam. If an issue about someone taking the gold in exchange for passage, complaints could be directed to the local police. All of the police happened to be former Viet Cong.

The escape-Viet-Nam industry in the late 1970s lacked refund policies, rain checks for last-minute cancellations and insurance for boat or occupant. It was all or nothing for pilot and passenger. A friendly welcoming return policy in Viet Nam after April 30, 1975, ceased to exist.

Victorious Hanoi won South Viet Nam and defeated the former-great United States of America. The new Viet Nam cut all ties to non-communist countries and ignored the plight of the people it believes delayed their victory. Many of these were ethnic Chinese of South Viet Nam.

After Sai Gon fell, Viet Nam engaged in disputes with Cambodia and China. Amid many complications restoring civilization in Viet Nam, the regime had many distractions. Amid an unreliable currency and imprisonment if not murder of all former civic leadership, the plight of the refugees ranked low among government priorities.

Flight solved one of Hanoi's problems. It purged dissidents from Viet Nam. Vietnamese were dying by the thousands each month in the South China Sea. Hanoi lacked sympathy or sought revenge by inaction.

Refugees were marked as enemies of the state, evidenced by the fact they escaped. Eventually, China petitioned Hanoi to reduce harsh treatment of ethnic Chinese. This enabled a safer departure to reduce the tragedy.

The program, known as the Orderly Departure Program (ODP), began in 1979. It started up slowly and took more than a decade before perilous escape by boat ended.

A one-way transport of a family of six was very costly and the addition of one more, Nguyên Loan, became awkwardly expensive. Lam and Anh had committed all of their money and goods. If they backed out that night, they had little to live on if they remained on shore after that night. If Lam avoided prison, it might take decades to scrape together what they needed to attempt escape again. Lam and Anh knew they faced many years in a chaotic country run by unpleasant government. It was getting worse and appeared to run for more years than they could endure.

Between Rocks & Hard Places

Anh and Lam were in a difficult situation. They had to choose between enduring medieval Viet Nam and flee East, South or West. Word among the few connections to the outside world, travel by land to the west through Cambodia grew increasingly dangerous. The Khmer Rouge replaced an existing Cambodian kingdom and was much harsher than Hanoi's revolutionary government. Independent-minded people who posed a perceived social or political threat to Khmer Rouge control disappeared in what later became known as the "Killing Fields."

Estimates of the deaths in Cambodia: 1.7 million died. Other millions were displaced.

If a fraction of the rumors were true, Cambodia went far more medieval than Viet Nam. Viet Nam's extrajudicial executions and artificial famines paled to the wholesale slaughter of administrative and educated classes in Cambodia. Where Hanoi's revolutionary government attempted a balance between applying "carrots and sticks" to re-construct Viet Nam's political and economic structure, Cambodia applied only "sticks".

The two choices squeezed down to the only option that had some chance of working for a couple with four small children: Find space on a boat that could make it to the East or to the South, to the shipping lanes in the South China Sea and beyond. Between two difficult issues endured by the few that fled before them, escape to the east and south was their only choice.

Through "back-door" communication from the otherwise internationally isolated Viet Nam, they heard from other parts of the world. American short-wave radios ceased operating shortly after Sai Gon fell. Ad hoc authority junked the American-made equipment.

Vietnamese technicians retrieved the equipment from junkyards. They replaced disabled tubes and transistors with working versions previously removed from the other working equipment.

Word went out through a narrow conduit of trusted felons. Vietnamese that fled before the fall of Sai Gon found new existence in Australia, Israel, France, and North America. Adapting to western ways was difficult. Yet, the generosity of the "white devil" surprised many.

As Sai Gon was about to fall, in the early hours of April 29, 1975, the United States initiated a helicopter-based evacuation program code named "Frequent Wind" to air lift out the remainder of Americans and vulnerable Vietnamese they could reach.

Many doomed Vietnamese made it out. Unfortunately, it was too little and too late. By the end of 1975, the US resettled 130,000 Vietnamese through one of four military bases. The intermediate re-location helped Vietnamese to adjust them to life in America before moving into communities across the country. It was only a beginning. In the first ten years, 823,000 Vietnamese settled in the 48 contiguous states.

After Sai Gon fell, another program under the same name grew to intercept Vietnamese refugees wherever and whenever possible and relocate them to safer environs. The term "asylum-seekers" was used for extra-legal reasons as well. Vietnamese that declared themselves as political refugees from communism or were in the employ of American operations in Viet Nam found passage to North America and Australia. Unqualified others languished in holding camps in the Philippines and Malaysia for years.

Civic, Catholic and Protestant organizations across the United States provided remarkable assistance to Christian and Buddhist Vietnamese providing homes and communities to aid the assimilation of Vietnamese into the United States and Canada. Communities throughout North America with small Asian populations developed "Asian Districts" to accommodate new arrivals. The demographic mix of communities in New York, California, Texas, Oklahoma, Kansas, and Arkansas, to name a few, acquired a new Asian component alien to their own experience. Americans embraced the refugees from Viet Nam, the land of a nightmarish war they seldom understood and wished to forget.

For their part, Vietnamese had to travel across east across the South China Sea to the Philippines or farther south and east toward Singapore, or somewhere into Malaysia. All the Vietnamese had to do was cross anywhere from six-hundred to over one thousand miles of warm pirate-infested storm-ridden seas. That is all they had to do. No biggie, eh?

Early stories of success filtered back into medieval Viet Nam by illegal short-wave radio. Some messages came in from South Vietnamese that left in American aircraft and by American sea-craft. The early stories failed to include the larger danger of evil human intervention.

The early stories of success gave hope and impetus to desperate people that otherwise might have re-considered such a decision given more accurate discussion and detail of the risks. Communication from other parts of the world was sporadic and it only confirmed those who made it to landfall somewhere else.

Failures went unreported distorting the estimation of success. The numbers of people that failed to make landfall also failed to illustrate the extreme hazards of such a trip at the wrong time of the year and the monsoon season. Just as in the gambler's world where people declare successes and hide losses, limited positive information overwhelmed the dearth of negative data discovered on Philippine and Malaysian shorelines.

If a body didn't wash up on shore, often a person's clothing did. Vietnamese clothing and belongings littered the southern and eastern Asian coastlines for years.

Escape by boat, any boat of any type and size, was seductive. Forced relocations, summary executions, and famines, artificial and otherwise, compelled rational people to make irrational commitments.

Vietnamese refugees made decisions to flee that defied logic to someone living secure in food, life, and liberty. Try as North Americans might, we fail to conceive of a situation forcing us into an insanely dangerous journey.

Despite North American myopia, over two million people attempted the journey. Thus began the largest sea-borne exodus of its kind across 600 miles of open sea riddled with treacherous humanity, fickle weather, and unreliable sea craft. *(Author's note: I note I repeat this a bit much. Perhaps it is my own form of process trying to grasp why people took such a risk.)*

Lam and Anh heard of successful escape from Vietnamese underground networks. What they did not know were the unreported large numbers of Vietnamese that were dying from a pirate's knife, drowning or washing up to die on a rocky Philippine coastline.

As a policeman, Lam knew of the Vietnamese returned by capture. Although inadequate to manage such a large task, Vietnamese patrol boats captured some of the "boat people" and repatriated those they did not kill outright. Life was worse for luckless refugees returned to Viet Nam. They were in version 2.0 of hell.

The refugees that didn't move far enough west to Thailand eventually fell victim to Cambodian killing fields or ended up imprisoned by communists in Laos. Horrors of Indochina continued despite the United States negotiation for amnesty and peace.

The consequences of the rapid fall of Sai Gon had only just begun. Loan had a "ring-side" seat on chaos.

Storms in the Forecast

In South Viet Nam, particularly around Sai Gon, the daily temperature ranges from lows in the 70° F to 'highs of 90° F in the afternoon with constant pervasive humidity. Afternoon high temperatures drop during the May to October monsoons by about 2° F.

By mid-spring, the weather that eventually results in the monsoon weather shifts over the region. This arrives in sporadic storms over the South China Sea that eventually evolves into the cycles of rainsqualls and typhoons of summer and fall.

Lies to a Young Girl

Anh lied to Nguyên Loan. She told her the family was going to Sai Gon by boat. This distortion misled Loan's understanding of her geographical location for most of the next four years.

Lacking formal education, she knew almost nothing about the rest of the world. To her, all land was called Viet Nam. No one told her where Viet Nam began or ended. All was Viet Nam so anything else she encountered could also be Viet Nam. She knew some of her family's origins from Shanghai, China and later from Hanoi, Viet Nam. Both cities, according to her best information were in Viet Nam. *(Author's Note: At 8 years old in 1962, all I knew of Asia is that everyone starved there and I had to clean my plate out of guilt. If I dug down real deep, I would end up somewhere in China on the other side of spherical planet and probably starve with the rest of the people. Loan hadn't learned yet that earth wasn't flat and had no concept of digging down and ending up in North America.)*

Language marks origins. Most everyone around Loan spoke Cantonese. Many adopted Vietnamese as a second language but among kin and friends, everyone spoke Cantonese.

Loan was the youngest child of ten all-blood siblings and four-plus half-blood siblings. She was an uneducated eight-year old girl who managed her thin understanding of the world, fragmented by constant movement from village to village every four to six months. Her mother moved often to stay ahead of avenging Viet Cong.

Consequently, Loan was unable to attend school for any length of time. Her brothers' education had priority. They were male and entitled to first opportunity for schooling. According to culture and tradition, Loan was accorded a life of service and breeding. Yet, that was not what her mother taught her.

Nguyên Maï was Nguyên Loan's mentor above all. Finding a way back to her home by whatever means was Loan's singular goal in life.

All Loan knew of value was to be with her mother. Subsequently, Loan's ignorance and desire to find her way home confounded her understanding of exactly where she was in the world. Crossing the sea, when the landmarks she knew disappeared were replaced with new land forms populated with similar vegetation and animals. She believed she was still somewhere in Viet Nam.

The Day Before – Being Sent to Sai Gon

Just before sunset, Anh asked Loan to talk to her in the front room of the house. Anh's face was hard. The mistress of the house and mother of four in a warm household had disappeared and before Loan stood a woman she hardly recognized. Anh's expression was painful.

Anh had a difficult task. She must send Loan back to Maï. She had to do this without revealing what Anh and her family were about to do. Anh had much to tell Loan but she could not take a chance that Loan could keep a secret. If plans fell apart, Loan might endanger everyone by telling the truth to a government entirely devoid of heart.

If Anh had the luxury of telling the girl anything, she might have told her that Lam's role in behalf of the losing side of the war might be discovered. She might have told tell Loan that the Americans left Viet Nam without protecting their allies such as her and Lam. The Viet Cong verged on figuring out Lam and perhaps Anh as enemies of Hanoi's revolutionary government.

Life was complicated if the VC even allowed them to live. In all likelihood in Viet Nam 1977, Anh and Lam die. Their children become orphans if not executed as an example to Viet Nam.

Without explanation, Anh walked Loan outside in the small court yard and stood at the gate. She thrust a wad of large blue paper money, five-hundred thousand Vietnamese đồng, into Nguyên Loan's hands. Loan had never held such money before. Anh interrupted Loan's amazement by setting bags of clothes and satchels of food at her feet.

Without apology, Anh told Loan she had to make her way home that night and pointed her in the direction of the train depot. Loan knew the drill. She had to purchase space on one of the flat-bed "cars" to ride back to Sai Gon.

Anh explained that something had come up. She tried to convey that they could not afford to have Loan work for them anymore even as Loan held more money than she had ever known existed. Loan had to leave now and make her way home.

Surprised by this abrupt change in plans, it took hardheaded Nguyên Loan a minute to absorb the news. She had only just returned to Rach Gia after three days on the flat bed of a freight train. She expected to stay for one year. Why this? Why now?

This characteristic of analysis served Loan well in the future. She did not accept sudden changes mildly and violated her Asian upbringing by protesting adult instruction.

Loan threw a fit.

Public and private objection was an unpardonable sin for a small Asian female. A young Asian girl never objects to an adult's instruction without consequences. Never.

Just as quickly as she was told she must go away, she instructed Anh she wanted to stay with them. As much as she missed her mother, she ate well with this family. She was also out from under the harassment of her brothers and older sister. Anh's young children had become her best friends. She rejected the change in venue on many levels. She handed the money back to Anh declared, "I am staying with you."

This was unexpected. Being of the old-culture Asian, Anh felt ambushed. Loan was by all evidence now Maï's daughter. Truly.

Anh hardened instantly telling Loan there were no options, stuffing the blue high-value bills back in Loan's hand. Anh handed the satchel of food and coconut juice prepared to feed the girl on a three-day journey back to Sai Gon. Anh had gathered Loan's possessions in a small bundle wrapped with some hemp twine for the journey. It was several hours before sunset. Loan had enough time to reach the freight depot and make arrangements to return home.

Before Loan could think of a better argument, Anh guided Loan to step outside and closed the gate on her. She heard Anh slide the steel bolt on the gate locking it. She was locked out!

They had cut her adrift to return to Sai Gon without any explanation. She had been told to leave the well-fed household she served and return to the rice-deprived and starving Cholon.

Loan possessed all her belongings, more money in her hands than she had ever seen and … rejection to a world back to life in Sai Gon. Her first reaction to this abrupt instruction: all that work in the family, her bossy brothers, along with the miserable diet of sweet potatoes and rice. *(Author's Note: If they could get rice. Viet Nam had imposed artificial famine on Sino-Vietnamese families in the Cholon. No rice for people disloyal to Ho Chi Minh.)*

Loan rejected this treatment. She stood outside the front door of the home, knocking on it for what seemed like an hour. Her frustration turned to tears, crying and begging to stay with them. Neighbors and passersby on the narrow street heard her objectionable wailing and knocking on the gate. Young Vietnamese girls shouldn't complain too much. It is very inappropriate.

It was uncharacteristic to see an eight-year old Asian girl make a fuss in public. Before very long, the neighbors might become curious about new events going on at the house of Lam and Anh.

Enemies awaited the downfall of mysterious Lam's elevated status with an improbable combat record. How dare he put the Sai Gon servant-girl out like that? Vietnamese tongues tend to wag.

Loan wanted to continue to eat well as she had with this family, to take care of the children who became her best little friends. She accepted nothing of the hand dealt to her that moment. She did not want to make the three-day journey home by herself a few weeks after coming back to this pleasant village outside of Kien Giang.

She missed her mother and her family. She knew that a return to home in Sai Gon meant the end of a warm bowl of steamed rice mixed in with chicken and pork in exchange for endless drudgery and a thin diet. At least with Anh and Lam, she endured drudgery better knowing she always had rice and meat each meal all day and every day.

Loan rejected the abrupt change of circumstance. She beat on the front door and cried. Emotionally exhausted, she slumped at the front gate on the front porch of the house, sobbing as she leaned against the freshly painted frame.

No one had a freshly painted gate in the village except for Lam and Anh. Everything she had seen since Sai Gon fell to the communists as it was shelled and destroyed by the NVA was rusted if not broken. Lam and Anh had the means to maintain appearances. They were rich.

By her standards measured by the war, Lam and Anh were wealthy. They had food and a good house they were able to maintain. They had electricity at least for several hours a day. Ceiling fans worked along with electric lights. Their telephone rang often. These people had prestige.

Late afternoon lapsed into sunset. No one inside the house stirred as Loan sat drifting between spells of crying and pouting at the front door.

Maybe out of concern of alerting nosey neighbors or curious pedestrians, Anh opened the gate and let Loan back in the house. Anh told her to be quiet. The children were already asleep. At that point, she told Loan that they were returning her to Sai Gon by boat later that night and that she must be ready to leave with them. She told her that if she were too noisy, they must leave her behind and neighbors would hire her.

Loan understood how to be quiet. This was going to be her fourth trip and she wanted to return to Sai Gon. It had only been a short time away but she wanted to see her mother more than ever.

Even as it worked to stay with Lam and Anh, Loan though it odd to leave as such a late hour. Regardless, her protest repaired the situation. She was happy to be with them. She'd sort the strangeness of the hour later.

Anh told Loan that she could continue to work for them and live with them in Sai Gon if she wished. She could see her family any time she wanted. Loan won the day and after the embarrassing outbursts had subsided, she thanked Anh for changing her instruction. Anh had not changed her mind; taking Loan with them was a mistake.

Loan went to sleep next to the three girls and the small boy, looking forward to new days with this family and being able to see her mother whenever she wanted. Life would be good now, so thought Loan.

The Tranh Exodus, Spring 1977

Late in the evening, Lam woke Loan and told her to in a whisper to wake up the children. He instructed her to limit noise that could wake the neighbors. It was rude make too much noise in public.

The family gathered their belongings without conversation. Polite quietness was an essential directive for tightly disciplined Asian households. Loan thought nothing of the instruction but she thought the hour of departure a bit unusual. She had never heard of someone finding public transportation at 2 AM. Even the roosters slept at this hour.

Restless Viet Nam usually had some traffic at such an early hour. Since May 1975, the regime imposed a sunset curfew. Loan knew to stay indoors after dark. Nobody ventured out until sunrise.

Lam among few in the village had what amounted to electricity, intermittently interrupted as it was. The aging American diesel-generators required rationed and expensive diesel fuel. Parts of the area and were usually shut off before midnight. That night, the electricity was on at the house.

Lam had turned out the fluorescent lights in the front room of the house to avoid drawing attention when they opened the front door. Loan with the four children quietly filed out to stand on the dark gravel road. Anh and Lam whispered a Buddhist prayer for the welfare of their house that provided them comfort and security.

With a painful expression on Lam's face, he grimly locked the heavy pad-lock on the hasp of the front gate. Anyone planning to return to the house a few hours later commonly did this. He secured the gate as a ruse. They weren't going to return to this house unless as ghosts.

Otherwise, late at night, the pad-lock was on the inside hasp of the gate. It was one more precaution to minimize detection of their plans. In his worst fears, Lam believed he was a few hours ahead of being arrested by the regime.

Completion of each small step of the plan relieved him of another increment of anxiety. They might yet escape. Lam and Anh were afraid to hope too much.

Lam joined his wife, their four small children, and their persistent young servant from Sai Gon in the street. He told the children to pick up their feet to avoid shuffling in the noisy laterite gravel on the best street in Rhac Ghia. They turned from the front of the house and moved silently down the road. It was after the start of curfew, the road was empty and quiet.

Anh and Lam rolled their motor-cycles with bags of clothing and food straddled over the seats. The wheels crunched through the gravel forcing them to walk slowly until they could reach a dirt road. The road was dry and dusty as it was the dry season, as it were, for the region.

Lam took an extra pre-caution the afternoon before. He gave the captain of the police station two large bottles of precious white whisky. He made up a reason for his sudden generosity. They knew of Anh's difficult wife. He had to hide it lest she find it in the house.

354

Knowing the men as he did, they drained the bottles at sunset. The liquor was 100-proof white lightning also known as Vietnamese moonshine. It inoculated the night shift of Rac Ghia police officers until late afternoon the next day.

A few days before, Lam transferred title of the property to one of his cousins in a sealed envelope. He told his cousin it was a copy of his will and that he should open it if something ever happened to him. Such was the nature of the times. Lam could not tell immediate family of his plans for escape from Viet Nam and Indochina. Trust as a signature component of Asian culture had collapsed in Viet Nam. No one could be trusted when it came to escape, even eight-year old servants such as Loan.

Lam's father had been killed during the fall of Sai Gon by Viet Cong and NVA shelling of the Cholon district. Lam's mother and sisters lived in Sai Gon and prospered due to gifts of food and money, benefits of Lam's inflated position with the Viet Cong.

Lam's mother would sorely miss those benefits. Unfortunately, he trusted no one including his mother and siblings with their plans.

Travel time was essential and they directed their brood and attendant to move quickly down the gravel and dirt roads that skirted the village. There was minimal light in the village at night. As expected, the electricity cut off abruptly and the few street lights in the village went dark.

Lam carried a green military flashlight that he had received in service to US Marines during the war. It was "western contraband" and dangerous for him to own it.

He kept it hidden and nursed the energy in the "D-Cell" batteries for just such an event. If authorities caught him with the flashlight, the American artifact incriminated his entire family. He might say he took it off a dead American half a dozen years before. It was the only excuse he could give.

Reckoning with Loan's memory and the Chinese calendar in 1977, it was six weeks after Tet which was February 17 to February 19 of that year. The Tranh family had embarked on this escape from Viet Nam in the first week of April 1977. This was well before the beginning of the summer monsoon. The deluges and continuously poor-to-bad was a month or two away.

They weren't traveling during the monsoon but the weather patterns in the region already began shifting toward the rainy part of the year. The outward flow of moisture across the South China Sea reversed and moved westward setting up the eventual heavy rains that inundated South Viet Nam.

Weather changes and the weather in Sai Gon seldom reflected the weather on the eastern side of the South China Sea. As it turned out, there is poor to bad guessing at weather patterns in this region of the world. The world of internet communication and satellite imaging was two decades away. Tropical disturbances on the South China Sea cropped up without notice.

Going Home to Sai Gon

Loan bought Anh's lie wholesale. She had no reason to doubt her master. More, she had no choice.

She was excited to return to Sai Gon to see her mother and older sister. She even welcomed her brothers, mean as they often could be to her. Her life had become exotic. They would ask her of what life was like in Rhac Ghia. For a brief period, she knew she would be the center of attention in her family.

She carried the boy Teo on her back. At two, he was half her weight.

Teo had been Loan's constant companion since first arriving fourteen months before. With him on her back, she carried nothing else but she had one hand free. Anh gave her some banana-leaf-wrapped bags of sticky-rice, which she held with her right hand. Her left hand behind her kept Teo situated on her back.

Lam and Anh rolled their Honda motorcycles beside them, laden down with tattered canvas bags holding cloths and food. The three daughters, Tsu, Ha and Tin carried satchels of cloths and food.

Loan and the toddler on her back walked in the darkness for a long time. They traveled down to the marshes on the edge of the village. As they approached the edge of the marsh they saw the glow of candlelight from a bamboo thicket.

Vietnamese men dressed in the ao ba ba *(black pajamas)* stood holding bamboo shafts with flaming cloth soaked in white gas. The men spoke in a mixture of Vietnamese and Cantonese quietly to Lam and Anh handing them long strips of black cloth for blindfolds.

Two of the men held the motorcycles while Lam removed the bags and set them on the ground. The men rolled the vehicles into the bamboo thicket.

Anh instructed the girls and Loan to wrap the black cloth around their heads. They could breathe through the coarse cloth but not see anything. The men held up a shuttered white-gas lantern that limited the light falling toward them. Other than the stars above, there was only moonless night sky to watch. The blindfolds changed little of what they could have seen.

As so often occurred in those years, the boat-people escaped in the middle of the night during a new moon. The few Hanoi-boats as they called them, patrolling for errant citizens, had greater difficulty finding culprits on a moonless night. Gasoline and diesel was precious and limited refugee patrols that motored out off the coastline and then shut off the engines and waited to see what might emerge from the rivers that flowed into the Gulf of Thailand and The South China Sea.

The strangeness of each event caught Loan up in the excitement of the mysterious men and the chances to go home again so soon and see her mother. The lie Anh told Loan worked as intended. Returning soon to her mother silenced most of the girl's concerns.

Loan ignored the odd hour of the night they were leaving. She gave the blind folds no thought as well. It was all part of a great new adventure. What great thinking to eight-year olds do?

Mysterious men with torches guiding them to a boat late at night made an exciting story to tell her brothers. This was her first ride on a boat. She had never been on the water. She would be able to see her beloved mother soon. The entire experience was glorious.

Anh gave Loan one of the large bags to carry. Teo's mother relieved Loan's back, carrying her son high up on her breast. They walked single file for another five minutes treading on the soft marsh grass and then waded into the shallow swamp water that deepened up to waist high on Loan.

Loan carried the bag high on her head. Blindfolded, she walked behind the girls hearing Anh's voice guiding them to step carefully and not stumble, steering them along soft grass and then through the smelly warm wet swamp water.

The night wind was breezeless. Loan smelled the foul odor of stagnant marsh water. It was not fit to drink and smelled of salt, sewage, rotting vegetation and fish. It was the first time she had been in the swampy area near the village. She thought it was a curious place to put a passenger boat when there were more pleasant places to embark up the coast.

The larger city of Kien Giang had a generous harbor. It was full of boats that might have been easier to board. Why did they travel to this boat and in this way?

She saw flashes of light around the edges of her blindfold as the men waved their torches around them. She cocked her head back to see anything. She was otherwise blind.

She felt the warm muck squishing between her toes and wondered if a creature in the bottom might bite her. There was always something in a marsh that could bite a careless girl as she remembered the instruction of her mother.

After what seemed to Loan like an hour, they waded through the foul water and up to a large wooden frame and heard whispering voices hovering just above her head. The voices were in a mixture of Vietnamese and Cantonese. A hand grabbed Loan's shoulder and guided her to a wood frame. She felt the rungs and realized it was a ladder.

She felt the bag lift off her shoulder and someone told her to climb the ladder and step onto the deck. In her masked blindness, mysterious hands guided her as she stepped up the ladder. The mysteriousness excited her. This was already a good adventure.

She lifted the blindfold to see the rungs and in the flickering light, she climbed the ladder and stood on the open deck of a large fishing boat with a high prow. More mysterious hands motioned her shoulders forward to stand next to a railing. Stern voices reminded everyone to remain silent, remove their blindfolds and stand still. She found they stood on the top of a large fishing vessel with a broad deck, a high forward prow, and a structure in the middle, a hut that covered a diesel engine. The wood smelled of fish, diesel oil and cellulose rot. The boat smelled old.

Loan stood among a silent crowd of people of all ages sitting or squatting Asian-style *(butt sitting on heels)*. They were illuminated by dim flickering light of bamboo torches.

Men gave them buckets of water with small bowls and rags to wash off the foul water from their legs and bellies. Loan's pajama-like pants were soaked. She had a dry pair in one of the cotton satchels that Anh carried. Loan was reluctant to change cloths among so many strangers. She'd "make do" for the moment. The wash of water on her legs was cool and pleasant to the point of a chill.

The night air was cool. Yet, she decided to sit and shiver and see what else was going to happen before she asked to change to dry clothes.

Loan believed the boat was the largest vehicle she had ever seen. It was twenty meters (65') long with a wide wooden deck and the engine hut sitting back from the center of the deck. A rudder-man stood on a high rear platform and held a long steel rod that went connected to a large metal blade. Two weathered steel masts, one forward of the engine hut and the other mast aft carried cloth-wrapped booms. It was a two-sail boat. It was huge.

One rusted metal pipe ran out of the top of the hut with a rain cap. The top of the high side rails were eight feet above the water and four or so feet above the deck. Loan had to stand on her toes to see over the side. Even then, she barely saw where the stars ended in blackness that was the horizon.

Men directed Lam, Anh and the children to the port side *(left)* of the boat one third of way down from the bow. They set down their belongings against the wooden side *(gunwale)*.

Lam recognized one of his neighbors in the village, now sitting quietly in the dim light from torches mounted on the sides of the boat. The two men made eye contact and nodded to each other. Lam gave a shrug and cracked a nervous smile. Here he was, the leading village policeman they knew too well, escaping with them. Others noticed him as well nodding in his direction. Civilization in their village, as all aboard the vessel confirmed, was coming apart.

Lam knew of a curious western phrase about "rats leaving the ship" before it sank. In this case, it was turned around. This time the rats were at the helm of Viet Nam, people were leaving the country as it sank. People fled the sinking vessel that was his beloved Viet Nam. The vermin, so to speak, stayed aboard, but not all of them.

Viet Nam: A great luxuriant fertile mother of a country that had year-round growing weather and good soil had slipped through the loyalists' grasp. Some portion of that tragedy was evident in the faces of men and women on that deck.

The desperate condition of the passengers appeared obvious among the men's exchange of glances. Lam took heart that his family was on board. Not everyone on board brought wives and children. Such was the desperation that husbands, fathers and sons fled alone to remain alive. Such was the desperation that wives and daughters shipped out separately so that mother or father, sister or brother might make it out from Viet Nam.

They had moved out the village undetected. The next challenge lay in moving out to sea without notice.

Loan was curious about all the people. She expected something different. Too many people crowded the boat deck. Where can she go to pee?

Maï taught her daughter to conceal her distinct gender parts. Female privacy among a crowd was a huge Asian issue. Nursing mothers fed their babies openly in public. Exposure of anything else was a different matter.

Anh asked Loan to "hold it" until they could figure out a "properness." Loan envied little Teo, he relieved himself wherever he wanted. She and Teo's sisters had to wait for proper arrangements. Boys have all the luck of life.

Loan was accustomed to public transportation being crowded when she traveled by flat-bed rail cars between Sai Gon to Kien Giang. Yet, there was something wrong about this boat deck carpeted with people. This was a working deck meant for fish and fishermen.

Anh saw the questions surfacing in Loan's gaze and motioned Loan to maintain silence, giving her the commonly understood side-waving hand sign she could talk shortly. Other people settled into assigned places on the deck for another ten minutes. As people settled into position, one by one, they assumed the Asian squat sitting comfortably on their heels.

The boat lurched backwards and Loan could hear men breathing heavily over the side of the boat, down in the water. A number of men down in the water on both sides and behind the boat strained to move the laden boat out of the mud. The exerted themselves noisily as they pushed the old hull backwards out of the shallows.

The boat floated silently backwards, halting at first stuck in the muck and then shortly moving smoothly as it cleared obstructions in the shallows. She heard the heavy breathing of the men fall behind as the boat built up its backward movement. It drifted silently into the black night for a few minutes.

The movement seemed to change as it floated into moving water. The hour approached low tide and the water in the tidal marsh flowed out to sea. They floated backwards and sideways in the flow for another few minutes. The stink of the marsh faded as the boat moved out into the flowing water.

A rusty-sounding whine of an electric motor, an engine-starter-motor broke the silence. It stopped and then started again. Stopped, and then started again. A large iron reciprocating engine under the deck of the mostly-wooden boat resisted waking up.

The diesel engine under the hut in the center of the boat was old. The big-iron block Korean-made truck diesel finally took hold. Muffled by the engine hut, its knocking was loud. Calm river water carried any sound to the shore. The engine noises made adults nervous.

It revved up to a predictable 1,500 RPM. Vapor blew from an overhead exhaust pipe above the hut, a rain cap rattled, opened, ejecting a cloud of oily black smoke invisible in the low light. The boat continued to drift backwards as the engine ran for a minute, warming up. The exhaust pipe in the center of the boat puffed more black smoke into the night sky above them. One of the two sail masts rested near them with long horizontal poles, spars that held rolls of ratty Dacron sailcloth. The wrap of material had patches on top of patches. Replacement sails of Dacron became impossible in 1977 Viet Nam. Parts of bed sheets and parachutes were stitched in for lack of an alternative sail repair.

Loan figured those were sails. She had seen boats such as this in the Sai Gon River before. This was the larger of most fishing boats she had seen. Dirty and crowded as the boat deck appeared, she was excited to be on such a magnificent vessel.

Something thumped under the deck as a clutch engaged the engine to a propeller shaft. Water churned noisily in the blackness behind the boat. The sound of the engine settled down as it gained the load of the propeller putting out now a comforting thrum. The boat's backward drift slowed as its over-loaded bulk began to reverse direction to stop and then move forward slowly turning to starboard. *(Right side).*

Loan felt the vessel's turn to starboard in the black landscape. She sensed the motion but saw nothing beyond the lanterns except a few stars that ended at a rough gray-black horizon. The city lights of Kien Giang up the coast were out, the usual evening to morning blackout of electricity. Viet Nam's inflating currency made larger purchases of diesel nearly impossible. Electric lights were a luxury few could afford to purchase.

Loan looked across a shallow harbor over the shoulders and heads of the passengers dimly lit by torch light and the starboard rail of the modified fishing-boat, nothing else. Otherwise, the boat was dark. The deck was a mass of invisible strangers except for her and Teo in her lap and the three sisters lying by her side, sitting on a dark hulking mass moving out to sea.

Lam's tensions eased. He, family and Loan were now in the boat headed out to big water. All that was left … pass the shore patrols undetected. More than twelve miles out, the patrols seldom challenged the boats. Otherwise, capture meant death for him, imprisonment for Anh and orphanage for their children.

Two years after Sai Gon fell; the bitterness of the war was strong as ever. Far as he knew, anyone captured escaping Viet Nam seldom returned alive or free.

Beyond twelve miles or anywhere out of sight, Vietnamese and Thai pirates lurked. He was somewhat prepared. Under balls of sticky rice in his satchel, Lam hid his forty-five caliber American pistol. His Springfield Armory version of the famous 1911 and six 7-round clips lay wrapped in banana leaves. He traded his AK-47s and ammunition for gold used to purchase passage on the boat. His big guns might have made a better answer two days later to fend off pirates.

In a few hours, he knew that escape was accomplished. Then, avoiding a series of small islands strung out between Viet Nam and the Philippines, it was otherwise a straight eastward run to Manila.

Lam possessed enough gold plates sewn into his pants to negotiate a better life than most of the refugees after they all made landfall. Anh did not know about the additional gold. Lam did not want to explain how he had the gold.

Lam was a good liar. Unfortunately, Anh possessed a penetrating stare that stripped his lies naked. She could ferret out his best stories. His best strategy was avoiding sensitive topics with his wife.

There was more than just a vengeful Viet Cong bearing down. Lam cheated customers on vacant Sai Gon property he sold before moving to the coast a year before. The income enabled them to hire Loan to tend to their children without taping his gold.

Fate raced to kill him. It had been a contest between family with a blood oath to find and sort restitution with him and the Viet Cong to find and kill him for war crimes. His crime: lying to Hanoi.

Buddha gave Lam more days than he probably deserved. He knew many men that took their own life as Sai Gon fell. He knew others that were dragged from their homes and shot in the street in front of their families. At times, the entire family was murdered.

He was not sure who was going to catch him first. Finally on the water passing out into the South China Sea, neither the VC nor men from an angry family could find him.

He gave time a few more hours before he could boast, if only to himself, that he had beaten all of them. He reached down along the outside of his thighs touching the plates of 24-carat gold sewn into his pants feeling the security of the precious metal. All in all, he carried pounds of the soft precious metal sewn into the blouse and shorts of his ao ba ba.

The boat picked up speed. Loan felt that motion along with a refreshing breeze now from the bow. The salt smell of The South China Sea displaced the stink of the swamp. New breezes blew in from the East. The cooling land mass drew in the night air off the sea.

As the boat ceased turning, the stars on the horizon stopped moving and the sails on the spars ruffled in the building breeze. The boat churned into the blackness of an unlit evening that was passing away from a socialist-communist night.

Politics were meaningless to an eight-year old girl. Loan knew she headed back to the Cholon on the southern outskirts of central Sai Gon, to home and to her mother.

A man on the front of the boat held a large shuttered white-gas light that shown out in front of the boat. Loan saw insects and dust floating and flying in the beam, nothing else. There were few land reference points to compare motion in the night. A satellite image of Viet Nam in 1977 at 2 AM, if available, showed a dark country. A small portion of Sai Gon remained lit through the night. Every community in South Viet Nam shut off its generators several hours after sunset and only restarted them for industrial needs a few hours after sunrise. Such was the progress of a medieval command economy dictated from Hanoi.

As the boat moved out on the deeper riverbed, the crew wrapped wet cloth on the bamboo torches near the passengers to extinguish the light, save for the boxed-light shining out on the bow. They reduced the diesel engine to an inefficient 750 RPM to reduce the noise emitted from the exhaust stacks and conserve fuel. The flow of the river ebbing out at low tide added a few knots to the boat's progress.

The vessel with its silent passengers packing the deck shoulder to shoulder moved now in the dark to settle in for the voyage. It motored noisily out into the night and toward large open water. In silhouette, the boat appeared to be a fishing vessel conserving fuel as it eased out to sea for a day's work.

After the engine started and covered their conversation, Anh whispered to Loan to remain quiet and to hold Teo. He had fallen asleep in Loan's arms. She covered him with a thin cotton blanket Anh had pulled out of one of the satchels. Teo's body warmed her ending the shivers in the chilling night air. She could not remember a time before where she was chilled and shivered so much as tonight.

Anh then told Loan it took days by boat to get to land and that she would greet her mother shortly after that. As for right now, she advised Loan to rest. Loan needed to rest and watch over the three girls as well. Tsu, the oldest daughter remained awake, sitting up with her sisters curled at her feet, Ha and Tin slept curled up on the deck beside her.

The boat moved steadily in the flow as low tide drew marsh water into the sea. The crew made a few course corrections before Loan heard small waves curling over in the darkness. She felt the roll of the seas as the boat moved out on the outward flow of water.

The boat cleared the shallows at low tide and entered the deepening waters of the South China Sea. An onshore breeze brought in small waves, adding the sound of water breaking off the bow. Loan was now outside of the confines of the land of her birth, moving out of the cloying grasp of communist Viet Nam. Of this, she had no knowledge. All she knew was that she was returning to Sai Gon by boat.

Fully ignorant of the geography and geo-politics of the world, Loan was denied this knowledge for the next forty months. The full measure of Anh's deception took decades for her to understand. She was only aware of the distinctions between the accent of Vietnamese from the North, from the central high lands and South Viet Nam. She knew of the white people but never understood where they lived. Yet, she was moving inexorably toward that part of the world.

As the boat churned through the darkness, the noisy diesel and night somehow lulled Lam's family and most of the passengers to sleep. The early hours passed without event as the vessel rolled along in outflow of the river that flowed south of Kien Giang out into the South China Sea.

It only had to move south of the Hon Meiu Island and angle eventually to the east. This was 4:00 AM and a thin ribbon of red glow of the sunrise was now delineating the eastern horizon above the South China Sea. If the engine had been quiet, they could have heard the crow of roosters in the fishing villages on the coastline of Hon Meiu.

Moving eight knots through the river outflow with a two-knot current, the fishing vessel gained speed in open water to ten knots if they didn't have a large head wind. In that region, the wind generally prevailed from the west during the morning.

Southeast head winds were common that time of day and switched to the southwest by mid-morning. Regardless, with the sails furled and at that rate, the old fishing boat left sight of land and the view of land-based authorities before sunrise.

Luck holding, they slipped unnoticed past the few government boats that patrolled the shoreline. With all that accomplished, they sailed in a world free of uncle Ho Chi Minh and Viet Cong.

Anh finally relaxed, sitting against the port rail with Lam and her children nestled around them. They sat cocooned among strangers all attempting to find a comfortable position to sleep on the crowded deck.

Anh regretted her lies to Nguyên Loan. In this circumstance, what else could she have done for the girl? Loan was stubborn. Anh felt trapped into lying to the girl. Loan's tough-minded innocence exposed their plans.

Anh and Lam trusted no one in their village with their plans. Now, Anh saw that some of her neighbors mistrusted everyone one else. Her revolutionary neighbors spoke openly of the merits of the new Viet Nam. The same fans of Hanoi and uncle Ho fled on this fishing boat.

Stealthy conspiracy was essential for leaving the coast of Viet Nam and this was before the exodus of people began in earnest in 1978.

Their expedition was one of the first waves of people to flee. A year later, the flood of boat-people caught world-wide attention.

Anh knew the cost to buy passage on this boat. She was surprised that her neighbors had enough gold for passage. Her neighbors had similar thoughts about her and Lam.

Such were the ways of ethnic Chinese in Viet Nam after 1975, keep a low profile, hoard gold, carry cash, and avoid debt. If they had to borrow money, they usually did business with family and close friends.

Viet Nam's banking system shared little with Western banking. When Asians need money, they borrow from relatives in 1970s Asia. Asia remains a cash-economy neglecting debts owed to relatives.

Chinese Asians borrow money and pay it back. If they squander the loan on frivolous and indulgent things, lending family gave warnings and direction. If they lose the money, often as not, they were expected to rectify their debt in one form or another. Servitude, banishment, and suicide are among the debtor's options in such a culture.

In Asia, "flash" seldom meant cash. Showy money became suspect. Smarter wealth kept modest appearance in public. Only the undisciplined rich showed off their money.

Inscrutability originated in Asia. Asians owned the concepts of discretion and deception. In this regard, Anh had been indiscrete. She had made too much show of being able to hire "domestic help." Hiring young Nguyên Loan from Sai Gon was "over the top" even though it was really doing a favor for her mother as an excuse to provide an allotment of regulated rice distribution.

Nguyên Loan's contentious behavior on the street posed hazardous exposure to all of them. Her unhappy lonely presence in the small village telegraphed that something was amiss in Lam and Anh's household.

As it turned out, much was amiss throughout the village. Hanoi's revolutionary dictum directed families to de-urbanize Sai Gon. Resistance to relocation meant time in the "re-education" camps north of Sai Gon. Unrepentant loyalists were sent to "development zones" with insufficient support on worthless soil and meager resources. Everyone schemed to avoid what amounted to perpetual punishment.

Loan's satchel of clothing and food meant she was returning to Sai Gon in less than two weeks after her arrival. Anh did not understand the full extent of Lam's transgressions, but she knew him well enough to suspect the worst. He was a charming scoundrel.

Lam told Anh they had a day or two to make their escape. Villagers noticing Loan's plight could trigger curiosity and solicit undesirable action from Lam's enemies. Loan's presence compromised a margin of time Anh thought they still possessed.

Lam manufactured his personal history and gained prominence in a small community dominated by former Viet Cong. Adding to the rub, he cheated investors in Sai Gon on some real estate sales. They happened to be well connected to NVA and VC well place in Sai Gon. To them it was Ho Chi Minh City.

Loyalists ethnic Chinese were locked out of most business activities after the fall of Sai Gon. They could not buy real estate. Not so for Lam who manufactured a war record to hide in plain sight. Lam cheated former Viet Cong adding significantly to his profile on an enemies list. If revelations from the CIA's Phoenix list failed to find Lam, angry clients could.

Revelation that someone of his position in the community was possibly leaving alarmed and mobilized political operatives. The boat was due to depart in less than ten hours. Perhaps it was enough time to escape.

Unfortunately, this was in a Viet Cong community that worked to midnight and did not put off to tomorrow what they could do today. With the right motivation, they dropped everything to intercept their enemies.

He had moved out of easy reach of VC-city-officials in Sai Gon that he had cheated a year before. Now, he lived among VC who felt slighted by his move from Sai Gon that took an entitled positioned from them.

Two months ago, he became aware of interest in his history in the war. Hanoi was piecing together a different story about Lam's military accomplishments.

Lam felt cornered. Discovery of Loan's crying and carrying money for travel could upset their plans before the end of the night.

While the Viet Nam government poorly managed its porous coastline, it hunted prominent enemies of the state. Anyone identifying a traitor to Ho Chi Minh's declaration on counter revolutionary principles received a bounty. This declaration of death for counter-revolutionaries began in 1945, re-iterated in 1967 and established as national policy in 1976.

Lam manufactured his reputation as a war hero. He built his house-of-cards on the stories of NVA and VC that, as dead men, could protest no different.

Lam was a double-agent in hiding. Anh's identity rode high on a similar "enemies list."

Before long, Lam became considered a fugitive spy. He would be shot as a traitor. Anh faced a similar fate. Their four children became orphans if they were allowed to live.

Both Lam and Anh were as-yet confirmed enemies of the state. It took only one suspicious neighbor or former Viet Cong patriot to sort out Loan's problem. Lam and Anh figured they needed most of twelve hours of invisibility to make their escape. Loan's protest inadvertently shortened their schedule to mere hours.

Life remained far easier for everyone if Nguyên Loan had only taken the money that night and quietly made her way to the train station. Lam thought that their remote community might escape Hanoi's purges for at least another year.

Hanoi steadily improved its grasp on an uncooperative populace. People disappeared more often. Lam sensed their time was up.

When the "carrots" didn't work, the "stick" had to be applied to sort out conflicted populace and convert them to the new religion of socialist-communism. Odd enough, Lam accepted the "carrot" to move to rural communities. It removed him, Anh and their children to the most remote community from Hanoi. He figured they should be out of sight and about as far from Hanoi as one could move.

The remnants of CIA documents left behind were duplicated and distributed to every communist party office and outpost throughout South Viet Nam. Lam, in his true identity, was a high-value prize to a vengeful Viet Cong.

Undetected departure on the boat that night was little assurance of success. Hanoi might attempt to intercept the vessel out at sea.

He had to admit to Anh within the last two days he was wrong about their future in Kien Giang. They would not have permitted Loan to return in view of the change in circumstances. Lam and Anh concluded they were exposed in hours. He and perhaps she could be dead in a day. They considered all this as they heard Loan crying outside their front gate.

Lam and Anh made a most painful decision they have ever made in their lives. Life's cold algebra was simple: they traded Loan's future in Viet Nam for the safety of their six lives. Loan will come with them.

Mail Service from Rac Ghia, Kien Giang to Sai Gon

Sending a message to Nguyën Maï in Sai Gon that Loan was going to be traveling with the family became unlikely. Rural utility structure, much of it improvements made by the Americans, fell apart from poor operation, minimal maintenance and fuel shortages. The Russians were "in-country" as it were and could have helped Hanoi restore and maintain many of the systems. In reality, they served only their interests, which was to enjoy a warm coastline away from the Russian winters and the hospitality of Vietnamese whores. Unlike the Americans, Canadians, Australians and British, Russian money didn't go far. Once Hanoi had consolidated the country, Russian largesse withered.

Russia had bigger problems as their third-world economy attempted to compete with western economies. The complexity of Soviet states and western satellite states consumed their energies. If Russia was so great, why was there a wall that kept them inside the Soviet sphere and unable to express their wonderfulness more openly to the world?

The Russian males that came into the conquered South Viet Nam were Russian Politburo dim witted men. They were dolts of the first order. They had been raised in a communist-bloc universe of structure and papers and pre-scripted lives to manage a cash economy without papers and vastly different expectations. Asian culture identified more with western-style management than Russian command-economy dictations.

Political rewards placed politically astute Russians in place to help the Vietnamese rebuild the economy. The Russian dolts were assigned to assist Vietnamese dolts. The math is simple: Dolt times Dolt equals Dolt-squared. The civilian infrastructure declined.

Consequently, phone service across South Viet Nam fell apart. Most of the working systems connected to post offices where banks of telephones were installed in lieu of providing private service. The new regime parceled out working phone calls for five to ten minutes depending on call traffic and number of working lines.

A phone call was either low-cost or free but it had to be arranged in advance by both parties, most of all calls monitored by the new regime. Vietnamese utilized the mail service to schedule most phone conversations between parties. It was relatively expensive, slow and sometimes failed delivery for many reasons. Many of the Vietnamese postmasters were heroic soldiers of the NVA that could barely spell their name when drafted at the age of 12 from a village in North Viet Nam or a hamlet in the Mekong Delta. Fragmented linguistic skills limited a postmaster's skill sets. Communication between communities was erratic at best and untrustworthy all the time.

Functional post offices became rare. Making or receiving a five-minute phone call often required traveling for thirty minutes to several hours to a location with a working phone system. This all assumed the phone service and erratic electric service worked simultaneously.

Postal systems often failed particularly during the monsoon season. The frequency of utility breakdowns increased significantly after April 30, 1975. Commerce depends on communication which became a seldom thing across Viet Nam, circa 1976 and from there on.

Bottom-line: Sending an important message quickly to Nguyên Maï became impossible. She was still in hiding in March 1977, checking in on the children for a few hours late at night. The "regime" looked for her until late 1979. She expected them to summarily execute her in what westerners termed "extra-judicial executions" if they found her.

Her husband Toan was also hiding in another location. The VC frequently visited the house beating the older boys with sticks asking them about the whereabouts of their parents. They mainly asked about Maï but gladly dragged Toan off for beatings as well when they found him.

The children remember times when Toan had been captured by the VC, returning to the house with bloody long wounds all over his arms, chest and back made from thin wooden whips. He lacked Maï's stealth and cunning.

After a few beatings, Toan developed the knack of concealment. Regardless of the beatings, he kept her locations to himself … if he even knew where she was hiding.

In actuality, Toan and the family seldom knew where she was staying during those years. Mai never talked about who helped her. To her dying day in the fall of 2006, Mai never spoke of her "sponsors" as she called them.

Anh may have tried to send a letter to Mai the night their plans changed to include Loan. She had to put the correspondence in the mail at a post office six kilometers from their home. Door-to-door delivery was erratic unless a citizen paid for the service. The post office with the public phone system was located next to the local police station. One-hundred percent of the staff was former NVA and Viet Cong. All mail was opened and read, all conversations were heard if not recorded.

Lam knew the VC listened in on phone conversations and opened the mail. Spying on citizen communication was part his job. That is how he had learned the state of Hanoi revolutionaries' enemies closed in on him.

Sending mail or making a phone call created one more tip-off that they were escaping. Nguyên Maï never received a message of any kind saying her eight-year old daughter had left the country to destinations unknown. Within two years, Maï concluded that Loan died in typhoon or some other disaster. It was the only way she achieved closure on the loss of Nguyên Xuân Loan.

Decline of Civilization in South Viet Nam

Viet Nam went medieval as Hanoi purged South Viet Nam's management of qualified South Vietnamese. Ignorant unskilled soldiers assumed positions emptied by suicides, summary executions, imprisonment and banishment.

Loyalty to the revolution and participation in the fight was prerequisite to state employment. Unfortunately, conquering comrades made poor administrators, planners, engineers, architects, physicians or anything resembling skilled training and conduct.

Accountability broke down along with the utilities, delaying replacement of unqualified personnel. This reduced efficient modernization of Viet Nam for years.

The rapid fall of Sai Gon surprised both sides of the conflict. Hanoi was ill prepared to manage the southern half of the country with an equal population and twice the land area of North Viet Nam. The ethnic Chinese of Sai Gon, the mandarins of Viet Nam, knew how to operate and sustain modern civilization. They were also members of the resistance to unification of North and South Viet Nam. As a single group of South Vietnamese, ethnic-Chinese *(Sino-Vietnamese as they are otherwise known)* received disproportionate punishment.

Between January 1965 and April 1975, VC murdered ethnic-Chinese that worked for the Americans. Vietnamese of any ethnicity that worked for the CIA were exposed to death sentence by VC and NVA operatives at any time.

Viet Cong surfaced in Sai Gon to assassinate ethnic-Chinese. This gained world attention during the Tet Offensive in 1968 when VC death squads brazenly killed civil and military leadership along with their entire families in the Cholon districts.

After the fall of Sai Gon, ethnic Chinese, particularly in the Cholon district, became broadly persecuted, locked out of commercial enterprise and imprisoned. Military leaders, key politicians, and former CIA operatives were executed wholesale.

Everyone that sided with South Viet Nam was denied work in the new government. The government owned all of the utilities that had been operated by the same people no longer allowed to hold their old jobs. In addition, the VC cadre locked up, killed, or forced into hiding people who knew how to rebuild and run South Viet Nam. Electricity, water, sewer, storm sewer, phones, mail, radio, television broadcast systems fell into disrepair. Infrastructure destroyed in the battles to capture Sai Gon remained broken for decades.

Hanoi won. All of Viet Nam lost. The country went medieval. Anybody that could flee … fled. The remainders endured until civilization returned.

South Viet Nam Merit System

Viet Nam's revolutionary management set up centralized authority based in Hanoi at the northern end of the country, 1,100 miles north of Sai Gon. The primitive phone network, inadequate roads and railroads were seldom improved by B-52 raids up until 1973. The mail system was erratic at best and worse thanks to scrutiny of an untrustworthy government. Hanoi read everyone's mail and listened to available conversations among its citizens.

Hanoi mixed in the spoils of war by staffing southern cities and districts with party members and warriors, regardless of skills, abilities, and experience. Loyalty and heroics ranked higher than competence and created bureaucrats and technicians immune to criticism. Accountability suffered.

Hanoi made thousands of executive mistakes each month to which the country's population lacked an agency of relief. In the first years after it fell to the communist forces, Sai Gon, formerly considered the Paris of Asia, descended into disrepair.

The region fell into darkness as electric utilities went down. Basics of civilization such as sanitation ceased. Urban citizens defecated in canals when the city sewers ceased working.

Former Viet Cong and NVA soldiers as new bureaucrats had minimal *(a.k.a. - zero)* civil management skills. Lacking civility along with training, they directed the maintenance of interconnecting utilities between urban and rural communities. Villages and towns electrified by South Viet Nam and the Americans went back to oil-lamps and manual mechanisms.

Humanity shit in the streets. Trash filled the water ways. People disappeared for no reason. Viet Nam went dark on all levels.

Land use efficiency collapsed. Pumps that fed clean water and removed sewage operated intermittently or stopped. Road repairs and construction projects often interrupted city drainage flooding areas of Sai Gon even during the dry season. Irrigation systems that enabled higher rice production failed and remained out of service. Essential food production withered as farming communities returned to old-world methods. Agricultural technology introduced in the 1960s ceased to function in the late 1970s. South Viet Nam with enviable fertile soils and year-round growing climate struggled to feed itself. Some of the famine was artificial but much of it was real enough.

Vengeance distracted the revolutionary government from improving Viet Nam. Hanoi punished the conquered population to excess and forced many to flee in order to survive.

Similar to communist China's blueprint for reform in five-year plans, they coerced city populations into "northern economic zones" (NEZs). Hanoi confiscated property at will handing homes and land to NVA and Viet Cong cadre.

Sai Gon politburo denied Sino-Vietnamese, Hmong and Montagnard rice rations. Hanoi killed active objectors in the first few years. NVA imprisoned passive objectors for years that often died under cruel working conditions. Tallies vary on the mass suicides, extra-judicial executions and death from imprisonment. In the first two years, at least 300,000 died without due process of civilized law.

South Viet Nam's economy and food production fell as they de-urbanized the city populations under the guise of economic development. Hanoi considered any complaint or non-compliance as criminal based on decrees make back to 1945.

Conversion of reluctant citizens of the newly united country actually never occurred. To this day, local government tracks people that were pro-South house-by-house. Hanoi keeps tabs on the political alignment of the population.

Hunting participants in the counter-insurgency against North Viet Nam eventually ended. Despite a national declaration of amnesty for loyalists four years after Sai Gon fell, it has never been fully implemented. Viet Cong hatred of southern resistance was immense; their witch-hunts were intense. Hanoi's effort to achieve payback became full time obsession after April 30, 1975.

Hanoi expanded tighter control over remote provinces and suppress potential uprising of the urban populations. They honed their skills starting with the final attack on civilian Sai Gon.

The programs were simple: terrorize the civilian population by killing or imprisoning former civil leadership including village chieftains. Fragment communities through re-location of urban populations to rural areas. Keep the remnants of civilian resistance off balance.

As they entered Sai Gon in April 1975, the NVA bombed civilian areas. They indiscriminately shelled three or four districts that made up Cholon in particular. They flattened entire neighborhoods killing hundreds if not thousands in a few days. It is hard to erase the memories of the piles of civilians buried in mass graves after May 1, 1975.

Sai Gon's new leadership opened up internment pits in the neighborhoods to deal with the dead. Mass burials and cremations dealt with incriminating evidence. Hanoi buried their victims and the destroyed the evidence of the rape of South Viet Nam in the spring of 1975.

Viet Cong cadres slaughtered key political and military leadership as they located them from lists prepared months in advance of the invasion. At the same time, they collected lesser offending civilians

374

and stored them away in the "re-education" camps, many of whom remained incarcerated for years.

Many were told the re-education period should last three weeks. It was a total state lie. Many were imprisoned until they died or finally re-emerged two decades later withered and beaten. To this day, some who did not spend time in the re-education camps cannot leave the country because they did not pay their "dues" to the regime in Hanoi.

When some say the above is a lie, then it is a remarkable lie. Many Vietnamese have told me of these situations for years. Somehow, all these different people got the same story straight.

Vengeance was first objective. Determine who of its most virulent enemies were left to locate. As it turned out, this was not hard to do. America's CIA failed to destroy key records as North Viet Nam fell upon the cities of Da Nang, Nha Trang and finally, Sai Gon.

America's CIA left behind files with lists and descriptions of tens of thousands of Vietnamese on America's payroll. The CIA failed to destroy all of its records of its counter-insurgency program known as Phoenix.

That list accelerated Hanoi's ability to sort and locate the most heinous of traitors, the double-agents within the NVA and Viet Cong. The CIA's failure to destroy its records shaved months and years off the time it took take to sort out Lam and others similar to him. They dragged others, hiding in new identities similar to Lam, out of their houses and businesses, killing them in public to intimidate neighbors unless torture produced more names for their enemies list. Then they killed the traitors exhausted of useful intelligence.

The terror continued over years. Former Viet Cong and NVA executed Vietnamese citizens without due process, in part to expose others who were listed on the documents the CIA managed to destroy. They didn't know what documents they were missing and resorted to extra measures to fill in the blanks.

The creaky network of social control rapidly improved. Hanoi steadily closed in on less visible enemies.

Spies infiltrated the NVA and Viet Cong, just as they had within South Viet Nam's government, press, and military. Lam successfully infiltrated the Viet Cong and subsequently the NVA. He had the knack of invisibility. Unfortunately, Hanoi took the time to scrutinize everyone.

Both sides treated spies severely during the war. Most were killed. After the fall of Sai Gon, Hanoi focused on the civilian counter-insurgents more than spies. As it was, both targets were considered versions of the same enemy.

Hanoi viewed counter-insurgency by South Vietnamese as particularly heinous. They were Vietnamese civilians that should have known better than to work for the Americans. To Hanoi, their crimes against the state justified summary executions.

This attitude ignored North Viet Nam's own record of phenomenally egregious activities against its southern brethren between 1958 and 1975. Hanoi purged records of their own atrocities from Vietnamese history (*and later in Viet Nam's internet*), the only villains were the counter-insurgents of Phoenix.

As the state surrounded its targets, outrageous public assassinations created desired secondary effects. It forced hidden traitors to act sooner than later. No one was certain who exactly was on the CIA documents left behind. One ambush might flush another traitor Hanoi had missed. Similar to quail in the brush startled to flight, Vietnamese names on the American CIA's lists flew to sanctuary.

Lam and Anh made the only safe move within Viet Nam they could find. They hid in plain sight with trumped up Viet Cong credentials in a small village south of the Mekong Delta.

Safe cover was offshore. That was if they could abandon their ancestors and post ninety ounces of gold for a one-way trip to the Philippines.

Lam and Anh misread deteriorating conditions in Viet Nam and their own circumstance. It was a mistake to hire Loan to serve them for another year. The necessity of escape presented itself sooner than expected.

Word in Sai Gon was that Hanoi had become curious about Lam's wartime record. Anh learned of this when she returned to Sai Gon to secure Loan's assistance for another year. She paid Maï another 200 kilos of rice shortly after the 1977 Tet celebration.

Mail and telephone calls were difficult, slow and being read and heard. It was expedient to ride her Honda motor-cycle the one-hundred miles to arrange the payment in rice and negotiate Loan's return to her village. While in Sai Gon, Anh's family's network of connections told her of their concern about Lam's future. He was about to be caught.

Anh believed Lam had more time. Unfortunately, she learned that she was being scrutinized as well. Time ran out for both of them. Her own record was becoming known.

Having Loan with them meant they saved the expense of her train ride back to Sai Gon. It was a vacant thought.

The deflating Vietnamese currency held minimal value in the world. The half-million-Dong notes Anh gave to Loan for the bus-ticket and food for the three-day journey was nothing compared to the additional fifteen ounces of gold Lam had to pay for her presence on the boat.

Lam counted on that gold to improve their options in the Philippines. Instead, he gave it to shady men operating an over-loaded old boat. He knew there was a risk adding one more person to an overloaded boat.

Anh's conscience about Loan resisted peace. Their danger: An eight-year old girl on a return trip to Sai Gon by herself revealed flight. With or without them, Loan's presence jeopardized their future.

Silence was essential for escape. Anh made a difficult choice about an aged parent behind in Sai Gon. She was unable to trust her mother with their plans for escape. Her mother's infirm mind could not handle a dangerous truth. Her conversation was a liability. Loan's unguided conversations with strangers on a return trip to Sai Gon added another liability.

Somehow, Anh meant to find a way to contact Nguyên Maï when they arrived in Palawan, Malaysia or Manila in the Philippines. She planned to tell Maï the whole story once they were situated in another country.

Nguyên Mai had been on the run hiding from Hanoi for two years. By what means Anh would locate Maï was uncertain at best. She decided to address the letter to Toan and he could relay it to Maï at the appropriate time. Could he be trusted to understand her coded references? It became moot as she ran out of time to send the letter.

Maï's exchange of letters with Anh timed with each new moon and Buddhist tradition. Anh sent letters precisely on that cycle. It took two new moons before Maï became alarmed about the welfare of her daughter. The chaos in South Viet Nam for the last two years created lapses in communication.

After three months of no communication, Maï went into full alarm. Viet Nam's erratic mail system no longer excused the silence.

She and Lam traveled by motor cycle to Rach Ghia in October 1977 to investigate at great risk of being picked up by the government. To their horror, they found the house occupied by another family. It had been confiscated and given to someone high up the government administration. Maï and Toan's daughter had disappeared without a trace.

Toan inquired publicly while Maï stayed out of sight. They turned up nothing other than the house had been abandoned six months earlier. When the Tet celebration arrived in 1978, Maï and Toan had zero information about Loan's disappearance. Relatives of Anh and Lam living near them in Sai Gon knew little else. After six months, Maï and Toan presumed Loan had died. It was inconceivable to them that she left Viet Nam on a boat and fled to America.

Viet Nam experienced great tragedy in the last few years. Maï and Toan sought closure. Maï was pregnant and due in November 1977. If she bore a girl, she would be named Loan. The New Year's celebration of 1978 was more a funeral and a request for guidance by Buddha over Loan's life.

Nguyên Loan was a durable and bright-minded girl. Maï and Anh knew this. After she turned eight, Loan lacked formal schooling of any kind. That fact weighed on Maï more than Anh. Loan knew little about the world. Any adult thought ignorance was a liability for the child. *(At least in Loan's case. Her ignorance of the world may have been a blessing more than a liability. Her innocence proved a benefit over time.)*

Anh imagined the horror of Maï when she realized Loan had disappeared. Anh asked Buddha for guidance and forgiveness, leaving a small bit of sticky-rice as an offering on the small shrine at the prow of the boat. It was small comfort. Something about this whole situation annoyed her specifically because the hasty departure settled nothing.

Anh cursed the abruptness of leaving so hastily. She suspected there was something Lam failed to tell her. He held back reasons why their plans changed so quickly. Regardless, they had acted and Loan was with them on a passage into the world.

Lam and Anh sought Buddha's guidance and protection for their family. They added the solicitation of acceptance for inadvertently taking Nguyên Mai's youngest daughter with them. They avowed to find a way to return Loan to her family by all means possible.

Viet Nam's borders were porous so it should be possible to get her back in the country the same way. Lam planned to ask the boat's pilot to return Loan to Viet Nam shortly before they landed. The unspent Vietnamese money should ease the negotiation for Nguyên Loan's return to Sai Gon. They planned to amend this trespass with Mai and all of Loan's family once they were succeeding in America.

Anh had only just learned that Nguyên Maï was pregnant again with one more child, her eleventh. Toan managed to impregnate Mai again despite the fact she was constantly on the move. At some point, Anh planned to tell Loan that a younger brother or sister will greet her when she returned to Sai Gon.

Lam and Anh shook their heads at the thought of a Chinese woman bearing eleven children and adopting six children by her errant husband. Seventeen children, make that sixteen due to the loss of Cüöng, was an unimaginable family size. The durable Nguyên Maï was fifty years old and expecting another child after bearing ten children with her difficult husband.

Loan should know about this soon. They planned to tell her all of the details at some point as their journey to America progressed.

As they left Viet Nam, they decided that it was too soon to tell Loan of new events in her family. They needed to keep peace on the crowded deck. They had enough of Loan's persistence for one day. Soon enough, they could tell her they were head to another country, to another part of the world. They also planned to tell her they had a plan to get her back to Viet Nam. The lies kept coming.

First Morning on the South China Sea

The modified high-prow fishing boat was able to navigate invisibly through the night without incident. The sun rose above the thin rolling edge of the eastern sea. This was early-April after the vernal equinox *(March 21)*. The sun rose above the tropic of cancer, a little to the north of east.

The sun in the tropics rose quickly and illuminated a carpet of inert bodies on the deck. A few of the adults had remained awake through the night helping the crew stand watch for government patrol boats.

Evil targets the unwary. They heard unfounded rumors about pirates raiding refugee boats. They stayed awake reasoning that sleeping invited trouble. It was not an exclusively Asian idea but still a persistent one. Now out of sight of the shoreline and soon to be out of reach of Viet Nam, the boat rolled on gentle swells churned west at first, then south around the southern tip and then east north east toward the Philippine coastline.

The crew's navigation system consisted of several sizes of compass. One was large and well-constructed. It was American made and incriminating evidence if they were caught. They steered in a direction keeping the Vietnamese coastline barely in view.

The crew possessed a faded nautical map of the southern tip of Viet Nam. It was printed in English showing magnetic compass correction graphics on three parts of the map. It also had lines showing depths and shallows. Most of the navigation information was meaningless to the crew.

The crew relied on their compass and their eyeballs. Unfortunately, none had ever been out of sight of land. When the land began pealing back to the north, they were told in Vietnamese to head to the right of the compass bar, to go "Thông dụng," to go slightly north of due east.

Sunrise

The passenger's spirits lifted with the sunrise. They had been quiet. Many of their emotions conflicted between elation of escape and leaving Asia perhaps never to return. Sorting their minds kept them silent.

There were many reasons why each passenger was on board heading into an alien world. Some had family waiting for them in North America and Australia. Others had no choice but flee or suffer if not die.

If any of them were in Lam's predicament, they and he were keeping it secret. If the boat was captured by the communist regime, they interrogated everybody. He knew most of the passengers faced prison. He was a dead man. He could put those fears finally to rest if they continued running east without incident.

Lam was giddy with delight to be on the water moving away from Viet Nam. He was no longer anxious about hearing a midnight knock on the door to find a gun in his face. He wondered what the village might think finding their house empty. From the looks of the passengers on board, his village had more than his family's disappearance to think about.

Better for him, he had plates of gold sewn into his pants. It was enough to make a start in America. Some of it came from ill-gotten gains in Sai Gon. He made it out with most of his gold save for what he had to spend to bring Loan on board.

Anh, on the other hand was trying to find solace as she watched over her four children sleeping, curled up against her. Loan lay wrapped around the children feigning sleep.

Her attitude might have been different at that moment if Loan had taken the money and headed back to Sai Gon the night before. Once they made landfall, she could tell Loan the truth. They could sort out their options in Manila first and then get word to Loan's mother by any means possible. Their future was highly variable.

All of the passengers left their homes and their country that night. Almost all knew only South Viet Nam. Most of them were upbeat by the fact they had passed out of the coastline with ease. They knew the next schedule: run like hell to the east and locate safe harbor.

The adults had several days ahead of them to sort out where they had been and where they were going. A few of the adolescent children knew they were leaving their country of birth and were told to keep facts to themselves. The younger children were on a voyage to another part of Viet Nam.

Fishing boats worked off the coast before dawn. The crew knew they had been seen.

Fishermen kept their silence. Standard Vietnamese ship-to-shore communication was a flashlight, a waving hand, or a flag made of colored shirts to distinguish Vietnamese from Thai.

The fisherman might report a large fishing craft headed out to sea, nothing more. A question remained whether another boat could see all the people on the deck, hidden by the high gunwales. A sure giveaway was the way the boat was riding in the water. Fishing boats go out empty and ride high and returns loaded and ride low if the fishing had been good. This boat was headed out into deep waters loaded and low with a five thousand kilo cargo of smuggled humanity.

Within a few months, tens of thousands fled each month. It was hard to ignore boats tied up on river or anchored near shore that disappeared never to return. The exodus emptied entire villages and hamlets. The population thinned in the cities and towns. Traffic patterns changed in part due to rationing of fuel and lower population.

Most of the passengers aboard carried food for a week and money assumed to sustain them for a month, enough for a start if they found work in Manila. The United Nations relocation camps were two to three years away from operating to handle the influx of refugees. The only hope was making safe landing in Manila or at Subic Bay.

Any job, no matter how menial, was salvation in a place where you could still find work and keep what you earned. They knew the chaos they left behind. Anything had to be better than what they were escaping. They knew they could make it to Thailand, the Philippines and Malaysia and that others had made it to the western countries.

Tens of thousands of Vietnamese boat people fell upon struggling third-world economies with high unemployment and squalor. The first-landing countries did not welcome the sudden influx of Vietnamese. No one in those countries welcomed strangers on their shores.

If they made it to America, Australia or to Canada, the rumor was they would ask themselves why they waited so long to escape. By American standards, the emigrants lived in near-squalor. Westerners, they thought, had a poor measure of what real squalor could be when the country endured artificial famines, persecution, torture and murder such as they had in Viet Nam in the last two years.

They Fled Asia

For some, this was the second exodus after migrating from Southern China two or three decades before. For the first time in all of the passenger's lives, they left the continent of their origins and the lands of their birth. They began their exodus from Asia by boat.

Over long unrecorded histories spanning hundreds of thousands of years, a pre-Asian people had migrated out of Africa and spread across northern and eastern land masses. The original people that settled the eastern lands changed and adapted to the new lands, evolving different appearance in their skin, size, facial features, and languages. They developed unique cultures with advanced civilizations, some with six-thousand year histories that predate the Egyptian empire that built the pyramids and embalmed their kings. The largest segment of the population of the eastern lands was ethnic Chinese, a people with the longest surviving language and culture in the history of the world.

They became the people connected to a land mass known today as Asia which starts essentially east of Constantinople and runs to the International Date Line. Their connections went deeper than geography. It is the land of their ancestors. The bones in the graves, the monuments to their families and the spirits of their ancestors held them to those lands.

Asia is more than real estate. It is an environment of long ethnic blood lines, of ancient traditions, of families, their feelings for the land and their spiritual home.

They were Asians leaving their most beloved mother. They fled Asia.

Most bet their lives on making it half-way around the world to another continent populated by different peoples, culture and language. They bet on North America, a continent of a few nations with a working history barely 400 years old. It had been everything else but a home to Asian people.

Caucasians dominated the population of North America in 1977. Yet, it possessed people of every race known to man, among the least being Asians. Americans spoke English, a language far different from every Asian language.

Vietnamese bet their lives on establishing life in an alien world where they were a minority among minority populations. Nothing in America was familiar.

Most of the passengers had lived and traveled within 100 kilometers of their birthplace. Now, they embarked on a journey to a continent 15,000 kilometers away, on a boat intended for river travel in the sheltered waters of the Mekong Delta. They expected to connect to other Vietnamese who made it to America on airplanes and ocean-worthy ships before the fall of Sai Gon.

These passengers embarked on a river fishing boat to cross 800 kilometers of open water to the Philippines as their best opportunity to gain asylum. They had to avoid the rumored Thai and Vietnamese pirates that plundered and murdered refugees.

They assumed on limited knowledge they could find sanctuary by heading east to Manila. After a time, they believed they could find a means to reach America.

Many of them had some idea of what it was to migrate and settle unwelcome in another country. Older passengers had moved to Viet Nam from Southern China before and after World War II (1938-1945). Ethnic Chinese's ancestors had settled in Viet Nam over centuries. At times, the native Kinh people of Viet Nam rejected Chinese openly but the immigration overwhelmed Southeast Asia. It became one of the sources of tension that fed civil war aspects of the Viet Nam War.

Surprise of the Americans

Hanoi promoted from radio broadcasts and via village assemblies that America intended to colonize Viet Nam for decades. As a former French colony, it had an aspect of truth as the western people exploited Asia in the previous centuries. Yet the propaganda fell on deaf ears among the Vietnamese that fought with the American military.

Many witnessed an unexpected openness of the Americans. Some of them had fought North Viet Nam side-by-side with the westerners. Americans G.I.s seemed to only want to survive their "tour" and go home. In effect, they were tourists. This was not the attitude of soldiers seeking to make Viet Nam their next new state or colony of America.

Americans were an array of all races of man. Outside of military rank, social class among a particular race lacked distinction. Some Vietnamese were aware of separation between white and black Americans even though the United States ended slavery a century before. Yet, America's military was populated with different races down to platoons. ARVN units had one-race-only military units. The United States did not.

Among the "white countries," Americans appeared more casual as compared to the British and perhaps less irreverent than Australians. One thing stood out, the Americans spent their money as freely as anybody seldom haggling over price as was the custom of Asians. Enterprising Vietnamese prospered in association with the Americans. The generosity left an indelible mark in South Viet Nam for decades to come.

As in any society that has many levels of good and bad manners, there were ugly Americans capable of poor behavior and cruelty. On the whole as an ally during the war, America left positive impressions among the South Vietnamese. Years later, an "Amer-Asian" young man characterized it simply, "The Americans came, they built, they fought and died with us, and they left."

All of the Vietnamese knew of the tens of thousands of Americans that had died or left the battlefield gravely injured, returning to America, fate unknown. American soldiers fell far short of sainthood. Yet, no other nation or people of the earth had done that with or for the Vietnamese. No liberal historian can argue this. America left its blood and treasure in the soil of Viet Nam and went home.

There was no evidence that America planned to annex Viet Nam. Yet, Viet Nam became a part of the American heart. The men and women that returned home alive and dead place an indelible mark in their American sense of history.

Many Americans that got out in the nick of time, so to speak, were relieved but their next thoughts went to those who were left behind. It was one of those "Oh My God Moments" when they realized all the Vietnamese massed at the U.S. Embassy gate that couldn't leave and had to return home to wait out the worst days of their lives.

The collapse of South Viet Nam went badly. Many blamed America for insufficient support. Yet, as the dust settled after the fall of Sai Gon, the stories of the massive American airlift and boat-transport of people circulated on the streets of Sai Gon.

United States transport pilots were totally exhausted as they risked death to extract vulnerable Vietnamese out of Viet Nam. As the North Vietnamese Army shelled and bombed neighborhoods in Sai Gon, the transports and helicopters flew in and out down to the last possible minute. I mean this ... down to the last possible minute.

Regretfully, Americans failed to rescue over fifty thousand Vietnamese deemed immediately vulnerable to North Viet Nam's vengeance. Even so, they evacuated over one-hundred and thirty thousand Vietnamese in the last few weeks of April 1975. By the numbers though, there were 19 million Vietnamese who preferred to be somewhere else than in South Viet Nam.

Something was different about the Americans. As complete and competent saviors, they screwed up. To its credit, the United States of America tried to save as many as they could before the communists took over. Their effort continued after the fall of Sai Gon. Americans continued to intercept and transport Vietnamese refugee that made it out of Viet Nam. Without exception, any Vietnamese refugee that met the criteria of at-risk-politics was transported America. No other country could boast of larger effort. Never in the history of the world has such an effort been documented.

Yes! America blew it! But no other country attempted to make amends as did the United States of America and its allies.

Unpredictable Receptions

Knowledgeable passengers expected to pass through a gauntlet of unpredictable receptions in the Philippines and Malaysia. Outlying countries had their own struggles. Refugees in such numbers were unwelcome.

Older passengers expected difficulty. Ethnic and religious differences posed unpredictable conflict. Much of Malaysia was Muslim. This boat was loaded with Buddhists, Catholics and Protestants. Making landfall in the Philippines, largely Catholic in Manila, was more tenable.

There might be danger for them on Malaysian shores. Unfortunately, there were jungle tribes throughout the archipelago that wanted nothing to do with the Vietnamese. Those stories are for another edition of these books on the Vietnamese exodus.

The Philippines possessed a variety of friendly religious cultures. Unfortunately, it was an impoverished country with simmering and active civil conflicts. Some of the older men and women on board expected trouble. Yet, they paid their gold for the voyage expecting to take their chances with the unknown.

It was too much to hope that a passing ship would intercept them and bypass the whole sub-Asiatic mess. They had to make landfall somewhere to the east or south of Viet Nam.

American military naval and air bases in the Philippines provided one deciding factor. The United States was one of the biggest payrolls in the Philippines. Therefore, Americans had some influence in Manila over the fate of Vietnamese refugees.

Many Vietnamese figured the Americans would have figured out how to get them to America. There were emerging mechanisms to transport Vietnamese to the United States once they landed on Philippine soil. It would not be fully in place until 1980.

The uncertainty of their prospects and the painful separation from their Asian heritage posed endless grief. It is simply impossible to express the sadness of leaving after so much hope and sacrifice. With no relief in sight, the only choice for a better future lay in flight.

Dwelling on the utter chaos, heart breaking losses and wasted lives of the last two years produced nothing. The only mechanism to preserve their sanity was to make an effort to improve their future. It was better to look forward to assure anything at all.

They had lost their beautiful verdant fertile Viet Nam. Losses are temporary if they could change their circumstance. In the Anglo-countries of America, Canada, Britain, France and Australia, they could prosper. With prosperity, they will find a way to return and fix their broken paradise.

South Viet Nam was only conquered. It could be retaken. All the land and most of the people remained. As long as the Asian people remembered it as a freer place and survived, and then thrived, they had a chance to turn Viet Nam into something better.

Some on board that boat, which had only just left, made plans to return. The only reason they were passengers on an over-loaded boat is they had run out of options or were about to die.

The crew had rolled up the sails on the spars, waiting for a favorable breeze. The wind had to exceed four knots from the right direction to assist the work of the sixty-five horsepower diesel engine. The tail wind failed to rise. Later in the morning, they unfurled the sails to shield the passengers from the sun.

Families made do with little more than a few pairs of clothes, bulging satchels of sticky rice, beans, bean curd and sweet potatoes mixed together. The passengers moved about the deck to stretch and reposition their belongings. Before long, people picked their way among the crowded deck on the way to the stern to use the ship's "latrine." The crew shifted people to create aisles for moving about on the deck. There was little room on board to do much else. The deck was jammed with human cargo.

Men watched the horizon for other ships and other than passing fishing vessels that lacked ship-to-shore radios to notify authorities. It appeared they evaded Vietnamese shore patrols. The only expected obstacles ahead lay weather and, if such existed, pirates. Barring the issue of pirates, the race was on to cover the long stretch of sea between them and the Philippine coastline. They needed to be close to shore before weather changed.

Diaspora: The Vietnamese Exodus

Fishing vessels out on the open sea witnessed the passing of another refugee boat, one more vessel laden with passengers headed out to other countries. The fishing would not return with food to feed a persecuted population verging on starvation. It was the beginning of hundreds of thousands of desperate Vietnamese that fled in the same manner. One selfish thought of the fisherman that watched the passing of their countrymen out into the world: another fishing boat fell out of service to the country. The real and artificial food shortage grew with one less working-boat and its crew.

Merchant ships and fisherman faced eventual government prosecution and deteriorating quality of life. Life on the water gave some margin of freedom but they still asked the same question, "When might they be able to make the same run for a better life? "

There was one main reason most fishermen were reluctant to flee. They knew the risks more than most anyone else. They had better knowledge of the danger of passage on a long run across the South China Sea. Fishermen lost count of the debris fields from another submerged boat, bloated corpse and bloodied empty hulls stripped of valuables and set adrift, whereabouts of the passengers and crew unknown.

Ruthless Vietnamese, Thai, and Malaysian pirates worked the South China Sea brutalizing and killing the men and raping the women with impunity. Fishermen knew of the boats adrift with children that died of starvation after the adults had been killed. Could this passing boat over-loaded with adults and children make it? By all accounts, they knew that roughly one third of the passengers ended up at the bottom of the sea.

It did little good for party loyalists to report the refugees to authorities. The vessel was out of practical reach of the Vietnamese patrols. Viet Nam lacked the economic resources to pursue every boat that crossed the twelve-mile international boundary.

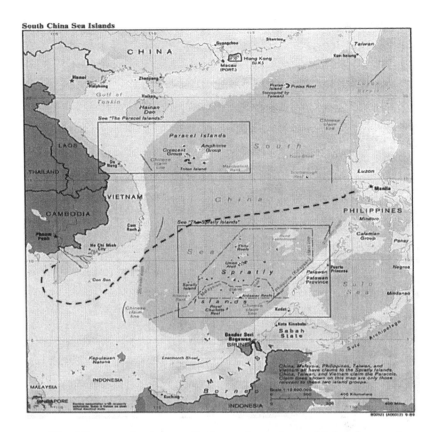

South China Sea Islands

Viet Nam made claims of a larger boundary which other nations ignored. Viet Nam was powerless or unwilling to contest much of anything on the open seas. Regardless of Viet Nam's illegitimate claim of territory, the British and American ships that could help the boat people gave the larger boundary some credence.

Russia operated naval craft with the North Vietnamese. Boundary issues could escalate into international incidents. The sensitivities of the cold war reduced the aid government navies might provide to refugees when they needed it most. Before they had crossed half of the east-west expanse of the South China Sea, no local nation supported their flight to freedom.

In difficult waters, refugees hoped to intercept a passing Japanese or western freighter. The ships had to be of a size and weight to easily pick up the refugees or provide assistance. Merchant boats could provide assistance.

Oil tankers were less viable rescuers. An oil-laden tanker took ten miles to stop. Captains had their orders. The Vietnamese were damned to watch the behemoths sail on.

Failing rescue, the refugee boats continued to the Philippines or south to Malaysia. Malaysia was closer but less accommodating to refugees than the Philippines.

The vessel churned on through the late morning to raise its sails to exploit a strong tail wind and reduce fuel consumption. The passengers came to know each other a bit. There was little else to do but talk to pass the time. They all sat on a crowded deck as the boat cranked on to the east, no longer under the ominous watch of Hanoi. Regardless, they guarded their conversations out of habit, exploring more than opening up with strangers.

The ethnic mixtures were mostly Chinese including the crew. Some were a blend of French and Kinh. There were few elderly people on the boat. The rest of the passenger list was made up of parents and children. Of the twenty plus children on board, most of them were under the age of twelve. The only childless adults were the young crew, three of which were first cousins to the captain. Of the one-hundred-and-four passengers and crew, few could swim or tread water.

The vessel maintained the sails until the wind settled down by midday, resuming engine use through the afternoon. Once out of sight of land, there was less urgency to make time to an uncertain landing.

The cloudless night was full of stars. These stars were more numerous and as clear and Loan could ever recall. For the first time, she could see the Milky Way separate from the humid haze of the coast near Kien Giang. She wanted to know the name of what others called the "The Milky Way" but Anh and Lam were ignorant about this curiosity of the sky. The drudgery of a hard life left little time for contemplation of a larger universe. Loan was entertained by the magnificence of the heavens until she fell asleep.

They ate, slept and used buckets of sea water to clean themselves. They ate sparingly from their stores of food uncertain of when they could resupply. Unable to carry much water of their own, they drank from sour-tasting drinking water stored in barrels in the vessel's hold. They had a toilet set up in the stern with partitioned areas where men and women sat over the water and cleansed themselves as necessary from a bucket with an aluminum ladle that had the shape of a frying pan. There was no such thing in 1977 Viet Nam as toilet-paper for the poor and the refugee.

Asians, particularly Sino-Vietnamese are fussy in the extreme about a quality diet and cleanliness. They made do with what they had on the vessel to manage the unpleasantness of a body in the tropical heat but it was not in their nature to be unwashed. Anh's primary focus was on keeping her children clean and she manipulated the crew to bring her fresh sea water to keep her daughters and son clean. She nursed the lye soap sparingly. She made sure her family was cleaned up as much as possible. Some of the passengers were beginning to have embarrassing odor. Anh tolerated none of that from her family.

Lam was a different issue, Asian men not wanting to appear run by their wives, but at the end, he succumbed to sponging off his body. In the heat of the day, it served to cool him off. His resistance to Anh's instructions was mostly for show.

Asian men ran the show but their Asian women know where their men stored their pride. In regards to hygiene and the management of Asian wives, a sharp word preceded a swift kick to the balls. Prudent Asian men knew this risk of pushing their dominance too much.

Anh wanted Lam to change his clothing while there was a laundry on board (the bucket of seawater). To Chinese women, body odor could not wait for landfall. Clean up or take a small fist or foot to the crotch. No issue here. Lam cleaned up.

The passengers had little else to do but watch the horizon and chat about what they might find in another country. Few of the adults had ever traveled outside of Viet Nam. Some knew of the Philippines and a limited geography beyond. Many could converse in either or both of Vietnamese or Cantonese. Few could read or write both languages. Many that worked with the Americans, British and Australians learned to speak, read and write English. Regardless, the basic knowledge of the scale of the world was unknown to most of the passengers. Many younger than fifty had known war in Viet Nam most of their lives. It disrupted and molded their education.

The appearance of the round-eyed white men from Europe, particularly French colonists and Catholic Missionaries and then English speaking white and black men and their women from Australia,

England and North America were a part of what was to them an anomaly. The round-eyed non-Asians, mostly from America, might as well have been from Mars. They invented telephones, television, cars and powered flight. Americans had gone to the moon and back. They were wealthy beyond measure. How would they treat people who developed and accomplished none of that?

Of all the non-Asian people in their experience, the Americans fought *__beside them and died beside them__*. The French were conquerors and administrators.

This bears repeating: The Americans *__fought beside them and died with them.__* The Americans, for all of their failings, left behind hospitals, roads, and bridges. They built electrical and sanitation systems better than anything they knew. Many Americans became brothers in the trenches with the South Vietnamese. Each wanted to have a life of their own after their "tour" was up and out of the hell hole of Viet Nam.

Americans wanted to enjoy their produce without having to share their productions with self-entitled bureaucrats. Compared to the other communities, the Americans gave of their lives and their wealth. The Vietnamese who knew them were uncertain whether they received anything for their sacrifice of 58,000 dead and 400,000 wounded. Who were these Americans? Why did they look similar to the French and the Russians, yet act so differently? Was there not a specific expectation of how white males act?

When Sai Gon and the south fell, why were the Russians that on the whole looked much like Americans but acted worse than the French. The Russian men were coarse and poor by comparison. Many of them were perpetually drunk and without manners sober or not.

After the fall of Sai Gon, the Viet Cong legacy ran the show as best they could. The Russians came in and served themselves. It enlarged the apparent differences between the Eastern Block and the Americans. The Russians were all about themselves, the Americans appeared to strive to a higher ideal.

The difference in approach to life: produce and reap what you own versus produce and give to others. It seemed to be the mechanism behind why the Americans appeared so rich. The Russians were assigned to a life. The Americans chose among their possible lives. By Vietnamese standards, the Americans were as free as anyone could hope.

Those that had worked with American and British forces learned more of the western world but largely for most Vietnamese, few had a clear picture of the world beyond Indochina and Asia. They only knew the way out by rote, make it to Manila, and file papers with the United States and other allies of the Viet Nam War.

Big Rule: Don't stay in the Philippines. Get there and get out. Above all else, they knew to seek out Catholic charities where possible, particularly in Manila. There were Baptist and Methodist Vietnamese but above all, most of the Christian segments of Viet Nam were Catholic.

Beyond that limited knowledge, they speculated on what they knew about life in Australia, Canada and the United States. All they believed or knew was that it was likely better elsewhere in the world than it was in Viet Nam. Much as they all loved the intensely green and fertile country they used to know, it was gone for now.

Intolerable evil occupied the land. They could only look forward to cross the sea and start another life among a people in a country mostly made up of non-Asians.

The Storm

Approaching the second afternoon after thirty-six hours at sea, hazy blue skies gave way to the billowing tops of clouds on the horizon. The western horizon darkened quickly in the late afternoon. Anh instructed Loan to help everyone to eat earlier than normal. She insisted they eat in case it rained and ruined exposed food.

More than just rain was coming their way from the looks of the sky. Squall lines blossomed west of the boat. A placeless panic rose in her as she watched the clouds build in to a dark slate-colored wall many miles west of the east-headed vessel. There was something about the boat's stability.

The Vietnamese man on shore that had been listening to a news radio channel on the long-wave radio had been right about the weather. Predicted storm clouds rose to the north. Loan sat there on the deck with the children doing as she was told, taking care of them, playing with the girls, holding Teo, thinking now and then about going home.

Loan was eight years old. What else do girls at that age think about? Mostly, she played with the little boy and teased the girls with small outrageous things about Teo's mastery of their future lives.

She noticed the building clouds to the west of the boat. She thought that the slate-blue and gray wall of clouds behind them was beautiful in the afternoon sunlight.

Weather on the South China Sea had a wild beauty best appreciated from shore. The grandeur of the open sky changing into a storm was lost on the make-shift crew of men. Building thunderheads to the west of them meant big winds. Clouds rapidly blew up into squall lines in the late afternoon as the atmosphere began to cool.

The rising seas threatened them. They had rested in the afternoon assuming the evening's duties might be full. Their duties might become impossible.

All of the adult passengers and older children on the deck of the vessel noticed the buildup of clouds behind them. As Anh watched the darkening west wall of clouds, it occurred to her that she should tell Loan the truth about where they were headed. She considered if it was better to tell her now in the middle of the passage or later as they entered Philippine waters. Loan believed she was getting closer to Sai Gon. Was it better for Loan to know the truth now or later? As the weather changed, she thought that Loan should be less distracted believing they headed to Sai Gon.

Wind gusts rose as the front shifted to birth confusing crosswinds. The weather changed faster than Anh anticipated. She postponed her confession to Loan until after the storm passed. The boat was riding the water well. There would be better time to talk in a few hours.

The wind change introduced small sprays of water off the tops of waves wetting the passengers. In the hot sun, the cooling water was welcome. In the late afternoon without direct sunshine, the sprays of water brought unwanted chill.

The storm fronted a series of squall lines that traversed the South China Sea whipping up the seas into choppy large waves ahead of it. The small waves built quickly into chop. A prolonged wind across of a fetch of several hundred miles enlarged the waves. The combination of swells and waves built on top generated larger rough seas. The sea appeared to rise.

The conditions exceeded the structural capabilities of a traditional coastal fishing boat. This was a converted river boat with gunwales augmented with rough lumber, stiffened with scrap discarded during the war. It had been refitted in secret by farmers and merchants.

It had been operated by young men who were now dead. Now, the boat was operated by Vietnamese men who had never run a boat on the backwaters of the Mekong Delta or the open sea.

The heavy old vessel was ill suited for a rough sea like the one blowing up. For all its modifications, this was a fishing boat, not a passenger boat. The deck was loaded with thousands of pounds of humanity and their belongings. The vessel lacked inert ballast to stabilize the top load. The lack of sub-deck ballast enabled the old boat to ride differently, top heavy, adding abnormal stresses to the keel and deck-work.

As the storm loomed up behind them in the west, the overloaded vessel seemed to shrink. Under stress of the impending weather, it was no longer a powered escape vessel. It was apparent to most of the adults that they were now at full risk. Some passengers knew the boat's weakness in rough seas and passed on their opinions to others ratcheting up anxiety among the adults.

As the vessel began its turn into the wind to reduce taking on water, it broke. Its bones cracked nearly all at once within the first minutes of plowing into the waves.

In another circumstance, the crew retired this boat retired to an inland waterway to wait out storms. It was five hundred miles out from the farthest point it had ever floated in all its existence as a fishing boat and river barge. It was now a passenger ferry. It was failing its assignment as a floating vessel of any kind. Its dead wood was water-soaked and softening to a point of failure. The boat was doomed to become an anchor.

Anh looked at Nguyên Loan with eyes mirroring the horror now falling upon them, hard sharp eyes expecting absolute obedience to her last instruction to Loan. It was all that was that was left for Anh to do, could do, for Loan and her longtime friend, Nguyên Maï.

Anh had postponed mailing a letter to Mai, planning to correspond from Manila about the circumstance of her daughter. She knew they'd die here. The letter ended up at the bottom of the sea. Nguyên Maï would have to wait two decades for real word of her daughter's welfare.

Anh's heart was collapsing, breaking, as certain catastrophe fell upon her family, her friend's daughter, the overloaded fishing boat and all of its too-many passengers. Generations of family were about to perish.

Afloat in the South China Sea

Those were all the last moments of the boat that was now going over and over in Loan's thoughts, the sudden swelling of the storm and the loss of everyone counting herself. She was in the water and afloat.

Loan focused on three tasks:

(1) Hold on to the board,
(2) Stay on top of the board and
(3) Pick the best time to draw a breath.

Loan could only think of the next moment and the simple tasks she had to manage. She dutifully kept repeating in her mind the last instruction from Anh, "Hold on Loan, Hold on." She said. She whispered it in Vietnamese when she exhaled, "Nắm chặt Nắm chặt." and repeated the phrase in her mind when she cautiously inhaled.

The image of the last scene on the boat burned into Loan's memory. Anh stood there on the deck with the smaller children on her hips, the boat tilting to starboard. The big waves breaking over the port gunwale of the wallowing boat rendered the authoritative self-reliant ever-instructive ever-deceptive Lam entirely helpless.

He held the older girls in his arms with the right side of his head still stained in blood from his lopped-off ear. The pirates had hacked his right arm as well and the congealed blood stained him down to his waist. He lacked any means of protecting them standing there with Anh the younger two children, dutiful Loan standing by them. Lam did this knowing he had sewn fifty ounces of gold plates into his clothing. He didn't know how to swim, yet he carried two kilos of gold on his body. The gold might as well have been lead.

Lam had no swimming skills. He kept the gold in the end as he lost his life. He held two of his children and drowned with them in seconds.

That was the last images of the family Nguyên Xuân Loan had before she was washed across the tilting deck and into the water. Lam held the girls as the boat frame went under water. Anh held Teo and the other daughter for seconds above the surface. Without swimming skills, Anh sank below the surface seconds after Lam. Their daughters and son sank with them. With arms full, Loan believed Lam and Anh sank like stones clutching their children until their life stopped.

Loan did as she was told, clinging to the precious rectangle of deck plank. Her legs dangled in the water, the waves rolling up and down, the froth of the wave tops and the wind driving stinging rain into her face and arms. The tropical sea water was cool, cold to her skin but warm enough to sustain her. The coolness of the water reduced the pain of her forearms rubbed raw where she gripped the rough edges of the plank. She repositioned her arms to ease the pain trying to find an easier way to hold it to her chest.

The sea churned by the squall broke up what was left of the boat that remained near the surface. Most of the wood was saturated. Without intrinsic buoyancy, most of the boat sank.

Loan had grabbed a dry section that could sustain part of her body above water. If the wood had been a bit larger, she might not have been able to reposition it without having to loosen her grip every time and risk losing it in the churn of the sea. Had the wood been smaller, it might not have kept her afloat well enough. It was enough to grasp and keep her forty pounds and forty-two inch length afloat. It was barely sufficient to help her keep her head above water. As it turned out, it was just enough and not too much.

A wave crested and rolled her over where she kicked her legs in the water to reposition the plank beneath her. She experimented with the motion of her legs as she didn't understand how to move them to propel her body. For the next twelve hours, she rolled over with the waves every ten to fifteen minutes. All she kept in her mind was to right her body on top of the plank and hold on, sucking air in carefully to avoid inhaling sea water.

Loan knew nothing of thermodynamics and hypothermia. Ignorant of how to move her legs preserved her body heat. Keeping her head and chest out of the water seemed more chilling. Yet, she kept her head high to breath. This behavior kept her from losing heat to the water. She tried to breathe without choking on sea water. The sea was warm enough. Her metabolism stirred by staying on the board balanced her heat loss. She chilled but slowly.

She experimented with her position on the board. Waves knocked her over when she rode the board too high. She had trouble breathing when she lay on the board too low.

Except for the sound of the wind and the frothing tops of waves breaking over, it was quiet. The voices, the cries of the others had ceased. Lam, Anh and the children fell into the water behind her as she was sucked under by the vortex of the sinking hull. When she surfaced, the family was nowhere in sight.

Before she surfaced, something, perhaps the plank had struck her head. She bled from a cut on her forehead, tasting iron in the blood that briefly flowed down her face. As she focused on using the plank, it took minutes of her attention away from Anh, Lam and the children. When she finally thought to look for them, they were gone.

The tops of the waves concealed anyone or anything floating nearby and the wind carried off sounds made by anyone alive and calling for help. In the troughs of the waves, she felt as if she was down in a pit looking up at the high tops of the waves.

Heavy showers in the squalls added to the noise as heavy raindrops noisily roiled the surface of the waves. The surface of the water took on a rough look until the rain stopped. It chilled her but refreshed her attention. Had she known, she would have tried to catch the water in her mouth as it was free of salt.

After being packed on the deck of the boat with the remaining ninety-some souls, she was suddenly alone. She had little time to think about her isolation. She focused solely on staying on top of the plank of wood and drawing a breath when her mouth was clear of the sea.

After a time in the water, Loan ceased looking for anyone. She concentrated on keeping the board beneath her and breathing amidst the rain and the splash of the waves.

The sun was setting and created a new concern. How would she manage in the darkness?

Tropical darkness arrives quickly. All that Loan could do was stay atop the board and breathe. The darkness reduced her sense of up and down requiring new attention to the slightest information that told her she was oriented above the plank of wood. All was blackness with a boundary between air and water she felt but could not see.

She had little time for distraction. The last hours of terrifying events replayed in her mind at brief moments until another wave reminded of her basic tasks.

The tumbling motion of the sea overwhelmed her senses and numbed her thoughts. She managed a simple summary of her predicament. She was an obedient eight-year old girl stranded by herself in the warm salty South China Sea. She was holding onto a chunk of wood that could barely sustain part of her body and head above water.

She concentrated on basic tasks. Stay on the plank, draw a breath carefully, and exhale it. Draw another breath. Stay on the plank. Hold on in the light. Hold on in the dark. Hold on when the sun rises again.

Hold on … Hold on … Hold on … Hold on.

Boat and Wave Collision: The Sinking

Two hours before, as a line of dark clouds gathered to the west in the afternoon overhead, the wind came up quickly. Against all prayers, the feared storm arrived. The wind gusts arose from behind the vessel, raking the surface of the waves in large fans of ripples. The sea appeared to rise as the waves grew.

The boat enjoyed a tail wind all day. They used the sails to help the engine and conserve fuel. Yet, when it began gusting from behind, it could over-stress the frame of the boat. They reefed the sails. The fan-shaped patchwork canvas sails were lowered to the spar that rattled over the heads of the passengers huddled on the deck.

The Vietnamese refugees, "boat people" as they would be known to the rest of the world, headed east making for the Philippine coastline. The storm blew from the northwest and the growing waves washed over the stern if they continued in the same direction. Turning into the wind to ride out the weather took them in the wrong direction.

The older men believed they were close to the Philippines. They lacked basic navigational tools as the pirates had taken anything of value including the right ears of all the surviving men.

They could only guess at their location. This was a great dilemma for the inexperienced ad hoc crew, make for the Philippine coastline or turn into the wind to stabilize the boat.

As the waves increased, water came over the stern and port gunwales soaking the passengers. Bilge pumps and manual labor fell behind. The bottom of the boat filled with water. This reduced their choices to two, sink on a run for land or turn into the wind and remain afloat.

As the waves washed over the stern, the Vietnamese man now in command at the center of the boat caught the attention of the other men that had assumed the duties of crew. Then he motioned with his right arm moving in a large counter-clockwise circular motion over his head. His crew watched him as he motioned with his left hand, thumb pointed down, to slow the motor before they began the maneuver. The crew watching the first man moved about the portside preparing for the turn to face into the wind.

The boat was steered by a man on the back pushing and pulling on a large pole shoved into the water to roughly guide the metal blade in the water. The rudder control might have worked well enough in the rivers and in calm seas along Viet Nam's shorelines. Unfortunately, this was the first time it had been used in heavy seas while in motion. The newly-drafted rudder-man at the stern shifted the long bamboo-bundle rudder arm to turn the lumbering vessel left, to port and slowly into the wind and the growing waves. In calmer waters, they could have stopped to fully restore the steering gear. The pirates had seen to the damage well enough. The rudder was half effective wobbling under stress.

This was Loan's first experience on a boat, it was also the only time she had ever seen rough water. Regardless, she was excited by the newness of the sudden shift in activity. The men were strained to steer the boat, their right ears missing, their bodies stained with blood.

The original crew had been killed and thrown overboard. The older girls and women were quiet from trauma having been brutalized and raped. Yet, the boat was alive with activity as the boat wallowed in the growing waves.

She failed to sense tension in the helpless passengers as she wanted to ask someone why they changed direction. She remained silent and watched Anh clutching her daughters as she studied Lam and the other men manage the boat's direction.

The crew ignored everyone's suggestions. They were all business about turning the craft into the wind. Loan clutched the two-year old Teo, and watched the crew scramble to tie the sails to the spars as the boat rolled in the turn. The boat's lurching turn into the wind and into the waves jostled the boat. The young men bounced around on the spars as they lashed the sails. The man at the rudder struggled with the make-shift bamboo shaft at the back, shoving it to the starboard side to get the boat to turn to port. The boat lurched a bit as it turned to port.

The man in command in the center watched the prow of the boat as it swung into the wind, then looked back at the man on the rudder. The vessel began to shake as the sea buffeted the port side, water splashing high over the gunwale. This was the first time the boat, a craft that plied the Mekong Delta and calm coastal shoreline, had encountered large waves head-on.

Refugee Boats & American Aircraft Parts

The vessel was fragile, even by Vietnamese standards. It was constructed of wood with metal frame here and there added to it when the Americans with all their excess goods and supplies were operating throughout South Viet Nam during the war. The boat yards of many communities swelled with useful discards and debris of war. Discarded American war craft made good reinforcing materials.

Much of the equipment was stripped to refit native industries. This boat was named in Vietnamese "Lan Thu Hai" or roughly in English, "Second Chance." Others might cannibalize this boat if the recycled American parts had not permitted additional life. The pilot and crew called the vessel "Lan" for short.

The Lan was a commercial boat constructed for coastal fishing and river traffic. It was never intended to be on the open seas without being able to run to shore when weather threatened. The Lan was ill-equipped for bad weather. It was unworthy of passengers, and certainly not for one hundred and four of them. Most of all, it was an old boat with essential/critical structural repairs impossible to make in the difficult times of South Viet Nam.

The communist government confiscated materials needed in the reconstruction of Viet Nam after the Fall of Sai Gon in the spring of 1975. The thuggish regime and rattling economy rejected trade with the rest of the free world. It was forced to cannibalize its own resources for priorities. It was similar to releasing prison inmates to become new administrators of the region, most of which had no clue on how to administer a village let alone the southern half of a country.

Useful metals, fasteners and welding equipment out in the open had been taken at will as party officials deemed necessary. It was a country managed now by mercenaries promoted to civic administrators. The career upgrade lacked training, particularly for a hostile population. They had little training to account for resources. Their previous skills largely involved stealth, coercion, and murder.

What was left to the population was salvaged from refuse. The once-abundant but depleting refuse of American and British materials left over from war had to suffice. The rest of the boat was made of native woods including bamboo and other natural lumber that grew in abundance in the central highlands north of Sai Gon.

Vital fasteners needed to hold a boat together in heavy seas were scarce. The owner of the boat made do for what needed to pass for safety in the sheltered coastal waters of Viet Nam.

Many types of boats had left the coast line loaded with refugees over the last year consumed vital materials. The theft of boats for refugees harmed the rickety post-war economy and the production of food as any boat even barely worthy of crossing a calm South China Sea was put into illegal service for escape. Many of the refugees began leaving in 1976. Unfortunately for boat maintenance, hoarding and consumption of structural materials began in the spring of 1975. The Lan was held together by leftovers.

The regime kept watch on the commercial boats. Yet, the coastline and waterways south of Sai Gon proved to be impossibly porous. There were too many open areas to manage and the inefficient Marxist bureaucracy was poor match for the ingenuity and guts of a desperate population.

Homes, bamboo thickets and jungle coastline became conversion factories for escape boats. Vietnamese converted unlikely vessels to South China Sea transportation. Holding as few as two people, some of the boats barely resembled a canoe with a sailing mast. Regardless, Vietnamese adopted these risky craft of all shapes and sizes and fled.

Desperation and guts make for weak glue on an old hull. Many unworthy boats attempted the passage to the Philippines starting in late spring of 1975.

The Lan was one in a long series of river boats making the perilous journey, betting on luck in lieu of solid structure pitted against a merciless sea. They had to exit to the west along a canal and then out to sea traveling south and then east.

The Diesel Heartbeat

The old engine below deck chuffed out black smoke. Combinations of extended cylinder wear and marginally refined fuel mixed with oil as an inexpensive "power" additive. The exhaust had the hint of vegetable oils often used to extend petroleum-based diesel fuel.

The muffled steady operation of the engine transmitted a soothing rhythm similar to a mother's heartbeat. The sound resonated throughout the boat. As the passengers lay on the deck during the first night, the engine noise lulled Loan to sleep. It was the first sound to which she awoke the next morning.

To Loan, the engine thrum had become the music of passage home, back to Sai Gon, back to her family, back to her mother. She became accustomed to the thrum of the engine, the smell of the diesel smoke, the mild stink of the fish that permeated the wood, the smell of sweat of the passengers crowded together and everything on the boat including the motion of the sea.

Strangely ... her growing familiarity of the boat's steady motor operation settled early fears. The constant sound of the engine along with the smells of the boat assured wellbeing. The sound of the engine betrayed her trust.

Now there were new noises as the boat creaked under the strain of the turn into the wind. The old frame underneath popped as it forced to twist into the on-coming waves pushed out ahead of the storm. The passengers could feel as well as hear the cracks and pops of the wood frame structure. The wind had whipped up spray off the tops of the waves. It stung unprotected flesh as the boat was now sideways to the wind and waves.

The Lan rolled in the waves a bit and continued its slow chugging turn when a large wave rose up over the port bow. The wave crested as the boat was not quite fully turned into it and the rising water and old wood frame collided.

The boat and wave collided badly. The wave slammed into the hull and sides and jarred the boat as it broke over the bow. The boat plowed through, water flowing down on the open deck and the passengers in front.

Deep inside the boat's frame, the thirty-year-old keel snapped. The vibration of its fracture shook everyone on the deck. The sound was loud. It was similar to the sickening crack of someone breaking an arm. The sound of the structural failure was in the giant spine of the vessel, in the keel beneath them.

It was an unsettling disturbance. It was also fatal.

Moments after the crash with the last big wave, the crew looked at each other with helpless expressions. To be out on the open sea in an old fishing boat, a Vietnamese river vessel, with its worn out diesel engine, with the deck carpeted with people and their belongings, they had few options. Worse, if they had any real options, they now had run out of time. They were doomed. Most all of the passengers had less than minutes to live.

Within a minute, the forward motion of the boat ceased. The heavy thrum of the engine and the clacking and chuffing of the exhaust pipe suddenly went quiet as seawater overwhelmed the hold suffocating the power plant.

The reassuring heartbeat of the vessel stopped. The engine was dead. It was also beyond restarting. Seawater poured into its water-proof air intakes choking it into silence.

The boat no longer moved forward and as it had not finished turning into the wind, the waves were pushing the bow to starboard to roll parallel to the crest of the waves. In seconds the rising sea was rolling the top-heavy vessel. Wave washed over the port side where Loan was standing. The waves grew taller. The troughs sank deeper. The floundering boat rapidly dissolved into the sea as it fell apart.

With the keel broken, the boat structure rapidly failed. Inadequate patches of bolts and screws fitted into metal bands below deck barely deserved to be called structure in calm seas. Every strap and bolt came apart.

Lack of parts for basic maintenance over the last few years forced "make-do" repairs until better fittings turned up. Better fittings never turned up. Fundamental components shredded under the stress.

The stressed framework rapidly disassembled as it wallowed in the rough water. The center of the boat broke. The long old frame bent downward at the center, hinged loosely by brittle wood that held it together.

Seawater rushed through central parts of the deck, spurting out of the engine hut doorway. The vessel became part of the sea.

Loan knew little else to do. Anh had her two older daughters in her arms. Lam took Teo from Loan and held him along with their youngest daughter. Loan stood by herself as her adoptive family embraced their own children. It was the first moment she was in effect now an orphan with no parent able to guide or shield her from the world.

She looked at the parents and the fear in their faces gave no advice on her next task. Without the children in her care, Loan became purposeless. She didn't know what else to do but stand by the family waiting to follow the next instruction.

She had been with the family for many months but at this moment she felt the severe pang of overwhelming loneliness. They had gathered their children up in hopes of saving them.

Loan was not one of them.

Her mother was untold miles away essentially on another part of the planet. Loan stood by herself on the deck of a sinking boat crowded with screaming frantic people who now became all strangers struggling to save themselves.

They could not help her, they could not help themselves. She was now starkly alone with only the last instruction "Hold on to something that floats." It was small comfort as comprehensive instructions go she would recall years afterward.

She did not have time to dwell on this selfish thought of her discomfort and loneliness as a wall of water slapped down on the deck splashing her and the family almost knocking them to the deck. As she later told in her best Brooklyn English, "Shit hit the ceiling fan." She knew at that moment she would die in this hour.

The waves leapt over the left side of the wallowing boat, its deck sloping leeward, to starboard as the port side seemed to rise. Starboard sank into the water.

In moments, the deck tilted enough no one could stand on the wet deck. Water washed over the port rail and shoved people, tumbling over each other, to starboard. Passengers fell over the lower side rail into the sea. In another moment, a huge wave broke over the high side washing over Loan and the family, soaking them completely.

That was when Anh gave her last instruction to Loan, "Hold on to something, Loan. Grab something that floats. Hold on Loan, Hold on." Anh's instruction became the last adult words Loan heard for the next thirty-nine months.

Lam and Anh held their children and tried to grab the remaining satchels with the food and clothes, now soaked and heavy. Anh, her arms carrying the youngest children, motioned Loan to grab the food.

She motioned with her head to Loan as she clutched the children. Everyone was yelling and screaming. Loan barely heard her. She made little sense of Anh's head motion toward the satchels.

Another wave washed their food and clothes out of reach and across the tilting deck toward the people piled up against the starboard rail. The people on the starboard rail fell into the sea and sank flailing into the depths. Their food and clothing fell on top of them.

She never saw them resurface. The flailing strangers sank into the gray-green water as if stones. No one or anything returned to the surface. Everyone and everything sank.

Lam and Anh tried to stay on the higher side of the deck. The increasing slope and the next wave proved too much for them. They slide across the deck, Anh and Lam losing their firm hold on the children and trying to stop the slide with their feet. Other people now lying down against the side rail were flailing, holding on to the rail or people or anything they could grab. The family and Loan fell into them, heads, bodies, arms, and legs moving uselessly everywhere.

For a few moments, screams were heard all around them, waves and foam splashing down on them. All was chaos.

Somewhere in the chaos, another wave came over the port side. The water cascaded down the sloping deck and lifted Loan over someone, into the air and over the side of the boat. She splashed into the water backwards and sideways sinking immediately below the surface. As she sank into the dark water, she thought first about finding Lam and Anh and the children. She needed to get back to the surface. Her intent disconnected with the situation.

Loan was totally ignorant about swimming. She tried making motion with arms and legs that might move her one direction or another. She was underwater, without air, and could only guess at how to move her body to the surface to get more air.

A swimmer must observe a non-swimmer to understand that people who have never been in the water don't know how to move their limbs to move about. For humans, swimming is a learned experience. Four-legged creatures including dogs have the instincts to do the dog-paddle from birth. Humans have to be taught to stay buoyant, their heads above water and taught how to move under their control.

Loan flailed. In her poorly coordinated strokes, she managed to come up to the surface. She was only able to keep her head above water for a few seconds paddling in panicky and poorly effective strokes, choking on the sea, trying to breathe. She wanted to find the family in one fleeting useless thought but something tugged her underwater. Her next thought was now that she drowned. She knew that she died in that moment.

As the vessel broke apart, water flowed into the frame dislodging pockets of trapped air. Buoyancy disappeared. The dead engine became an anchor overcoming any remaining floatation of the broken hull. The shattered deck slipped below the water gaining speed as it sunk, developing downward currents that pulled on anything or anyone near the hull. As the deck sank below the surface, currents sucked Loan into warm suffocating darkness.

Loan moved arms and legs to minimal effect. In her eight years, she had stood in water up to her knees running in a ditch after a heavy rain. She bathed out of bucket or under a shower. She had never sat in a bathtub or waded in the sea. The mechanics of swimming, using her hands and feet to claw or push water around her was foreign.

She could not propel herself in any direction. As for direction, she had vertigo. Loan only knew to hold her breath knowing little else to do but flail. She wanted air but knew not to inhale in the bath-water warm sea.

Confused by what was now up and down, she continued to move her arms and legs. She needed to take another breath as she floundered five feet beneath the surface as the boat sucked her deeper into the sea.

Loan was at the mercy of the water and roar of the blood in her head from the panic was all she could think. Her urge to breath began to burn in her lungs. She knew taking a breath under water meant death. She was out of options.

A large plank of deck wood broke loose from the sinking hull. It snaked and wormed to the surface. One corner of the plank struck Loan in the forehead. Stunned and flailing, she had the presence of mind to grope for the offending plank. Although it cut her forehead and nearly knocked her unconscious, in a flash of instinct, she latched on to the thick wood. She found something to grab, something to hold.

She did as Anh had instructed. Loan held on to something that was floating to the surface.

Barely able to hold her breath, clutching to the wood as it floated upward, she surfaced with the buoyant plank. In seconds, she felt the coolness of the air on her face, her head was clear of the water. Loan exhaled and sucked in a large breathe, paused, exhaled and took another breathe.

Her eyes stung from the salt water. She kept them closed. After drawing a few more breathes as she clutched the plank, maneuvering with it to keep her head above water. The cut on her forehead bled down her face.

Loan coughed for a few moments clearing her lungs and throat. The buoyant plank bobbed high on the water with Loan clutching one side with both hands. Not knowing how to kick, she barely kept her head above water. She moved one hand then the other to in search of better support from the plank. Finally, she worked from one end and pulled herself on top with the plank beneath.

Loan was small and thin weighing forty or so pounds and standing less than 42 inches. The thick plank, wider and longer than her torso buoyed her body half way out of water.

She cracked open her left eyelid and looked around. With her head a foot above the board, the rolling horizon was crest of gray-green waves and troughs under an overcast sky. The sky cleared to the west with a band of yellow as sunset approached. When a wave rolled under raising her five feet from the bottom of the trough, there was nothing to see but waves white capped by the wind and the valleys in between.

To her surprise, the boat was gone. She believed she was underwater for 15 to 20 seconds. Now, the large wooden boat and all the people on it were nowhere to be seen.

Loan thought maybe it had resurfaced and sailed on without her. She had little clue as to what had happened.

Loan was right about one thing, the boat had moved on without her. It sailed down in pieces. The boat and most of its passengers drifted to the bottom of the South China Sea. The seafloor near the west cost of the Philippines ran 12,000 feet deep. The boat and most of its passengers sank out of reach and recovery.

The wind blew the tops of the waves into noisy curling foam. Above the noise of the wind and the curling tops of waves, she heard were noises of splashing around her. It was solely the churn of the waves.

Loan was surprised to be alone in the water. The waves quickly dispersed floating debris. Anyone nearby could be concealed by the tops of waves.

Lam, Anh, and the children disappeared. Everyone lacked swimming skills on a boat without life preservers or life rafts. Loan tightened her gripped plank of wood and thought of nothing else but to hold on and breathe carefully.

She focused on drawing each breath without choking on seawater. She lay on her belly half submerged resting on her elbows with a tight grip on the sides of the plank. If she rode too high on the board, the waves toppled her over. She balanced her position just enough to inhale without ingesting seawater and stay on top.

A wave broke over her and in a few minutes, another wave did the same. She held on to the wood timing when to draw a clear breath.

After fifteen minutes, she felt a bit more stable. The wound on her forehead quit bleeding down her face. After each inhale, she thought in fragments about where she was until taking the next breath.

She was alive. She was alone. The water was warm. Take another breath. She was alive. Where are the others? Take another breath. It will be getting dark soon. Hold on to the wood no matter what. Hold on. Take another breath. I didn't die yet. It's getting darker…on and on.

As the sun set, she kept up the cadence of breathing. She quit kicking her legs other than to shift an inch or two on the plank or resist being rolled over by a wave. The simple task of breathing displaced her panic. It gave her mind something to do besides dwell on the unknown. Her universe of concerns distilled to two tasks, stay on the plank, take another breath and after five seconds, take another breath and stay on the plank. Hold on. Hold on.

Seawater splashed around her not suffocating as before. She figured out how to inhale with her face down over the plank.

The water was warm. The cut on her head didn't sting anymore or she quit thinking about it.

The offending piece of wood was below her, her grip tight on its front edge. She felt the cut of its roughness into her forearms. She disregarded the pain in a larger effort to keep it below her and maintain her head above water.

It had broken loose from the deck of the sinking ship. It was barely buoyant enough to sustain her head and upper torso. As she held on to it and controlled her breathing, she looked around for any-thing different from the water and the darkening sky.

She could have been mistaken about its sinking. It probably cor-rected itself and took everyone on board on its way. She could only be sorry now about missing the boat.

They knew she was not on the boat. They should be looking for her. They should hurry as the sun was setting.

Her thoughts varied between hope and reality. Loan had hoped the boat resurfaced carrying Anh, Lam and the family on to where it was going, back to Sai Gon. That thought opened up sorrow. How could she get to Sai Gon now? Lam and Anh needed to find her? Where did they go?

Yet, she knew in her core that the family she served, the parents and the four small children were lost. In the few minutes she had to think about everyone, she realized it was just her, the waves and her piece of wood, about six feet square and an inch and half thick. It was barely enough to keep her afloat. But it was enough.

It failing daylight in the South China Sea, Loan believed she was in the Sai Gon Sea. She had never seen a coastline in daylight even though she grew up an hour away from Vung Tau, a popular seaside town on the South China Sea.

It might as well as been called the Sai Gon Sea. It was the water that should take her back to her mother in Sai Gon. Anh had told her so. Between inhales, she wondered how she could get to Sai Gon if the boat failed to retrieve her from the water.

The storm had come up in the late afternoon. Loan knew tropical darkness came quickly. She needed to tightly hold on to the plank of wood, lest she lose it in the rolling waves and the darkness. The plank was her only connection to life. Lose it and everything ends. She held on to it to see her mother again.

It was large enough to help her raise her head above water along with her shoulders and upper half of her torso. She pulled herself up to lie on top of it, lying on her belly clasping both sides of the wood. If she rode too high on the plank, the waves broke over her regularly upsetting her position. She experimented with the plank, repositioned herself again and again. For the rest of the night, she was able to stay on top. She reset her position every ten minutes or so after a curling wave rolled her over.

411

Loan doesn't recall to this day if she fell asleep through that night. She remembers endless hours in the water, in the dark, righting her torso to have the wood plank below her, more afraid of tiring than being tired. Somehow, she held on.

After the first hour in the dark, she quit thinking about Anh and Lam's family or the return of the boat. Every moment centered on when to take the next breath. It became a mechanical process of listening to the wind and water, figuring out the best moment to take a breath and exhaling at any moment, take another breath when the air was clear.

Regardless, she still choked on inhaled seawater; salty snot ran out of her nose. She did not chance letting go of the plank with either hand to wipe salt water from her face. When the waves nearly rolled her, she kicked one leg or another to stay above the plank.

Above all she gripped that rough wooden plank like it was a baby sister. As the night wore on, Loan quit thinking of anything but to hold on to the plank.

She remembers becoming slighting chilled and that moving her legs warmed her up. The sky had begun to clear giving her some detail to watch in the otherwise pitch-black water. Points of light appeared in the velvet-black sky.

The stars came out later that night dimmed by the tropical atmosphere. Other than starlight, she was in a threatening darkness being jostled constantly by unseen waves. The sea was rough all through the night but after the stars came out, the wind died down and the surface grew calmer, still rough still but less agitated. The roll of the ocean moved her up and down but became less threatening as the night wore on.

She spent the next hours righting herself, breathing carefully as the water splashed over her and trying to keep as much of her body out of the water as possible to stay warm. To this day, she believed she hung on because she was too ignorant to know anything else to do, including giving up and just letting the sea take her during that long night.

It was a long night. She only remembers watching the stars more than ever in her life. She had no idea what the points of light might be. No one told her, even her mother, about what was in the sky. They might be eyes watching over her.

The night's cloak lifted quickly as the tropical sunrise approached. The horizon began to glow at first a thin band of red sky cut on the horizon by the silhouette of wave tops. Then the sun came up quickly.

Out on the ocean after a storm, it might have been an inspiring sunrise, but Loan doesn't recall if she noticed it. She was pleased to see the water's surface again. It made it easier to adjust to the roll of the waves. The sea crested less with foam. She worked less to stay on top of plank.

The sky was big and open. Although the surface was much calmer, she was busy rolling in large swells with a steady wind pushing her to the East toward the rugged jungle coast of the Bataan peninsula on the western shores of the Philippines.

Loan believed she was somewhere off the coast of Viet Nam. She lacked formal education of any kind, certainly without sense of geography beyond what she knew of Sai Gon. She had two points of reference in her eight years, Sai Gon and Kien Giang. Travel to Kien Giang and back to Sai Gon took three days on the railroad to travel the one-hundred-and-twenty miles. It had not been a full three days since they left Kien Giang so she hadn't been out long enough to make it to Sai Gon.

She hoped to be floating toward shore and reckoned it was near her home. Because it took about three days to travel between those points, she thought if the boat hadn't run into trouble, she should be home by now. When she made it ashore, she assumed it would be somewhere along the Vietnamese coast. She could find someone to help her when she made it to land.

Loan vaguely knew of other people, the Americans, the large white and black men with the curious round eyes, some eyes that were brown like hers but also blue and other colors. She saw them at times talking to her mother. That was before they moved to Tay Ninh. Perhaps she might find one of them to help her return to Sai Gon.

A few years later, the strange men no longer came to the house. She had no idea where in the world those white and black men lived exactly other than it was America, some other part of Viet Nam called America. It was only different, similar to Kien Giang only with large white and black people that spoke poor Vietnamese.

She had no knowledge of the fish that might be in the sea, not fish to eat or fish that ate human flesh. Lying relatively motionless on the plank provided some measure of protection, largely by avoiding attention of a passing predator below. Loan's forehead cut quit bleeding and her arms, while rubbed raw, were not bleeding, not giving up the scent in the water for predators. Loan appeared as nothing more than storm-blown debris.

Her dangling legs might have exposed her to the attention of sharks. She did not know how to use her legs to propel forward in the water. The only shark-attractive commotion she made in the water was when a wave destabilized her and she had to reposition herself.

Everyone else had drowned. She did not know that. The bodies of the remainder of ninety eight or so people that drowned distracted some of the predators that might have otherwise noticed her. There was plenty of meat to satisfy undersea carnivores and scavengers.

The South China Sea sustains nearly one hundred varieties of sharks, many of them smaller and less threatening to people. Regardless, nearly all are carnivorous predators. There was an abundance of easy pickings in the water that day.

As she became accustomed to floating with the board buoying her, the return of daylight, Loan's thoughts turned to a building thirst and discomfort. Cold crept into her body.

In such a warm sea, it took many days of exposure to drop her body temperature to dangerous levels. Sleep presented the largest danger in warm sea water.

She kicked in the water briefly to warm up and clear her mind. Her need to sleep was seductive. All she needed was a short nap on the plank. Just a short nap resting on the plank was all she needed. A short nap meant death.

Loan's fear of waking up without the piece of lumber jogged her back to consciousness. The rough plank of deck lumber was her lifeline. Lose it and all that she knew ends.

Her lack of motion contributed to preserving precious body heat. Stirring the water warmed her up briefly but the heat bled into the surrounding water at the same time. If she even knew how to propel her in the water, why? Where could she go?

She remembers crying in the darkness for brief moments. Loan tried not to think about the four children she tended. In her heart, she knew they could not swim. They drowned. Deep down, she knew the little boy and the girls died.

She asked herself, even if Anh and Lam could swim, how could they stay afloat and still keep those four small children from drowning?

She did not know Lam had sewn gold plates into his clothing exacerbating his inability to swim. The family and its precious gold now rested 12,000 feet below the surface.

She did not want to think they could be dead, drowned along with the remainder of the people that had set out two days before from the swampy shore near Kien Giang, Viet Nam. Another wave jostled her. She redirected her energy to stay on top of the plank.

Most westerners, particularly Americans and Europeans learn how to swim. Not knowing how to swim is more the exception than the rule for western civilization. Western affluence enabled recreational swimming pools and developed shorelines that enlarged water recreation.

Western countries spent more leisure time around water requiring swimming as a social skill if not essential to personal safety. Western civilization required life preservers and safety equipment on every form of watercraft. Not so in Asia 1977. Asians as a quasi-general-rule don't know how to swim. Not everyone else in the world learns to swim. Throughout 1970's Asia, maybe one in seven could swim at all.

In Viet Nam of 1977, the ratio of swimmers to non-swimmers might have been less than five percent. Disasters involving floods and sinking ships killed many throughout Asia due to a broad lack of swimming skills and non-existent safety standards.

Given the circumstance in post-Sai-Gon-Fall-in-1975-Viet Nam, escaping across a long stretch of water in unseaworthy boats was apparently not as difficult a choice as remaining in Viet Nam and living with the threat of starvation, persecution, and death at the direction of the revolutionary government. Learning how to swim was not a prerequisite for becoming boat people. It was normal among Vietnamese that none could swim.

Swimming-impaired Nguyên Loan bobbed helplessly adrift in a warm sea lying on a barely-large-enough piece of wood floating toward landfall. The vessel had managed to cross most of the South China Sea and come within a dozen miles of rugged Philippine coastline.

The mountainous western Philippines on the Bataan peninsula included primitive areas with prehistoric volcanic soils. The terrain had treacherous chasms hidden by jungle.

Civilization was close but mountainous jungle and rough forbidding coastline stood in the way. The destination city of Manila might as well have been a million miles away from Bataan.

Western Philippine coastlines varied widely between open sandy beaches to forbidding rugged seawalls of cliffs and boulders generated by volcanic events thousands of years before. Loan floated along with the waves toward the latter. Odds for safe landfall were slim.

Mountainous regions near the South China Sea bore steeply sloped sides that intersected the sea without transition other than promontories that jutted into the sea along with broken cliffs and boulders. There was no beach in long stretches of coastline.

The crucial matter to a non-swimmer was there were few places to wade the last 20 feet to land. They had to swim at least briefly to negotiate landfall. The danger to non-swimmers was absolute on the rugged Philippine coastline.

Swimming skills meant having the power to propel a body a desired direction on the surface of the water. It might be said that swimming is aggressive treading. Unfortunately, treading water is not swimming. Treading water is a stand-off situation between air and sea. Losing meant death.

Loan lacked swimming skills. If she abandoned the life-sustaining plank, she drowned. She was flotsam adrift and entirely at the mercy of the waves, tides, and unfriendly coastline. This was the plight of hundreds of thousands of Vietnamese that faced crossing an expanse of water.

The rocky shores of western Philippine islands and peninsulas were dangerous to approach in a boat, worse for someone washing up to them hoping to get through the treacherous rocks in calm water. Untold numbers of people had survived pirates, starvation, and sinking boats to crash on the rocks. Knocked senseless or crippled, would-be survivors died within feet of dry land.

The waves pushed Loan into the cliffs and boulders guaranteeing her destruction. Auspiciously, she arrived on a high tide that varied as much as four feet from low tide. At 40 pounds, she and her plank of wood bobbed high in the waves.

The sea bottom rose up at a steep angle to the shoreline. There was no reef or sand bar to temper the waves. Waves broke at the water's edge. The breaker's position preserved the height of the wave's crest to the last moment. In heavy surf, the waves slopped its top water onto the lower cliffs.

Tide and storm-driven waves converged in a two-hour period as the sea pushed Loan into the cliffs. If she was to survive the landfall, the water had to throw her high on to tops of cliffs. Otherwise, her broken carcass would feed sea life at the coastline.

Loan did not know she moved toward the cliffs until she heard the roar of waves crashing on the seawall. She felt the unfamiliar chop of reflected waves pushing her back to sea. The forward rhythm she had felt for more than a day was now in contest with its reflection. Her forward motion slowed the closer she moved toward the cliffs.

She was exhausted and surprised she had held plank for so long. There was no remaining option but to hold on to the wood. The waves struck the shoreline at an angle with the crest of the wave tracing along the cliffs and stumbling over the boulders at the base.

She heard the crashing water roaring through a maze of boulders. She was too tired to be afraid. There was no other option but to hold on. She was literally along for the ride.

A few of the waves caught her at crest. She rode high then slid down the front of the wave, board, and body tumbling in the wave's collapse. She righted herself again and bobbed toward the rough shoreline.

She was close to the ledges that rose above her head between three and eight feet. She believed that at times, the crest of the waves carried as high as the lower ledges.

Timing of her arrival was everything to her survival and nothing Loan could control. If Loan rolled in low to the first object and hit it hard, her journey ended there at land's edge.

Her best chance lay in washing into a shallow spot where she could stand up and scramble to high ground. She had been in the water for a day. Will her legs work when she needed them?

Loan carried only one thought. Hold on to the plank. She was at the mercy of the physics between a turbulent sea and land.

Loan clutched the plank with aching hands and bleeding arms. She girded herself for what the sea threw at her in the next moment. She would deal with the next moment after that if she survived the coming event.

Some would call the next moment a miracle. In poker, Loan drew a royal flush. Her bet: All in. Otherwise, the game was over.

A large wave rolled in carrying her with its crest into the face of the cliff. She felt the acceleration as the contest of waves and rocks squeezed sea water into a narrowing slot.

One large wave rolled past a higher ledge sending her through a gap with a lower ledge. The rolling wall of water broke through the breach carrying her six feet above the rocky surface. The water rushed through the short pass of the cliff running up to the jungle's edge. Loan rode atop the surge on her plank of deck wood.

The wave roared over the face of the rock, splashing up high in the air, carrying Loan clinging to her plank. She rose up with the water and as it broke on the cliff's edge, the mass of water fell away. She fell hard on top of the cliff clutching the wood. The impact stunned her. The plank slapped her chest and knocked the breath out of her.

Her battered rib cage squeezed the air out of her lungs. Stunned muscles resisted contraction. For a moment, she could not inhale. She struggled to draw a breath. After managing to breathe carefully for a day, she could not inhale. She panicked.

Loan's aching grip on the plank broke. She bounced once more and slumped in the second landing. On a shallow slope of rock that drained to the sea, a thin layer of seawater water slid around her inert form on its return to the South China Sea. Stunned, semi-conscious, she finally drew a shaky breath and passed out.

The last thing she recalled was flying into shore on the mass of the wave and then hit a rock surface hard with a sharp pain and then blackness. Loan made landfall in the fullest meaning of that term.

It was mid-morning, more than three days after sitting outside Anh's home begging for a chance to stay with the family as they returned to Sai Gon. Loan left the Vietnamese coastline aboard the vessel later that night along with one hundred and three passengers and crew. Three days later, alone and near death, Loan lay immobile on a rocky shelf on a wilderness coastline of the western shore of the Bataan peninsula in the Philippines. Battered and bruised, she drifted between dazed exhaustion and unconsciousness.

Waves roared in crashing on lower rocks. One last large breaker shoved her inert body inland. The spray of the waves breaking on the seawall wetted her perhaps as a last attempt to coax her back into the water. She was out of easy reach of the South China Sea.

The Plank

The receding water wrested the board that had sustained her body for most of a day and night and then again a morning out of her grip. It left her high up on the rocks above the fading churn of the surf.

The plank washed back out to sea on one of the last breakers that broke over the edge of the cliff before the sea settled down. The plank had been her only companion in the one and only day she had ever been in deep water by herself.

Loan has never entered deep water alone since that day and still does not know how to swim.

Consciousness Returns

Loan drew quick shallow breaths ready to purge the breath if seawater splashed on her mouth. She had been doing that for most of a full day. Even on land face down on the rocks, the sea reached out to her. Wind whipped sprays of white caps in the bay wetted her back as she lay face down on the hard surface of the cliff. Her lungs burned. Her stomach cramped. She had inhaled and swallowed seawater. Her belly muscles ached from throwing up the poisons. There was little she could do for her lungs except cough.

Loan was paralyzed by exhaustion. She had become immobile and had not moved so much as a few inches since the last wave pushed her inland.

In the sunlit morning of a tropical day, Loan, inert and in great discomfort was stuck to the top of the cliff. Stiff from hypothermia and low blood sugar, her arms, and legs ignored commands to move. She lay there able to breathe but do little more than move her head now and then to see her surroundings.

The hard red rock beneath her along with array of discomforts reminded her she was still alive. The thought left a question, "For how long?"

She was cold. Shivering competed with thirst for attention. In all her days living in South Viet Nam, she had never known such cold. She shivered uncontrollably at times as her muscles involuntarily contracted to rebuild internal temperature. The sun heated her back but not her shivering core.

Yes. She was alive. She thought it was not for long.

The wind blew constantly and gave no comfort. It had a bite. The sea spray turned to salt stung her open sores. The wind off the South China Sea hurt.

Loan was severely dehydrated and sick from ingesting seawater. Lying on her stomach, she could barely raise her head enough to look around. She attempted to rise up on her arms or move up on to hands and knees. Her spent body was incapable of movement. Dehydration had disabled motor control. She was within feet of infinite water she could not drink.

On the edge of a jungle, she could see up and down the shoreline. The land rose up steeply from the sea. It was a mountain covered in verdant jungle under a blue-white morning sky.

She lay on a rocky ledge that overlooked a curving bay. There was no sign of anything human. She thirsted for water and without the ability to get up and move, she had no way to find something to drink.

In fleeting moments of consciousness, Loan concluded this was where she would die. It was the second time in two days she had drawn this conclusion. The first realization came when the boat's deck was awash with seawater and chilled her legs. She knew at that moment on that boat, she would die. Decades later, she recalled those thought in dreams.

Alone and lying on the rocks too weak to save herself again, she knew she would be dead soon. Her most painful summary of the circumstances was that she could never see her mother again. She began to cry before passing out again. Tears drained away precious fluid her body could ill afford to spend.

Loan lay there on the rocky cliff for most of that day. As the day wore on, she woke up less and less. Even though the tropical sun beat down on her back, her weakened metabolism failed to heat her body. She shivered uncontrollably even as her skin cooked red in the sun. Her muscles consumed precious resources needed to sustain the rest of her.

Someone coming upon her body later that afternoon would conclude she was dead. The coastline was littered with bodies in the bay and among the rocks. No one else had come ashore alive. Either from her boat or another sinking, there were some other bodies in the rocks below.

Boulders and rocks trapped the bodies of other passengers. Remains of some rolled in the rough surf washing in and out breaks in the cliffs. Of the half dozen passengers' bodies that had washed ashore that morning, only the bodies of children made it to this boundary between land and sea. Adult bodies rarely made the shoreline, just the bodies of children.

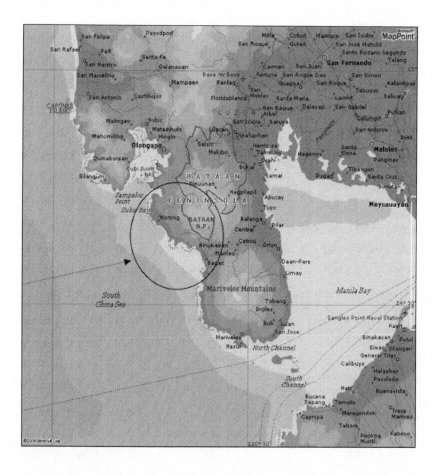

Vietnamese Angels: Thúy and Huė

Two naked Vietnamese girls with long black hair, thirteen-year-old Nguyên Thúy (*Thúy pronounced "Toowee" with emphasis*), and eleven-year-old Tu Vo Huė (*Huė pronounced "Hu-way" with short small emphasis on the front sound*) searched that afternoon among storm debris in hopes of finding something useful, maybe even someone alive. Odds favored finding something useful.

Thúy and Huė had been the only living human beings on this stretch of the Bataan coastline for nine months since coming ashore. The only artifacts of civilization within reach were the wrecks of fishing boats, flotsam, and jetsam that washed into the shoreline. The only other human beings to make landfall died.

The two girls had hardened themselves to tragedy. They were the only survivors of the sinking of an overloaded fishing boat that ran aground a hundred yards from shore. Their families and the remainder of 49 passengers drowned within reach of this shoreline.

After they sorted how to exist on the isolated coastline, Thúy and Huė explored the area attempting to find a village or adults to help them get out. Other than freighters passing by in the shipping channels miles to the west, there was no sign of civilization. The shallow bay between major promontories ran roughly several miles in a gentle arc. No other land was visible. This bay composed their entire world.

Treacherous deep ravines and sinkholes cut into ancient volcanic deposits up the steep mountainside that rose to the east from the bay. Jungle growth concealed many deadly traps that littered the steep slopes. The nearest outpost of civilization was roughly several miles inland. It might as well have been a thousand miles away.

If the shoreline had been friendly to foot traffic, they could have walked one direction or the other until they found a fishing village. Unfortunately, the shoreline was an obstacle course of boulders and cliffs terminating at the edge of the South China Sea. Shoreline for miles in either direction lacked continuous open beach.

Unable to swim out around promontories jutting into the sea, the girls gave up after several attempts to climb up and down the rocky shoreline. If they had been able to swim, they were ill equipped to fend off predatory sea life. Everything from jellyfish to sharks posed fatal threats.

On occasion, smaller boats passed by closer to shore than the freighters. Unfortunately, the boats never came in close enough to see the girls waving and yelling. The wind blew into the bay most of the time often full of choppy waves and carried their calls for help into the jungle. Likely, they were from a fishing village somewhere up or down the coast.

Neither Thúy nor Huế knew how to swim. Had a Philippine fishing boat seen them, it could not get close to shore for fear of submerged boulders that could wreck their boats. The girls could not swim out to the boat.

The rough western coastline had become their home. It might as well been an island prison.

The landscape against the sea forced Thúy and Huế to stay in the same area and live off the jungle. They remained close to shore in hopes of rescue from the fishing boats that passed nearby.

After each storm passed, they explored the shoreline searching for useful flotsam that washed ashore. Wooden crates and pieces of tarpaulins were among the most common finds.

Thúy and Huế grew accustomed to finding bodies of people who had made it into the bay alive but died in making landfall. The bodies of others that had tied themselves to tire inner tubes and bamboo rafts as make-shift life preservers washed into the bay. Their bodies ended up dashed against the rocks. The inner tubes and life preservers failed at preventing concussions.

In a matter of days, creatures in the sea and flew over the water removed most of familiar parts of the victims. Gruesome remains tied to floating objects that had been out at sea no longer resembled human beings.

The girls kept count of the dead at first. After a few months, they lost count and refused to think of the number that had lost their life on this shoreline. This was year two in the fifteen-year period of the insane Vietnamese exodus by boat. The term "boat people" had yet to take hold in most of the world.

The first of several bodies Thúy and Huế found among the boulders and rocks that day were children. If the bay waters were calm, the girls retrieved the remains they could reach in shallow water. A fall into deep water a few feet from land was a death sentence for either girl.

The girls moved a child's body to places north or south of their camp depending on the prevailing wind or the time of the monsoon. Burial in the rocky coast was not an option. Rock cairns were their best means of internment.

At times, the numbers of dead Vietnamese overwhelmed them. On most occasions when this many dead floated ashore, they moved to another part of the bay for a few weeks upwind of the smell or rotting flesh.

The girls performed a rough algebra sorting between nursing their meager resources to live another day and serving the influx of dead Vietnamese. If they had enough to eat, they spent free time scavenging the shoreline and tending to the dead. This kept their minds off their predicament.

Huė spotted another inert form high up on a ledge above the water. Thúy being the oldest and having by virtue of her seniority became the decider, at least more than Huė, whether to move the body or leave it to nature. Thúy assumed the worst expecting to find another dead Vietnamese child. If the child had been in the water for a short time, it would appear like themselves but dead.

Thúy puzzled on how the child's body had been deposited so far up the ledge. A ragged line of trash and flotsam higher up on the rocks indicated heavy seas at high tide. She assumed the morning's storm waves deposited the body with the rest of the debris. It had landed between cairns the girls had laid before on other bodies.

Rock cairns thwarted marauding animals without sealing off the odors of decay. Upwind of their camp, Thúy and Huė had to move the body downwind before covering it with rocks. The body appeared small enough. They should be able to move it.

Among the many chores living on this desolate coastline, touching a dead Vietnamese child was the grimmest. If the body was in an advanced state of decay, relocating it became a horror. No child should see the state of another child in such condition. By superstition and tradition, they could not touch an adult body. As it was, adult bodies seldom made it to dry land.

Without digging tools and deep soft soil, Thúy and Huė lacked practical means to bury anything. Throwing a body back in the sea accomplished nothing. Prevailing easterly winds blew debris to shore. It remained in the bay if not being re-deposited on the cliff.

Asian culture prevented Thúy and Huê from touching remains of dead adults in order to avoid trifling with their ghosts. As children had unfinished spirits, they moved the bodies of children as they wished.

When they had sufficient rocks or suitable debris, the girls covered the adults in place with a rough cairn. A dozen such "graves" dotted the ledges since arriving nine months before.

Thúy decided to move this body to a position downwind of their camp. The girls girded themselves for its condition. Hopefully, it was more fresh and intact.

Incredible Providence

The task of dealing with the dead girl's body on the high ledge changed everything for the two girls. Incredible providence postponed if not denied history another tragedy. To their surprise, the girl's body was warm and soft. Rigor mortis and rot had not taken hold. The girl had not yet died.

This little girl was still alive. Unconscious, she panted in shallow breaths.

She looked terrible. A head injury had scabbed over and some of her hair was missing from prolonged exposure to salt water. Her knees and forearms bore contusions with fresh scabs, injuries made when she landed on the ledge. The tropical sun baked her salt-blistered skin red.

They made plans to do what they could for her. They had learned to expect little of people that had been in the water for what might have been days. Everyone in such condition always died.

She was a bit smaller than they were, wearing the ubiquitous dark pajama (*Vietnamese: ao ba ba*), a commoner's clothing. She was a rural girl from what they could determine.

Thúy and Huê believed every victim whose body landed on the coastline in the bay was from Viet Nam. That assumption stems from ignorance. They thought the shoreline was a part of Viet Nam. They didn't know it was called Bataan and on the island of Luzon in the Philippine archipelago.

Deteriorating conditions in Viet Nam interrupted schooling for Thúy and Huê. Declining resources went to their brothers first. Neither knew regional geography and circumstances reinforced Thúy and Huê's ignorance. Their better-educated brothers along with their parents died on this shoreline nine months before. With them died the knowledge of where in the world the girls now lived.

Of the dozens of bodies that had floated ashore in the last month, all appeared to be Vietnamese. Hence, they were in Viet Nam.

If this girl survived, they hoped she could explain to them why so many Vietnamese bodies ended up on this shoreline. Even more, maybe this girl could help them find their way back to Sai Gon.

Thúy rolled over Loan's limp body and picked her up by her armpits. Huè lifted her by her feet.

In similar situations, if a body had turned stiff, Thúy and Huè moved the child as if transporting a tree limb. In other situations, the body had rotted to the point they carried segments wrapped in elephant-ear leaves. If the body had lost coherence such that it no longer resembled a human being, the girls left it to finish its return to nature.

Thúy and Huè made big adjustments since leaving their privileged life in Sai Gon. Their well-connected fathers developed business with the Americans up until 1974. For a time, they prospered.

Then Sai Gon fell to the communists in 1975. A year later, they fled for the Philippines to make their way to Manila and the U.S. Consulate to gain asylum in America.

The boat was over-loaded and ended up in the rocks on this shoreline nine months before. Thúy and Huè alone made it ashore. Their families' bones litter the shallow bay as there was no one to tend them as they do now.

They moved the unconscious girl up the rocky slope in stages, taking breaks to catch their breath. Loan weighed less than forty pounds. Thúy and Huè weighed maybe ten or fifteen pounds more. It took most of an hour to set the girl down in their camp on the edge of the jungle.

Their camp set in a shallow cave set back in from the shoreline. It was more of a deep recess in a rock ledge. It was out of the sun most of the day and somewhat protected from rain.

Thúy and Huè positioned parts of weathered wood pallets as a barrier on the open sides of the recess. They piled small tropical apples and coconuts in a corner along with two stacks of rocks. The rocks were armament to repel packs of feral dogs. A series of giant elephant ear leaves cradled in bamboo frames held rainwater collected during the previous day's storm. The elephant ear leaves held water well enough saving them the trip up the mountain to collect water from springs.

A pile of stones on the edge near the barricade smoldered. Empty coconut shells fueled their "fire-pit." They made fire by striking a soft green rock with a dark stone making sparks on dried banana leaves. Huế's mother taught her how to make fire after the fall of Sai Gon rendered matches a luxury. The girls utilized sparking-rocks to build a fire instead of maintaining it day after day.

Except for hapless lizards they could catch, Thúy and Huế seldom cooked anything with the fire. In the heat of the tropics, the warmth of a fire meant little. It broke the darkness as needed and sharpened the tips of sticks meant to fend off dogs and boars. Most of all, their ability to make fire restored their singular link to civilization as they knew it.

Not by choice, Thúy and Huế had become a new generation of troglodytes, cave men in a modern era of super-sonic aircraft and of a world that had sent men to the moon eight years before. They were the cave-girls of Bataan verging on the initiation of a new member to their tribe.

Two water dragons, large iguana-like lizards tied up by thin vines thrashed against the corner. One of the lizards was today's meat in their diet. Their new arrival postponed cooking the lizard. If the girl lived, they should cook both of the lizards in celebration.

Thúy and Huế laid the girl on her back atop a white-gray cloth placed on layers of dried banana leaf. The "bedding" was a fragment of rough Dacron sailcloth they found on the shore. Brass eyelets in a seam revealed its original purpose. It was a sail on a two-mast Vietnamese fishing boat such as brought them here. (*Vietnamese fishing boats used the wind as often as possible to move their boats saving their fuel for emergencies. After April 30, 1975, fuel became expensive if available at all. Precious resources were allocated to members of the Communist party and anyone who could purchase it on the black market. On the South China Sea, the wind was nearly ceaseless.*)

They covered Loan with giant elephant-ears leaves to keep her warm and dry. They used banana leaves to shed water and elephant-ear leaves to store it. During storms and without other means of staying out of the rain, the giant leaves served as umbrellas and rain coats.

Thúy bent over whispering in Vietnamese, do you want some water? She waited a minute, and then asked again. Huế waited with rainwater cupped in a piece of elephant-ear leaf.

Loan slipped in and out of consciousness. In semi-conscious moments, she grew aware of her surroundings. She felt the Dacron sailcloth on her back. Her head throbbed and skin burned. She shivered from hypothermia after more than a day afloat in the sea. (*The South China Sea is perpetually warm as bathwater to a tourist taking a swim. Water is 1,800 times denser than air, which means it draws heat from a human being with a skin temperature of 93°F to seawater at 83°F. A body at rest in the South China Sea continuously loses energy to the seawater. It is possible to die of hypothermia in such warm water.*)

Her vision, blurred from exposure to salt water, made out the shape of Huế leaning over her as Thúy repeated the question. "Do you want some water?"

Loan whispered out one word. "Vung!" (*Vietnamese: Yes!*) Thúy and Huế smiled at each other. It was the first time they had heard another human being's voice beside their own in nine months.

Thúy propped up Loan's head as Huế poured some water on her parched lips. Loan felt the liquid on her lips and she closed them fearing more seawater. She tasted a drop and open up her mouth. Huế poured a little and stopped.

Loan held the water in her mouth for a moment. Then she swallowed it. She coughed as the sensation of fresh water shocked her throat. In a moment, she uttered. "Khac nuc." (*Vietnamese: Thirsty*).

Thúy cautioned Huế to give her a little more. Too much could choke her. The girls knew little else to do but sit beside Loan and give her small doses of water. They spent the rest of the day sitting on their heels tending Loan keeping her covered and giving her water in small doses.

Thúy and Huế expected her to be hungry. They had learned to avoid giving anyone anything but fresh water in limited amounts. They had never gotten this far with other Vietnamese making landfall. They always died.

They had other people, adult women and children, come ashore barely alive. Thúy and Huế administered what aid they could. It was trial and error. Each of the previous survivors from the sea died within the day.

Many rural and city Vietnamese unaccustomed to the sea may not have understood that seawater is toxic. With several times the

salt level of human blood, seawater poisons blood chemistry and ultimately the nervous system. Seawater acidity and human blood have
identical acidity (PH) levels. Unfortunately, it slakes desperate thirst
at a horrific cost.

Previous Vietnamese survivors of landfall were always in distress if
not in shock and unconscious. They could not talk. More than likely,
they ingested too much seawater. Prolonged exposure and poisonous
minerals doomed them to a strangulated death on the shore. They died
under the girls' care unable to say anything. Thúy and Huẻ were powerless to change the outcome of anyone who ingested too much seawater.

Thúy and Huẻ debated whether to leave the girl and check for
more like her on the shoreline. Thúy decided better to tend to this girl
now. Huẻ agreed as they had already walked most of the bay. It was
better to focus on the one they knew was still living.

Toward sunset, Thúy and Huẻ believed the girl might live. Yet,
they were afraid to hope too much. If she lived through the night,
they set about the task of nursing her back to health.

They elicited three more words out the girl before nightfall. They
asked her, "What is your name?" (*Vietnamese: Tên của bạn là gì?*)

Loan's body was sore but the throbbing pain in her head had
subsided. She was no longer as thirsty but terribly hungry. The girls
gave her have a few bites of a bittersweet fruit that resembled a white
potato. They told Loan she would get sick if she ate too much too
soon. They asked about her name again.

Loan managed a hoarse, "Nguyên Xuân Loan." *(Pronounced: "Win
Soon Loan")* Thúy and Huẻ smiled at each other pleased to hear a familiar Vietnamese family name. The girl might have news of Sai Gon.

After the girls learned of her name, they told Loan to save her
voice and rest.

As she lay in her dark shorts and blouse, Loan's vision returned
well enough to notice a few oddities about Thúy and Huẻ. In the fading light of sunset, she realized that Thúy and Huẻ had dark skin for
Vietnamese girls. Vietnamese women wore the conical-shaped non la
to keep their skin light. Thúy and Huẻ were very dark.

In addition, their silky black hair ran down to their waistline. Such
long hair was impractical. They had banded it in one long pony tail
with vine. Still, long hair was a luxury of rich adults, not of young girls.

Most of all, they were naked. As they fussed over her, Thúy and Huể made no effort to conceal their private parts. Loan wondered what their parents must think of such improper behavior.

She must ask them about these things. Then she fell asleep.

Thúy and Huể ate some apples saving the water dragons for their main meal tomorrow or the next day after that. They sat "Asian-style" on their heels studying their new little sister. They barely contained their delight in finding someone alive and, Buddha providing, on the mend.

After nine painful months on this coastline, this might be their first good news. Thúy, always the "big sister" (*wet-blanket in western parlance*) chided Huể not to hope too much. Huể thought without saying it, "You too, big sister, you too."

For nine months, neither Thúy nor Huể had smiled and laughed so much as that evening as they tended their camp. (*Vietnamese: trại*). In actuality, they tended their house, which was more a term for home. (*Vietnamese: quê hương*). Despite their mutual cautions, Thúy and Huể already hoped too much.

Thúy shifted the crates to form a barrier around them. The stone cliff formed a back wall and the barrier encompassed some straggly trees able to grow in the rocky seawater-washed perimeter of the jungle. The barrier bought them time to scramble into the trees if a pack of dogs appeared.

After a big storm, the dogs seldom appeared for days. The grim reason: jungle animals had plenty to eat all along the "Vietnamese" coastline as they called the shoreline of the Bataan.

Loan quit shivering. Nevertheless, the warm sea air at night chilled an unprotected body at rest. Thúy and Huể assembled their sleeping mats of banana leaves around Loan and lay next to her covering themselves with elephant-ear leaves. Thúy and Huể lay on each side of their new companion to share their body heat.

A breeze blew in from the northeast settling the sea. Spent storm waves rolled into the shallow bay crashing on the rocks and boulders below.

Loan woke at times to hear the sea churning the coastline. The unfamiliar sound jolted her memory of where she was (or wasn't). The unknowns of the pitch-black jungle coastline replaced the horror of floating adrift in the sea clinging to a plank of wood.

431

Panic rose in her for an instant. Then she felt the comfort of the girls lying next to her keeping her warm. She was no longer alone. The animal warmth of the girls' bodies next to her reminded her of her mother's embrace. The moment was benign without agenda. They were together to endure the night, confront the sunrise and manage the next day.

Regardless of the intellectual exercise to come, human contact postponed Loan's fears in the alien darkness until sleep overcame her again. She woke several times in the night to be assured by her new sisters and returned to sleep.

Night falls fast in the tropics. The sky cleared and Venus led the charge of stars to appear in the west above a sliver of light running on the horizon. Thúy and Huế often studied the sunset horizon to spot the silhouettes of freighters plying the shipping lanes of the South China Sea.

When night fell, the sea became a black velvet horizon below the mantle of stars except for the bay. Below them, waves stirred luminescent microscopic organisms that glowed faintly in the surf giving the bay a faint green shimmer.

Miles out over the churning bay; they frequently spotted cabin lights of freighters plying the shipping channels. When the wind and sea calmed, they could hear the low thrum of immense low-RPM engines above the background noise of the surf. The heartbeat of and engine of commerce radiated over the water provided unexpected comfort to the girls. Civilization was close.

Thúy and Huế remained silent witness that despite their primitive circumstance, civilization continued. The rest of the world was oblivious to the tragedy they lived daily. Evidence readily confirmed this. Four miles west of them in the freight routes of the South China Sea, world commerce passed them by unaware and unable to help.

By providence of Buddha, they were alive. By his guiding instruction, perhaps tomorrow Loan will rejoin the ranks of the living. They sorted their options about returning to Sai Gon after Loan could tell them how to get off this coastline.

In their hearts, Thúy and Huế knew beyond hope that she could not guide them out. Loan was too young to have such capabilities. From her appearance, she might be too frail to be of consequence in their lives. Time would tell.

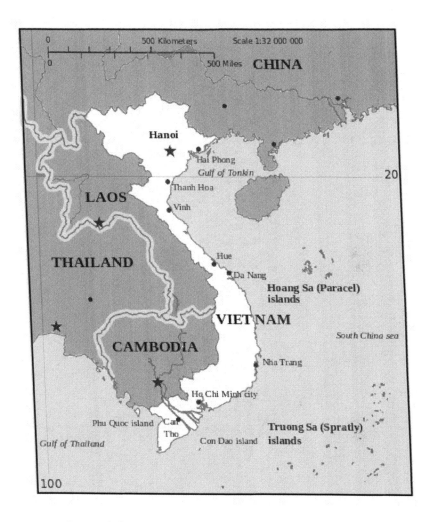

Exhausted from a momentous day, Thúy and Huế fell asleep as their bodies' yielded healing warmth to the little girl, thinking similar thoughts. They now had better purpose than to tend the dead. They finally had a way out of the wilderness.

Tomorrow, they would do everything possible to save little sister Loan.

THE END of FIRST PASSAGE

Recommended Reading & YouTube Videos

Books:
Decent Interval   Frank Snepp
Tears Before Rain

Video:
Sixty-Minutes, Ed Bradley, Vietnamese Boat-People, 1979